AN AMERICAN VEIN

D1570950

AN AMERICAN VEIN

CRITICAL READINGS
IN
APPALACHIAN
LITERATURE

Edited by
DANNY L. MILLER, SHARON HATFIELD,
and
GURNEY NORMAN

OHIO UNIVERSITY PRESS   ATHENS

Ohio University Press, Athens, Ohio 45701
www.ohio.edu/oupress
© 2005 by Ohio University Press

Printed in the United States of America
All rights reserved

Ohio University Press books are printed on acid-free paper ⊗ ™

12 11 10 09 08 07 06 05   5 4 3 2 1

Library of Congress Cataloging-in-Publication Data

An American vein : critical readings in Appalachian literature / edited by Danny L.
Miller, Sharon Hatfield, and Gurney Norman.
    p. cm.
Includes bibliographical references and index.
ISBN 0-8214-1589-1 (cloth : alk. paper) — ISBN 0-8214-1590-5 (pbk. : alk. paper)
    1. American literature—Appalachian Region—History and criticism.   2. Authors,
American—Homes and haunts—Appalachian Region.   3. Appalachian Region—
Intellectual life.   4. Appalachian Region—In literature.   5. Mountain life in
literature.   I. Miller, Danny, 1949–   II. Hatfield, Sharon, 1956–   III. Norman,
Gurney, 1937–
PS286.A6A83 2005
810.9'974—dc22   2004023207

CONTENTS

PREFACE

The idea for this collection of critical essays about Appalachian literature was hatched at the 2000 Appalachian Studies Conference at the University of Tennessee–Knoxville. Gurney Norman, a writer of fiction about Appalachia and one of the region's chief spokespersons in the last thirty years, and Danny Miller, author and teacher of Appalachian literature for the past twenty-five years, lamented the fact that Appalachia as a literary landscape is almost entirely absent from the American literary canon and that Appalachian literature is celebrated almost exclusively only in the region itself. They discussed the need for a collection that would highlight the significant contributions of Appalachian writers and literary scholars to American literature. Upon deciding to move forward with an anthology, Norman and Miller were joined by scholar and writer Sharon Hatfield. We three editors have spent four years compiling this book and have thoroughly enjoyed our collaboration.

Preparing our book has been an exciting and rewarding experience. We have learned a great deal about the subject of Appalachian literature, and we hope that others will do so as well. We have had stimulating discussions, among ourselves and with other scholars and writers of the Appalachian region, about many of the issues underlying a study of Appalachian literature, such as the fundamental question of what it is that makes (or does not make) one an "Appalachian" author, why the American literary establishment and canon-builders have shunned Appalachian authors, and what it is about "regionalism" that makes it seem less valuable than "mainstream" or "high" literature. These discussions formed the foundation for our choices in this book. Some of our editorial decisions are explained in the introduction; others are perhaps inexplicable, but were guided by our instinctive feelings about Appalachia and its literary history. We specifically chose to focus our attention on literature and literary criticism of the twentieth century, beginning with those writers who first wrote with authority about their native place—Jesse Stuart, James Still, and Harriette Arnow. We then brought our study of Appalachian literature to the twenty-first century. Most of the essays in the book are reprints; some of these have been slightly revised for this collection. We commissioned other essays on authors or topics we felt to be significant.

We cannot name here everyone who has helped us formulate our ideas about Appalachian literature and its authors. However, we know that this book would not have been possible without the support, creativity, and encouragement of many of our colleagues and friends. In addition to the authors of the articles presented herein, with all of whom we have had the most congenial dealings, we wish to thank two of our fellow editors and scholars in the field for their assistance. John Lang, editor of the *Iron Mountain Review* at Emory and Henry College, and Sandy Ballard, editor of *Appalachian Journal* at Appalachian State University, were especially helpful to us, and we extend them our sincerest thanks. Sandy read the manuscript, as did Betty Pytlik, and both offered excellent suggestions for its revision.

We are extremely indebted to our general editor at the Ohio University Press, Gillian Berchowitz, whose supportive editorial expertise is matched by her warmth and good humor. Gillian kept us going on this project, and without her it would not have been accomplished. Others at the press we wish to thank are David Sanders, Nancy Basmajian, and Christy Johnson. Additional assistance was kindly and patiently supplied by Tim Smith at Ohio University's Alden Library.

On a personal note, we wish to acknowledge the support of Jack Wright, Nyoka Hawkins, and Darrell Hovious.

INTRODUCTION

It has been said that the people of the Southern Appalachian mountain region are the most written-about but least understood people in America. Well before 1700, early hunters and explorers described in letters and diaries the wondrous beauty of the ancient Appalachian forest and its abundance of wild game, good soil, lush vegetation, and pure water. The majestic mountains and their meadows and valleys struck some as a kind of Eden.

By 1800, many published descriptions of settlers on the Appalachian frontier represented them as heroic, larger-than-life Americans leading the new nation in its expansion to the west. This heroic image would evolve into the national archetype of the noble pioneer.

In the decades following the Civil War, readers of books and magazines in the urban East were offered a less flattering picture of Appalachian people. Travel writers, journalists, cartoonists, and writers of "local color" fiction with little knowledge of mountain culture began the construction of a narrow, distorted, and often malicious negative portrait of Appalachian people. Descriptions sent home by some missionaries, educators, and other would-be servants of the people who came to the mountains from the East also contributed to the stereotypical "hillbilly" image that has become deeply rooted in the American consciousness.

In the twentieth century, movies and television shows and a continuing flow of books and magazine articles perpetuated this inaccurate and damaging perception of the people of Southern Appalachia. Such representations have, sadly, found broad acceptance among scholars and the general reading and viewing public.

It was not until the late 1920s and early 1930s that poets and fiction writers native to the mountain region began to render the experiences of ordinary Appalachian people realistically, honestly, and sympathetically. In the 1930s, Appalachian writers such as Jesse Stuart, Harriette Arnow, Don West, and James Still found national audiences for their novels, short stories, and poetry drawn from their experience of living in the mountains. By the

1960s, these writers had become literary heroes and models for a dynamic generation of young Appalachian writers just then coming to maturity.

The decade of the 1960s released powerful new cultural energies all over America, not least in Appalachia, as an old order of life was ending while a new one was beginning. It was and still is a painful transition. By the 1960s, mechanization of the mines and mills had left thousands of mountain people out of work. Young families were forced to leave the mountains to find economic opportunity in another of the waves of out-migration that mark Appalachian history. The loss of jobs left tens of thousands of mountain people dependent on welfare programs. Labor unions lost members and much of their power. Strip mining and later mountaintop removal mining caused monumental environmental damage. Many mountain people were driven to despair in those dark days, but others were able to rally and form citizens' groups to offer political and cultural resistance to dominant global forces. Citizens' groups went to Washington and to state capitals to lobby the legislatures. Many of these same people sought to shut down working strip mines.

Other resistance came in the form of artistic expression. Newly educated sons and daughters of displaced farmers, miners, and mill hands came home to the mountains with a burning desire to work in solidarity with local people struggling against corporate exploitation and political and social oppression. Many of the returning artists and political activists were veterans of the Vietnam War. These young people quickly discovered—or rediscovered—that in their home communities much of the old mountain life they had known as children still remained. Local people still told the old stories, played music from "deep in tradition," and danced the old dances in the spirit of local community celebration. Young returning writers, political activists, filmmakers, photographers, video artists, performance artists, painters, playwrights, and actors, as well as lawyers, doctors, educators, and scholars, appreciated the vitality of the traditional mountain storytellers, musicians, singers, songwriters, quiltmakers, weavers, potters, whittlers, wood-carvers, chairmakers, and dulcimer and banjo makers and a regional society where most of the people still knew how to work with their hands.

Included in the storytelling were accounts of strikes and picket lines, of hunger and violence and death during the struggles to establish unions in the coal mines and textile mills earlier in the century. As the 1970s unfolded, a cultural transmission, a modern-day "handing down" of cultural knowledge from one generation to another, took place as a modern Appalachian sense of *identity,* at once old and new, burst across the mountain ranges. From this decade of creative foment came a remarkable Appalachian literary and cultural renaissance.

The editors of *An American Vein,* Danny Miller, Sharon Hatfield, and Gurney Norman, have had the good fortune to be a part of this experience, having participated as writers, activists, editors, and teachers in their region's expanding literary field for the past three decades. Danny Miller grew up in Ashe County in the mountains of western North Carolina. Sharon Hatfield lived her early years in Lee County, Virginia, that state's westernmost county, which ends at Cumberland Gap. Gurney Norman, the son and grandson of coal miners, is a native of the eastern Kentucky and southwest Virginia coalfields. They, like thousands of other young people of their generation who grew up in the heart of the hills, first became aware of their region's literary tradition in school and college. It is a life-changing experience for new generations to discover that their own local landscapes, their families and communities, have been truthfully portrayed in books by writers whose backgrounds are similar to their own.

Despite growing enthusiasm for Appalachian literature among readers who know it, there is no denying that this unique part of American literature remains largely unrecognized by the rest of the country. Many individual writers from the mountains have found success and acclaim beyond the region, but awareness of the *region itself* as a thriving center of literary creativity is not widespread. It is hoped that this collection of critical essays will help new readers, nationally and internationally, discover Appalachian literature and its relevance to our times.

The sheer number of excellent writers who have established the Appalachian literary tradition has made the task of choosing writers for inclusion in this book difficult indeed. In no time at all the editors made a list of fifty twentieth-century Appalachian authors worthy of consideration by critics. Much discussion and some argument went into the process of selecting the authors for critical attention.

We recognize that the scope of this volume, like that of any anthology, must necessarily be limited. Some readers may wonder why certain famous contemporary Southern authors, some of whom are internationally recognized, are not included in *An American Vein.* Throughout the making of this book, the editors have relied as much on instinct and personal knowledge as on a rigid methodology. The authors selected for critical attention reflect the editors' knowledge of Appalachian cultural history and overall sense of the development of Appalachian literature. Other readers may wonder why many of the newer literary voices are not discussed in these pages. The editors consider this book to be a foundational text for future Appalachian scholarship; hence the focus on twentieth-century writers. Clearly, more scholarship and more anthologies similar to this one are called for to do justice to the many fine writers now at work in the Appalachian mountain region. These writers, some in midcareer, others quite young, represent a challenge and an opportunity for a new generation of scholars who recognize the power of contemporary American letters.

As *An American Vein* celebrates writers who have contributed to the Appalachian literary tradition, it also celebrates the many small literary journals, the regional magazines and presses, and the dedicated people who created and operated them for their indispensable contributions to the rise and development of Appalachian literature. Since the 1930s hundreds of such publications have come and gone, but in doing so they have brought into print the work of many creative writers, scholars, and journalists. *Mountain Life and Work, Appalachian South, Hemlocks and Balsams, Wind, Mountain Review, Laurel Review, Appalachian Journal, Appalachian Heritage, Mossy Creek Reader, Journal of Kentucky Studies, Journal of Appalachian Studies,* and *Iron Mountain Review* are but a few of the scores of regional publications that for decades have offered Appalachian writers and scholars a range of outlets for their work.

Another important contribution comes from the pioneering editors of earlier anthologies of Appalachian literature and criticism. In 1976 a pamphlet called *Appalachian Literary Criticism: Critical Essays* was published. This little book contained five essays chosen by noted West Virginia scholar Ruel Foster, to whom the present generation of Appalachian critics owes a great debt. *Voices from the Hills* (1977), an anthology edited by Robert J. Higgs and Ambrose N. Manning of East Tennessee State University, gathers a broad range of Appalachian fiction, poetry, historical notes, and critical commentaries. Twenty years later, Higgs and Manning were joined by Jim Wayne Miller to compile the two-volume *Appalachia Inside Out*, a sequel to *Voices*. *The Poetics of Appalachian Space* (1991), edited by Parks Lanier Jr., is a collection of literary essays based on the ideas of Gaston Bachelard.

As the twenty-first century began, *The South in Perspective: An Anthology of Southern Literature*, edited by Edward Francisco, Robert Vaughan, and

Linda Francisco (Prentice Hall, 2000), broke new literary ground and gained a fresh audience for Appalachian literature. To the surprise and delight of many writers and readers of Appalachian literature, *The South in Perspective* featured a 104-page section called "Appalachia Recognized." The ten-page introduction is an important contribution to a general understanding of modern Appalachian literature. In particular, the introduction establishes the ways in which Appalachia is part of the South but also separate from it.

Other valuable new books in the fledgling century spotlight a panoply of writings by mountain women. *Her Words: Diverse Voices in Contemporary Appalachian Women's Poetry,* edited by Felicia Mitchell (University of Tennessee Press, 2002); *Listen Here: Women Writing in Appalachia,* edited by Sandra Ballard and Patricia L. Hudson (University Press of Kentucky, 2003); and many other important anthologies, large and small, represent major milestones in the development of Appalachian literature and the creation of a modern consciousness in the region.

It is clear by now, after decades of discussion, that the concept of "regional" literature in America will always mean different things to different people. For example, even in this new millennium, many professors of American literature, on hearing the words "regional writers" and "American regionalism," will automatically register "late-nineteenth-century local color movement, Mary Murfree, John Fox Jr., Brett Hart, Mary E. Wilkins Freeman, Sarah Orne Jewett." Certainly the great American "regional" writers of the post–Civil War period have an enduring place in the nation's literature. Nearly a century and a half later, however, "region" and "regional literature" have taken on new, more fluid meanings. One meaning that many Appalachian writers and scholars agree on is that regional writing is truthful writing from and of the region, not merely about it. An Appalachian writer is someone who writes knowledgeably and honestly about the Appalachian mountain region and the people who live there. Life in Appalachia is not static, as some have assumed. The Appalachian region's literature reveals a modern, rapidly changing world that retains many aspects of traditional rural life. It is hoped that the essays in *An American Vein* will stimulate fresh discussion not just of Appalachian literature but of the concept of regional literature itself.

A sense of design underlies the organization of the essays in *An American Vein,* especially those at the beginning and the end of the book. The first two essays, by Cratis D. Williams and Jim Wayne Miller, are general introductory pieces intended to situate the reader in an Appalachian context. Williams is often referred to as "the father of Appalachian literature." His 1962 PhD dissertation, "The Southern Mountaineer in Fact and Fiction," is regarded as the most influential critical work in the region's literature. Miller, a generation younger than Williams, was a leading poet, fiction writer, and essayist who did much to spark the quickening of Appalachian literature in the final decades of the twentieth century. The collection closes with an essay by Rodger Cunningham that may surprise many readers and stir considerable discussion. A writer of both fiction and nonfiction, Cunningham is the author of *Apples on the Flood* (University of Tennessee Press, 1987), in which he traces the roots of Appalachian regionalism to twelfth-century Scotland. His insightful essay on John Crowley's novels breaks new ground in Appalachian literary criticism. In this new millennium, both Crowley and Cunningham suggest new possibilities for the region's literature in times to come. Together they make the radical announcement that in fictional Appalachia, postmodern werewolves have arrived and brought with them powerful new metaphors.

Other essays in addition to Cunningham's point to new directions in Appalachian literary criticism. One important positive change in the past twenty years is the belated recognition of the contributions to Appalachian literature and culture of African American writers and artists. Black people have been part of Appalachia since before the "white" settlement of the eighteenth century, but it is only in recent years that white Appalachians have begun to know something of the experience of African American mountain people. Readers of the region's history learn that large numbers of slaves escaped from their plantation "owners" and joined the Cherokee and other tribes in the mountain South long before Daniel Boone shot his first deer in the transylvanian wilderness. Black Appalachian writers often draw on family and regional lore as they create a vibrant new space in the region's literature, a "space within the space," as Kentucky poet Frank X Walker puts it.

African Americans are one of several population groups who have shaped the Appalachian story from its human beginnings and continue to do so today. Native American people have been present in the Appalachian mountains for thousands of years. European immigrants have come to the mountains one by one, in families, and also in great waves. One of the greatest of these waves came in the early years of the twentieth century with the arrival in the Appalachian coalfields of trainloads of European laborers to lay the railroad tracks and dig the coal in the new industrial mines. Now at the beginning of the twenty-first century, a new wave of immigration to the Appalachian region is in full swing as people from all over the world find their way to the mountains, bringing with them the full diversity of the world. As in the rest of America, the growing Latino population especially is rapidly changing the demographics of the mountain region. It will likely not be long before new writers emerge from these populations and make their own contributions to the region's and the nation's literature.

In putting together this collection of essays, the editors established several goals: (1) to bring Appalachian literature to the attention of literary scholars; (2) to gather into one place some of the critical writing about Appalachian literature for use by future generations of readers, writers, and scholars; (3) to exemplify the quality and range of Appalachian literature; (4) to provide representative essays that illuminate the work of leading Appalachian authors of the twentieth century; (5) to illustrate different literary critical approaches to Appalachian literature; (6) to provide something of value to teachers of Appalachian literature; (7) to offer resistance to the negative stereotyping of mountain people; (8) to provide essays that are generally accessible to a wide range of readers, both scholarly and general; and (9) to present Appalachian literary criticism as a vital part of the American literary tradition.

It is for readers to decide the extent to which these goals have been met. Of one thing the editors are certain: *An American Vein: Critical Readings in Appalachian Literature* unearths a mother lode of literary treasure that runs through the Southern Appalachian Mountains, its veins shooting out in all directions.

Danny Miller
Sharon Hatfield
Gurney Norman

New Directions

Folk or Hillbilly?

CRATIS D. WILLIAMS

Although touches of realism in the newer fiction had been given to the Southern highlanders by Elizabeth Madox Roberts in *The Time of Man* (1926), in one or two of the more recent novels by Charles Neville Buck, and in T. S. Stribling's *Bright Metal* (1928), realism in the contemporary sense of the word was first introduced into the treatment of the Southern hill people by Fiswoode Tarleton in *Bloody Ground: A Cycle of the Southern Hills* in 1929. It contains twelve "pieces"[1] about life and characters in Leeston and its surroundings, notably Porky Ridge, where the soil is so rich and the water so sweet that the best moonshine whiskey available is made there; Misery Mountain, where the poorest and weakest of mountain folk are forced to live; and Little Congo, to which the Negroes have been driven, for the people of Leeston do not permit them to dwell within its limits.

The setting of the stories is not identified with a particular state. But the title of the book, the frequent references to feuds, the names of the characters (notably Sheriff Jett), and such place names as Leeston (Lee's College is in Jackson, Kentucky), Meddlesome Creek, Misery Mountain, etc., all suggest "Bloody Breathitt" County, Kentucky.

The stories overflow with stereotypical notions of mountain life and custom. The mountaineers are moving toward physical degeneracy through

From "The Southern Mountaineer in Fact and Fiction—Part IV," chapter 8, "New Directions: Folk or Hillbilly?" (edited by Martha H. Pipes from the author's 1961 dissertation), *Appalachian Journal* 3 (Summer 1976): 347–57. Copyright © 1976 by *Appalachian Journal* and Appalachian State University.

intermarriage.[2] Their lore keeps alive a fierce pride in their blood strains, their daring, their cunning.[3] Their chivalry is in the blood, for their ancestors had fought with the Stuarts and with Washington and had followed Boone over the Wilderness Trail (298–99), but wherever chivalry is marked, slanderous gossip "evolves into a horrible, twirling monster" (284). The mountain folk are unable to articulate their deepest emotions (235). They possess the "cold pride of the hills, where the word 'love' is seldom heard, where affection is stifled, where dignity's an unwritten code and not even death draws a kiss" (222).

The Leeston folk congregate in the county seat on election days and Saturday afternoons, and for such special occasions as revivals and traveling carnivals held in the grove of elms that serves as a town park. The description of the county seat at such times differs little from that of similar seats in previous fiction (55).[4] It is on occasions such as these that feuds break out again, that knifings, fistfights, and violence occur. Particularly, election days are dreaded by sheriffs and town marshals, for "killing is a part of getting men into office" and people come to see "who's going to be killed" (63). The ballad-makers turn all these tragedies into minstrelsy in this land "with a page from Chaucer in every stark hill" and where the genius for ballads is unweakened by time from "King Alfred to the present" (70).

As to its structure and its central purpose, *Bloody Ground* is in the tradition of Sherwood Anderson's *Winesburg, Ohio.* The stories are all told in present tense in terse sentences and pungent fragments. The compelling style, the use of the same general setting, and the movement of some of the characters from story to story, as well as the sense of community evoked through a fresh use of stereotypical material and skillfully handled dialect, give Leeston and its surroundings a unity of impression comparable to that achieved by Anderson in *Winesburg.* The same sense of attrition between the old and the new as well as an underlying sickness of provincialism is achieved.

Tarleton's novel, *Some Trust in Chariots* (1930), though written in a realistic vein, is a dishonest sort of book and a failure structurally. The essential elements of the plot are derived from high-pitched and far-flung incidents appearing in the novels of Lucy Furman and Charles Neville Buck, all of which place *Some Trust in Chariots* in the "quare women" tradition, but certain emphases on the attitudes of mountain folk, whom Tarleton calls "hillbillies" or simply "'billies," suggest that it more appropriately belongs in the "hillbilly" tradition. To one who has read *Bloody*

Ground and who is acquainted with Buck and Furman, it is disappointing. With its artificiality of plot and its exaggerations of character, customs, and dialect, it lacks conviction, in spite of its realism, and fails to sustain reader interest. There is no central character. At first it would seem that Joel Welkin's struggle for an education is to be the central theme and that Joel is to be the protagonist; then the struggle of Patricia Fanton, the principal of Thessalonia Settlement School on Fretful Creek, to prevent the school from being abandoned by the mountaineers who have become resentful of Yankee charity, appears for a time to be the central purpose of the story; but finally, it would seem that the theme of the story is an ultra-romantic one—the fruition of the innate honor and nobility of character of a most dissolute and dismally ignorant hillbilly (named Daniel Boone), after he attempts to put out the fire that burns the school building, because he is convinced that it has been set by one of his enemies in order to incriminate him. The clumsy manipulation of plot machinery by which Daniel is jock-eyed into attending the school himself, thus restoring it to favor with the hillbillies, does not approach the neatness with which Buck handled such things nor the integrity with which they were presented by Lucy Furman.

It is painfully obvious that Tarleton was in the main simply writing a novel when he wrote *Some Trust in Chariots,* a novel compounded largely of what he considered the striking things he had gathered from novels he had read, but he discovered and revealed two or three important recent changes which had taken place in the mountaineers. Dan Boone's rat-house, guarded by outposts to prevent raids of the revenue officers,[5] was a meeting place for a new kind of mountain rowdy who had come to recognize himself as a hillbilly (89), the depraved and extremely ignorant stay-at-home whose limitations were such that he could not join the migrations of his people to the centers of industry during the prosperous 1920s and whose presence at home hastened the disintegration of community organization in a decade marked by a resurgence of moonshining in the mountains. Mountain stock had begun to degenerate as a result of cousin marriages,[6] and the highlanders had become severely sensitive to outside criticism (91–92). On the very eve of the Depression that was to convert them to the Democratic Party through the saving grace of the New Deal dole, they were skilled at elaborating their resentment of "indirect" charity (26, 72). Because there was increasing contact with the outside world, it was generally known in the mountains by 1929 that the public relations officers of the mission schools and settlement centers were misrepresenting the highlanders in the emphases they were making in order to raise funds to support the schools and centers. This misrepresentation led generally to resentments and reprisals, which Tarleton was in the forefront in presenting in fiction but which probably contributed very little toward the closing of large numbers of the schools and centers during the Depression.

The Tennessee mountaineers have been reduced to misery and moral bankruptcy in Anne W. Armstrong's *This Day and Time* (1930), an honest tale of lechery, fornication, incest, murder, and betrayal as they touch the life of Ivy Ingoldsby and her son. After Ivy, abandoned by an irresponsible husband, starves out of a textile town, she returns to a miserable shack on a rocky scrap of a farm in a socially disintegrated mountain community to contend with poverty and the hacking lechery of the passion-ridden men who live around her.

This Day and Time is essentially a study in contrasts. The title, a much-used expression of the mountain folk in that section of East Tennessee (taken over lately by the Federal Government in the development of the Tennessee Valley Authority), sets the difference between the hard life the mountain folk were living on the eve of the Great Depression and that easier life, circumscribed by the comfortable certainties of an isolated social structure based on a subsistence economy of an earlier day, such as was described by Mary Noailles Murfree.

Although the primitivism in *This Day and Time,* which antedated Erskine Caldwell's *Tobacco Road* by two years, is something new in mountaineer fiction, the naturalism, with its emphasis upon the inexorable forces which plot the fate of Ivy Ingoldsby, is, like Murfree's naturalism, freed from the genteel restrictions of her time but with biology added.[7] In her selection of materials (i.e., character types, homes, customs, and activities) Armstrong is in the tradition of Murfree, but in her use of superstition and proverbial lore, all of which has the pure ring of authenticity, she owes much to the Chapmans, whose Glen Hazard books were showing the most clearly defined direction being taken by mountaineer fiction at the time her novel appeared.

Armstrong's book, the most radical departure in the direction of naturalistic primitivism in mountaineer fiction down to the time of its appearance, possesses stretches of genuine power. It is a more significant novel than any of the better-known Glen Hazard books in that there is no laboring of a tenuous thesis, no effort to exhibit the mountain folk as quaint and "interesting," no recommendation of a formula for the salvation of the depraved highlanders, but a genuine effort to present honestly and fearlessly the social and moral decay of a community without psychic resources and strangling in the cesspool of its own social and cultural excrement.

Grace Lumpkin's *To Make My Bread* (1932), a simply written but powerful proletarian novel similar in structure to Steinbeck's *Grapes of Wrath* (1939), should be included, along with Fox's *The Heart of the Hills,* Heyward's *Angel,* Anderson's *Kit Brandon,* and Arnow's *The Dollmaker,* on the list of required reading for the social worker who seeks to understand the problems of the mountain migrants in adjusting to civilization in contemporary America. A long novel, *To Make My Bread* follows the destinies of the McClure family from their insulated life, stripped by privation to its elemental terms, in the South Mountains in North Carolina to their ultimate bitterness, disillusionment, and ruin in Gastonia (called Leesville) in the labor troubles of 1929. Effective contrasts, drawn without sentimentality, are made between the poverty-stricken but independent and self-respecting McClures deep in the South Mountains in 1900, before the lumber companies drove them from their land, and the struggling, toil-ridden, exploited McClures, crushed in spirit, dying of pellagra, victims of violence, and disintegrated as a family, in the textile town in the late 1920s.

Lumpkin's book makes two extremely significant points relative to mountain migrants: because they are not prepared for work in the industrial world, they find it necessary to accept places at the bottom of the economic and social ladder when they arrive in industrial centers; and, with their proud independence unsubdued by experience in cooperation, they become troublemakers quickly in the presence of industrial strife. John and Bonnie's abiding sense of justice placed them in the forefront as leaders in the strike, but Sam McEachern's long experience at defying law and decency prepared him well for his role as a strikebreaker in the pay of the managers. That John is flirting with communism at the end of the book does not so much impugn the patriotism of mountain people as underscore the raging indignation of mountaineers at social injustice, the same sort of indignation that made of the mountain man's ancestors such excellent patriots at Alamance and King's Mountain, at New Orleans and Santa Cruz, and at Chickamauga and Gettysburg. Implications are clear: the solution to the mountaineer problem is simply educating the mountaineer *in the mountains* for the work he is to do when he grows up and migrates. To do this the local school system must receive through federal taxes financial aid from the industrial centers to which mountaineers migrate.

Olive Tilford Dargan, the North Carolina poet, short story writer, and novelist, turned from exquisite portrayal of mountain character in a series of idyllic stories collected in *Highland Annals* (1925) to a bitter attack upon capitalism and a frank avowal of Marxism in two powerfully written but emotion-packed proletarian novels of the early years of the Great Depression. *Highland Annals* includes eight distinguished stories and sketches of life in the Nantahala Mountains west of Asheville just at the time civilization was marching into the highlands.[8] Dargan, although not a native mountain woman, perhaps caught more accurately the isolated Carolina mountaineer's dialect, essential character, and habits of mind than any other writer of fiction ever to attempt to interpret Carolina mountain folk.

Dargan's proletarian novels, *Call Home the Heart* (1932) and *A Stone Came Rolling* (1935), were published under the pseudonym of Fielding Burke. *Call Home the Heart,* the more successful of the two, follows the fortunes of a remarkable mountain woman, Ishmalee Waycaster, from girlhood through her marriage to a handsome, happy-go-lucky mountain orphan, Britt Hensley, to her elopement with a neighboring mountain man, Rad Bailey, to Winbury (Gastonia), a textile town in the Piedmont section of North Carolina.

In *A Stone Came Rolling* Ishma and Britt and their handsome son have moved to Dunmow (Burlington?) in the Piedmont. Britt, who is too much the mountain man to become a mill worker, is a tenant on a farm surrendered to renters after two hundred years by a Quaker family whose ancestor had been hanged by Governor Tryon's men in 1771 on the tree by the gate. Ishma becomes a relief worker. Because her communistic convictions are strong, she sees the dole as an opiate to drug the senses of the poor in order to prevent them from organizing to demand the overthrow of capitalism and establish their own rights.

Although Dargan was most successful in capturing and identifying those facets of the character of the Carolina mountaineer which have been associated with the spirit of freedom and independence of his Revolutionary ancestry, with his outrage in the presence of injustice and exploitation in the mill villages, she was not so successful as Grace Lumpkin in motivating the mountaineer's protest against grinding injustice. Because the McClures suffered personally the debilitating poverty and the pulverization of mind wrought by labor in the textile mills of the twenties, their reasons for moving toward Marxism were more valid than Ishma's. In *A Stone Came Rolling* particularly, it seems that Ishma is little more than a convenient vehicle, like Lanny Budd in Upton Sinclair's novels, for wheeling Dargan's heavy load of social propaganda into place. Yet, Dargan's underlying assumption is a logical one. Mountain character shaped in an atmosphere of permissiveness toward independence, justice, and freedom, as conceived by the founding fathers, moves easily toward Marxism when it is liberated by education from the stultifying limitations of superstition and prejudice indigenous to the mountaineer's colonial religious fundamentalism, and particularly so in the presence of fascistic controls in the hands of the capitalists.[9]

Dargan's mountain fiction shows its preeminence not in the social propaganda with which it is overlaid[10] but rather in the consummate skill with which she captures the mountaineer in his own setting. By the time she was completing *A Stone Came Rolling,* however, the Depression had clouded her vision of the mountaineer in his own place, for she had begun to express the wistful yearning of the "back to nature" movement that stimulated a new admiration for Henry David Thoreau. The simple life of the mountaineer sharing his one-room slab abode with fourteen others is contemplated as a restorative, offering therapeutic value to the struggle-worn outlander who finds his way to the remote coves.[11] Sentimental regret that progress has reached the mountains (355) and a sudden revelation that the unschooled mountaineers are "folk," possessing the psychological complex of the primitive whose intelligence amounts to little more than a set of impulses suspended in an emulsion of ignorance and witchcraft (369), indicate that Dargan, after all, was sensitive to the odors of new literary styles wafted aloft by the breezes that brushed Cloudy Knob.

After Sherwood Anderson moved to Marion, Virginia, to become an editor of two small-town weekly newspapers, he became interested in the plight of the poor Virginia mountaineers living in the desolate cabins flung among the upper coves and along the high ridges of the Clinch Mountains and the Blue Ridge near Marion. Included among the stories collected in *Death in the Woods and Other Stories* (1933) are three slight pieces which might be considered Anderson's finger work for *Kit Brandon,* one of the major studies in fiction of the mountaineer during the Depression. In "A Jury Case," the best of the three stories, Anderson portrays in broad strokes three mountain types: the congenital criminal, the sly troublemaker who knows how to induce others to take vengeance for him, and the sensitive but volatile mountaineer who is gentle when sober but a terror of violence when intoxicated.

Anderson's unique prose style, developed around his western rhythms, when applied to the flat average of poor-white mountaineers in the stories included in *Death in the Woods,* certainly produced a new way of seeing the mountaineer as but another American, subject to the same sort of frustrations and compulsions as Americans everywhere. When Anderson turned again to the mountaineer in *Kit Brandon: A Portrait* (1936), he had served an apprenticeship in portraying a new type which became the subject of his best structured novel and one of the most compassionate novels ever written about Southern mountaineers.

A picture of the big moonshining era in the upper South in the 1920s, *Kit Brandon* also presents snapshots of textile mill workers and mountain ridge people, all in an effort to explain the good sense of those who entered the bootleg racket. Bootlegging, with its powerful and complex gang organization, is presented as the obverse of a familiar old pewter token, called individualism, whose converse bears the image of the big-time robber baron of the latter part of the nineteenth century. The novel centers around Kit Brandon, who tells her story to the author while she is driving his car through the Dakotas.

Anderson had gone into the history and social conditions of mountain folk carefully before he set about to write *Kit Brandon.* In Kit's long account of her origins and her struggles with poverty and hardship, the essential facts and the main notions, true and false, about Southern mountain people are recited. The sentimental and romantic concepts of Southern highlanders are dismissed hurriedly.[12] The positive aspects of their culture and background are recognized briefly, but Anderson finds them an exploited and abandoned people, their lands denuded by lumber companies and their mountains gutted by coal corporations (27–28), just at the time that their reputation for distilling excellent whiskey (218) makes it possible for them to choose between the poverty, more abject than what they have known, that becomes their lot in the Southern mill towns and the dangerous but lucrative occupation of manufacturing and blockading moonshine whiskey (40–42). Although they are dominated by Scotch-Irish character, possess pioneer virtues, and cling tightly to their old-fashioned individualism in their native coves and hollows (118–20), in the mills they are poor whites selling themselves as cheap and unskilled laborers to factories which have moved down from the North to "lap up the cheap labor of hill billies" (41). The mountain people are forced by circumstances to abandon their denuded acres, load their shabby belongings, their numerous children, and their slovenly wives into their creaking wagons, and drive down to some mill town where the children go to work and the husband, too old for work in the mill, sits "at home with the fat wife" (131–33).

Ellen Glasgow's brief side glances at the Virginia mountaineers in *Vein of Iron* (1935) rest upon poverty and degeneracy. Ada Fincastle, the heroine of the novel, had heard in her girlhood the familiar claim that in colonial days the ancestors of the mountaineers were "a stalwart breed." Although the Virginia mountains were described as Alps-like,[13] they were inhabited by a run-out race. In some instances idiocy was the result of cousin marriages;[14] in others, of unwise marriages with degenerates.[15] But even the proud Fincastles were not shocked unduly by the increasing number of degenerates, for they believed that people could not do anything about idiots.[16]

In *Absalom, Absalom!* (1936) by William Faulkner, the ambitious imposter Thomas Sutpen, who in 1833 had set himself up in a strange mansion located in the center of a hundred-square-mile plantation in Mississippi, is revealed as a mountaineer from southwestern Virginia. Born and reared in one of those log cabins "boiling with children" in which men and grown boys "lay before the fire on the floor while the women and older girls stepped back and forth across them to reach the fire to cook,"[17] Thomas's basic trouble was the destruction of his innocence. After his father, following the death of the boy's mother, had taken his half-naked brood back to the Tidewater country, Thomas saw his sister run over by a coach driven by a proud Negro (231) and was himself driven by a Negro from the front door of a Virginia mansion and ordered always to come to the back door (232). Thomas knew then what he had to do in order to "live with himself for the rest of his life" (220). Fourteen years old at the time, he ran away to devote his life to taking his revenge on the social order that had so dramatically relieved him of his innocence. The sordid story of Sutpen's climb to position is the main level of Faulkner's novel. That the house Sutpen builds should fall to ruins in ignominy, his blood having mingled with that of Negro, aristocrat, and poor white—following his death at the hands of a poor-white tenant, Wash Jones, whose daughter old Sutpen had seduced—but measures the dimension of Faulkner's scorn for what he considered a most vicious variety of poor whites. Sutpen is such a skillfully created character, one half regrets that Faulkner could not forgive him for being a poor white and half suspects that all of Faulkner's noise about poor whites is in part a device to delude the pickers standing at the foot of his own family tree, from which he prefers himself to pick the fruit he wants displayed.

Glenn Spotswood, the Marxist labor organizer in John Dos Passos's *Adventures of a Young Man* (1938), spent some time in Slade (Harlan) County, Kentucky, assisting the striking miners of the Muddy Fork Local.[18] While there he became intimately acquainted with one mountain family, the Napiers, who were still living in a primitive cabin.

Glenn Spotswood found the Kentucky mountaineers vulnerable to the false doctrines of "piecard" organizers precisely because the Kentuckians were unwilling to join unions tainted with marxism. Sheriff Blaine's army of deputized thugs suggested that the prevailing view of the Kentucky mountaineer was anti-union and that he was still eager to work for his boss on a personal basis.

The Southern mountaineer as he appears in the fiction examined in this chapter is a folk character cavorting like a ballad hero, or an angry worker protesting against exploitation by greedy capitalists, or a poor white either sinking into awful degradation or poisoning the gentle society into which he has sneaked. It is interesting to note that these interpretations of the mountaineer, though at times artistically achieved by accomplished hands, were made by outsiders. By the time the fiction emphasizing the folk quality of the mountaineer had excited a new interest, labor troubles in Gastonia, North Carolina, refocused attention upon him as a migrant worker. Beginning with Lumpkin's *To Make My Bread* in 1932, he tended more and more to become a proletarian figure as the Great Depression rolled across the decade. To distinguish him from other proletarians, his interpreters identified him as a hillbilly. In the past, only two or three native voices had joined the chorus of interpreters, but the hillbilly himself, becoming articulate at last, was to lead the chorus by the end of the Depression. Sherwood Anderson had perceived that even hillbillies are people. Vitally concerned with neither labels nor sharp differentiations, the new voices, those of Hubert Skidmore, James Still, Jesse Stuart, and Harriette Arnow, are voices of the mountain people themselves chanting songs of themselves and their kind, be they what they may.

Notes

1. Previously published in *The Forum, The Golden Book, Adventure, McClure's Magazine,* and *Plain Talk.*

2. Ked Fallon, summoned home from the mines to take up the cudgels in his family's feud with the Cherrys, muses before the fire in his father's cabin: "All they think about here is keeping blood-ties strong. They want me to hitch with Caroline [his first cousin] and have

young ones that stare at the fire all winter long, boys that plow in circles and girls like my sister Ora that do the bidding of hill boys, when they are grown. Marry first cousin like my pap and grandpap, marry Caroline so I'll have a boy like Matthias [his half-witted brother]." (*Bloody Ground* [New York: L. MacVeagh, 1929], 40.)

3. *Bloody Ground,* 103–4. The Taneys on Porky Ridge chronicle by firelight old tales of feudal barons, duelists, chieftains, hunters, and heroes at King's Mountain.

4. The streets are lined with lean horses, mules, wagons, sleds, and oxen. Hogs wallow in the streets. Cows roam about turning over rubbish heaps with their noses. The people themselves are perhaps better portrayed than writers usually succeed in portraying them: "Under the porticos of the business stores men, women and children make groups. Some stare silently at newcomers who hitch their mules to the racks. Some whisper among themselves. Legs swing over portico floors and eyes stare from under bonnets and wide-brimmed hats. Some hill men and hill women sit under the big elms in the courthouse yard. Men lie flat and women lean their backs against tree-trunks. Men whittle or whisper. Women nurse their least-ones. Boys and girls wander around the grove wide-eyed."

5. *Some Trust in Chariots* (New York: L. MacVeagh, 1930), 104–11.

6. The slow-witted Hicks boy who sets fire to the school building because of a grudge against a student is degenerate. His father and grandfather had married their first cousins. (Ibid., 166.)

7. *This Day and Time* (New York: Alfred A. Knopf, 1930). A counterpart of the sordid account of the death of tubercular little Bertha Jane, made pregnant by her sanctimonious but brutal father, who refuses to send for a midwife (247–56), had not appeared in mountain fiction, but there is much factual evidence to indicate that many pious widowers like Uncle Abel Dillard found their animal passions too powerful to control in those crowded little mountain cabins. That such a classic theme had not been used reflects the state of America's reading taste rather than a dearth of applicable materials in the hills.

8. The first seven of the stories had appeared in the *Atlantic Monthly* from 1919 to 1924. The eighth one had appeared in the *Reviewer.* In 1941 the eight stories, together with an additional one, "Uncle Hiram's Cure," were republished, with fifty photographs of Carolina mountain life by Bayard Wootten, under the title of *From My Highest Hill.*

9. Discussing the response of intelligent mountain youths to intellectual life on college campuses, Dargan said: "Mountain lads who were strong enough to break out of the coves and seek the highways, were usually of a mind to assimilate to truth wherever and however it was uncovered to them. If they found their way to Chapel Hill they did not stand debating by the stream of modernity crackling through the walls of the old University. They plunged in, and without pain cleansed themselves of the mental barnacles fastened upon them by the ebbing ancestral tide. Sometimes circumstances forced them into a college of more modesty and retirement, where only limited thinking was acceptable. Here they succeeded in ruffling the pools of acquiescence around them, and made their final exit noisily enough but trailing no honors." (*Call Home the Heart* [London and New York: Longmans, Green, 1932], 158.)

10. An eight-page speech summarizing the philosophy of communism is gulped by a volant mob of textile workers, "eager as burnt fields scenting rain" (ibid., 285).

11. *A Stone Came Rolling* (New York and Toronto: Longmans, Green, 1935), 278–79, 352.

12. *Kit Brandon* (New York: Scribner's, 1936), 6. "Not much chance among these defeated women, slovenly and dirty, for such romances as *The Trail of the Lonesome Pine.*" See also p. 114.

13. *Vein of Iron* (New York: Harcourt, Brace, 1935), 80–81.

14. John Fincastle, as he lay dying, was disturbed by the memory of a family of idiots, "inbred until it was imbecile," which had gathered about him. "Two generations of blank,

grinning faces and staring eyes and driveling mouths danced and shouted round him as they pressed closer and closer" (455).

15. One old mountain man had married an idiot girl from the poor house. "They had four idiot sons, who worked in the cornfield" (ibid., 167).

16. "It was God's law . . . that married people, no matter whether they were half-wits or not, must bring all the children they could into the world to share in the curse that was put upon Adam and Eve" (ibid., 167).

17. *Absalom, Absalom!* (New York: Random House, 1936), 221.

18. *Adventures of a Young Man* (New York: Harcourt, Brace, 1938), 187–235.

Appalachian Literature at Home in This World

JIM WAYNE MILLER

While the varieties of Protestantism found in the Appalachian region often differ sharply with regard to certain theological points, denominations share a decidedly otherworldly outlook. On this point sociologists, missionaries representing mainline Christian denominations, and others interested in programs of regional uplift have generally agreed. Jack Weller, a Presbyterian minister and missionary to Appalachia, has suggested that the different Protestant denominations in Southern Appalachia constitute a single folk religion so otherworldly in outlook as to be an obstacle to progress and social action—because believers look for a better life not in this world but in the next.[1] The region's literature might be expected to reflect something of the thoroughgoing otherworldliness of the folk religion. Yet Appalachian literature is—and always has been—as decidedly worldly, secular, and profane in its outlook as the traditional religion appears to be spiritual and otherworldly.

The notion that Appalachian literature is particularly worldly in its orientation will strike most people as wrongheaded. Sut Lovingood, who puts the lizards up Parson Bullen's pants leg, is a worldly fellow, everyone will agree.[2] The preacher himself, who is describing the agonies and sufferings of hell, is clearly Sut's opposite; the preacher is otherworldly in his view. But is he? A. O. Lovejoy maintains that talk of heaven and hell is

From *Iron Mountain Review* 2 (Summer 1984): 23–28. Reprinted by permission of the estate of Jim Wayne Miller; Mary Ellen Miller, literary executor.

this-worldly in the extreme, despite its ostensible vision of joys and agonies in a beyond:

> To be concerned about what will happen to you after death, or to let your thought dwell much upon the joys which you hope will then await you, may obviously be the most extreme form of this-worldliness; and it is essentially such if that life is conceived, not as profoundly different in kind from this, but only as more of much the same sort of thing.[3]

Lovejoy's insight leads us to suspect that both Sut and the preacher share the same worldly view, the only difference being that the preacher has been constrained by occasion while Sut has not.

The religion of the frontier tradition only seems to be otherworldly. When people in this tradition think of heaven, not with imagery that has come down from impoverished desert nomads—pearly gates, streets of gold—but with imagery derived from their own experience, they imagine a heaven very much like the place they know and are content with. The preacher on the Kentucky frontier is revealing in this respect when, endeavoring to picture heaven to his congregation, he exclaims: "Why, heaven is just a Kentucky of a place!" Certainly that is the conception of Big Eif Porter in Jesse Stuart's "300 Acres of Elbow Room." Big Eif, contemplating death, wishes for nothing different from what he already knows. His heaven is a transplanted Kentucky: "I hope there is a farm in heaven where I can work and I hope they have winter, summer, springtime and fall just like we have here."[4]

But if heaven in traditional Appalachian culture is often no more than the familiar, known world, the important thing is that this world and the next are nevertheless strictly separated. The varieties of Protestantism that have flourished in the region quite logically assume, given the premise of a transcendent God, a clear demarcation between this world and the next. There's a better world a-waiting, but it's off yonder in the sky. In the meantime, we are here, in this life, and we should not expect much help from God. Religion and life in this world do not have much to do with one another. Religion certainly has nothing to do with "worldly" things, but rather with "spiritual" things.

The strict division between this world and the next can be noted in the views of people who have moved from Appalachia to midwestern and northern industrial centers. Robert Coles's *A Festering Sweetness,* a collection of "found" poems taken from transcripts of interviews with Appalachian and other migrants, contains two revealing statements in this regard, one from a mountaineer's wife, a resident of Chicago since 1967, and another from a Kentuckian on his way to Chicago in 1970. In Chicago the mountain woman felt truly godforsaken: "In Chicago God isn't right at your side," she says. But then she expects little help from God, in Chicago or back home in the mountains, because "God has more on his shoulders / than us in Down Bottom Creek." The man's views are similar but even more explicit with regard to the division between this world and the next. Although he is a Bible reader, and although he prays on his way to Chicago, he does not really expect help from God, and repeatedly tells himself not to expect too much, for, as he says, "God looks after you in the *next* world."[5]

This world and the next are still for the most part separate in the contemporary folk culture of the region. Consider the contents of a program of country music. Most of the program will be given over to the alternating joys and sorrows of fornication and adultery, and to the celebration of place ("Good Old Rockytop"). The program concludes typically with a "sacred" or "spiritual" number. Lester Flatt could routinely sing "I Live the Life of Riley—When Riley's Not Around," and close with "Will the Circle Be Unbroken?" There is no inconsistency here. The program reflects an assumption of two spheres, this world and the next; the lack of transition or middle ground between them suggests the two realms have little to do with one another in spite of the fact that they are juxtaposed.

Nor is it necessarily important whether the otherworldly or the worldly view predominates. Both views are present, and strictly separated. The religious tradition has tended to remain separate from secular traditions. In the lives of individuals, particularly men, one frequently finds a secular phase followed by a religious one. The energies and enthusiasms of youth and one's more vigorous years are devoted to secular pursuits: drinking, fighting, fiddling, "swarping around." Later a man may become exceedingly devout, moving from the world of "Old Joe Clark" to that of "Amazing Grace."

The most vigorous literature of the Appalachian region, the writing which is an expression *of* the region and not a report *on* it, is concerned very much with things of this world, situated squarely in the secular realm. Literature is not "spiritual." It is "worldly." The earlier literature expressive of life in the region includes Davy Crockett's autobiography, Longstreet's

Georgia Scenes, Harden E. Taliaferro's *Fisher's River Scenes and Characters,* and George Washington Harris's *Sut Lovingood's Yarns.* It is a literature reflecting frontier conditions and attitudes, oral secular traditions, and is most alive in print when it deals with worldly matters: bear hunts; politicking; horse swapping; whiskey; brawling; play-parties; quiltings; corn shuckings; land speculating; gander pullings; fornication and adultery.

It may be that literature in Appalachia had no choice but to persist in a worldly, secular tradition, since fundamentalist Protestantism had no place for it. Traditional ballads were popularly known as "love songs" and were frowned upon—still are—by the devout. And those caught up in secular pursuits thought just as little of the devout and their activities. Play-parties and camp-meetings, quiltings and prayer-meetings were indicative of the two traditions. And the worldly preferred fornication to salvation. As Sut Lovingood observes in "Mrs. Yardley's Quilting": "One holesum quiltin am wuf three old pray'r-meetins on the poperlashun pint."[6]

Sut's dislike of preachers stems partly from his keen sense of hypocrisy and injustice. In "Rare Ripe Garden Seed" he asks a preacher why it is that he, Sut, feels so good knowing he could never become a sheriff and

> sell out widders' plunder, ur poor men's corn, and the thought of hit gives me a good feelin; hit sorter flashes thru my heart when I thinks of hit. I axed a parson onst, what hit cud be, an' he pernounced hit to be *onregenerit pride,* what I orter squelch in prayer, an' in tendin church on colleckshun days. I were in hopes hit might be religion, or sense, a-soakin intu me.

But Sut's abiding hostility toward religion is based, ultimately, on a thoroughly worldly view of things, a view which can be grimly naturalistic or deterministic. Sut observes that where there is not enough to eat, bigger children take from the smaller ones. Thus it is the world over, he generalizes; bishops eat elders; elders eat common people; common people eat cattle such as himself; he eats possums; possums eat chickens; chickens eat worms; worms eat dust;[7] and dust is the end of it all.

Sut denies the existence of the soul, of a beyond. Man is an animal, as his comparisons of children to pigs at a trough, of widows to smooth pacing mares, of himself to a rooster or a horse imply. The burial of Mrs. Yardley, killed when run over by a horse Sut has deliberately bolted, is no more to Sut than "a durn'd nasty muddy job," no more than salting her down, "fixin her fur rotten cumfurtably, kiverin her up wif sile [soil], tu keep the buzzards from cheating the wurms."[8] Sut's view is, to say the least, a view of this world and no other.

How is this situation best understood? What critical concepts would be most fruitful in dealing with such a literature? A useful approach is based on the distinction made in traditional societies between myths and tales. Anthropologists such as Malinowski and students of myth such as Eliade have long known that members of traditional societies are careful to distinguish between their myths, which they consider "true" stories, and tales, which they consider "false" stories.

Myths and tales deal with different kinds of reality, and narrate different kinds of "histories." Myths narrate sacred history; tales secular history. The former deal with the realm of the holy, the supernatural, the transcendent, things absolute, unconditional and beyond time; they tell of the other world. Tales are generally concerned with everyday happenings and events in time. The teller of tales may introduce elements of the supernatural or imaginary creatures such as fairies and giants, but even when these elements occur there is a matter-of-factness about the story. For even when dealing in fantasy, the tale tends to remain within the limits of the familiar, everyday world. Wondrous things may happen, strange beings may appear, but they do so in familiar surroundings and circumstances. The teller of tales delights in and illuminates this world and the things of this world, makes them stand out and shine in the foreground. Tales stand in a secular tradition, and their tellers, even when they are extremely sophisticated, are folk artists employing literature to reveal, through art, what reality may obscure.[9]

Our ability to distinguish between myths and tales, and between different kinds of reality rendered by these fundamentally different types of telling, suggests that we might consider works of literature as expressions of two different traditions, one concerned with sacred history, the other with secular history. These two traditions, although they coexist in a society, require different critical standards of judgment for their proper understanding and appreciation.

The worldly, secular tradition of Appalachian literature, rooted in the frontier experience, persists in the work of those "native voices" who began to be heard in the 1930s: Jesse Stuart, Harriette Simpson Arnow, and James Still. The essentially worldly view of Big Eif Porter in Stuart's "300 Acres of Elbow Room," noted earlier, is more explicit in Stuart's story "Snake Teeth," a spoofing of otherworldly visions and powers: the otherworldly beliefs of the pretty female preacher are destroyed when the young man lets her believe the snake that strikes her repeatedly is poisonous, only to inform her afterward that the serpent was defanged, and therefore harmless.[10] In Harriette Arnow's *The Dollmaker,* a novel about mountaineer migrants, emphasis is increasingly on things of this world, not of the next.[11] Like the mountaineer migrants to Chicago interviewed by Robert Coles, the novel's heroine, Gertie Nevels, feels godforsaken. Increasingly caught up in a bewildering and brutal web of worldly circumstances, she makes dolls to earn money and is unable to finish her carving of Christ because she can no longer visualize Christ's face. The otherworldly vision is dimmed and rendered impossible, in an almost deterministic fashion, by harsh and unrelenting circumstances of this world.

In the poems, short stories, and novels of James Still one finds the most artful expression of the worldly, secular tradition of Appalachian literature, as well as the clearest and most emphatic distinction between worldly and otherworldly views. Still's earthy hill folk typically assume the existence of a beyond. Brother Sim Mobberly, in the novel *River of Earth,* is a mountain preacher who, when he preaches the funeral of the Baldridge baby, says: "We have come together to ask the blessed Savior one thing pine-blank. Can a leetle child enter the Kingdom of Heaven?"[12] But while the novel accommodates this otherworldly view, other characters offer little affirmation of it. The notion of a beyond is irrelevant to their immediate concerns—and to the novel's thematic and imagistic structure.

Still's people are rooted in this world. No less than plants and animals, they are a part of the landscape, their lives shaped by natural forces, conditions, and cycles. Their lives are dusty with the land. Their experiences are such that the notion of a beyond is necessarily peripheral to the press of immediate needs. They subsist, persevere, and survive in this world. The father in *River of Earth* assumes a beyond but advises his son, the narrator: "There ain't no sense trying to see afar off. . . . It's better to keep your eyeballs on things nigh, and let the rest come according to law and prophecy" (16). Uncle Jolly's view of death is as crassly matter-of-fact as that of his literary ancestor, Sut Lovingood. Expressing his dislike for coal mining, Jolly says: "I'll be buried a-plenty when I'm dead. Don't want bug-dust in my face till then" (21). Anticipating her own death, the grandmother leaves instructions for her burial that are, like her son Jolly's view of death, matter-of-fact, and determined more by relationships in this world than by any considerations involving an afterlife. Feeling neglected by her family, she says bitterly:

When my dying day comes I'm right willing to be hauled straight to Flat Creek burying ground and put beside my man, buried down and kivered against [before] any o' my blood kin was told. My chaps won't come when I'm sick and pindly; they hain't use in coming to see me lay a corpse. (70)

When she dies, her grandson, the narrator, has no notion of her having gone to heaven. He can only visualize her "in the dark of my head where I could see her living face." He asks: "Grandma . . . where have you gone?" (127).

Here the narrator echoes the word he used when his grandmother mysteriously disappeared from the house and he feared she might be dead. "She [the grandmother] was gone and I couldn't think where" (77). The narrator's question, "Grandma . . . where have you gone?" also recalls questions asked by Brother Sim Mobberly, the preacher; by his mother; and by his Uncle Jolly. In a sermon Brother Mobberly speaks of the hills as "jist dirt waves" and asks: "where air we going on this mighty river of earth . . . ? Where air it sweeping us?" (42–43). The mother complains of "[f]orever moving yon and back, settling down nowhere for good and all, searching for god knows what. . . . Where air we expecting to draw up to?" (30). While teaching the young narrator to plow, Uncle Jolly asks: "What's folks going to live on when these hills wear down to a nub?" (71).

Brother Mobberly's vision of a "mighty river of earth" and of the hills as "jist dirt waves, washing through eternity" may seem quite otherworldly in contrast to the very practical and worldly concerns of the narrator's mother, who longs to settle down, and of his Uncle Jolly, who speculates about the effects of soil erosion. Yet while Brother Mobberly in his person and actions represents an otherworldly point of view—namely, fundamentalist Christianity—his words actually express a natural cycle of birth, reproduction and death—a cycle which requires no other world, no beyond, for its completion. Mobberly's vision is, furthermore, of a river of *earth*. Death does not translate people into another realm; rather, the dead continue on the river with the living. Mobberly describes humanity as moving on "this mighty river of earth, a-borning, begetting, and a-dying—the living and the dead riding the waters" (43).

The young narrator's question at the end of the novel, "Grandma . . . where have you gone?," seems already to be implicitly answered in Mobberly's sermon and by the cumulative impact of detail woven into the cyclical structure of the novel. Early on the narrator witnesses the birth of a colt and knows for the first time "the pain of flesh coming into life." The colt dies, leaving him "bitter with loss" (20). At the end of the novel, when his grandmother's coffin is hauled away, he observes wagon tracks that mark "where death had come into our house and gone again" (127). At that moment a newborn baby cries in another room of the house. Between these two scenes—the birth of a colt, followed by its death; and the death of the grandmother, followed immediately by the birth of a child—between these two scenes the natural cycle of birth, reproduction, and death described in Brother Mobberly's sermon is repeatedly emphasized. Because the family is on the verge of starvation, the father hunts rabbits in the spring. While cleaning a rabbit the father has killed, Euly, the narrator's sister, finds "four little ones in its warm belly" (10). This interruption of the natural cycle serves to emphasize it. The father, in response to his wife's complaint about the difficulty of raising guineas, generalizes about the inevitability of premature death: "Bounden to lose some," he says. "It's the same with folks. Hain't everybody lives to rattle their bones. Hain't everybody breathes till their veins get blue as dogtick stalks" (32). His observation is borne out in the death of one of his own children, from croup, the following spring (88). Shortly before the grandmother dies, the narrator, living with his family in a coal camp, goes to a neighbor hoping to see two blind mules. But the mules have "been tuck away," he learns. They were "old, blind, and puny," the neighbor explains, and because they required so much feed and times were hard, they had to be "put out of their misery." The narrator is disbelieving. "Gone?" he asks. (His question anticipates "Grandma . . . where have you gone?") Again he asks, "Gone?" And the answer comes, "Gone to dirt." The repetition of the word "gone," together with other verbal echoes (the mules are "old, blind, and puny," the grandmother is "sick and pindly"), link the death of the mules and the death of the grandmother (119).

Closely identified with the earth, the hill people of James Still's poems and prose narratives are subject to the same natural conditions—often harsh and perilous—as plants and animals. People and place are rendered as parts of one subtly interdependent whole. The condition of people in the poem "Spring on Troublesome Creek" resembles that of the animals and plants that have also endured winter: "We are no thinner than a hound or mare, / Or an unleaved poplar. We have come through / To grass, to the cows calving in the lot."[13] The physical features, characteristics, and qualities of people mirror their environment. In the poem "On Troublesome Creek" men wait "as mountains long have waited" (17). People are like the hills; the hills resemble people. The ridges in "Journey beyond the Hills" are "heavyhipped" (13). The hills in the poem "Court Day" are so near they seem like people drawing close at the open courthouse window (21). A similar personification occurs in *River of Earth*. On his seventh birthday, acutely aware of how much he has grown, the narrator thinks "the hills to the east of Little Carr Creek had also grown and stretched their ridge shoulders, and that the beechwood crowding their slopes grew down to a living heart" (13). Such consistent identification of people with their natural environment serves to root people in this world no less than trees. Still expresses this sense of identification with a particular spot of earth, this sense of rooted attachment, in the poem "Heritage": "Being of these hills, I cannot pass beyond."[14]

Though rooted in a particular environment, Still's people are forever journeying through the world. (The motif of the journey is implicit in the central "river of earth" vision.) Still's characters are frequently eager for a view of the wider world, for the experience described in the poem "Apple Trip" as "a worldly wonder."[15] The young narrator of *River of Earth* models himself after a local legendary figure, Walking John Gay, described as "traipsing and trafficking, looking the world over" (30). The boy dreams of "going to the scrag end of creation" (76). After his father moves the family into a coal camp, the narrator says: "I tramped the camp over. I saw what there was to see" (116).

But for all their interest in "worldly wonders," Still's people do not wish to pass permanently beyond the boundaries of their familiar, known place. In fact, journeying out into the world serves only to heighten the sense of belonging to one familiar spot of earth. Leaving home, the narrator of *Sporty Creek* says: "I experienced a yearning I could not name. I knew that Sporty Creek would forever beckon me."[16] In the poem "White Highways" the speaker has "gone out to the roads that go up and down / In smooth white lines." But like the mother in *River of Earth*, who yearns to "set down in a lone spot, a place certain and enduring," he has come home with a sense of the wider world, happy to live quietly now in peace "curved with space / Brought back again to this warm homing place."[17]

The attempt to reach a "warm homing place" is the subject of one of Still's finest stories, "The Nest." A little girl, Nezzie Hargis, becomes lost trying to cross a ridge to stay with her aunt and uncle. The actual terrain Nezzie covers is limited; she is never far either from her home or from that of her relatives. Yet her small world symbolizes the great world; her failed attempt to cross the ridge capsulizes the metaphorical journey from childhood to adulthood. ("Be a little woman," her father had told her when he sent her over the ridge.) Nezzie dies from exposure on the ridge, where wind "flowed with the sound of water" through trees, and within hearing of her father's fox horn—details suggesting she is one with "the living and the dead riding the waters" of the river of earth.[18]

Even when journeys to imaginary or otherworldly places are dealt with in Still's work, he renders them (in the tradition of the teller of tales or "false" stories) in familiar worldly terms. The imaginary Biggety Creek in the story "Mrs. Razor" is a whimsical parody of a very familiar world. For Biggety Creek, the father tells his children, is a place where "heads are the size of water buckets, where noses are turned up like old shoes, women wear skillets for hats, and men screw their breeches on, and where people are so proper they eat with little fingers pointing, and one pea at a time."[19] In *Jack and the Wonder Beans,* Still's retelling of Jack and the Beanstalk (a quintessentially "false" story), the giant, though he lives in another world at the top of the beanstalk, is rendered in terms familiar to an Appalachian Jack. The giant has "feet like cornsleds, hands like hams, fingernails to match bucketlids, and the meanest eye ever beheld in this earthly world."[20] As a critic has pointed out, the use of such details to describe this "larger-than-life creature allow the giant to come closer to the familiar, making the story more of this 'earthly world.'"[21]

In one instance Still deals with a situation in which the distinction between "this earthly world" and the next is brought into question. The result is a short story, "The Sharp Tack," which is both humorous and instructive regarding the worldly orientation of Appalachian literature. Jerb Powell, a mountain preacher, writes to Talt Evarts, who has recently returned from service in World War II, to warn the returned soldier he is within "singeing distance of hell-fire and eternal damnation" for claiming to have been to the Holy Land. The Reverend Powell is upset by Evarts's claim because, as he explains, he has spent half his life preaching that "only the dead and the saved ever journey to that Country. . . . The Holy Land is yonder in the sky and there's no road to it save by death and salvation."

For the Reverend Powell the Holy Land is one of the "true" stories—a sacred myth; it is, in fact, the most important of the true stories. He is not distressed by other tales returning soldiers tell. For instance, when Powell's grandson claims to have climbed a tower in Italy called Pisa, that was "out of whanker, leaning on air, against nature and the plan of the Almighty," or when others tell stories of seeing twenty-foot snakes in Africa or of a tombstone in Egypt that covers thirteen acres, the preacher is tolerant and understanding. These are just exaggerations. "Wonders grow a mite big in their mouths." The soldier boys are just "trying to see how big [they] could blow the pig's bladder before it bust." These are "false" stories (like Jack and the Beanstalk, or like the father's tale of Biggety Creek in "Mrs. Razor"), relatively harmless because they do not blur the distinction between things of this world and the next.

The Reverend Powell's geography and general knowledge of the world may be imperfect, but his theology is sound. His God is transcendent (the Man Up Yonder), and everything associated with Him, the Holy Land included, belongs not to this world but to the next. When the Reverend Powell loses the respect of local people as a result of his interpretation of the Holy Land, he seems to modify his view. He writes to Evarts:

> I'm not claiming now you didn't go to a country bearing the name "Holy Land." I'm a fellow with brains enough to turn around when I've learned I'm headed in the wrong direction. What lodges in my craw is the mixing of Up Yonder with a place in this world.

His way out of this personal and theological dilemma is to conclude that "the Holy Land on earth is a namesake of the Country above," an interpretation which saves face yet preserves the all-important distinction between true stories and false stories, and between this world and the next.[22]

Still's "The Sharp Tack" suggests that the firmer and more fervent the belief in the next world, the starker will be the distinction between things of this world and those things which have to do with the beyond. In such a situation, a worldly literature of "false" stories will be worldly with a vengeance (though Still's Reverend Powell is dealt with more gently than is George Washington Harris's Parson Bullen, who must endure the merciless Sut Lovingood and his lizards).

But from its beginnings in the frontier experience and in oral traditions, literature of the Appalachian region has been a worldly literature in the tradition of the "false" story or secular "history." From Sut Lovingood's revenge on Parson Bullen to the Reverend Powell's theological dilemma (posed by Talt Evarts's visit to the Holy Land) the literature of Appalachia has persisted in the folk mode, very much at home in this world, concerned with what Fred Chappell has called "the literary possibilities of the obvious." The poems, short stories, and novels of James Still are a distinguished, unified body of work, at once unique and universal, illuminating a particular place, people and way of life by providing a poetic vision of the facts. Still's Appalachian hill folk, swept along the "mighty river of earth," constitute a metaphor for the essential human experience.

Notes

I wish to thank Professor Lester Woody, Union College, Barbourville, Kentucky, for helpful suggestions and assistance in preparing an earlier version of this essay.

1. Jack E. Weller, *Yesterday's People* (Lexington.: University Press of Kentucky, 1965). See also Weller's "Salvation Is Not Enough," *Mountain Life and Work* 45 (Mar. 1969): 9–13.

2. George Washington Harris, *Sut Lovingood's Yarns,* ed. M. Thomas Inge (New Haven, Conn.: College and Library Press, 1966).

3. A. O. Lovejoy, *The Great Chain of Being: A Study of the History of an Idea* (New York: Harper Brothers, 1960), 24.

4. Jesse Stuart, *Head o' W-Hollow* (Lexington: University Press of Kentucky, 1979), 7.

5. Robert Coles, *A Festering Sweetness: Poems of American People* (Pittsburgh: University of Pittsburgh Press, 1978), 24–25. Perhaps Coles should have called these poems *by* American people, for they are "found" poems—statements taken from tapes of interviews conducted by Coles.

6. *Sut Lovingood's Yarns,* ed. M. Thomas Inge, is the best source of the Lovingood stories. However, this passage and subsequent ones cited in this essay are found in *The Literature of the South,* Randall Stewart, gen. ed. (New York: Scott, Foresman, 1952), 400–401.

7. Ibid., 405.

8. Ibid., 399.

9. Eric Auerbach, *Mimesis: The Representation of Reality in Western Literature,* trans. Willard Trask (Princeton: Princeton University Press, 1953). See chapter 1, "Odysseus' Scar." See also Fred Chappell, "Two Modes: A Plea for Tolerance," and Bob Snyder, "Colonial Mimesis and the Appalachian Renascence," *Appalachian Journal* 5 (Spring 1978): 335–49.

10. Stuart, *Head o' W-Hollow,* 105–17.

11. Harriette Arnow, *The Dollmaker* (New York: Macmillan, 1954).

12. James Still, *River of Earth* (New York: Viking Press, 1940; Popular Library, 1968), 94–95. Page references are to the Popular Library edition.

13. James Still, *Hounds on the Mountain* (New York: Viking Press, 1937), 20.

14. Ibid., 55.

15. James Still, "Apple Poems," *Appalachian Heritage* 4 (Spring 1976): 1.

16. James Still, *Sporty Creek* (New York: G. P. Putnam's Sons, 1977), 123–25.

17. *Hounds on the Mountain,* 46.

18. James Still, *Pattern of a Man and Other Stories* (Lexington, Ky.: Gnomon, 1976), 43–52.

19. Ibid., 1–6.

20. James Still, *Jack and the Wonder Beans* (New York: G. P. Putnam's Sons, 1977), unpaginated.

21. Rebecca Briley, *"River of Earth:* Mythic Consciousness in the Works of James Still," *Appalachian Heritage* 9 (Fall 1981): 75.

22. *Pattern of a Man,* 53–89.

JESSE STUART AND JAMES STILL

Mountain Regionalists

DAYTON KOHLER

A curious parallel links the careers of Jesse Stuart and James Still. Products of the same general environment, graduates of the same small college on the Tennessee side of Cumberland Gap, they live less than one hundred miles from each other as the crow flies in the mountain section of eastern Kentucky. This is the region of ridge farms and lonesome hollows about which each has written, first in poetry and later in prose. In a way this similarity is misleading, for the effect of their writing is completely unlike. James Still is realistic where Stuart is melodramatic, poetic where Stuart is often sentimental. Between them, however, they have given shape and life to their green Appalachian hills.

The background of their work is familiar enough. At the end of the century Mary Noailles Murfree and John Fox reclaimed the Tennessee and Kentucky hill country as a segment of older America. But one can describe a region without participating in its life. Today this sense of participation is the very center of all regional matters. A generation of local-color writers from Miss Murfree to Maristan Chapman exploited only the picturesque and sentimental in the lives of mountain characters; their stories failed to reveal the essential humanity of the people themselves.

Jesse Stuart and James Still have an advantage over these earlier writers in having been born into the life they write about. They use the materials

From *College English* 3 (Mar. 1942): 523–33; reprinted by permission of the publisher.

of the local colorists, but it is clear that much of their freshness and gusto derives from a sense of identity with a place and its people. We can mark a stage in the development of Southern fiction if we put one of their books beside one by Miss Murfree, for example. The older writer demonstrates a landscape literature: bright scenes of local color enlivened by quaint dialect. Her stories are about a place rather than of it. No writer's notebook, filled with tourist observations of dress, weather, sayings, manners, crops, could give the casual yet familiar picture of a way of life which we find in Stuart's and Still's best work. Even their language has emotional roots in the common experience, for it takes its color and rhythm from the speech of people who have lived a long time in one place. This writing has value quite apart from its importance as regional documentation.

Like the best apple butter, good regional writing is always made at home. Jesse Stuart has written five books without going far beyond the borders of W-Hollow in his native Greenup County. Ten or twelve families live in the hollow, and he has written poems and stories about all of them. These real people behind his stories would make an interesting article in themselves. There is the old railroadman in "Huey, the Engineer." He operated the small train on the thirty-six-mile branch of the Eastern Kentucky Railway, and Stuart used to wait to see his engine come puffing out of Barney tunnel. Uncle Fonse of "Uncle Fonse Laughed" was a country schoolteacher whose children Stuart himself taught later on. Having known these people, he says, he tries to tell their stories as vividly and truthfully as he can.

Stuart came into literature in 1934 with an amazing collection of 703 sonnets, *Man with a Bull-Tongue Plow.* Many of these poems were pure description, a re-creation in lyric language and mood of the Kentucky landscape in all weathers and seasons. Others told with innocent frankness of the adventures, loves, and dreams of Jesse Stuart, poet and plowman of the hills. Then in the third section the book came roaringly to life when the writer resurrected more than two hundred dead in Plum Grove churchyard to tell the stories of their humble lives. The method suggested *Spoon River Anthology,* but these stories—grim, humorous, profane—had nothing in common with Edgar Lee Masters's studies in pessimism and defeat. The poetry was often trite and prosy and crude. It was also as native as a whippoorwill and as full of provincial flavor as a persimmon. Critics, viewing Stuart's book with mixed feelings, tried to account for his earthy vigor by calling him a Kentucky Robert Burns. The true explanation of his talent, I believe, lies closer to home. These poems and the prose which followed show us something of the pioneer experience as it has survived on a ruined frontier. In everything he has written we can find evidence of a tradition which goes back beyond the Sut Lovingood papers and Augustus Longstreet's *Georgia Scenes* to the anonymous storytellers of the frontier.

The early American was by nature a storyteller. The realities of pioneer living and his own hard comic sense created a literature of oral anecdote which flourished in the trading post, the groggery, the trappers' rendezvous—wherever men met on the edge of the wilderness. Folklore and fantasy appeared at every halt on the westward march, and the best hunters and rail-splitters passed into legend: Davy Crockett, Dan Boone, Honest Abe. More fabulous heroes—Paul Bunyan, John Henry, Pecos Bill—came out of the common experience and imagination. These stories had a geography, a mythology, and a lingo of their own. Some were streaked with ballad sentiment. Others crackled with bawdy humor. But mostly these tales were comic elaborations of character or drawling reminiscence in which the frontiersman dramatized himself with shrewd appraisal and salty enjoyment.

This literature was of the country and the times. Through the frontier yarns goes a procession of hunters, traders, prophets, settlers, land speculators—the raggle-taggle of a nation on the move. The musterings, auctions, infares, feuds, and frolics are here, the holdup, the war whoop, eagle oratory, revival shouts, hard work and hard times, and every aspect of pioneer morality from the bashful lover at the bean pot to the camp-meeting baby. Behind all this is an awareness of the beauty of river and forest which gives our literature its most authentic theme. It is the brief, westering American dream in the language of the people who lived it.

In his short stories Jesse Stuart has caught the echoes of this frontier world. *Head o' W-Hollow* and *Men of the Mountains* are filled with pioneer tags of realism and rough humor. Sometimes he reports on local custom, such as the rowdy charivari described in "Bellin of the Bride." His mountain politicians are as shrewd as in the days of Davy Crockett. Uncle Casper is a homespun state senator who wins a vote by telling tall stories. Another backwoods candidate tricks two feuding families with some political skulduggery that might have come out of Crockett's dealings with the electorate. Religious fervors shake his people. In "300 Acres of Elbow Room" a Forty-Gallon Baptist gets the word that he will die that night. He invites all of his Free-Will neighbors to be present so that they can see the error of their belief. The leader of an uncouth shouting sect digs up the body of his dead wife but is bitten by a copperhead in her coffin. A constable arrests him on a charge of public indecency for violating the grave. Red Jacket, the shade of a murdered Indian, upsets a spiritualist meeting by telling sly crossroads gossip. Patterns of violence are always present. Grandsons of the men who shot it out with squirrel rifles break up a dance with guns and brass knuckles. Thickety laurel hides a smoking still. The farm wife of "Woman in the House" spends a night of terror in a cabin with her brutal husband and drunken brother. The hero of "Whip-Poor-Willie" can never get a wife because he had an eye shot out at a church meeting. "Dark Winter" records a season of poverty and hunger in the lives of the humble Powderjays.

He has a frontiersman's delight in tall talk and tall deeds. "The Blue Tick Pig" has weird overtones of the Paul Bunyan legends in its account of a runt that learned to milk cows. There is genuine folk fantasy in the story of a quiet tramp, a champion worker in the cornfields, who is finally arrested for stealing all the brass in the neighborhood. Grandpa Grayhouse asked his family to keep his body salted down in the house for six months while they held a party every week in his memory. These doings become the scandal of the countryside. "Huey, the Engineer" and "Uncle Jeff" belong to the John Henry tradition, stories of strong mountain men beaten in the end by the machine. These tales have the tall-story blend of sharp, dry realism and fantastic invention.

Jesse Stuart tells his stories without apology or comment. Whether grimly realistic or wildly humorous, they bear the manner of tales that have been common for a long time. Part of this effect comes, I think, from his use of the present tense and a first-person narrator through whom the experience is presented. These stylistic devices make it plain that he thinks of the short story as a narrative told, for on the printed page they approximate the tones of voice, the pauses, the decisive accents of speech. His colloquial language adds also to the oral manner that we find in frontier yarns. Sometimes this style makes for vivid reporting:

Mom comes to the door with me. She takes a piece of pine kindlin and sticks it between the forestick and firebrands and gets a tiny blaze with a tiny black smoke swirlin up. She lifts the lantern globe and wipes off a speck of mud with her checked apron. I can see the tears roll down her cheek without the curve of her lips for cryin.

Less expertly handled, it falls into the flat, declarative rhythm of meager prose.

> Tarvin sees the redbird on the bank above him. It sings in the leafless brush. It is a pretty redbird. It is the rooster redbird. Its feathers are red as beef blood. It sings to its mate. The mate answers the rooster redbird. She is up on the hill picking up straws.

In *Beyond Dark Hills* he tells of his own life on the arrested frontier. A provincial innocence and cocksureness touches the chapters on his hardy ancestors and his boyhood, and the account of his struggles to get an education reveals a provincial distrust of cities; but his pictures of mountain life are written with great feeling and sincerity. There had been no book quite like this in our literature since Hamlin Garland described another late frontier in *A Son of the Middle Border*. Stuart's autobiography is pure regional writing, simple in finish and tone, and more effective than his novel in showing us the piety and violence of his people. *Trees of Heaven* presents another phase of the frontier experience, the old grudge fight between the settler and the squatter. Anse Bushman is a patriarch of the hills, proud of his cleared acres, his cattle, his crops. Boliver Tussie is a squatter living in idleness and squalor. When Anse buys the tract of land on which the Tussies live, he tries to hold his shiftless tenant in line with a bill of particulars to which the Tussies must conform. But the quarrel between the man of property and the landless man takes a new turn when young Tarvin Bushman falls in love with Tussie's daughter, Subrinea. The romance of this backwoods Romeo and his Juliet ends, as all such stories must, with the feud settled forever. At times the novel reads like a parody of all the hillbilly fiction ever written. Its faults are obvious. Its plot is sentimental and trivial, its dialogue extravagant, its social problem unresolved. Stuart's imagination is free and vivid, but sustained passage work between the scenes of his novel is impossible for him. *Trees of Heaven* lives only in single episodes like the frolic at a sorghum boiling or the night watch in a blizzard when Tarvin and Subrinea nurse the newborn lambs.

After five books his writing remains a frontier talent for anecdote and character drawing, and the chief impression from his work is one of much power poorly controlled. He is by turn a reporter, an atmosphere man, a poet, and a racy fabulist. He has the mixed strains of pioneer fatalism and broad humor which produced the lonesome ditties and tall stories. He also has the pioneer's morbid concern for death, a subject which he treats either with sentimentality or with the cruelty of casual humor. At his best he seems to know instinctively the meaning of life in terms of a people and a place, and he can describe the look and feel and smell of things with joyous certainty. But as an artist he is without discipline—perhaps incapable of it. The truth may be that he is not temperamentally a writer at all but a conversationalist with a quick eye and ear and a lively gift of expression. As such, he stands at the end of a tradition in American storytelling rather than at the beginning of a new one.

If Jesse Stuart has escaped from strict localism by a renewal of frontier types and themes, James Still has gone beyond local emotions through the working of a poetic imagination which finds in regional experience the feelings common to very simple people everywhere. This was also the method of Elizabeth Madox Roberts, the one novelist to whom Still can best, although imperfectly, be compared. He is like her in his ability to join outward realism with intense inwardness of mood.

In Still we confront a serious writer. He has specifically those qualities that Stuart lacks: the precision and restraint which reflect a literary discipline of humility as well as sincerity in the handling of his material. The writings of both men exhibit the same regional theme, the relationship between man and his natural world. In Stuart's fiction this kinship of man and nature leads him at times into vague landscape mysticism. Still has wisely given his sensibility a frame of reference and a point of view. In his novel and short stories, his narrator is a boy whose recognition of objects in nature becomes a measure of his awareness of the world about him. This sensibility is effective because it sets a contrast between a boy's knowledge of the familiar natural world and the bewildering, mysterious world of human relationships.

The territory of Still's fiction is the region of hill farms and coal camps scattered along the branch waters of Little Carr and Troublesome creeks. For him this is adopted country. Born on Double Creek in the Alabama hills, he came into Kentucky by way of Tennessee. His boyhood ambition was to be a horse doctor like his father, and among his earliest recollections are nights he spent with his father while they nursed a sick animal on some neighbor's farm. At Lincoln Memorial University, where he worked in a rock quarry and in the school library to pay his way, he became interested in writing. After some postgraduate study at Vanderbilt he went to Hindman as librarian at the Hindman Settlement School. There one of his duties was to carry boxes of books over mountain trails to supply one-room schools that had no libraries of their own. He has tramped over every ridge and hollow mentioned in his books. At Hindman he wrote his first poems, published in 1937 as *Hounds on the Mountain.*

These poems are minor but authentic. Their subjects are those of much regional verse—people, a horse-swapping, a court day, the sights and sounds of nature—but the quiet tones of his lines surprise us with a sudden sharp image that reveals the true poet. His descriptions of the hill country are always warm and homely and clear. There are overtones of music and emotion in "Mountain Dulcimer":

> The dulcimer sings from fretted maple throat
> Of the doe's swift poise, the fox's fleeing step
> And music of hounds upon the outward slope
> Stirring the night.

"Earth-Bread" tells of the miner's life: "This is the eight-hour death, the daily burial." "Year of the Pigeons" stirs ancestral memories. "Heritage" is his regional affirmation:

> Being of these hills, being one with the fox
> Stealing into the shadows, one with the new-born foal,
> The lumbering ox drawing green beech logs to mill,
> One with the destined feet of man climbing and descending,
> And one with death rising to bloom again, I cannot go.
> Being of these hills I cannot pass beyond.

One way of becoming an artist is to accept those limitations of material imposed upon the individual by the nature of his social experience. This acceptance implies an act of discipline, the necessity of the writer to distinguish what is his own from what he admires in other men's books. It was this discipline which Thomas Wolfe, for example, could never learn, but which turned Willa Cather from the Jamesian manner of *Alexander's Bridge* to a use of native materials in *O Pioneers.* James Still has known this discipline from the first. All of his writing is of one piece, for it comes straight out of the region which has shaped his own life. Perhaps that is why he reverts to a boy's world in *River of Earth,* where the experiences of a growing boy make the regional pattern clear.

River of Earth covers two years in the life of a mountain family. The novel begins shortly before the boy who tells the story has his seventh birthday, and it ends two winters later, after he has learned something of a man's responsibilities. The boy is one of Brack Baldridge's young ones. Brack is a miner, moving his family about from one coal camp to another as he follows the precarious wages the big companies pay. Although he will take to farming when work in the mines grows slack, he has no desire for the homeplace his wife talks about. She wants a house with windows and a real puncheon floor, a garden patch, and some trees without smoke-grimed leaves. She is one of the mild Middletons, but she speaks her mind when Brack's worthless cousins and lazy old Uncle Samp come to live with them at the end of a hard winter. But Brack says, "As long as we've got a crust, it'll never be said I turned my folks from my door." Mother has another plan. She moves the furniture into the smokehouse and burns the cabin. It is a life of hardship and violence. School closes when the teacher is shot for whipping one of the pupils. After Uncle Jolly has been taken off to jail, the boy goes to Lean Neck Creek to look after Grandma Middleton through a starvation winter. At seventy-eight Grandma is still spryly carrying on her secret feud with the man who killed her husband years ago. Next spring the baby dies. In September the Baldridges hold a funeralizing, with Preacher Sim Mobberly from Troublesome Creek to preach the text. "Oh, my brethren," he begins, stroking his white beard, "we was borned in sin and saved by grace." Lifting his hands toward the sky, he thunders, "We have come together to ask the blessed Savior one thing pine-blank. Can a leetle child enter the Kingdom of Heaven?" In Blackjack they face another hungry winter after the mines close. Then Grandma Middleton dies. "Send nary word to my chaps," she says. "They wouldn't come when I was low in health. No need they haste to see me dead."

From incidents like these James Still has made a simple but moving regional novel. There is no dramatic structure to his book, for it is a boy's story that falls into a clear pattern of memory as he tells what he saw and did during those two full years. He has learned the feel of tools in his hands and back-breaking labor in the fields. Birth and death, men's anger and hate, women's tolerance for clumsy masculine ways, summer's plenty and winter's hungry pinch have become as much a part of his life as the sights and sounds of mining camp and farm, the smells of plowed ground, an empty house, cooking food.

River of Earth is regional, but it is first of all a novel about people, not more literary business about folkways in the manner of so much regional literature. People are never folk to any but outsiders, and Still happens to be writing about friends and neighbors into whose lives he has entered with the instinctive knowledge and feeling of true imagination. They belong to the life he himself shares. The signs are hopeful for his future. The writer who can reveal the life of his own region with perception and meaning usually ends up by writing about the world.

Beneath the regional feeling of the novel there is another meaning which is never put into words because it lies just outside the boy's understanding of his world. Brack's son can describe his mother's fears and his own hunger, but he can only listen to talk of puzzled resentment and bitterness when men are out of work. He knows Uncle Jolly's anger over good farmland ruined when the timber was cut off, leaving the plowed fields to wash away in gullies during the summer storms. But if he is too young to realize what is happening, the reader can understand the terrible importance of work and food to America's dispossessed. The Baldridges are not Joads or Lesters; nevertheless they speak to the social conscience of our time.

On Troublesome Creek is a collection of short stories in the same clear, luminous pattern of measured emotion and unstudied drama. At first glance it may seem that Still is trying to write a lesser *River of Earth* in these stories, for some use the same background and the same theme and all are loosely linked by the bright-eyed boy who tells them. Although the book as a whole is likely to give an impression of sameness because the point of view does not vary, most of the stories, taken singly, will stand on their own merits. In any collection like this, each reader must find his own favorites. One of the best is "I Love My Rooster," in which the boy's longing for a gamecock and a striped shirt becomes an expression of the desires of an inarticulate class in which the sense of possession is strong but seldom satisfied. "Snail Pie" is a pathetic picture of old age. "Brother to Methusalem" shows that Still can write fantasy and humor in the tall-story tradition. A boy's revenge on a miserly cattle-driver gives another kind of humor to "On Quicksand Creek." "The Moving" tells what happens to these people when the mines close, and several of the stories deal with the hardships of finding a new home in a new place.

James Still has been praised for his simplicity. Much of the effectiveness of his writing comes from a clear and often lovely style with the occasional incorrectness of folk speech in its idiom. This is the best kind of style that a regional writer can have, for it shows the habits of thought and language found in the sayings, stories, and proverbs that indicate the history and simple wisdom of a region. "Even come spring," says Grandma Middleton, "we've a passel chills to endure: dogwood winter, redbud, service, fox-grape, blackberry. . . . There must be seven winters, by count. A chilly snap for every time of bloom." Still's style is flexible enough for more than one effect. It can bear a considerable burden of emotion that is within a boy's range of response, and it can record sensory impressions with poetic finality. Here is a picture of the back country in autumn:

> Fall came in the almanac, and the sourwood bushes were like fire on the mountains. Leaves hung bright and jaundiced on the maples. Red foxes came down the hills, prowling outside our chicken house, and hens squalled in the night. Quin Adams's hounds hunted the ridges, their bellies thin as saw blades. Their voices came bellowing in the dark hours. Once, waking suddenly, I heard a fox bark defeat somewhere in the cove beyond Flaxpatch.

In Preacher Sim Mobberly's sermons this style broadens with homely metaphor into rude folk poetry. It can also weight a situation with a deeper meaning that adds to our understanding of life. In *River of Earth* there is a scene in which Brack, newly hired at the mines, brings home several sacks of food from the company commissary. The mother sits quietly touching the meat and flour and then suddenly throws her apron over her head as she bursts into tears. The words of that passage are not the language of realism, but something as flat and final as the realist can offer has been said about a way of life.

Perhaps one should not grow too critically solemn over the books Stuart and Still have written. Stuart has probably shown us the whole range of his talent. Still has the manner of a young writer feeling his way, and as yet he has not attempted a direct portrayal of the larger adult world. But as regionalists they have added another panel to the long record of American life, for in their books the southern mountaineer has found his own voice for the first time. This regionalism is as genuine and untainted as any we have in America today.

THE CHANGING POETIC CANON

The Case of Jesse Stuart and Ezra Pound

CHARLES H. DAUGHADAY

In summarizing the origins and characteristics of "mass culture," Ruel E. Foster writes, "the industrial revolution and modern technology upset the balance" between the two modes of "high art" and "folk art," thereby generating a new, third type: "mass art, designed to palliate the boredom of the masses and condition them to accept the dubious blessings of mass culture." The resulting mass art, Foster continues, "debases" the standard of taste, thereby brutalizing the senses, boring and depersonalizing its audience, and contributing to the decline in ethics. As a result, "mass media, the great agency of mass art, alienates people from personal experience and intensifies their moral isolation" (20).

If this analysis has validity, it would raise the question as to how a technological society producing "mass art" still manages to identify and perpetuate a preferred status, a "high" art, while simultaneously relegating other art to a less acceptable or "low" status.

Certainly the arrival of literary modernism began to usher in a new poetics, a new mode of high art, displaying multicultural readings and bookish allusions. The chief practitioners and exemplars of this new poetics were Ezra Pound and T. S. Eliot. As the poetics succeeded on the American

From the *Journal of Kentucky Studies* 8 (Sept. 1991): 111–21. Reprinted by permission of the author and the publisher.

scene, it began to displace and devalue the popular, traditional, and regional poetry like that of Edgar Lee Masters and Jesse Stuart.

There were several factors that gradually worked to establish and then make pervasive the views of Pound and Eliot regarding what the new "program" or poetic canon of high modernism was to be. First, the influence throughout academia by way of textbooks and criticism of the "new critics" seemed without precedent. These new critics stressed the necessity of objectivity in the reader's confrontation with literature. In part, these critics were attempting to reclaim an epistemological respectability for poetry, in the wake of a world increasingly scientifically oriented. With this new critical value system and emphasis came a distinct lessening of value accorded to the "other" American poetic, best identified as traditional, grounded in nature, a specific locale, which spoke directly to its audience, within a commonly accepted moral frame of reference in a common language. This traditional mode of poetry became the "low" mode to better illuminate and define "high" modernism. Who can ever forget the Brooks and Warren reading of the Kilmer poem "Trees"? Until this kind of reading, a poem in the tradition of "Trees" had, ironically, no need of a critical intermediary; neither do most traditionalist poems. But high modernism was to create and sustain great need of critics.

A second factor in the success of Pound's and Eliot's program was their stress upon the importance of a multicultural past, which could only be reached by books, and then presumably best reached through their cultures' literary writings. Such preferences were to lead to the heavy employment of bookish allusions, fragments, paraphrases, and "translations" in high modernist poetry.

Thirdly, both Pound and Eliot were consciously seeking to formulate a new poetic style, which would reflect the modern world's sense of time, place, and urban setting. Thus, the use of allusions, fragments, and paraphrases lent themselves readily to the kind of obliqueness and juxtaposition Pound was to teach in his reworking of Eliot's *The Wasteland.* Pound and Eliot sought, in the manner of the new critics teaching, to dissolve, or at the very least obscure, the narrative basis of traditional poetry; and thereby, as authors, they could "withdraw" from their work, as James Joyce would describe the process, to be far removed, like God, paring one's nails. The program of high modernism, then, was double-pronged; on the one hand, it valued and demanded an intellectual, literary-centered poetry; on the other hand, it devalued emotional, experience-centered poetry. Such a program was the goal of Pound in his "Imagist" period as he sought to rid poetry of all decoration, description, and expressions of the poet's subjectivity. Similarly, this was the project that led to such a seemingly logically structured essay as Eliot's *Tradition and the Individual Talent.*

And here we arrive at the fourth factor in the triumph of high modernism: both Pound and Eliot created an aesthetic or theory to accompany, sustain, and justify their favored poetic canon. Their aesthetics were to change and differ over their careers, and their canons were different, but the poetic devaluation they achieved remained constant. The measure of the degree of success and the pervasiveness of the establishment of this program of high modernism on American poetics is registered seismologically in the 1938 "Preface" to Robinson Jeffers's *Collected Poems.* In this important poetic manifesto, Jeffers seeks to *reclaim* for poetry no less than what he believes constitutes *reality*—the human experience of the material creation, not the mind's creation of its own thoughts. In order to return poetry to its original ability to deal with reality, Jeffers says the poet must reclaim the right to employ narrative once more, to speak directly to his audience. He convincingly argues that the Pound/Eliot poetic program has made a virtual eunuch of modern poetry. With his reclamation Jeffers was to create a poetry that was to encompass all of Pound's "sailing" after knowledge as well as Eliot's pilgrimages to classical and medieval times. Learned in medicine, astronomy, geology, and the modern sciences in general, Jeffers was to construct a poetic cosmology worthy of a modern Dante. The moral of all this is very clear: our poetic tastes, our critical values, and our literary (poetic) canons—be they those of the new critics, of Pound and Eliot, or of the structuralists and deconstructionists—are arbitrary; they largely succeed (or enjoy the perception of success) because the proponents of the "new" are able to create a new vocabulary and invest it with their own emotional meanings, while cleverly disguising the emotion with the pretense of a more respectable intellectuality. And just as inevitably, the raising of a new canon or poetic to the status of "high" art is accompanied by a corresponding devaluing of other canons and critical views to a status of "low" art. Even Derrida cannot escape such a set of circumstances with his "play."

This study will seek to demonstrate that even in our age of "mass art," a separation into "high" and "low" modes of art still occurs; and on the American poetic scene just such a separation can be vividly traced in an unlikely poetic connection between Jesse Stuart and Ezra Pound in a time beginning in the late forties and ending in the early sixties. Much of the focus will come to bear on the same poetic award both poets received, the $5,000 Academy of American Poets award, which went to Jesse Stuart for 1960 and to Ezra Pound for 1963.

At first glance no two American poets would seem more dissimilar than Ezra Pound and Jesse Stuart. Pound was a native of Idaho, yet lived largely the life of an expatriate, and later an exile, punctuated by a thirteen-year stint at St. Elizabeth's Hospital for "insanity." Seemingly nothing was ever sufficient to contain or satisfy Pound. He was always moving on—to a new culture, a new literary movement, or a new literary project. He desired to write the greatest poetry ever written; he wished to write an epic of the human race. Nothing was ever too large for Pound to undertake; he held opinions on all matters; he presented himself as an expert on most matters, a teacher in many.

For a long while in his life, Ezra Pound sought knowledge; he wanted to know the best that was ever thought or written, and he set up art in the place of religion to convey his findings. He desired that the arts should legislate to mankind. Even after his performances over Italian Radio during World War II, after the trial, and after he had "pulled down" his vanity, his incarceration at St. Elizabeth's Hospital still kept him in the public eye, and it was not until his release in 1958 and subsequent return to Italy that he lapsed into despair, self-doubt, and at last, silence. Knowledge had failed him.

On the other hand, Jesse Stuart was as attached to a specific locale in and around W-Hollow near Greenup, Kentucky, as Ezra Pound was to his nomadic wanderings. Moreover, Stuart exemplified the kind of union of the practical life of the body and physical labor demanded by husbandry with a life of the imagination called forth by the American Transcendentalists like Emerson and Thoreau. Jesse Stuart was also a teacher. Jesse Stuart was much closer to and conversant with the dead of Plum Grove Cemetery than Ezra Pound was with Homer's Hades and Tiresias. While Pound imitated his poetic way via various personae through an esthetic period, said "goodbye to all that" in *Mauberley,* and at last turned to his epic *Cantos,* Jesse Stuart, in the words of Jim Wayne Miller, "did not develop as a poet—at least in the ordinary sense. Instead, he unfolds, revealing what was there in embryo from the start" (xxi).

Each year, a large number of tomes dealing with Pound's work appear, attempting to discover, to recommend or reject his "program," or to explain or otherwise reconcile the shipwreck of Pound's life with the undertakings of his work. In contrast, the poetry of Jesse Stuart is by and large relegated, mostly by critical neglect, to the status of a regional or "low" poetry. Miller suggests that Stuart both changes and remains the same (xxi).

This is not to say that Jesse Stuart *is* a minor poet; he came to believe, as many poets have, that the sum of all knowledge (Ezra Pound notwithstanding) amounted to a "formative experience, a palpable realization of the reality of death" (Miller, viii). Jesse Stuart, that is, sought wisdom rather than knowledge *per se;* he valued the heart more than the head.

These general points of comparison and contrast can be pursued into more specific and revealing areas. For instance, the watchword of modernist poetics was "craft," which referred to the use of intricate structural devices and the attention to style as previously discussed. With this poetic, the emphasis shifts from *what* to *how,* from content to structure. Behind all this shifting and changing, of course, the moral and ethical dimensions of poetry are being replaced by a posture of scientifically mandated "objectivity." The high modernism of Pound and Eliot became an intellectual puzzle to be solved by the mind; freed of its author's subjectivity, it could become a "text" connecting with other texts (with regard to Wimsatt and Beardsley). In the case of Pound and Eliot, reading poetry became an erudite, intellectual experience, thereby according a new respectability to poetry, enabling both poets to make epistemological claims that would enable poetry to be competitive with science. Surely such art seemed to predict profound discoveries about weighty matters, yet Eliot in his late plays, like *The Elder Statesman,* teaches the simple theme of "love," while Pound's last effort in the *Cantos* is aimed at reaching "light." Both arrived at unexpected conclusions to the earlier poetic journeys they embarked upon.

In revealing contrast, Jesse Stuart depended heavily upon one very traditional literary form—the sonnet—and, "like Whitman, was always engaged in writing one book" (Miller, xxi), and the controlling ideas of his work can be expressed in the themes of *carpe diem* and *memento mori* (Miller, xxvii).

The unlikely connection between these two poets, representative of mass culture's versions of "high" and "low" art, Ezra Pound and Jesse Stuart respectively, lies in the fact that they both received within a three-year period the same prestigious poetry award—the $5,000 award given by the Academy of American Poets. Stuart received it first, by majority vote of the jury, for the year 1960. The award was apparently the Academy's attempt to affirm the value of traditional poetry in the face of the mounting tide of poetic modernism. In 1963 Ezra Pound received this award, and the values of traditional poetry affirmed in the award to Stuart seemed no longer to have a public voice. There is an interesting story behind each award, which reveals that even in a time of "mass art" the cultural apparatus of teachers, critics, journal media and university presses is constantly engaged politically in redefining the poetic canon. These stories, then, reveal much about the importance of critical biases in establishing this canon in a particular moment.

We begin with Jesse Stuart. Because he was so imbued with a consciousness of death, the brevity of life, and the "trick" nature works on man, since it is capable of endless renewal as man is not, Jesse Stuart was also keenly aware of "the passing of the old ways and the intrusions of new ways, especially through popular culture" (Miller, xii). Moreover, he felt we had "forgotten the struggles and achievements of the pioneers and settlers" (Miller, xiii).

Thus, like the high modernists such as Pound and Eliot, Stuart sought to preserve in his poetry the values of his past. In so doing, he struggled for public recognition of his efforts and achievements; when the symbols of such recognition came, late though they might be, Jesse Stuart interpreted them as a victory for traditionalist poetry as opposed to the "obscurist" or "high" poetry of the literary establishment, exemplified so vividly in Pound and Eliot. The story of Stuart's interpretation is vividly captured in several of his unpublished letters, dating from late 1960 until early 1962. Many of Stuart's remarks directly concern the Award of the Academy of American Poets for 1960, but many others are pieces of exchanges with friends and fellow artists and even critics, which finally form a composite portrayal of the increasingly rapid displacement and devaluation of traditionalist American poetry by the new modernism. The fact that two such dissimilar poets could receive this award within a three-year span, with the majority of the jury members overlapping,[1] suggests this period may be an appropriate place to locate a significant turn in the history of American poetics and its canon.

We may begin with a letter to Jesse Stuart from Ruel E. Foster dated 16 December 1960,[2] in which Foster observes, "I finished re-reading *The Year of My Rebirth,*" a journal dealing with Stuart's recovery from a 1954 heart attack; "this . . . human warmth is passing and being lost in the vast welts of mass gadgets and in the mass hysteria of modern shopping. . . . I'm glad you put it down, before it was lost forever." Stuart, then, wrote of values rapidly disappearing. Most readers of his poetry felt similarly.

Another ingredient in Stuart's interpretation of achieving a victory for traditionalist poetry with his Award lay in his relationship with the Vanderbilt-based Agrarian group. Although he had studied with many members of this group, he remained more true to their professed principles than most of the Agrarians themselves did. Stuart addresses this concern in a letter to Ruel Foster dated 6 January 1961. Here, Stuart records his disillusionment with them, calling their views "sweet theory" to one who really practiced it. He further observes, "I have never been able to understand an Agrarian movement by men . . . not one living on a farm." Stuart quotes an unnamed source saying of Alan Tate that he "didn't have anything creative to offer . . . only what he borrowed." Later Stuart adds that "no one has changed position as much as he. And where did he go? He left the South long, long ago." In a similar vein, after having met Robert Penn Warren for the first time in fifteen years, Stuart says he "hardly knows him . . . and his attitude had completely changed." Jesse Stuart felt money lay at the root of this change.

About two weeks later in a letter dated 21 January 1961, Ruel Foster responded to Stuart's letter by underscoring his agreement with Stuart's judgment of the Agrarians. But Foster expands the indictment to include their role in the new criticism and in establishing the new poetic of modernism. Foster initially objects to the Agrarians' dismissal of God and then their "talking in grand terms of the need for religious humanism . . . and religious myth." Foster goes on to identify these Agrarians as the "literary establishment," John Crowe Ransom as its "high priest," and the *Kenyon Review* as an "attenuated" journal which publishes only each other and praises only each other—"a sort of critical incestuous relationship." Foster concludes that "the new critics have been utterly blind in overlooking [Stuart]; they have done [Stuart] a great disservice in refusing to evaluate [his] work. But the tide will change . . . and most of their stuff will topple while [Stuart's] will ride out the shifting winds of change."

After Stuart received the Academy of American Poets award, Foster again wrote to Stuart, on 31 March 1961, that he was "still musing over [Stuart's] great poetry award victory, because it is a victory in the world of literature. It's a victory for the traditional world where good is good and evil is evil." He adds that he knows the survival of America "hinges on the survival of the family and families can't survive in a world where moral anarchy is the rule." Thus, we see the truly conservative and moral nature of the traditionalist poetry Stuart represented. In contrast, the high modernism of Ezra Pound initially sought to identify and preserve values largely esthetic in nature; Pound believed art could re-establish lost connections and provide answers to questions essentially spiritual; Stuart was not so tempted.

Some of Stuart's correspondence of this period widens the circle of indictment of the new criticism even more. For instance, Margaret Carpenter wrote to Stuart on 16 April 1961 that "[Ciardi] is not the only poet I could name who had some talent and then went completely off the deep end to get into the lunatic world of 'modern poetry.'" She continues (and she could be speaking of Pound as well) by saying that Ciardi also "developed a Jehovah complex about being a literary critic—and given a high position of power, he had used it to assassinate anyone who happens to hit his eye. He is truly the McCarthy of the literary world."

Robert Hillyer, who pinioned the backroom manipulating meant to gain public awards for Ezra Pound in order to rehabilitate his reputation, wrote to Stuart on 18 April 1961, "As usual with my books, the 'new' critic group have done their best to murder it [Hillyer's *Collected Poems*]. One of them, Cleanth Brooks, at Yale, went so far (I am told) as to tell the bookstore not to carry it." It would seem that for the high modernists and their able support groups of new critics and academic professors, the "enemy" was more often than not traditionalist or "low" poets rather than common elements both groups had distaste for, elements rapidly making for an all-pervasive "mass society." It was increasingly the high modernist camp members who assumed positions of authority in matters of poetic taste and criticism.

Stuart, himself, is one of the most effective spokesmen for the position of American traditionalist poetry at this time. In a letter to Robert Nathan (a member of the committee or jury making the awards to both Stuart and Pound) dated 28 August 1961, Jesse Stuart observes that "once in my life back before *Man with a Bull-tongue Plow* was published, I won the Janette Sewell Davis Prize for 7 poems published in *Poetry: A Magazine of Verse*. This was it. Now, this Academy of American Poets Award for Poetry. . . . I've had about 1,600 poems published but [I] never made one of the big American Anthologies." The point is clear: traditional poets like Jesse Stuart were read, were published, and were beloved by great numbers of readers, but such actions and responses were not significant recognition factors for the rapidly rising elite of high modernism. In this same letter Stuart concludes, "Believe me, people can make fun of the poetry that came from an earlier age, the twenties, for instance, and some of our finest poetry came from that decade. . . . [P]oetry [then] had meaning and beauty. Now, I believe the trend is changing . . . but so many fine American poets have taken a beating." Stuart does not feel he is one of those poets taking such a beating, but he "is for them and if I belong to a trend it is this one." Stuart erred in thinking his award represented a trend favoring traditional poetry, or even a victory in such matters, but he was certainly correct in identifying his work as well as his sympathies with traditionalist poetry.

Robert Nathan wrote Stuart on 29 August 1961 regarding "today's poetry": "it seems to me as if the poets were simply playing with words, less interested in what they were trying to say than in how fancy they be, saying it." Indeed, this is one of the hazards of high modernist poetics.

These attitudes of exclusiveness, selfishness, and arbitrariness ascribed to the high modernist poetry establishment by Stuart and his fellow traditionalists are returned to in letters to Jesse Stuart from August Derleth, dated 23 December 1961 and 2 January 1962. In the earlier letter Derleth states that "these [establishment] people in poetry don't trouble me so much as the coterie poets or the you-scratch-my-back-I'll-scratch-yours academic poets who freeze out of their classes, their teaching, and their anthologies/textbooks all those who don't belong to their groups." In the later message he writes, "It is really up to a great many of us to get poetry out of the cages in which professors have confined it."

These samples of Stuart's correspondence reveal two important facets about the scene of changing American poetics at midcentury: First, Jesse Stuart, as well as a number of respected and prominent men and women of letters, valued a traditional poetry which seeks to address a common audience directly by using value-based (i.e., moral) language to articulate the feelings and perceptions of mankind that the traditional poet believes form the common bond that unites us all. Second, both the content and the private mode of these expressions amply testify to the degree to which the poetics of high modernism had become officially "established" and gained control of the major forms of public expression. In other, more familiar words, high modernism had successfully marketed itself.

When we realize that in a scant three years (1963) Ezra Pound was to receive the same award from the Academy of American Poets, we may well register surprise. And we may recall that in the time between the two awards, Robert Frost accepted the invitation to read a poem at the inauguration of John F. Kennedy (1961). Presumably, such an invitation and reading was an acknowledgement and recognition of the values of the common people's poetry, since Robert Frost's narratives and lyrics dealt with the same values and spoke with the same assumptions and to the same audience as those previously identified with the traditionalist poetry represented by Jesse Stuart.

As we shall see, an entirely different set of circumstances was at work when the Academy made its award to Ezra Pound in 1963. These circumstances had their origins in the Bollingen Prize awarded to Pound in 1948.

E. F. Torrey recounts that James Laughlin wrote to Pound in 1948 advising him that a claim of insanity was "the best strategy for eliciting public sympathy and avoiding responsibility for his broadcasts over Rome Radio" (234). Laughlin further argued to Pound that "the public was unable to understand Pound's political and economic teachings" (Torrey, 234). Torrey then recounts, using a variety of sources, how a group of Pound's influential friends developed a strategy of manipulation ultimately designed to gain his release, by creating a new literary award, the Bollingen Prize, subsidized by the Pittsburgh Mellon family, and naming Ezra Pound as the first recipient. The goal of this manipulation was to "dramatize his [Pound's] situation and [put] the government, and particularly the Department of Justice, in an awkward if not untenable position" (Torrey, 234). As a result, a virtual literary and political storm arose.

Robert Hillyer, writing in the *Saturday Review of Literature* a year later (1949), sought "to consider what elements in modern American poetry and criticism are sufficiently stagnant to serve as a breeding place for influence so unwholesome" (7). First, Hillyer indicts the Bollingen jury for limiting all discussions to "esthetic values merely"; next, he criticizes the values and practices of the high modernist poetics. He notes their "current preoccupation" with a "new vocabulary that has no purpose but its own creation"; he follows with an indictment of their analysis of "disillusioned irony, word by word" to a world "eager for the clearest vision of poets"; and finally he argues that they are guilty of subtly undermining the "reputations of our greatest poets such as Robinson and Frost, lest they destroy the bases of their propaganda" (8). Hillyer also criticized the new critics for "a common snobbery" which excludes the public from their resulting "pathetic substitute for aristocracy" (8). He concludes by protesting the "blurring of judgment both esthetic and moral," and sees in this contrived Bollingen Prize of 1948 for Ezra Pound "the mystical and cultural preparation for a new authoritarianism" (38).

Rather than helping Pound as intended, the 1948 Bollingen Prize culminated in controversy and actually retarded his hopes for early release by "reminding the public what he had said and done for Mussolini and Fascism" (Torrey, 235). Still, Torrey claims that Pound was "happy at St. Elizabeth's" (236), a claim Eustace Mullins disputes (329–31).

Then, after the elapse of another six years, during a period when "America was in a forgiving mood," Ezra Pound's friends "renewed their efforts to effect his release" (Torrey, 254). This renewed effort was more ambitious in particulars than the initial effort, for now Pound's friends sought the Nobel Prize in literature for Pound. Torrey observes, "Given the fiasco brought about by the Bollingen Prize, one might have thought that Pound and his friends would have been wary of a Nobel Prize strategy. But still, they forged ahead, engaging the aid of Archibald MacLeish and the Secretary General of the United Nations, Dag Hammarskjöld" (254). But neither did this strategy succeed. It was not until April 1958 that the indictment against Pound was dropped. Seemingly, with his release, Pound's life more or less collapsed. Thus, when James Laughlin visited Pound in the fall of 1959, he found Pound "melancholic, preoccupied with becoming mentally ill or dying" (267).

Torrey believes that Ezra Pound "equated his failure as a poet with his failure as a person," and that "he had confused paradise with the satisfaction of his personal desires" (270). Torrey finds another important source of depression for Pound after his release, and one that was a "constant reminder of his professional failure," in the lack of major honors and public recognitions of his poetic accomplishments (271). Yet Noel Stock presents an impressive listing of Pound's works, publications, and reissues between 1958 and 1964 (256–57). Evidently, the acclaim for Pound was still insufficient for his own lofty ambitions. Even with his *Poetry* award in 1962 and the Academy of American Poets award in 1963, Pound still coveted the Pulitzer and Nobel Prizes, which so many of his friends had won (Torrey, 271).

These two literary accounts, tied together by the Academy of American Poets awards for 1960 and 1963 to Jesse Stuart and Ezra Pound, respectively, demonstrate that the literary values behind the 1948 Bollingen Prize were no longer operative in 1963, for Pound had been released since 1958; but the assumptions made about the value of his kind of poetry had become the public mode: "high modernism" had won out over low, traditionalist poetry. Between Pound's release in 1958 and the Academy of

American Poets award in 1963, there were continuing efforts to "rehabili-tate" Pound's highly soiled and suspect reputation, so his poetry and poetic could be gathered safely into the modernist canon. The rehabilitation at times contains the satiric and pathetic ingredients of the story "Grace" of Joyce's *Dubliners*. In this regard, Pound's 1963 award stands as the fulfill-ment of the feelings registered and the charges leveled against the new criticism and poetry of high modernism by Jesse Stuart and his friends and fellow artists.

Should we run the reel forward, we will recall how the modernists' legacy did not escape its Romantic condemnations or achieve an "episte-mological" ground; rather it left a privatized, introspective, and subjective verse which has taken over the literary canon.

Charles Altieri traces modernism back to two sources: romanticist (rep-resented by Wordsworth) and symbolist (represented by Coleridge) (29). He demonstrates that the modernists rejected seeing nature as reflective of moral or teleological functions, like Wordsworth, and instead opted for the symbolist impulse of Coleridge with its allegiance to "the creative mind as the source of value" (37). Without question, this option and shift by the modernists committed them to an even more pronounced degree of subjec-tivity than the Romantics they supposedly rejected. In 1975 Jesse Stuart was nominated for the Pulitzer Prize for poetry. The winner was John Ash-bery with a volume of poems appropriately entitled *Self-Portrait in a Convex Mirror*.

In one of the poems of this volume, "Ode to Bill," Ashbery writes,

> What is writing?
> Well, in my case, it's getting down on paper
> Not thought, exactly, but ideas, maybe:
> Ideas about thoughts. Thoughts is too grand a word.
> Ideas is better, though not precisely what I mean.
> Someday I'll explain. Not today though.
> (50)

Move it further still to our contemporary setting and we have the near total dissipation of literature into politically charged critical theory, con-tinuously engaged in manufacturing its own vocabulary, perpetuating it-self in texts and university presses, and in short, in becoming the new "establishment." Literary theory today has replaced the high modernism of Stuart's time, and literature itself, with a final irony, has become "low," trivialized because the critics have determined it is a mere activity of language; unfortunately these critics missed the reality of the plow, the land, and the world outside of the self that Stuart and his successors like Wendell Berry offer us. This contemporary example of critical literary hubris suggests a repetition of the rise of high modernism, which is now one of its own whipping boys.

In an age in which the concept of the human being, so laboriously composed from our Western heritage of the Judeo-Christian tradition, has been utterly dismantled and degraded to the status of inferior chemical/electrical machine, we need not wonder that Jesse Stuart's works seem to suffer from critical neglect; indeed this situation may actually signify his lasting value, for the reader Stuart addresses does not require the intermediary of a critic. J. R. LeMaster observes that Jesse Stuart wrote on average a book a year and that each book, "regardless of genre, is merely another chapter in the larger chronicle, a record that seems to have neither beginning nor end." And though LeMaster suggests that Stuart's emerging chronicle is "highly reminiscent of Pound's *Cantos*" (14), we would perhaps make a fairer comparison by suggesting the similarity of life and art that exists between Stuart and Thoreau.

Michael Reck locates "an aspect of Pound's greatness" in his "international spirit," which makes him somehow more pertinent to a "shrinking" world (153). Then, Reck argues that "Pound cultivated a cosmopolitan, universal spirit *and* his Americanism at the same time. . . . [H]e tried to keep his American roots—and succeeded better than many good poets who stayed at home!" (155). Such a claim does not square with the facts of Pound's verse or his life. Roots depend on locale, tradition, and the spirit: the American poetic tradition from its beginnings has emphasized these values. For Jesse Stuart, "the earth is a book, and poetry exists in that which is alive to the senses—beyond words" (LeMaster, 209). Contemporary literary theory denies not only language's ability, but man's ability to register in literature anything beyond the solipsistic expression of desire. It is hoped this study casts a small light on a brief period that reveals how long and diligently we have labored to reach our current critical dead end. As Jerry Herndon observes, Stuart's "works deal with real people in a real world, in which *everything* matters" (119).

$\mathcal{N}otes$

1. The committee members for the Stuart award were J. Donald Adams, W. H. Auden, Hugh Bullock, Wittar Bynner, Henry Seidel Canby, Max Eastman, Randall Jarrell, Marianne Moore, Robert Nathan, J. G. Niehardt, Frederick A. Pottle, and John H. Wheelock. The members for the Pound award were W. H. Auden, Louise Bogan, Wittar Bynner, Randall Jarrell, Robert Lowell, William Meredith, Marianne Moore, Robert Nathan, J. G. Neihardt, Frederick A. Pottle, John H. Wheelock, and Richard Wilbur.

2. The Stuart letters used in this study are part of Murray State University's Special Collection of Stuart Papers located in the Pogue Library. I am indebted to the Stuart curator, Dr. Jerry Herndon, for his indispensable aid and advice in this project.

$\mathcal{W}orks\ Cited$

Altieri, Charles. "From Symbolist Thought to Immanence: The Ground of Postmodern Poetics." In *Enlarging the Temple: New Directions in American Poetry.* Lewisburg, Pa.: Bucknell University Press, 1979.

Foster, Ruel E. "Flight from Mass Culture." *Mississippi Quarterly* 13 (Spring 1960): 69–75.

Herndon, Jerry A., and George Brosi, eds. *Jesse Stuart: The Man and His Books.* Ashland, Ky.: Jesse Stuart Foundation, 1986.

Hillyer, Robert. "Poetry's New Priesthood." *Saturday Review of Literature,* 18 June 1949, 7–9.

LeMaster, J. R. Introduction to *Jesse Stuart: Essays on His Work,* ed. J. R. LeMaster and Mary Washington Clarke. Lexington: University Press of Kentucky, 1977.

Miller, Jim Wayne. Introduction to *Songs of a Mountain Plowman,* by Jesse Stuart. Ashland, Ky.: Jesse Stuart Foundation, 1986.

Mullins, Eustace. *This Difficult Individual, Ezra Pound.* New York: Fleet Publishing, 1961.

Reck, Michael. *Ezra Pound: A Close-Up.* New York: McGraw-Hill, 1967.

Stock, Noel. *The Life of Ezra Pound.* New York: Pantheon Books, 1970.

JAMES STILL'S POETRY

"The Journey a Worldly Wonder"

JEFF DANIEL MARION

It's a familiar scene: late afternoon at a small southern town bus stop, already the bus filled with various sojourners, mostly rural folk returning home, a few others going longer distances, but all travelers settling back for miles of rolling hills, lush valleys, landscapes familiar to most, new to some. The engine whirrs and whines; the journey begins. But before the bus can make its turn away from the station, a lone straggler runs to the door waving his ticket and pecking on the window. He comes aboard and takes the only remaining seat beside a young man with a book balanced on his knees. Settling, the late arrival introduces himself and notes with pleasure the book perched on his traveling companion's lap. He offers the young man a magazine from his coat pocket, says there's a selection in it he'd like him to read. So the two settle back for the journey: one to read the passing landscape, the other to journey in a world of words.

And so it is in poetry—but remember that poetry is both vehicle and destination, both journey and place of arrival. Nothing new in that idea— it's a familiar scene. When we enter the landscapes of James Still's poetry, it's a familiar scene but one that etches itself indelibly in memory, a journey that routes its way across a terrain more than mere passing scenery, a terrain

From *Iron Mountain Review* 2 (Summer 1984): 17–21. Reprinted by permission of the author and the publisher.

of the heart and mind in the process of discovery, knowing, understanding, and enduring. As Still himself has noted,

> When I have done a thing it often seems that it pre-existed and had only to be discovered. The creative act involves a person wholly. More even than he knows about himself, or could guess. The work of the great mental computer which has registered every mini-second of being from the moment of birth. Creativity involves the total experience, inherited characteristics, learning. The joys, the sorrows, the horrors.

Consider, then, some of the places of his poems.

Farm

In the deep moist hollows, on the burnt acres
Suspended upon the mountain side, the crisp green corn
Tapers blunt to the fruiting tassel;
Long straight shafts of yellow poplar
Strike upward like prongs of lightning at the field's edge,
Dwarfing the tender blades, the jointed growth;
Crows haggle their dark feathers, glare beady eyes
Surveying the slanted crop from the poplar boughs,
Opening purple beaks to cry the ripening feast,
And flow from their perch in heavy pointless flight.
A lizard, timid and tremulous, swallowing clots of air
With pulsing throat, pauses at the smooth trunk
And runs up the sky with liquid feet.[1]

This is no cozy scene, no placid Eden, no cornucopia of eternal delights. The language itself is *alive,* energetic, moving. In an interview Still cautioned the budding writer to be wary "of static words in composition—words registering little change. Someone has calculated that Zane Grey's work is ninety-five percent static while James Joyce's is only five percent." Note that here the acres are "burnt," the corn is "crisp," the "tapers blunt." Indeed, even the yellow poplar trees tower over the corn, dwarf it, not only in size but also in energy, as suggested by their similarity to "prongs of lightning." And as every farmer/gardener knows: If the crows didn't visit the field as the corn was barely thrusting through the earth and pull it up shoot by tender shoot, pecking the germinating seed at the root, then the corn will not be thinned out. At harvest time, these returning furies will then "haggle," "glare," "survey," and "cry the ripening feast." But in a poem whose energy has been generated primarily by active, sensory verbs and nouns, the central irony resides in the adjective *pointless*: the crows "flow from their perch in heavy pointless flight." Destinationless, yes, but also the crows do not fly in a distinct formation, pointless. "Pointless" vividly contrasts with "tapers," "shafts," "edge," "prongs," "blades," "beaks," and "perch." But the most telling contrast is in the final three lines: the "timid and tremulous" lizard. In a poem in which we expect images such as "hollow," "acres," "corn," "crows," and "ripening feast," the lizard comes as a surprise. We react much as we might upon seeing the lizard itself. Or, as another poet has put it: "His notice sudden is." This unexpectedness quickens the pulse, sharpens our senses, focuses our perception.

But Still's attitude toward the land and its power is more than an ironic vision of the thin line between the crows' boldness and the lizard's timidity, the lightning-like yellow poplars and the dwarfed corn stalks, or the tightrope the farmer walks between hardship and harvest. In "Heritage" the persona senses other claims.

Heritage

I shall not leave these prisoning hills
Though they topple their barren heads to level earth
And the forests slide uprooted out of the sky.
Though the waters of Troublesome, of Trace Fork,
Of Sand Lick rise in a single body to glean the valleys,
To drown lush pennyroyal, to unravel rail fences;
Though the sun-ball breaks the ridges into dust
And burns its strength into the blistered rock
I cannot leave. I cannot go away.

Being of these hills, being one with the fox
Stealing into the shadows, one with the new-born foal,
The lumbering ox drawing green beech logs to mill,
One with the destined feet of man climbing and descending,
And one with death rising to bloom again, I cannot go.
Being of these hills I cannot pass beyond.
(*WP*, 82)

Here the land is both prison and home. The power it exerts on the speaker is such that he feels compelled to find in language an equal power to match the strength of its claim. Surely this is the claim of an artist/writer who does not see himself as separate from the land he writes of but instead is *one with* the fox, the new-born foal, the lumbering ox, the destined feet of man, and ultimately death itself. The catalog is a revealing one: craftiness, cunning ("fox stealing into the shadows"), innocence ("new-born foal"), awkwardness of raw power ("the lumbering ox"), the arduous struggle of man ("destined feet of man climbing and descending"), and finally "death rising to bloom again." This artist refuses to reject any of the qualities of his heritage. He recognizes the universal in these local details. There is the implicit understanding that even if the hills, forests, valleys, and ridges were to be swept away, he will remain forever in place. The place is *in* him. It is thus his locus, the source he will neither deny nor abandon. This is not to say that Still's artistry depends on the source of his subject matter, however. Dean Cadle so astutely reminds us that "[Still] would be an artist in any hollow in any country. All that finally matters is the always whirling life in the ever-fresh vision in Still's mind; and once he gets it on paper there is little reason for concern over whether it ever actually existed, for hopefully neither time nor reality will erode it."

"Wolfpen Creek" is yet another representation of Still's vision of the land.

Wolfpen Creek

How it was in that place, how light hung in a bright pool
Of air like water, in an eddy of cloud and sky,
I will long remember. I will long recall.
The maples blossoming wings, the oaks proud with rule,
The spiders deep in silk, the squirrels fat on mast,
The fields and draws and coves where quail and peewees call.
Earth loved more than any earth, stand firm, hold fast;
Trees burdened with leaf and bird, root deep, grow tall.
(*WP,* 71)

So the particular quality of light in a landscape enters memory, that bright pool the speaker will draw from, drink from, for a long time. And, yes, how it was in that place is reflected in this pool, this lyric of praise for "earth loved more than any earth."

How it was in that place: the journey of Still's poems is not one of landscape only. We long remember, long recall the characters and the rituals by which they live in that place, Still's world. The ritualistic processes through which we expend our energy, pass our time, find our joys, fulfill our hopes, or realize horrors are suggested by the titles of several poems: "Fox Hunt," "Horse Swapping," "Court Day," and "Dance on Pushback." Even though these poems are significant in accurately documenting cultural and social mores, folkways, their value ultimately lies in their artistry, the ways the poems themselves journey in language to substantiate reality. As Robert Frost has told us: "The figure a poem makes. It begins in delight and ends in wisdom. . . . [I]t inclines to the impulse, it assumes direction with the first line laid down, it runs a course of lucky events and ends in a clarification of life. . . . It finds its own name as it goes and discovers the best waiting for it in some final phrase at once wise and sad." Notice how "Dance on Pushback" fulfills Frost's description.

Dance on Pushback

Rein your sorry nags boys, buckle the polished saddle
And set black hats aslant the wind down Troublesome,
There are doings on Pushback at Gabe Waye's homeplace
And the door hangs wide, the thumping keg bubbles
With gonesome plumping in the elderberry patch;
The cider brew strains against red cob stoppers
And the puncheon floor is mealed for the skip and shuffle,
Ready for the stamping, waiting for the hopping,
The Grapevine swing, the ole Virginie reeling
In the grease lamp's fuming and unsteady gleaming.
There are jolly fellows heading toward Pushback
In the valley's brisk breathing, the moon's white bathing,
In the whippoorwill's lonesome never answered calling.

Gabe Waye has six fair young daughters
Who dance like foxfire in dark thickets,
Whose feet are nimble, whose bodies are willowy,
As smooth as yellow poplars in early bud,
And their cheeks are like maple leaves in early autumn,
And their breath as sweet as fresh mountain tea.

Gabe Waye has six full-blooming daughters
With dresses starched as stiff as galax leaves,
Awaiting the dancing, awaiting and hoping.

Rein-up the filly boys, hitch-up the stallion
And heigh-o yonder toward Pushback Mountain,
The katydids a-calling, the hoot-owl a-hooting,
Thick hoofs are striking fire on the crookedy trail,
For feet are yearning for the heart-leaf weaving
And a sight of Waye's daughters doing the Fare-you-well.

Gabe Waye has three tall strapping sons
Standing six feet five in wide bare feet,
And with handsome faces where laughter's never fading,
And with swift limber fingers for silver strings twanging.
The tallest picks the banjo, the thickest saws the fiddle,
The broadest plays the dulcimer with the readiest grace,
And the three together set the darkling hollow ringing
While the harmony goes tripping over moon-dappled hill.

Spur-up the nags boys, the dance won't be lasting,
Tighten up the reins and set the pebbles flying,
Heigh-o to Pushback with a quick lick-a-spittle,
Night will be fading and moonlight dying.
(*WP*, 17–18)

The cast of characters we encounter in a journey through Still's poems ranges from Uncle Ira Combs, mountain preacher, who is a mountain of faith, to Bad Jack Means whose "sins / killed every fish in the river," a man so intolerable that he brings the narrator to question heaven with: "Are you up there, Bad Jack? / If you are, if He took you in, / I think I'll choose the Other Place." There are also those for whom music is essential: Banjo Bill Brewer is the quintessential artist who not only has shaped his banjo by his own hands but also sings his own song. Too,

This is his own true love
He grieves, these his winding lonesome valleys
Blowing with perished leaves and winds that starve

In the chestnut oaks, and these the deaths he dies.
His voice is a whispering water, the speech of a dove.
("Banjo Bill Brewer," *WP,* 39)

For this artist, Banjo Bill Brewer, music is the means by which he experiences both joys and sorrows ("It [the banjo] is his tongue for joy, it is his eyes for weeping.") On the other hand there is Clabe Mott, a man obviously not made for farming, for

the sun rakes the fields, your farm stands fallow,
The mould board rusts, the plowstock stands upturned,
The harness falls in heaps within your sagging barn
And your stock runs free upon the brambled hills.
("Clabe Mott," *WP,* 34)

Nevertheless, when this man takes out his fiddle and begins to play, the world is at his command: "The waters wait, the winds break their pace, / . . . / The oaks go down with thunder in the singing air." Not only do we experience the presence of those who live energetically in their pursuit of some moment of joy, but there is also the lingering presence of the dead. The narrator in "Nixie Middleton" achingly tells us, "I am alone and all the hills have eyed my sorrow, / And bird and fox have heard my breath along the slopes / Whistling your name." The narrator's journey is a search for his lost love, a pilgrimage that takes him "up Sand Lick, up Carr's clear waters / And the sixty-seven mile wandering of Troublesome Creek." The end of this quest is "the laurel-thicket hill / where my love sleeps. My love waits for me still." But perhaps the epitome of Still's world is Uncle Ambrose, a man whose very being has become one with the landscape in which he lives. Like the land, he *is* strength, stability, endurance.

Uncle Ambrose

Your hair is growing long, Uncle Ambrose,
And the strands of your beard are like willow sprays
Hanging over Troublesome Creek's breeze in August.
Uncle Ambrose, your hands are heavy with years,
Seamy with the ax's heft, the plow's hewn stock,
The thorn wound and the stump-dark bruise of time.

Your face is a map of Knott County
With hard ridges of flesh, the wrinkled creek beds,
The traces and forks carved like wagon tracks on stone;
And there is Troublesome's valley struck violently
By a barlow's blade, and the anti-cline of all waters
This side of the Kentucky River.

Your teeth are dark-stained apples on an ancient tree
And your eyes the trout pools between the narrow hills;
Your hands are glacial drifts of stone
Cradled on a mountain, rock-ribbed and firm,
On the Appalachian range from Maine to Alabama.
(*WP*, 44)

Frequently, details similar to ones we see woven into the life of Uncle
Ambrose become occasions for poems themselves, journeys into the nature
of things themselves. In the poem "Dulcimer" we see details of a world
drawn into the object: not only do we see the uniqueness of the object, but
by an amazing catalog of metaphors a context is also established whereby
we see the greater world in which the object exists. "Dulcimer" is, then,
microcosm.

Dulcimer

The dulcimer sings from fretted maple throat
Of the doe's swift poise, the fox's fleeting step
And music of hounds upon the outward slope
Stirring the night, drumming the ridge-strewn way,
The anvil's strength . . .
                              and the silence after
That aches and cries unhushed into the day.

From the dulcimer's breast sound hunting horns
Strong as clenched hands upon the edge of death,
The creak of saddle-bags, of oxen yoke and thongs,
Wild turkey's treble, dark sudden flight of crows,
O unshod hoofs . . .
                              and the stillness after,
Bitter as salt drenching the tongue of pain:

And of the lambs crying, breath of the lark,
Long drinks from piggins hard against the lips;
And with hoarse singing, raw as hickory shagbark,
The foal's anxiety is woven with the straining wedge
And the wasp's anger . . .
                              and the quiet after
For the carver of maple on a keen blade's edge.
(*WP,* 20)

Notice the blending of object, sound, and motion; notice the surge, the rush of everything toward "silence," "stillness," "quiet." This is the pulse of life itself, the surge poised against stillness and death, "the keen blade's edge." What William Heyen once said regarding Williams's "Red Wheelbarrow" could be said of Still's "Dulcimer":

This is one of the reasons . . . [it] . . . is so important; as object, as thing to engage the mind, it is always there, it is matter. Perhaps the steps are sight, speech, awe, and silence. "Revision," speech again, wonder and silence again, looking up in perfect silence at the stars again, as Whitman said, "The poet's art not to chart, but to voyage." Nature itself is the Zen master who sends us back day after day for as long as we live to study perhaps one inexhaustible leaf or sound or angle of sunlight.

Again and again Still's poems do voyage, take us on journeys of the self. In "With Hands Like Leaves" we find a narrator who wanders quietly in dark thickets and discovers:

This is not a mountain I walk upon. It is a ridge
of sleep or death, a slope hung on a night-jar's speech.
A child walks here with hands like leaves, with eyes
Like swifts that search the darkness in a perilous land.
He seeks a hill where living day shall stand."
(*WP,* 59)

This wanderer in the fearful dark seeks light, knows the precarious balance of the self hoping to endure. We do not know whether the journey will be successful. Closely related to this wanderer is the narrator of "Eyes in the Grass," who recognizes the separation of the self from nature, particularly from the grackle and the ant whom he observes. Through this journey the narrator reaches a moment of self-awareness and says,

> I think that neither the grackle's black eyes
> Nor the ant's myopic sight has found me here,
> Drowned in quivering stems lost in wattled twigs
> of grass-trees. O, I am lost to any wandering view.
> I am a hill uncharted, my breathing is the wind.
> I am horizon. I am earth's far end.
> (*WP,* 57)

Although there are some journeys (particularly in "Hounds on the Mountain" and "Pattern for Death") that end bitterly or with the realization that there is no escape, there is the seasoned traveler in "White Highways" who arrives at a paradoxical truth: his journeying has brought him back to the starting point with the realization "Here is my pleasure most where I have lived / And called my home." The road to discovery we find turns backwards. We rediscover Emerson's truth: "Man is a knot of roots."

And now our journey leads us back to the two travelers who have journeyed by bus across Kentucky. They have reached their destinations, and as they take leave of one another, they agree to stay in touch, to write to one another, for during this journey they have found that they have common interests. The young man who sat with a book perched on his knees and who read from his fellow traveler's magazine during the trip was Cratis Williams, known to many now as Mr. Appalachia, certainly one of the region's most outstanding spokesmen and interpreters. And yes, the words he read during the trip were those written by his fellow traveler, James Still. Although this first meeting of Cratis Williams with the man James Still and his words occurred nearly half a century ago, we can certainly say of that trip and of Still's poetry: "And O the trip was a sight to the world, / The journey a worldly wonder."

Notes

1. James Still, *The Wolfpen Poems* (Berea, Ky.: The Berea College Press, 1986), 5. Hereafter cited parenthetically as *WP.*

ON HARRIETTE ARNOW'S *The Dollmaker*

JOYCE CAROL OATES

This brutal, beautiful novel has a permanent effect upon the reader: long after one has put it aside, he is still in the presence of its people, absorbed in their trivial and tragic dilemma, sorting out their mistakes, rearranging their possibilities, pondering upon the fate that makes certain people live certain lives, suffer certain atrocities, while other people merely read about them. Because Harriette Arnow's people are not articulate, we are anxious to give their confusion a recognizable order, to contribute to their reality, to complete them with language. They are assimilated into us, and we into them. *The Dollmaker* deals with human beings to whom language is not a means of changing or even expressing reality, but a means of pitifully recording its effect upon the nerves. It is a legitimate tragedy, our most unpretentious American masterpiece.

First published in 1954, *The Dollmaker* tells the story of a dislocated Kentucky family during the closing years of World War II. The Nevels family comes to Detroit, so that the father can contribute to the "war effort" by working in a factory. The war is always a reality, though at a distance: real to the Kentucky women who wait anxiously for mail, dreading the arrival of telegrams, real to the workers of Detroit who dread its ending. But the "war" itself becomes abstracted from common experience as the Nevels family gradually is accommodated to Detroit and its culture of machines, the radio being the means by which war news is always heard, and also the primary means of entertainment. In the foreground is a life of

From "Joyce Carol Oates on Harriette Arnow's *The Dollmaker*," in *Rediscoveries*, ed. David Madden (New York: Crown, 1971); reprinted in Harriette Arnow, *The Dollmaker* (New York: Avon Books, 1972), 601–8. Reprinted by permission of the author.

distracting, uprooted particulars, everything dependent upon everything else, tied together magically in the complex economic knot of a modern industrial society. How can the human imagination resist a violent assimilation into such a culture? In Kentucky, the Nevels are themselves a kind of domestic factory, producing their own food; in Detroit they are the exploited base of a vast capitalistic pyramid, utterly helpless, anonymous cogs in a factory that extends beyond the brutal city of Detroit to take in the entire nation. They are truly American, as they become dehumanized—Gertie Nevels is encouraged to make cheap dolls, in place of her beautiful hand-carved figures, and her children are enthusiastic about selling themselves in various clever ways, knowing that one must be sold, one must therefore work to *sell oneself.* A pity they can't put up a sign over their door, they say, declaring this three-bedroom apartment to be the "Nevels' Woodworking Plant Number 1!" The enthusiasm of the children's acquiescence to the values of a capitalistic society is one of the most depressing aspects of this novel.

It is a depressing work, like most extraordinary works. Its power lies in its insistence upon the barrenness of life, even a life lived in intimacy with other human beings, bound together by ties of real love and suffering. Tragedy does not seem to me to be cathartic, but to deepen our sense of the mystery and sanctity of the human predicament. The beauty of *The Dollmaker* is its author's absolute commitment to a vision of life as cyclical tragedy—as constant struggle. No sooner is one war declared over than the impoverished, overworked citizens of Detroit anticipate the start of another war, the war against "communists," particularly those in Detroit— no sooner is one domestic horror concluded, one child mutilated and killed, than another horror begins to take shape. The process of life demands total absorption of one's energies, there is no time to think, no time to arrange fate, no time to express the spiritual life. Life is killing, a killing of other people or of oneself, a killing of one's soul. When the war is over, concluded by the drama of the atomic bombs, "Gertie could hear no rejoicing, no lifting of the heart that all the planned killing and wounding of men was finished. Rather it was as if the people had lived on blood, and now that the bleeding was ended, they were worried about the future food."

It is a fact of life that one must always worry, not about the "planned" killing and wounding of men, but about his own future food.

The Dollmaker begins magnificently on a Kentucky road, with Gertie in her own world, knowing her strength, having faith in her audacity—a big, ungainly, ugly woman astride a mule, ready to force any car that comes along to stop for her. She is carrying her son Amos, who is dangerously ill, and she must get a ride to town in order to take him to a doctor. Her sheer animal will, her stubbornness, guarantee the survival of her son; she is not afraid to cut into his flesh with a knife in order to release pus. She succeeds in stopping a car with an army officer in it and she succeeds in overwhelming this man by the determination of her will. But it is her last real success: after the novel's beginning, everything goes downhill for Gertie.

Basic to her psychological predicament is a conflict that has been an obsession in the American imagination, particularly the imagination of the nineteenth century—the twin and competitive visions of God, God as love and God as vengeance, a God of music and dollmaking and domestic simplicity, and a God whose hell quivers with murderous heat. The God of hell is the God worshiped by Gertie's mother, who is responsible for the tragedy of the novel. If the God of this hell rules the world also, and it is Gertie's deepest, helpless conviction that He does, then all of life is forecast, determined; and the fires of Detroit's steel mills are accurate symbols for Gertie to mull over. Gertie, like Judas, is foreordained to sin against such a God. The novel resolves itself in a bitter irony as Gertie betrays herself, giving up her unique art in order to make herself over into a kind of free-lance factory worker, turning out dolls or foxes or Christ, on order; she is determined to be Judas, to betray the Christly figure in the piece of wood she never has enough time to carve out, and the Christly figure is at once her own and that of the millions of people, Americans like herself, who might have been models for Christ. They do not emerge out of the wood, they do not become incarnated in time, they are not given a face or a voice. They remain mute, unborn. Man is both Christ and Judas, the sacred, divine self and the secular, betraying, human self, the self that must sell itself for "future food" because this is the foreordained lot of man.

"She thought she was going to cry. . . . So many times she'd thought of that other woman, and now she was that woman: 'She considereth a field and buyeth it; with the fruit of her own hands she planteth a vineyard.' A whole vineyard she didn't need, only six vines maybe. So much to plant her own vines, set her own trees, and know that come thirty years from now she'd gather fruit from the trees and grapes from the vines. . . ." Gertie's only ambition is to own a small farm of her own. In order to live she must own land, work the land herself. The owning of property has nothing to do with setting up boundaries (there are no near neighbors); it is a declaration of personality, an expression of the profound human need for self-sufficiency and permanence. Wendell Berry's *A Place on Earth,* also set during the closing months of World War II but dealing exclusively with those Kentuckians who did not leave home, is a long, slow, ponderous, memorable novel of praise for a life lived close to the earth, to one's own earth, a "place on earth" which is our only hope; the earth and human relationships are our only hope. In the government housing project in Detroit this desire is expressed feebly and pathetically in the tenants' planting of flowers, which are naturally trampled and destroyed, though a few somehow survive—the tragedy is that this desire lies beyond the reach of nearly everyone, and therefore identity, personality, the necessary permanence of life itself are denied. To be "saved" in this culture one must remake oneself entirely, one must sell oneself as shrewdly as possible. One's fate depends not upon his sacred relationship with the land, but his secular, deceptive relationship with society.

There are great works that deal with the soul in isolation, untouched importantly by history. Sartre's *Nausea,* which concerns the salvation of a historian, is an ahistorical work, a work of allegory; Dostoyevsky's *Notes from the Underground,* neurotic and witty and totally subjective, is nevertheless a historical work. It seems to me that the greatest works of literature deal with the human soul caught in the stampede of time, unable to gauge the profundity of what passes over it, like the characters in certain plays of Yeats's who live through terrifying events but who cannot understand them; in this way history passes over most of us. Society is caught in a convulsion, whether of growth or of death, and ordinary people are destroyed. They do not, however, understand that they are "destroyed."

There is a means of salvation: love, particularly of children. But the children of *The Dollmaker* are stunted, doomed adults, destroyed either literally by the admonition "Adjust!" or destroyed emotionally, turned into citizens of a demonic factory-world. There is another means: art. But art is luxury, it has no place in the world of intense, daily, bitter struggle, though this world of struggle is itself the main object of art. Living, one cannot be saved; suffering, one cannot express the phenomenon of "suffering." Gertie Nevels is inarticulate throughout most of this novel, unable to do battle effectively with the immense hallucination of her new life, and her only means of expression—her carving—must finally be sacrificed, so that her family can eat. So the social dislocation of these Kentucky "hillbillies" is an expression of the general doom of most of mankind, and their defeat, the corruption of their personalities, is more basic to our American experience than the failure of those whom James thought of as "freed" from economic necessity, and therefore free to create their own souls. Evil is inherent in the human heart, as good is inherent in it; but the violence of economic suffering stifles the good, stimulates the evil, so that the ceaseless struggle with the fabric of the universe is reduced to a constant, daily heartbreaking struggle over money, waged against every other antlike inhabitant of the city, the stakes indefinable beyond next month's payment of rent or payment on the car.

If the dream of a small farm is Gertie's dream of Eden, the real "Paradise Valley" (a Negro slum section of Detroit) is an ironic hell, and the "Merry Hill" to which she and her family come to live is, though segregated "by law," no different. Detroit is terrifying as seen through the eyes of this Kentucky farm woman. The machines—the hurrying people—the automobiles—the initial sounding of that ugly word "Hillbilly!"—everything works to establish a demonic world, the antithesis of the Kentucky hills. There, man can have privacy and dignity though he may be poor; in the housing development money appears and is lost, there is no privacy, everyone intrudes upon everyone else, the alley is "one churning, wriggling mass of children." The impact of this dislocation upon children is most terrible: Reuben, the oldest boy, becomes bitter and runs away from home, unable to "adjust"; Cassie, deprived of her invisible playmate Callie Lou, is killed by a train in the trainyards near her home. I can think of no other work except Christina Stead's *The Man Who Loved Children* that deals so brilliantly and movingly with the lives of children, and Mrs. Arnow has chosen not to penetrate the minds of the Nevels children at all but simply to show us their development or deterioration from the outside. It is a fact of slum life that children dominate in sheer numbers. The more impoverished the neighborhood, the more children to run wild in its streets and on its sidewalks, both powerful and helpless. The fear of anarchy, shared by all of us who have been children, materializes in the constant struggle of children to maintain their identities, striking and recoiling from one another: in miniature they live out tragic scenarios, the pressure upon the human soul in our age, the overcrowding of life, the suffocation of the personality under the weight of sheer numbers, noise, confusion. Yet no dream of wealth, no dream of a fine home in "Grosse Pointe" is too fantastic for these people to have; corrupted by movies, by the radio, by the mystery of the dollar, they succumb happily to their own degradation, alternating between a kind of community and a disorganized, hateful mass that cannot live in peace. Neighbors cannot live in peace with neighbors, nor parents with their own families, nor children with children. The basic split in the American imagination between an honoring of the individual and a vicious demand for "adjustment" and conformity is dramatized by the gradual metamorphosis of the surviving Nevels children. Gertie is still Gertie, though profoundly shaken by the loss of Reuben and Cassie, but her other children have come a long way, by the end of the novel, when they can laugh at a cartoon of a woman with a mule, having learned the proper contempt for a "hillbilly."

Gertie's husband, Clovis, with his liking for machines, adapts himself easily to the new culture. He takes pride in buying his wife an Icy Heart refrigerator (on time) and a car for himself (on time) and in "hunting Christmas" for his family in smelly department-store basements. It is part of the moral confusion of life in Detroit that Clovis, essentially a good, "natural" man, should become a murderer, revenging himself upon a young man hired to beat him up because of his union activities. There is no time to assess properly Clovis's act of murder—Gertie has no time to comprehend it, except to recoil from what she senses has happened. But the struggle continues; nothing is changed by the murder; another thug will be hired to take that man's place, by the mysterious powers with money enough to "hire" other men; at the novel's conclusion Clovis, like millions of other men, is out of work and we can envision his gradual disintegration, forced to look desperately for jobs and to live off his wife and children.

It is part of the industrial society that people of widely varying backgrounds should be thrown together, like animals competing for a small, fixed amount of food, forced to hate one another. Telling an amiable anecdote about factory life, Clovis mentions a Ukrainian: "He hates everything, niggers, hillbillies, Jews, Germans, but worse'n anything he hates Poles an that Polack foreman. An he is a good-hearted guy. . . ." Catholics hate and fear non-Catholics, spurred on by their famous radio priest "Father Moneyhan," but Irish Catholics hate Polish Catholics. However, the hatreds seethe and subside, especially in the face of common human predicaments of drunkenness and trouble; at any rate they can be easily united into a solid hatred of Negroes, should that need arise. Living in fear more or less constantly, being forced to think only of their "future food," these people have no choice but to hate the "Other," the constant threat. What a picture of America's promises *The Dollmaker* gives, and how unforgettable this "melting-pot" of economic democracy!

Mrs. Arnow writes so well, with so little apparent effort, that critical examination seems almost irrelevant. It is a tribute to her talent that one is convinced, partway through the book, that it is a masterpiece; if everything goes wrong, if an entirely unsuitable ending is tacked on, the book will remain inviolate. The ending of *The Dollmaker* is by no means a disappointment, however. After months of struggle and a near-succumbing to madness, Gertie questions the basis of her own existence; inarticulate as she is, given to working with her hands, in silence, she is nevertheless lyrically aware of the horror of the world in which she now lives. Behind her, now unattainable, is the farm in Kentucky which her mother talked her out of buying; all around her is the unpredictable confusion of Detroit. What is the point of having children? "What was the good of trying to keep your own [children] if when they grew up their days were like your own—changeovers and ugly painted dolls?" Throughout the novel Gertie has been dreaming of the proper face for the Christ she wants to carve. She never locates the proper face: instead she takes the fine block of wood to be split into smaller pieces, for easily made dolls.

The drama of naturalism has always been the subjecting of ordinary people to the corrosive and killing facts of society, usually an industrial one. *The Grapes of Wrath,* so much more famous than Mrs. Arnow's novel, and yet not superior to it, is far more faithful to the naturalistic tradition than is *The Dollmaker:* one learns a great deal about the poetic vulgarities and obscenities of life from Steinbeck, and this aspect of life has its own kind of immortality. *The Dollmaker,* however, is not truly naturalistic; a total world is suggested but not expressed. Mrs. Arnow, like Gertie Nevels, flinches from a confrontation with sexual realities. The frantic naturalism of such a work as *Last Exit to Brooklyn,* superimposed upon this little Detroit epic, would give us, probably, a more truthful vision of Detroit, then and now; but such naturalism, totally absorbed in an analysis of bodily existence, is perhaps equally unfaithful to the spiritual and imaginative demands that some people, at least, still make. So Gertie is an "artist," but a primitive, untheorizing, inarticulate artist; she whittles out figures that are dolls or Christs, figures of human beings not quite human, but expressive of old human dreams. She is both an ordinary human being and an extraordinary human being, a memorable creation, so real that one cannot question her existence. There are certainly greater novels than *The Dollmaker,* but I can think of none that has moved me more, personally, terrifyingly, involving me in the solid fact of life's criminal exploitation of those who live it—not hard, not sentimental, not at all intellectually ambitious, *The Dollmaker* is one of those excellent American works that have yet to be properly assessed.

THE CHRISTIAN AND THE CLASSIC IN *The Dollmaker*

BARBARA HILL RIGNEY

Because Christ was a man, his fictional counterparts have also traditionally been male, providing a central motif in patriarchal literature for centuries. Even contemporary male authors, nontraditional in many other ways, have focused on a traditionally masculine view of Christ as heroic reformer or at least as active agent in the melioration of the human condition. Theodore Ziolkowski, in his important *Fictional Transfigurations of Jesus,*[1] explores a variety of modern and historical literary Christ figures—none of them female or representative of a female psychology.

The female Christ-figure as a fictional device, whether explicit or only implied, is relatively recent in the works of women writers. While contemporary women novelists are now presenting a great many such transfigurations, these differ from traditional renditions in a number of ways. First, women writers are more conscious of an inherent irony in the depiction of Christ as a woman, and their works are often more pleasurably iconoclastic because of this awareness. Many feminist writers are also more fully cognizant of the political and psychological ramifications involved in the literary transfiguration of Christ; they recognize that women who are oppressed because of their sex often tend to identify themselves with those aspects of Christ which are traditionally associated with the feminine: the essential victim, the eternal sufferer, the innocent scapegoat sacrificed for the sins of an entire world.

From *Lilith's Daughters: Women and Religion in Contemporary Fiction* (Madison: University of Wisconsin Press, 1982), 11–16, 49–51. Reprinted by permission of the author and the publisher.

Simone de Beauvoir saw such an identification, whether in literature or in life, as a form of paranoid delusion. In *The Second Sex,* she explores women's perceptions of their blood-tie with Christ. As women bleed each month and in childbirth, so Christ bled on the cross; as women perceive themselves as sacrificial victims of men, impaled in the sexual act, so Christ was pierced by the spear:

> In the humiliation of God (at the crucifixion) she sees with wonder the dethronement of Man; inert, passive, covered with wounds, the Crucified is the reversed image of the white, blood-stained martyr exposed to wild beasts, to daggers, to males, with whom the little girl has so often identified herself; she is overwhelmed to see that Man, Man-God, has assumed her role. She it is who is hanging on the Tree, promised the splendor of the Resurrection. It is she: she proves it; her forehead bleeds under the crown of thorns.[2]

Phyllis Chesler states in *Women and Madness* that a common manifestation of female insanity is an identification with Christ, an identification "concretely rooted in female biology." According to Chesler, it is through the "blood sacrifice" of childbearing that women assume their role as martyr: "Women are impaled on the cross of self-sacrifice. Unlike men, they are categorically denied the experience of cultural supremacy, humanity and renewal based on their sexual identity—and on the blood sacrifice, in some way, of a member of the opposite sex. In different ways, some women are driven mad by this fact."[3]

A number of contemporary women writers have found their inspiration in the association of woman with Christ, the tree with the cross, blood with glory. The poetry of Sylvia Plath comes immediately to mind and has been frequently and thoroughly explored in this context.[4] A similar preoccupation with woman as victim, in this instance the blood sacrifice equally as complete as Plath's and more terrifying, occurs in Kate Millett's *The Basement,* a harrowing analysis of the actual murder by torture of sixteen-year-old Sylvia Likens in Indianapolis in 1965. Millett sees Sylvia's death, "this head with its frayed lips, this *Pietà,*" as a paradigm for the female condition: "You have been with me ever since, an incubus, a nightmare, my own nightmare, the nightmare of adolescence, of growing up a female child, of becoming a woman in a world set against us, a world we have lost and where we are everywhere reminded of our defeat. What you endured all emblematic of that."[5] To minimize the suffering of Sylvia Likens would amount to a perversity approximating that of her torturers; to see her as a female Christ and her fate as symbolically that of all women, however, is to internalize the psychology of the victim and to deny the reality of female power.

The transfiguration of woman into martyred Christ occurs also in Harriette Arnow's *The Dollmaker*,[6] a novel of immense emotional impact but almost totally lacking in what Ziolkowski calls "the ironic consciousness."[7] Without the detachment that might have been provided by either irony or psychology, Arnow reproduces the suffering and the sacrificial function of Christ in the person of Gertie Nevels, an immigrant from the hills of Kentucky displaced to Detroit during World War II. Gertie herself does not know she is Christ; rather, the transfiguration is imposed by Arnow from without.

The tree, in Arnow's novel, quite literally becomes the cross. Gertie is a wood carver, a sculptor of great natural talent. Throughout the novel, she carries with her, on both her physical and her spiritual journeys, an immense block of cherry wood, itself a kind of cross, from which she plans to carve the face of Christ. She is never to complete the project, however, even when she looks into a mirror or at the faces of her friends, women who also suffer and are Christ.

In the beginning of the novel, when Gertie is at home in the relative paradise of Kentucky, working the land, loving her children, talking to the trees, and at one with nature and herself, she envisions the potential face of her Christ as "a laughing Christ uncrowned with thorns and with the scars of the nail holes in his hands all healed away; a Christ who had loved people, had liked to mingle with them and laugh and sing" (64). Like Gertie herself, this Christ is a carpenter, a working person intent on the joy of work; the image is that of Jesus at the wedding of Cana of Galilee.

Unfortunately, Gertie too has gone to a wedding—her own—and her real cross is a patriarchal and religiously condoned concept of marriage. Gertie's mother, always a voice for patriarchal religion, hysterically admonishes Gertie: "'Leave all else and cleave to thy husband.' She's never read to them the words writ by Paul, 'Wives, be in subjection unto your husbands, as to the Lord'" (141). Gertie complies, packs up her five children, and follows her husband to Detroit, thus beginning a journey through the underworld: "the whirling snow, the piles of coal, the waiting cars, the dark tanks moving, all seem to glow with a faint reddish light. The redness trembled like a flame, as if somewhere far away a piece of hell had come up from underground" (168). For Gertie, Detroit is "a world not meant for people" (168); her breath on the frozen car window "was at times a reddish pink, as if bits of blood had frozen with the frost" (169). The blood is, of course, symbolically Gertie's own and literally that of her daughter, who is later run over by a train and killed.

In Detroit, Gertie can no longer conjure up her earlier visions of a loving Christ, and the aspect of her cherry-wood carving changes correspondingly. Her Christ is now an image of the crucifixion, an image which reflects the nature of her world, one determined by poverty, by noise and filth and lovelessness and a malevolent God. In her suffering, Gertie herself psychologically resembles this alternative vision of Jesus, "the head drawn back in agony, the thorns, the nails, each with a drop of crimson below it, a great splash of scarlet for the wounded side, the face bearing many wrinkles to indicate agony" (235–36). Gertie's former pride now reduced to abject humility, she stands to serve food to her seated family in Arnow's version of the Last Supper. Before, Gertie was capable of performing even the miracle of resurrection from death, as she saved her son by performing an emergency tracheotomy with her woodcarving knife; she now cannot even feed her family, let alone muster the power to protect them from death.

Finally, Gertie is reduced to mass-producing figures on her husband's jigsaw and selling them in the street. Thus, she sacrifices her art to necessity, literally and figuratively selling both herself and Jesus. Her still faceless block of cherry wood begins to resemble her own schizoid self, assuming the aspect of Judas as well as Christ. As Joyce Carol Oates has written in an afterword to *The Dollmaker*: "The novel resolves itself in a bitter irony as Gertie betrays herself, giving up her unique art in order to make herself over into a kind of free-lance factory worker, turning out dolls or foxes or Christ, on order" (603).

Gertie, at least, is a physical survivor. But, as I have argued with Arnow in an unpublished interview,[8] surely Gertie has, in emulation of Christ, sacrificed herself as well as her sculpture when, at the end of the novel, she takes up an axe and splits the cherry wood into pieces with which she will manufacture more assembly-line toys. Arnow replied, "She doesn't need it anymore." In retrospect, I think Arnow meant that Gertie has finally come to terms with a "real world" in which God, in fact, would demand the sacrifice of his own son as well as a multitude of nameless women. There is no room for art in Gertie's universe, only for survival. The only possible salvation for Gertie lies in the sisterhood she experiences with the women in her alley, in the human dignity which they help one another to preserve in spite of the overwhelming odds, which include the very nature of God.

Gertie's reward for her suffering is the mystic's vision of God: she ultimately sees in her neighbors' faces the image of Christ and, in her own, a reflection of a tragic human condition. Like Job, Gertie has experienced an insight into what Arnow, in accordance with the Old Testament, apparently sees as the actual and living God. Also like Job, Gertie remains a victim. She has been sacrificed, not so much by her own volition as by Arnow's grim and naturalistic world view.

Gertie Nevels embodies the tragic Christ figure, but her essential tragedy lies in her metamorphosis from Demeter to Christ, from nature goddess to victim of technology, from pagan deity to Christian martyr, from a representative of matriarchy to a refugee from patriarchy. The isolated hill region of Kentucky, as depicted in the early parts of the novel, has become a matriarchal society; World War II has claimed the male members of the community, leaving the women to farm their lands and survive on their own. Gertie, with her strong arms and amazon height (she stands well over six feet tall), has no problem with this arrangement; Arnow lovingly depicts her chopping wood, digging potatoes, joyful in gathering even a meager harvest. At home in Kentucky, Gertie clearly represents a creative principle as she forces the land to yield, carves tools and dolls from sticks of wood, bears and protects her five children. She has even resurrected one of her sons from death by heroically performing a tracheotomy. She celebrates her power, secure in the idea that "she might live and be beholden to no man" (139).

Gertie, at this point, is totally pagan, oblivious to her mother's threats of damnation and the rantings of the lay preacher, Battle John. She walks the land "with long swift strides," singing "at the top of her lungs, joyfully, as if it had been some sinful dance tune, 'How firm a foundation ye saints of the Lord.' She slackened her pace, but couldn't stop the song as she smiled at the stars through the pines. Her foundation was not God but what God had promised Moses—land" (127–28).

Behind Gertie walks her little daughter, Cassie, "her hair the color of cornsilk" (43). It is Cassie for whom Gertie yearns, more than for her other children, for Cassie is the wild, pagan part of herself, undisciplined inventor of fantasy and of the imaginary witch-child, Callie Lou. When Cassie looks into her mother's eyes, she sees herself reflected: "little bitty girls . . . little Cassies" (54).

The loss of Cassie is inevitable, given the analogy with Demeter and Kore. When Gertie weakens, succumbs to the patriarchal admonition that women must follow their husbands, and joins Clovis in Detroit, she has already entered the underworld. She has forfeited her power and can no longer protect her child. In Arnow's novel, Hades in his chariot come to rape and abduct is death in the form of technology, the phallic and powerful locomotive come to take Cassie into the darkness. Gertie's grief is like Demeter's—inconsolable, profound. Nature, too, reacts, even the April grass becoming merely "green paper" (419), artificial, infertile. But, unlike Demeter, whose power remains intact and enables her to seek out her daughter and regain her for at least the larger part of every year, Gertie only grieves. Adrienne Rich writes of Demeter and Kore: "Each daughter, even in the millennia before Christ, must have longed for a mother whose love for her and whose power were so great as to undo rape and bring her back from death. And every mother must have longed for the power of Demeter, the efficacy of her anger, the reconciliation with her lost self."[9]

Arnow's essentially tragic vision, then, precludes the efficacy of Demeter's power. The world of *The Dollmaker* is unmitigatedly patriarchal, dominated by husbands, the moguls of capitalism, and an Old Testament God intent on the destruction of women, children, and nature itself. Chesler's poetic projection of the fate of Demeter in modern times pertains to Arnow's novel and describes it poignantly:

> And it happened as quickly as this. Demeter was stripped of her powers, torn from her maidenhood, and exiled into history as a wretched, fearful wanderer. No longer was she a mother-goddess. Now Demeter appeared only as a stepmother, often a cruel one, or as a witch, often an evil one. . . .
>
> In our time, the stepmothers wander still—exiles, with no memory of what has gone before. Demeter has been known to curse at passing airplanes, to dress in shapeless mourning costumes, to talk to herself, to talk nonsense. . . . Often these days, when Demeter gives birth to a child, she abandons her then and there, turning her own face to the hospital wall. Sometimes, as in a trance, Demeter tries to keep her daughter at home with her again forever.[10]

The powerful Demeter is thus transformed, reduced, to Mary, the suffering figure of the *Pietà.*

Notes

1. Theodore Ziolkowski, *Fictional Transfigurations of Jesus* (Princeton, N.J.: Princeton University Press, 1972).

2. Simone de Beauvoir, *The Second Sex,* trans. and ed. H. M. Parshley (New York: Bantam, 1961), 636.

3. Phyllis Chesler, *Women and Madness* (New York: Avon, 1972), 31.

4. See Gary Lane, ed., *Sylvia Plath: New Views on the Poetry* (Baltimore: Johns Hopkins University Press, 1979).

5. Kate Millett, *The Basement* (New York: Simon and Schuster, 1979), 11.

6. Harriette Arnow, *The Dollmaker* (New York: Avon, 1972).

7. Ziolkowski, *Fictional Transfigurations,* 294.

8. This interview with Arnow took place in 1975 in Ann Arbor, Michigan.

9. Adrienne Rich, *Of Woman Born: Motherhood as Experience and Institution* (New York: Bantam, 1972), 243.

10. Chesler, *Women and Madness,* xix.

Social Criticism in the Works of Wilma Dykeman

OLIVER KING JONES III

Wilma Dykeman has written intelligently in various forms of print media, from newspapers to magazines to books. She is a respected historian, biographer, fiction writer, teacher, columnist, and book reviewer.

These accomplishments place her in a distinguished group, but her social criticism sets her apart from most members of that group during the 1950s and 1960s, when many writers avoided unpopular issues. This criticism was forward-thinking, not satisfied with the status quo, and it follows two general themes: race relations and the environment.

As a writer of both fiction and nonfiction, Dykeman has used her nonfiction to state clearly her beliefs and positions on these themes. These books, articles, and essays have value in their own right, as background and commentary on the issues she has promoted. The nonfiction also shows her determination to improve adverse conditions and to encourage mutual understanding. In most cases, she has then infused her fiction with these themes, not as sermons, but as natural elements of the stories.

She has faced considerable criticism in her approach to these issues. These were not the subjects a proper, Southern white lady mentioned in polite company, much less wrote about, in the 1950s and 1960s. She and her husband, James R. Stokely, were among those far-sighted Southerners who early in the civil rights movement declared their positions and had

Originally published in a slightly different form in *Iron Mountain Review* 5 (Spring 1989): 26–32. Reprinted by permission of the author and the publisher.

the courage to present them in an atmosphere that was often hostile. They were even ostracized by his family and many of their friends. In a 1965 letter to playwright Paul Green, Stokely notes:

> I suppose you know that Bill Sharpe & Co., and others of the Old North State official cultural custodianship, placed Wilma Dykeman Stokely in the literary doghouse some years ago because she was, and has continued to be, outspoken on the subjects of racial integration and civil liberties. (16 Nov. 1965)

In 1955, the year *The French Broad* was published, she was president of the Conference of the North Carolina Literary and Historical Association. However, between 1955 and 1965, she wrote four books and numerous articles dealing with civil rights, a theme that proved to be unpopular with this group.

Despite the resistance to the couple's work, their social criticism comes from an insider's perspective—both Dykeman and Stokely were born and raised in the South. Examined in retrospect, she was something of a prophet.

RACE RELATIONS

Wilma Dykeman began exploring civil rights issues early in her career. Her scope includes civil rights in the broadest sense—the idea that all people should have the right to be different, yet treated as equals. During the 1950s and 1960s, the most obvious civil rights issues revolved around equal opportunities for blacks.

Her first book with a civil rights theme was *Neither Black nor White* (1957), which she and Stokely co-wrote in response to the *Brown vs. Board of Education* case that desegregated the public schools. In that book (and others), she exposes long-standing myths and stereotypes about blacks and black/white relationships. These myths included the concept of a Solid, or monolithic, South; the belief that blacks did not really want civil rights; and the perception that the civil rights movement was a Communist plot. Dykeman shows the damage these myths did to the South, not just to blacks, but also to the national image of all Southerners.

Neither Black nor White strongly challenges the myth of a "Solid South." Although most Southern politicians may have voted as a block on civil rights matters, this book proves that many Southerners favored voting rights and desegregation and worked to achieve racial equality. Dykeman and Stokely point to such unlikely heroes as Dr. Chester Travelstead and Buford Boone. Travelstead, who was dean of the School of Education at the University of South Carolina, announced in a 1955 speech that "the enforced segregation of the races in our public schools can no longer be justifiable on any basis—and should, therefore, be abolished as soon as practicable" (180). His board of trustees promptly fired him. Boone, the publisher of the *Tuscaloosa (Alabama) News,* covered the initial integration attempts at the University of Alabama. He challenged his readers to reject the mob's violence and to recognize the legal rights of blacks. His stance earned him a Pulitzer Prize.

Another dissenting voice was the Association of Southern Women for the Prevention of Lynching. This little-known organization, made up primarily of housewives, applied behind-the-scenes pressure to politicians and businessmen (often their husbands) in an effort to stop lynching and to promote equal opportunities for blacks. In an article entitled "The Plight of Southern White Women," Dykeman and Stokely point to a common bond between these women and blacks—resentment of white male dominance (20–21). This bond, and deep disgust at lynchings and other crimes against blacks, caused many women to make a choice between safe, traditional acquiescence and public protest. By the mid-1960s, an increasing number chose the latter.

Dykeman and Stokely prove in *The Border States* (1968) that the South is not just currently diverse in its opinions on race, but has been for over 150 years. They point to the early conflicts between slaveholding planters and abolitionist Quakers in the South, adding that in 1827, "there were more antislavery societies in North Carolina and Tennessee than in any other state in the Union" (73). They also emphasize the animosity between the planters and the small backwoods farmer, who, despite his lack of political clout, represented most of the people in the South in his opposition to slavery on economic terms. It was this division that contributed most to Southern Unionist sentiments before and during the Civil War (73).

Another myth popular with opponents of desegregation held that most blacks did not really want equality, but that the idea was imported from outside the South, perhaps by Communists, certainly by Northern liberals. Dykeman and Stokely ridiculed both aspects of the myth, and contended that the desire for equal rights was real. For years most blacks kept silent about their dislike of subservient roles and unequal treatment, but the 1954 Supreme Court ruling on desegregation and the broad denial of these legal rights brought the "general discontent and desire for self-improvement . . . [from] beneath a veneer of friendliness and happiness" ("Sit Down," 9). The people who boycotted buses in Montgomery and staged sit-ins at Greensboro lunch counters were acting on inner convictions, not outside orders. As Dykeman and Stokely put it, "by his very struggle for equality the Negro is seeking, not alienation from democracy, but greater participation in it" ("Changing South," 11).

Dykeman was aware that most whites in the 1950s and 1960s had no idea what blacks wanted in terms of relationships with whites. In a 1957 article published in the *Virginia Quarterly Review,* she emphasizes this problem by using the example of a speaker at a courthouse rally who prods the crowd with "the specter of miscegenation . . . [and] the horrors of racial intermingling" ("Southern Demagogue," 558). What Dykeman, but not the speaker, realizes is that most blacks were no more enthusiastic about miscegenation than most whites. In another article, she and Stokely claim that a lack of communication between the races was partially responsible for the bitterness and violence. They cite a white Southerner's epiphany in discerning that

> these people we'd prided ourselves on knowing so well we didn't know at all. Oh, we had cooks and houseboys and we talked to them, but we didn't communicate with them. And now we find out that the Negro had ideas on everything, including his place in life—and he didn't like that place. It was we white people who were naive in the whole thing. ("Inquiry," 86)

The assertion of Communist influence, applied especially to Martin Luther King Jr. and his followers, but also to civil rights advocates in small towns, kept many whites wary of becoming involved. Dykeman and Stokely explained it like this:

> [The myth of silence is] designed to quell disagreement with a majority—or a vocal and often ruthless minority. It labels Southerners who wish to discuss their racial situation as "trouble-makers," disturbers of the peace at pleasant dinner parties and church socials and club gatherings. This, of course, is somewhat like saying that the diagnostician who pronounces his patient ill of cancer is a trouble-maker. ("Changing South," 7–8)

The authors showed the complete lack of evidence for these claims of Communist influence. They pointed out that one of the prime witnesses to this supposed influence was Manning Johnson, a "former self-confessed Communist" and fraud who was invited by segregationist groups to speak at legislative hearings throughout the South. His wild accusations delighted his hosts, but they were all based on rumors. Dykeman and Stokely likened the mood of these hearings to McCarthyism because of the almost religious fervor with which the supposed Communists were accused of treason and other crimes. And, as in McCarthyism, the victims were permanently tainted by the unproven accusations ("McCarthyism," 6–10).

What seemed to bother Dykeman most about the myths and stereotypes was their results. The primary result was a complete lack of understanding, with no desire to improve or change the situation. As long as the myths persisted, blacks were denied civil rights.

Another result was a tendency to associate the South with racism. Despite the widespread racism at the time, much of the nation assumed that racism was at its worst in the South, and that perception became a self-fulfilling prophecy. But Dykeman and Stokely used examples to demonstrate that the problem was no worse in the South than in the North or Midwest. In comparing race relations in Clinton, Tennessee, and Deerfield, Illinois, they conclude that racism among white Southerners had long been sanctioned and was less surprising, while "the white Northerner's racism, real and ugly as it may be, nevertheless exists without official sanction" ("The South," 227).

Dykeman's fiction reflects many of these civil rights themes through characters who either exemplify or refute the stereotypes discussed in the nonfiction. Her white characters have attitudes toward blacks that range from blatantly racist to idealistic, and her black characters are neither saints nor savages, but realistic and representative.

Using a strong theme of civil rights in a 1965 Southern novel was a bold experiment. *The Far Family,* which deals most directly with civil rights, centers upon black/white relationships and white attitudes toward blacks at the height of the civil rights movement. Dykeman sets the stage in the first few pages:

Everything that happened now between a white person and a black person became more than an encounter of individuals—it became a confrontation of groups, two races, two histories. (16)

In this novel, which is set in the mountains of North Carolina, a white man is accused of killing a black man. The plot is complicated when the accused, Clay Thurston, cannot remember whether or not he killed the man, and no one is sorry the victim, Hawk Williams, is dead.

Dykeman uses Clay and his three sisters to represent four common attitudes toward blacks. One sister, Frone, has been sheltered from blacks since moving to Connecticut. Out of ignorance, she is suspicious of the black maid, Naomi, and afraid Naomi is spying on the family. Another sister, Phoebe, is just the opposite in her misconceptions. As the wife of a South Carolina planter, she feels she knows all there is to know about blacks, yet she bases this knowledge on her relationship with her maid, Aunt Hettie. Unfortunately, she sees all blacks as either hired help or kindly mammies. She also claims her children consider Aunt Hettie "like one of the family," but the shrewd reader recognizes that phrase as pure cliché, which does not square with Phoebe's actions.

Clay is a realist; he has dealt with blacks outside of purely servant roles in his job and his hunting parties. He resents the lawyer's assumption that the murderer can get off simply because the victim was black. His major concern, after staying out of jail, is keeping the focus on Hawk's questionable character rather than on racial issues (79). Later, while his sisters express their differing opinions on how well they understand blacks, Clay sarcastically attempts to remove race as the issue: "Is it pretty much like understanding people in general . . . or is there some special trick to it with Negroes?" (128).

Clay's other sister, Ivy Cortland, who is also the novel's protagonist, is the idealist of the family, although she lives closest to the mainstream of Southern whites of the 1960s. More than any other character, she represents Dykeman as the social conscience of the novel. She is genuinely concerned that, despite her efforts, she might be a racist at heart:

And she was gnawed by a secret fear, so well buried she did not acknowledge it even to herself: Was any part of their fear and hate intensified because this was a Negro? As a family they had never been reared with any overt or stated prejudices—Grandfather Mark McQueen had fought with the Union in the Civil War—and they were the Mountain South, not Deep South, and yet . . . . She found it difficult to know herself. (34)

Ivy also worries about her relationship with Naomi. In a passage that accurately analyzes the employer-maid relationship, Ivy worries that despite their attempts at real friendship and their shared experiences, there was still a "barrier, visible only at certain times, yet always there. . . . [Ivy] had the impression that Naomi knew something she could not or did not want to tell her" (61).

In addition to presenting these representative characters, Dykeman also honestly explores the state of black life in Appalachia and much of the South. With Naomi, the reader sees the assumed familiarity with which servants have often been treated. Unlike the white characters, Ivy does not learn Naomi's last name until late in the novel, and then only in a reference. Neither Naomi nor any other black character is addressed as Mr. or Mrs., although the blacks are expected to use titles when addressing whites. Naomi is expected to give up time with her family when Ivy needs her, and because of the lack of opportunity in the South, her children are effectively forced to move to such places as Philadelphia or Detroit to find good jobs.

Hawk would be an unlikable person of any color. By using this unsavory character, Dykeman avoids the temptation of portraying blacks entirely as innocent victims of white oppression; yet she hints that his problems are partially a result of his environment. He is disliked by both whites and blacks, including his own family. His wife, Lorna, admits that "nobody [in her house is] able to cry because Hawk's gone" (148). Yet instead of scorn, Lorna seems to pity him, because she realizes he was treated no better than the meat he butchered, and that he believed and acted out the public's perception of him.

The person who ultimately admits killing Hawk is, perhaps appropriately, part-black. Homer Bludsoe, whose ancestors had intrigued Clay's grandmother, Lydia McQueen, in *The Tall Woman* (1962), provides the link to encourage progress toward change. His explanations of the toll miscegenation had taken on his family—a sense of belonging to neither the black nor white worlds, of prejudice from both sides, and of general powerlessness with the law—cause the Thurstons and the reader to feel ashamed for long-simmering attitudes toward the Bludsoes in particular and blacks in general.

Dykeman should be admired for not writing this novel as a "classic example of Negro deprivation and frustration" (217), as a young newspaper reporter wants to portray Hawk. Although she becomes pedantic on a few occasions, especially near the end of the novel where she attempts overtly to make her point, she lets the work serve more as a casebook on race relations and the resulting problems of poor communication and unequal opportunities. The net effect, like much of her nonfiction, allows readers to see an exposed, unattractive racism, and to see the possibilities when people attempt to overcome prejudice.

Dykeman uses race more subtly in *Return the Innocent Earth* (1973). This novel is really a *bildungsroman,* or novel of apprenticeship, which traces the growth and maturity of Jon Clayburn. Jon, who serves as both protagonist and narrator, discovers himself through exploring his family's history and its impact on him.

An important part of the Clayburn legacy involves relationships with and attitudes toward blacks. The two characters who best represent this theme are Lonas Rankin and Cebo, whose last name we never learn. Lonas is a Negro blacksmith who becomes subject to a pattern of prejudice by most members of the community except Dan and Jonathan Clayburn. Dykeman uses him to illustrate how easily ignorance leads to prejudice, which in turn can become violent. He is what many whites might call a troublemaker, although he does little to deserve their hatred.

Lonas arrives at the Clayburn's Riverbend Farm just after Elisha Clayburn has been murdered by two "blacks," who later turn out to be disguised whites. When an angry mob finds Lonas and prepares to lynch both him and Cebo, Jonathan Clayburn steps in and saves their lives, but Lonas is marked from that point forward. As one member of the mob warns him: "You watch your step, boy. . . . You hear?" (91).

As Lonas's relationship with Dan and Jonathan Clayburn improves, the citizens of Churchill, and especially the factory workers, fulfill the threat. Jonathan hires him to help with the original cannery, but Col. Wakely attempts to whip him and have him fired when Lonas accidentally spills some cannery waste on the old man's pants. Later, when Dan supports Lonas's desire to own stock in the factory he has helped build, the white workers threaten to quit if a black man is allowed the same privileges they are given. Eventually, after Dan is dead, Lonas is lured away from town and murdered when the mob mentality prevails.

The Clayburns' relationship with Cebo is quite different. Instead of a drifter, Cebo is a sort of "Father Earth," a superstitious, mystical figure who seems to have been around forever. Cebo is Jon's link to the past and to the land. His mother was a slave, and his father was Major Lawes, the white planter who built Riverbend Farm. In a scene that molds Jon's attitude toward blacks for the rest of his life, Cebo explains to a pre-teen Jon how his mother died. When she accidentally dropped her load of bricks, Major Lawes became furious, chained her to a tree, and flogged her. He then left her out in a thunderstorm, wet and bleeding, and she died of pneumonia soon afterward. As Jon later explains, "I had no knowledge to fit his words. . . . But I mourned his proud, industrious mother. God, I mourned her" (112).

Like Ivy Cortland, Jon is an idealist, and we see race relations in Churchill mostly through his eyes. Looking back, he recalls how the blacks who worked for his family shaped his attitudes:

> How else except through them and through a childhood of white innuendoes, nods, grins, frowns, approvals, rejections, could I have gained the love/fear, need/hate, identity/indifference sunk deep beneath my tanned and tended flesh? . . . [A] dozen of them moved through my boyhood—the proud strangers destined to stir unease and guilt and destruction, and the unassuming hands and feet, carrying and fetching, lifting and building, doing for—always for. (108)

Unlike Ivy, Jon admits he has had to overcome his family's practiced prejudice. Despite early warnings from his mother that blacks must be kept in their place, he recognizes her blindness to their needs and feelings, and he understands how that blindness leads to a lifetime of self-condemnation and psychological imprisonment (259).

Without forcing her point, Dykeman combines in *Return the Innocent Earth* believable characters and the effects of prejudice to warn others who consider themselves liberal on race relations that they have responsibilities to act on their beliefs. Jon's beliefs have placed him on a community human relations council and led him to institute minority-hiring programs at the Clayburn-Durant company, but they also leave him asking why he didn't act sooner.

Dykeman's forceful yet unforced exploration of race relations, starting early in the civil rights movement and extending until the early 1970s, indicates a genuine concern for social change while it avoids the temptation to sermonize. Most Dykeman critics, who have focused instead on her fiction as it relates primarily to Appalachia, have largely overlooked this theme. However, Dykeman considers her early advocacy of equal rights for blacks as one of her major literary contributions.

ENVIRONMENTAL CONCERN

Wilma Dykeman's concern for human resources matches her advocacy for preserving natural resources. In fact, she sees a definite link between the two:

> As we have misused our richest land, we have misused ourselves; as we have wasted our beautiful water, we have wasted ourselves; as we have diminished the lives of one segment of our people, we have diminished ourselves. (*Neither,* 5)

She has also called environmental conservation the South's second greatest problem, eclipsed only by the related need for self-government. In *The Border States,* she and Stokely complain that "the region as a whole has allowed its trees to be demolished, its waters to be poisoned and its air to be polluted with only the faintest of protests" (162). Their voices have added some much-needed legitimacy to these protests.

Dykeman's early interest in environmental conservation came at a time when most people had never heard of water pollution and considered strip mining progressive. She made her position known as early as 1955 in *The French Broad.* In that book, which explores the geography and history of the region around the French Broad River, she traces a pattern of abuse affecting the land and water. She castigates even the earliest settlers for their lack of foresight in clearing the forests:

> The bitterest irony of all the years of settlement is in the process by which a people so frugal they utilized every element in nature . . . could waste, with prodigal abandon, the vast harvest of centuries as if it were not only useless but also an enemy. (51)

She is no easier on the loggers and farmers who followed the first settlers. As the land was cleared for crops that the soil could not support, the topsoil eroded, leaving gullies on the land and silt in the creeks and rivers. She faults the massive hog and cattle drives of the nineteenth century for leaving an ugly mark on the land. The great popularity of the routes caused roads to be built and more crops to be planted, leading through bad crop rotation to even more erosion.

Dykeman also became an early and active opponent of strip mining. This practice, which has been used extensively in the coal mining areas of

Appalachia, uses explosives and huge shovels to expose seams of coal directly under the surface. In economic terms, it is both cheaper and safer than underground mining, but it can leave permanent scars on the land. Dykeman clearly expresses her views on strip mining in *The Border States:*

> [Strip mining is] a new form of destruction . . . [which renders] much of the mountain man's labor unnecessary and much of his land uninhabitable.
>
> . . . The coal country of Appalachia is becoming a blighted area whose landscape resembles the barren, blasted surface of the moon. As the green cover of the steep hills has been scraped away and overturned into the narrow valleys, roads and houses and streams have been engulfed. The raw dirt left behind after the coal is extracted is a thick sludge of mud in rainy weather and a choking bed of dust in drought. From one mountain slope to the next, the cuts run wide and deep and the wreckage accumulates. (116–17)

She is equally concerned with the way strip mining affects the people of Appalachia. The small family income from the mining-related jobs is easily offset by the diseases and accidents associated with mining, and many miners live at or below the poverty level. While the miners remain poor, the large corporations that own the mines reap large profits, and little money is reinvested locally.

She understands that most of the abuses have occurred in the name of progress, but she also sees the irony of people who are drawn to a place for its natural beauty yet end up wasting the land's resources until it becomes ugly. What sense does it make to pollute your home when the beauty of the place is one of your strongest ties to the land? Her strong statements about the pollution of the French Broad River underscore her convictions on this theme:

> One by one we allowed ourselves and others to begin the rape which finally (in places) ended in the murder of the French Broad. And it had come about precisely because the headwaters were so pure, so nearly perfect. (281)

At the time *The French Broad* was written, most experts considered controlling water pollution either unnecessary or too expensive. Several newspaper articles and governmental reports had documented the effects of pollution in the river, but these reports were generally ignored. However, Dykeman's treatment of this subject is much stronger and potentially more effective than these accounts because it is juxtaposed with several hundred pages of well-written history, biography, and geography, which build a strong bond between the reader and the river. This bond becomes sensitized when she points out that the French Broad basin "contains sources responsible for more that one-fourth of the total pollution in North Carolina" and that most of the pollution in the river comes directly from manufacturing plants, which "daily bring millions of gallons of clear clean water into their plants, use it, and turn it back into [the river's] channel discolored, bestenched, and loaded with oxygen-consuming litter" (*French Broad*, 284).

Instead of simply complaining about environmental pollution, Dykeman offers constructive criticism and suggestions for immediate improvements. In *The French Broad,* she calls on her readers to assume personal responsibility for both reclamation and prevention, and proposes laws calling for each town or factory to be held responsible for its own wastes. Today, with the Environmental Protection Agency and other watchdog groups, such laws have proven helpful in controlling the problems she encountered thirty-five years ago.

In each of her novels, Wilma Dykeman conveys a sense of respect for nature. While avoiding the pathetic fallacy found in many nineteenth-century local color novels, she emphasizes the natural beauty of the land and the intangible relationship that exists between the land and those who interact with it daily. She attempts to show the disparity between those who use the land properly and those who abuse it.

In *The Tall Woman,* Dykeman tells the story of Lydia McQueen and her family, who live in the mountains of North Carolina. The action takes place between the Civil War and the turn of the century. Lydia maintains a close, healthy relationship with the land and appreciates its fragility. When one of her children voices doubts that a mountain patch of ginseng could be scarred, she replies: "Not when folks set their minds to it. It would be a surprise to you how quick a thing can be killed out" (208).

Dykeman contrasts Lydia's appreciation for the land with Ham Nelson's disregard. Nelson thinks of land only in terms of ownership; Lydia values the land for its natural beauty and its potential. His farm is dried up and useless from years of neglect and from the harvest of most of its trees for a sawmill. A spring, which has sentimental value for Lydia, is clogged with silt and weeds. The effect of this juxtaposition is strong, because Lydia and her husband Mark rented the farm and used it responsibly earlier in the novel, renovating the dilapidated cabin, adding a rail fence and a new stone chimney. Ironically, Lydia dies from typhoid fever, which she contracts by drinking water from the Nelson spring.

Lydia's daughter, Martha Thurston, inherits her mother's appreciation for the land in *The Far Family*. Like Lydia, she is the voice of environmental reason in the novel. When economic conditions force her husband Tom to abandon farming in favor of starting a sawmill, Martha regrets the loss of trees and the way the mountainsides are scarred. She takes seriously the biblical exhortation to multiply and replenish the earth, and explains her belief to her daughter Frone:

> It means to replenish the earth of all you wrench from it, multiply the fruits instead of just subtracting them. Oh, I feel somehow that this timbering . . . is all wrong. He can't just take and take from the land and never give back. (163)

Dykeman's portrayal of Burl McHone represents both Martha's opposite and a common problem throughout Appalachia. She graphically describes his land:

> The steep hill, . . . once green with a cover of sturdy balsam and delicate birch, thick mosses and vines, . . . was now a mass of rubble and devastation. The hillside had been completely cut over, the large logs snaked away and sold, rich humus and topsoil destroyed, and then everything abandoned. . . . And dominating all the other squalor and waste and decay of this place was the automobile graveyard, littering with rusty wheels, torn tires and twisted pipes the cement-like dirt which could hardly be called a lawn. (226)

This scene, as disgusting as she could write it, is unfortunately not unique in Appalachia. As these scenes are played out all over the region, they lead outsiders to believe and perpetuate the stereotype of the lazy, dirty mountaineer. Although Burl McHone certainly matches that description, he is not representative of all Appalachians. But Dykeman also recognizes that many people in the region are apathetic to litter and erosion, and view them more as petty irritants than as major issues.

Dykeman uses environmental themes most strongly in *Return the Innocent Earth*. As in the other novels, there are characters who appreciate the land and others who abuse it. Laura Rathbone is Lydia's spiritual heir; she loves the forest and knows how to profit from its natural provisions without damaging it. When faced with a choice between Jonathan Clayburn and her woods, she chooses the woods; when her woods are sold to the Clayburns, she retreats farther into the mountains. Yet Dykeman saves her from becoming a token character who is too innocent to be believed. She finds a kindred spirit in the botanist the Clayburns hire to help them grow peas, and she leaves the mountains with him to live in Wisconsin. Her grandson, Lex Morrison, develops the chemical spray that poisons Perlina Smelcer and kills the plants instead of extending their growing season. This consequence may be Laura's revenge for plowing her land; regardless, it gives Jon Clayburn an opportunity to realize his own ties to and love for the land.

Jon's views on protecting the environment are similar to his racial convictions. When he first returns to Churchill, he sees how much the land of his youth has been abused to make his own fortune. Standing in a field, he compares the original Clayburns to their current descendants:

> I can remember hearing about the day Elisha Clayburn, my grandfather, stood not far from where I am tonight and let the rich black dirt filter through his hands, saying "The land outlives us all—" and within the month he was dead. Now Clayburn Foods has just about come full term. Now our tractors and cultivators and planters gouge up the earth, turn it to rows, beat the clods to dust, feed it, irrigate it, make it yield whatever those gleaming cans demand. . . . Now the using is all. (40–41)

Later, as he confronts his cousin Stull Clayburn, he suggests a system of accounting for "damage to air or water or land, to the health of a human being" (405). Although this scheme may be idealistic, he at least considers the human costs involved in manufacturing.

Stull considers such talk pure nonsense. He is everything Jon is not, especially in his mindset on the environment. This villainous characterization is one weakness with Dykeman's portrayal of Stull—he is too one-dimensional. He is the one responsible for using the poison spray in the first place, and his major concern is keeping the news of Perlina's death out of the papers and ensuring that Clayburn-Durant stock does not suffer. The effects on Perlina's family and on the land are of little consequence to him. He finds imaginative ways to avoid the FDA, and mocks Jon's personal interest in the land. As a man with no feelings, however, he is simply too evil to believe. While some corporate executives may resemble him, one has to believe they have some redeeming qualities.

Dykeman incorporates a strong sense of irony throughout *Return the Innocent Earth*. The Clayburn family depends on the land for its income, and although some family members use it wisely, others, like Josh and his son Stull, use it up, essentially "burning the clay." In other instances, she reminds us that even those with honorable intentions can tend to forget their convictions in the interest of business. These lapses include dumping canning waste into a creek and spoiled cans into the river. In both cases, someone notices that it might be wrong, but the problem is never fixed. When Jonathan notices an open waste ditch leading from the factory to the river, he comments: "We'll have to see about that—one of these days" (289), but Dykeman does not mention the ditch again, and one assumes that it remained polluted.

Dykeman has used her fiction to examine both race relations and environmental issues in the tradition of the sociological novel, or novel of protest. Holman describes this type of novel as "center[ing] its principal attention on the nature, function, and effect of the society in which the characters live and on the social forces playing upon them" (421). In American fiction, it includes Stowe's *Uncle Tom's Cabin* and Steinbeck's *The Grapes of Wrath*.

Dykeman devotes her attention in *The Far Family* to the effects of irresponsible timbering and poor soil conservation. These are not the novel's central issues, but they play upon the main characters, notably Ivy Cortland and Martha Thurston. In *Return the Innocent Earth,* she uses the land as both setting and victim of abuse. Most of the novel's characters earn their living from the land, either directly, like the early farmers and growers, or indirectly, like Jon and Stull Clayburn. The novel explores the dual effects of progress—developing more efficient growing techniques versus making the land useless through pollution and bad crop rotation. Dykeman clearly is concerned with the latter, but she allows the reader to choose his own interpretation.

SUMMARY

Dykeman's strength in her fiction lies in her characterization. With few exceptions, the protagonists in her novels are three-dimensional, and we see them change over time. Lydia McQueen, for instance, develops from a fragile bride into a strong, sensible wife, mother, and grandmother. Her general view of life changes little, but her manner of dealing with people and problems matures. Jon Clayburn grows from a young boy with few questions into a man who questions his own purpose in life, and his problems are those of most young executives.

Her most important contribution through characterization is her refusal to perpetuate the stereotyped mountaineer or black man. The Bludsoes in *The Tall Woman* and *The Far Family,* Burl McHone in *The Far Family,* and Janus Rathbone in *Return the Innocent Earth* come closest to the traditionally portrayed mountaineer—poor, uneducated, living in tumble-down shacks, what Wolfe would call "mountain grills"—yet they are clearly the minority in their largely middle-class communities. Likewise, while both Hawk Williams and Lonas Rankin are troublemakers who end up murdered, and their murderers are largely forgiven by the community at large, Dykeman strives to show that not all Southerners approved of these murders and that not all black males are troublemakers.

Dykeman's plots are successful chiefly because her characters are believable. Although many characters in her novels are representative of various viewpoints and experiences, they are not stock characters. In the five generations of Moores, McQueens, Thurstons, and Cortlands examined in *The Tall Woman* and *The Far Family,* we see her characters through Civil War, Reconstruction, birth, growing up, death, dismemberment, deforestation, rural flight, civil rights, murder, and suicide. These elements of plot, both macrocosm and microcosm, allow her characters a context in which to respond, and overall their responses are realistic, but not always expected. Laura Rathbone seems to be modeled on the traditional image of an untamed mountain girl, yet she responds to the encroaching farms by marrying a scientist and moving to Wisconsin, which is hardly a mountain state.

The charge often leveled at Wilma Dykeman is that she is "just a regionalist." Regionalism, in that pejorative sense, indicates an artist's inability to interest or affect readers outside that region. But the term can carry other meanings. Hugh Holman defines the concept with more positive dimensions:

Fidelity in literature to a particular geographical section; the accurate representation of its habits, speech, manner, history, folklore, or beliefs. A test of regionalism is that the action and personages of a novel . . . called regional cannot be moved, without major loss or distortion, to any other geographical section. . . . [However] in this century a concept of regionalism much more complex has developed, . . . and has expressed itself in literature through the conscious seeking out in the local and in the particular of those aspects of the human character and the human dilemma common to all people and in all ages and places. (373)

By this definition, Dykeman is undoubtedly a regionalist in the best sense. The themes brought out in her fiction—race relations, social stereotypes, conservation of natural resources, a sense of place and of the past—are universal and unlimited by time, even if not everyone agrees with her interpretation. They are as applicable in New England or California as in North Carolina and Tennessee. Yet the strength of the fiction is that the facts remain true to the region, but the truths are not confined to it. In that sense, Wilma Dykeman's regionalism is universal.

Works Cited

Dykeman, Wilma. *The Far Family.* New York: Holt, Rinehart and Winston, 1966.
———. *The French Broad.* Knoxville: University of Tennessee Press, 1955, 1965, 1966, 1973, 1985. Illus. by Douglas Gorsline.
———. *Return the Innocent Earth.* New York: New American Library, 1974.
———. "The Southern Demagogue." *Virginia Quarterly Review* 33 (1957): 558–68.
———. *The Tall Woman.* New York: Holt, Rinehart and Winston, 1962.
Dykeman, Wilma, and James Stokely. *The Border States: Kentucky, North Carolina, Tennessee, Virginia, West Virginia.* New York: Time-Life Books, 1968, 1970.
———. "Inquiry into the Southern Tensions." *New York Times Magazine,* 13 Oct. 1957, 20+.
———. "McCarthyism under the Magnolias." *Progressive* 23, no. 7 (1959): 6–10.
———. *Neither Black nor White.* New York: Rinehart and Co., 1957.
———. "Our Changing South: A Challenge." In *We Dissent,* ed. Hoke Norris, 3–14. New York: St. Martin's Press, 1962.
———. "The Plight of Southern White Women." In *White on Black: The Views of Twenty-two White Americans on the Negro,* ed. Era Bell Thompson and Herbert Nipson (editors of *Ebony* magazine), 19–28. Chicago: Johnson Publishers, 1963.

————. "'Sit down Chillun, Sit down.'" *Progressive* 24, no. 6 (1960): 8–13.

————. "'The South' in the North." *New York Times Magazine,* 17 Apr. 1960, 8+. (Also *U.S. News & World Report,* 2 May 1960, 2+, and *The New York Times: Background and Foreground: An Anthology of Articles from the New York Times Magazine,* ed. with an introduction and notes by Lester Markel, 220–28. Great Neck, N.Y.: Channel Press, 1960.)

Holman, C. Hugh. *A Handbook to Literature.* 4th ed. Indianapolis: Bobbs-Merrill Educational Publishing, 1980.

Stokely, James. Letter to Paul Green, 16 Nov. 1965. Paul Green Papers. Wilson Library, University of North Carolina, Chapel Hill.

CASTING A LONG SHADOW

The Tall Woman

PATRICIA GANTT

There is a dialectic between stories and experience. Stories give
shape to experience, experience gives rise to stories. . . . If
women's stories are not told, the depth of women's souls will
not be known.

—*Carol P. Christ,* Diving Deep and Surfacing

[Wilma Dykeman's fiction] is the result of a deep imagination
and considerable craft at absorbing and making images. Only
through reading her images sensitively and following her invi-
tations to lift our eyes from the page and dream can we begin to
comprehend her sense of place.

—*Jim Gage, "Poetics of Space"*

The years following the publication of *The French Broad* (1955) and *Neither Black nor White* (1957) were busy ones for Wilma Dykeman. The warm re-
ception accorded to both books placed her in demand as a speaker and
writer on Southern topics, and that demand continues to this day. Through
her investigation of the region, inspired by research for these two works of
nonfiction as well as by her interest in the South's cultural politics, Dykeman uncovered many inequities she wished to address further, particularly
those relating to conditions of the South's second-class citizens, blacks and
women. Continuing the balanced perspective displayed in these books, she
often spoke out on both the region's problems and its sources of pride.

Dykeman also wrote a number of essays for various periodicals. Although some of these articles, such as "Smoky Mountain Magic" in *Reader's
Digest* (1956) or "The First Day of School, Remember?" (1960) and
"Thomas Wolfe Comes Home" (1957) for the *New York Times Magazine,* are
simply nostalgic features, most of Dykeman's articles asked readers to look

seriously at the South's political questions. Among these essays are "Mc-Carthyism under the Magnolias" (*Progressive* 1959), "Patience Is Not Enough" (*Nation* 1958), "Face of the South" (*Current History* 1958), and "The Southern Demagogue" (*Virginia Quarterly Review* 1957). An article entitled "New Southerner: The Middle Class Negro" (1959) was one of the first of several dozen Dykeman was to write for the *New York Times* over the years. These politically oriented articles reveal her conviction that the South must acknowledge and deal with its social inequities.

Seven years after the publication of *The French Broad,* Dykeman turned to fiction with *The Tall Woman* (1962), the story of a heroic mountain woman, Lydia Moore McQueen. The genesis for *The Tall Woman* was Dykeman's wish to write about "the person who is not famous, who doesn't become well-known, [but] who influences so much of life" (Marius, 10). She decided to build a story completely around the sorts of middle-class people she had known personally and interviewed—in fact, the types of people she herself had come from—instead of focusing on a famous person or even on a lesser-known, local celebrity.

Dykeman set the book in the years following the Civil War "because that time posed the greatest problems for anyone who wanted to be positive and creative" and because the Civil War and Reconstruction era background, she said, "gave me imagination to let myself put a lot of the things I had discovered about people in these other two books [*The French Broad* and *Neither Black nor White*] into fiction" (Marius, 10). This setting also occupies the first of the contextual frames Dykeman desires for consideration of Appalachia—"that old South which has dominated the regional image" ("Appalachia in Context," 28).

The book was written at the request of the Southern Appalachian Studies Commission (SASC), a Berea College (Kentucky) consortium dedicated to marshaling resources "to help the Appalachian people know who they are and what contribution they [have] made" (Weatherford Papers). *The Tall Woman* grew in part from a 1959 conversation Dykeman had with SASC leader Willis D. Weatherford, a prime mover in the budding Appalachian studies movement; he, like Dykeman, wished to counter the negative popular image of Appalachia. They believed that this image had a debilitating effect on the people of the region and therefore could not be dismissed, since those who "had no idea that there was any culture" or "anything creative that had come out of the region" could not possess the "sense of pride that all people need" (Miller, 58). In one of the many letters Dykeman and Weatherford exchanged, he wrote: "We can probably restore [the Appalachian people's] sense of independence and self-valuation only by showing them what great capacity they have" (Weatherford Papers). Weatherford secured a grant from the Ford Foundation to underwrite Dykeman's work, and she began her "Appalachian novel" (Weatherford Papers). Soon James Stokely, Dykeman's husband, would confide to a friend, newspaper editor Mark Ethridge, that Weatherford was "quite excited about both the human and literary qualities of the story" Dykeman had under way (Ethridge Papers).

Dykeman chose the story of an Appalachian woman as her focus, convinced that "[b]etween all of these stereotypes, the Appalachian woman's had a rather difficult time being understood" (Miller, 49). Through her years in the mountains, Dykeman had "talked with wonderful women and . . . with men whose mothers and wives had meant so much to the region" (Marius, 10). She was excited about these women's potential as fictional heroes; her book, she decided, would concentrate on anonymous women who "were there . . . raising the logs on one side of the cabin . . . having their children on cornshuck mattresses . . . bringing the schools there, and they were nameless—a kind of unknown" (10). Accordingly, Dykeman chose to focus on "those other frontier people," anonymous individuals whose contributions had been marginalized or overlooked altogether (10).

In particular, she chose to create a fictional heroine who "had never been more than fifteen miles from home, had never been known in history, but whose life embodied all kinds of creative forces, one who really cared about the world around her—the natural world, the human world" (10). She decided that all the characters in her first novel would be similarly unknown, but—like her heroine—worthy of depiction. Dykeman, writing to Weatherford while the novel was in progress, expressed her ambition to "make the mountain mother live" (Weatherford Papers). Imbued with this strong sense of dedication to forgotten mountain women, Dykeman created the story of Lydia Moore McQueen.

With her presentation of the memorable Lydia, Dykeman carved out a literary territory that now remains almost exclusively hers: the mountain woman, drawn with realism and fire. Dykeman's portrait of Lydia comes, too, from an impetus "to try to deal with life, internal and external, in all its complexity" and to avoid "the tendency to compartmentalize thought and feeling, home and work, self and other," which Mary Belenky, Blythe Clinchy, Nancy Goldberger, and Jill Tarule associate with women writers (137). Lydia integrates concerns for self, home, and community.

The narrative spans events in the main character's life from her first pregnancy at nineteen until her death at fifty. These years (1865–96) are tumultuous both for McQueen and for her fictional Thickety Creek community. In her interactions with her community and family, McQueen encounters problems the entire Reconstruction South faced: healing or dealing with the scars of war; expanding as a community and region to take a greater place in national or world society, and anticipating economic and ethical dilemmas brought on by rapid progress, such as environmental waste.[1]

The postwar setting enables Dykeman to treat the progress of the region and nation, as well as the pleasures, struggles, frustrations, and contentments of the maturing Lydia McQueen. Dykeman parallels the growth and change taking place in Thickety Creek and in the nation with similar transitions in Lydia's life. Westward expansion and the search for gold, the push for public education, and rural flight for urban areas with greater economic promise all have an impact on Lydia's life, giving her greater opportunities for personal autonomy and showing her concern for Appalachia's future. Then, too, placing the action in this rural past allows Dykeman to use "the image of the family on the land" which Allen Tate perceives as the central metaphor for Southern literature (Rubin, 468). Like Eudora Welty, Dykeman feels that the family can "encompass" all the stories of humankind (Welty, 456). Dykeman's later works continue to use the family structure as their fictional base.

Dykeman took the title for *The Tall Woman* from a mountain saying, "A tall woman casts a long shadow" (9).[2] Inspired by actual matriarchs Dykeman had interviewed for *The French Broad*, Lydia is both physically and emotionally rooted in the mountains; she finds in them "a deep companionship she could not name or describe" (*Tall Woman,* 278). Regardless of her limited formal education, she knows a rich variety of practical lore, including the uses of medicinal plants. Dykeman casts Lydia as a midwife, partially to give her a skill realistic for her time, but also to create a woman with "the sense of nurturing"; she saw in midwifery a concrete means of making Lydia one of "the affirmers of life, rather than the destroyers" (Miller, 50). Both "healer and activist" for mountain schools, Lydia has unbending integrity that touches her entire community—even those who do not subscribe to her values (Neufeld, 6L). As Dykeman's admirable characters inevitably do, she finds her center in the family and the land, and fights to preserve both.

Dykeman opens *The Tall Woman* by establishing the ebb and flow of natural forces that dominate both Lydia McQueen's life and the novel: "The wind was a wild dark thing plucking at the trees outside, pushing at the doors and chinks of the house, then dying down still as death before another rise and rush and plunge" (13). The power of nature is something Lydia knows well and feels a part of. Lying cozily under piled-up quilts of her own making, she waits for her husband, Mark, to return from the Civil War and thinks—not of the winter night around her, but of a day the previous spring, when she and her mother, Sarah Moore, had spoken about Lydia's coming marriage. Of all the seasons, Lydia identifies most with spring; like her, it is unpredictable, "chancy," but she likes its chance and change (14). "One day," she recalls, "would be still and soft with the sun flowing like honey along the hillsides . . . with time slow and the bees buzzing somewhere in the sunshine—forever, forever" (14). Then spring reverses itself and becomes "fierce, with the wind tearing through the woods in gusts . . . piercing every crevice of house and clothing with a bitter chill, and time rushing with it down the valley" (14). These dualities do not threaten Lydia, whose passion for both sunshine and chill is palpable throughout the book. Lying in bed, she feels "the pleasure of her own body-warmth. Like a seed, she felt, one of those sun-warmed seeds in the spring ground, growing, ready to give forth new life" (13). Despite her mother's wise warning that "Nothing's ever taken, or given [that] doesn't have its price," Lydia at this point in the novel cannot foresee anything but happiness, and is content (16).

The young wife also recalls the day she first spoke to her mother about wanting to marry Mark McQueen. Opposing her daughter's choice of a man so harsh and brooding, Sarah Moore reminds Lydia of her ties to a strong matrilineage—of the Cornish immigrant who was Lydia's great-grandmother, and of Lydia's pioneer grandmother, a woman whose gentleness was worn away by the rigors of mountain life. Mrs. Moore desires an easier path for her daughter. More importantly, Sarah Moore tries to talk to Lydia about "something beyond even love, for a woman as well as a man. A body's personhood" (16). But Lydia, "being a girl only and a girl in love," does not know how to respond to her mother's "strange talk," and is impatient to get her consent (16, 17). "I never asked for easy, Mama," she responds (18). Lydia's choice of Mark as a husband is difficult for her parents to accept; they value formal education and gentleness and, finding evidence of neither in Mark McQueen, foresee more difficulty for Lydia than she can predict, caught up as she is in her domestic dream.

To complicate matters, Mark sets himself against the rest of Thickety Creek by determining to fight for the Union. Dykeman told Marius that one reason she wanted to write *The Tall Woman* was to set up the conflict Lydia's husband personifies, to "show that there was the little Civil War here inside the big Civil War. The bitterness of the struggle was reflected in ways that I think are not true anywhere else in the country . . . in the Appalachians" (11). Mark's choice, an ethical stand which Lydia admires, is problematic for her: it places her in opposition to her family and neighbors, all of whom side with the Confederacy; regardless of their stand on slavery, Lydia's relatives are unable to picture themselves fighting against fellow North Carolinians. The couple's wedding day is "overcast, with thin sunshine and clouds threatening rain," an omen Lydia chooses to overlook (18).

It seems at first that Dykeman is presenting a typically romantic narrative with the usual quest plot, an "ideological script" in which the "rightful end" for successful women is courtship or marriage—what Rachel Blau DuPlessis calls the "iconography of love, the postures of yearning, pleasing, choosing, slipping, falling, and failing" (1–2). In such traditional texts, the woman who does not satisfactorily "negotiate with sexuality and kinship" dies, her death brought on by her "inabilities or improprieties" as a negotiator (4). The reader sees, however, that Lydia McQueen is a departure from the usual gender-stereotyped heroine of romantic fiction—and of local color, where "the comely mountain girl" is the passive object of an outsider's attention (Miller, 49). The dimensions of Lydia's life transcend traditional gender patterns, as Dykeman builds what might have been a slight character from templates of romantic fiction into a powerful one who exerts substantial control over her world.

Dykeman begins the variation from traditional gender roles by having Mark go to war, leaving Lydia with responsibilities—and opportunities for decision and control—she would not ordinarily have. Absenting the male figure (away at war, in nearby woods, in a distant office, on a Western trip, or dead before the novel opens and therefore seen only through the lens of memory) would become a frequent device for Dykeman. Male characters appear—some with considerable substance—but, like Mark McQueen in *The Tall Woman,* they not only lack the dynamism of female characters, but are blatantly weaker than Dykeman's females. With Mark and the other adult men in the Moore family temporarily absent "from amidst their little patterns and permanences," a new pattern emerges as Lydia and her mother take charge (*Tall Woman,* 22). Lydia will retain her leadership role even after the war.

The cozy reverie with which the novel begins soon gives way to a deeper portrayal of Lydia as a woman of deep inner strength. Alone in her cabin, Lydia hears horse's hoofs; she rushes to respond to the first of a series of emergencies that come her way. Outliers, "raiders who banded together under no flag but one of robbery and cruelty" against Union and Confederate, have stolen the Moores' cattle and taken what food they can find. Worse, they have taken Sarah Moore to a nearby field and tortured her, attempting to discover where stores of precious supplies are hidden. Lydia's response to these trials illustrates her change from a girl with "wispy ways" to the strong mountain matriarch Dykeman set out to depict (14). As the first chapter closes, Lydia rushes to see what she can do, suddenly a woman who must be "steady and knowing," her easy life all in the past (31).

Mrs. Moore, physically battered, is also emotionally broken; delirious, she can only mutter, "I didn't tell them. I didn't tell" (32). Lydia goes outside and leans on the fence, aware that they will never know exactly what their mother has endured. Reminded by her sister that she is the family's only resource now, since the other Moore children are too young to carry much responsibility, Lydia dries her tears—the last she will shed for a long while—and gets breakfast going. She arranges to move her belongings back home, where she can stay by her mother and care for them all; she has "grown into problems larger than herself, into trouble beyond tears" (35). Lydia assures the little ones that the men "with their faces hidden" will not return; privately she wonders which of their neighbors has led the outliers to the provisions available at the Moore farm (35).

Walking back to her cabin to get her cow, Lydia glimpses a figure darting across the road to hide behind a laurel bush. The shock of curly black hair tells her she has seen one of the Bludsoes, a mysterious whiskey-making family who live secluded on the peak of distant Stony Ridge. Now Lydia speculates whether the fierce Bludsoes have anything to do with the outliers' raid. All her life she has heard tales of the Bludsoes' "cruelty and rage . . . their evil aura," which the Thickety Creek community attributes to their supposed slave origins (38–39). To Lydia, everything about them is shadowy, tentative, and fearful; because she fears them, her suspicions increase. She rushes home in the growing darkness. Dykeman's insertion of the Bludsoes in this early passage establishes the tensions between them and everyone else in Thickety Creek. Bludsoes and their descendants will figure significantly, not only in the remainder of *The Tall Woman,* as Lydia determines whether they have played a part in torturing her mother, but in the following novel, *The Far Family* (1966), a sequel that carries the McQueen family into a new century, this time with the Bludsoe family both victims and perpetrators of violence.

The weeks that follow the outliers' raid are worrisome for the Moores. Lydia sends for her mother's sister, Matilda MacIntosh, or "Aunt Tildy." Tildy is not sought just as an extra pair of hands, but for the "herbs and roots, the quarreling and the laughter, the tales and threats" that always come with the lively old woman, a person whose honesty and humor will hearten the family (34). Affectionate and blunt, she is reminiscent of vinegary Miss Kinzaida in Dykeman's early short story, "Summer Affair."

As soon as Aunt Tildy arrives, the reader is aware of her presence as a second nontraditional female paradigm to complement Dykeman's developing portrayal of Lydia. Separated by a generation, temperament, and marital status—yet more alike than any other two characters in the novel—Lydia and Aunt Tildy assume attributes of traditional heroic male characters: leadership in the family and community, courage, and particularly personal autonomy. Like the men in the family, Lydia and Aunt Tildy are revered for their skills and intellect, their advice, and their physical and emotional strength.

Dykeman initially presents Lydia as wife and daughter, relational identities important in patriarchal cultures. Lydia will continue to think of herself in these roles, but her sense of self expands as she becomes a voice for issues in the public mind of Thickety Creek. Her traditional roles provide a base from which to chart Lydia's "growth into autonomous selfhood," seen by Lucinda H. MacKethan as "delayed even more strenuously in the South than in other regions" (5). Participation in social reform—in Lydia's case building a school for Thickety Creek—becomes a means to autonomy. Lydia's increasingly strong public voice indicates an important shift MacKethan notes in portrayals of Southern women in fiction, a "determination to become, freely, themselves through creative acts of voicing" (6). Dykeman, in presenting the daughter-mother-wife/activist Lydia McQueen, seeks "an integration of mind and place that both celebrates and transcends gender" (11). Domesticity, threaded through situation and metaphor, figures in many female narratives. Some critics, however, inter-

pret domestic orientation as lessening the significance of characters depicted in such narratives. Carol Christ, considering the limitations of traditional concepts of heroes, speaks to the problems critics have often found
in reconciling a heroic character's power and impact with domestic narratives. Heroic quest narratives have typically disallowed female domestic experience, since those who cannot travel (that is to say, go on a quest) are
routinely barred from being heroes (9). Christ, with Carol Pearson and
Katherine Pope, sees the heroic plane extending to any spot where a character is involved in self-definition or redefinition of roles. This extension of
the usual (male) heroic paradigm is significant for a consideration of Dykeman's work, as well as that of so many other writers treating women's experience, which is often based in the world of home and family. Lee Smith,
who frequently chooses a domestic setting for her fiction, says that the subjects "women have often written about, which are deep kinds of rituals or
families or relationships . . . are just as important as some traditionally male
thing. I don't think there's a degree that makes it lesser" (Hill, 27).

The domesticity Lydia McQueen enjoys never decreases her viability as
a heroic character. She finds abundant adventures close to home, operating
from a position of strength, daring to fight for her homeland and the
people who live there. She battles fear, waste, ignorance, and prejudice (including her own against the innocent Bludsoes). Refusing to yield to Ham
Nelson's greed, for example, she is not satisfied until Thickety Creek has
both a new school and the community's commitment to the school's success. In fighting for the school, Lydia displays what Dykeman calls "an
honest anger [that springs from] the joy of confronting the opposition . . .
through ways that are not destructive . . . to overwhelm in a positive way"
(14 Mar. 1992). Often alone, always lonely, she lives a life of her own
choosing—second to no one, not even to her husband Mark, whose happiness is vitally important to her. As the narrator says of her: "If strength was
what was called for, then she could be strong. She would be stout enough
to carry every day as it came" (*Tall Woman*, 35).

The strength of her most famous heroine has led to the author's being
considered a feminist writer, a label Dykeman assiduously avoids. Even
while chafing about what he calls the "excesses" of feminism that may make
it "drift into faddishness," Fred Chappell commends Dykeman as "in some
important ways, one of the early feminists. . . . *The Tall Woman*, if it were
published today, if it exhibited explicit sexual detail and were set almost
anywhere else but Appalachia, might stand a chance of being recognized as

a landmark feminist document" (13). Dykeman has protested: "Mine is not a feminist world nor a masculine world—it's a *people* world" (Marius, 8). But in her depiction of a multigenerational cadre of strong women living autonomous lives, she demonstrates (and *will* admit to) an implicit feminism.

Dykeman does embrace women's issues as one of "the subjects that are of great concern to me" (letter, 2 Dec. 1999). However, asked if she belongs to any feminist caucus, since she has produced so many indomitable females, the author has disclaimed any such affiliation, saying, "I've been living it. I use my maiden name and I've made a career" ("Dykeman"). Dykeman, like the characters she has drawn, simply goes about living her life; she does not look for valorization of what she does every day. Nevertheless, her women can be almost exhausting in their ability to triumph over circumstance.

It is for that reason that the author's most famous heroine, Lydia McQueen, has also drawn the most critical fire. According to Doris Betts, having a single character dominate the novel (which Betts calls a choice of "microscope over telescope") allows McQueen to "obliterate every other character around" (3:5). Another reviewer states outright that Dykeman's mountain mother is "possessed of a nobility too vast for us pampered moderns even to dig [*sic*]—much less identify with. No one outside of a soap opera, you feel (half in guilt, half in irritation) could be so perfect, so long-suffering, so tolerant of the awful men in her life" (Stanback, 21 Oct. 1962). Certainly it strains credulity when Lydia can quite easily forgive the doctor whose clumsy delivery, a result of his drunkenness, results in the mental retardation of her firstborn, David. Later, she does not so much as demur when her husband sets off, leaving her with a dwindling food supply and a houseful of children, to search for inner peace out West. Further, she is never vindictive, in spite of the horrors she is privy to.

I would argue that the matriarch of Thickety Creek is consciously designed to be larger than life.[3] In her, Dykeman has fashioned a literary construct to serve as a powerful rejoinder to generations of stereotypes—a new hero from a reconstructed and gendered mythos. In *The Power of Myth,* Joseph Campbell explains the stature of characters invested with mythic power. He says they are "fixed stars" who give their societies "a known horizon" (12). Adding that "myths offer life models," Campbell continues: "Myths are metaphorical of potentiality in the human being. . . . The courage to face trials and bring a whole new body of possibilities into the field of interpreted experience for others to experience—that is the hero's deed" (12). It is clear that Dykeman, re-visioning Appalachian life, intended her heroine to have an epic dimension; her plans for distributing *The Tall Woman* upon publication indicate that intention. Writing to Weatherford, she details her choice of the *Christian Herald*'s subsidiary, the *Farm Journal* Book Club, as distributor of the book. With methods of distribution that would allow literary access to people in mountain places too remote for service by a bookmobile, this book club could "reach small towns and rural areas as an audience that might not be reached through other means" (Weatherford Papers). Dykeman made this choice presumably so this specified audience—not just those beyond the region or in large cities—could see a depiction of an Appalachian hero, this time a female one. Lydia does offer new boundaries of experience; her characterization also satisfies Julia Kristeva's demand for "equal access to the symbolic order" (12). Dykeman's protagonist is a literary mentor for women who may be wives or mothers, but who are also family historians, keepers of the culture, scholars (whether in books or in the lore of the woods), dispensers of folk wisdom and philosophy, healers of body and spirit, or bringers of genuine progress to their communities. This fresh image of the female hero is one Carol Pearson and Katherine Pope argue for as well: one who enjoys mastery that comes from understanding the world and coping, not from "dominating, controlling, or owning [it]," as is often true with traditional male models of heroism (5). Lydia so strongly exemplifies what Dykeman calls "that little flame of life" that she makes all human beings stand a little taller ("Dykeman"). Dykeman's presentations of females, even with their epic dimensions, are infinitely closer to a balanced reality than scores of depictions of mountaineers that precede or follow them.

Yet, if Wilma Dykeman's fictional world cannot be said to be militantly feminist, it certainly is one which foregrounds strong female characters in a family setting. Her characters encourage family solidarity. Those who subvert the family are abhorrent; they lose their chances at happiness, alienate the very people they hope to win, frequently fail in business ventures, or realize too late the emptiness of their lives. Dykeman's heroines suffer, too, but their suffering ennobles. Even though they acknowledge "the confinements of family and community and love," they are never callous about the benefits inherent in what they unswervingly feel is an essentiality—Family with a capital F (*Tall Woman*, 179). It is not just the rural world of the past that ties Lydia McQueen and Dykeman's other principal female characters to this domesticity, but their wish to express joy in family.

Notes

1. According to Robert Penn Warren, the idea of the South as a separate region began at Appomattox Courthouse; thus this historical frame seems an appropriate starting point for Dykeman's first major fictional rendering of the region.

2. Dykeman dedicated *The Tall Woman* to her mother, Bonnie Cole Dykeman, a diminutive lady whom Dykeman calls "the tallest woman I know" (7). In an address to the North Carolina Women Writers' Conference (14 Mar. 1992), Dykeman spoke of her "mountain mother," "Miss Bonnie," who died 19 January 1992, as being "formed of the root and flower of North Carolina."

3. Dykeman comments that *The Tall Woman* "*is* about a very strong mountain woman, as there have been many strong women from the Greeks on, before the Greeks, in all time" (Miller, 49). Another writer she admires for creating valiant female characters is Harriette Arnow, especially Arnow's Gertie Nevels in *The Dollmaker,* a work Dykeman calls a "fine novel . . . one of the universal tragedies of mankind" ("Dollmaker," C:2). Dykeman had not read *The Dollmaker* before she wrote *The Tall Woman* (letter, 28 Feb. 1992).

Works Cited

Betts, Doris. "The Long Shadow of a Woman." Review of *The Tall Woman,* by Wilma Dykeman. *Raleigh (N.C.) News and Observer,* 29 July 1962, sec. 3:5.

Christ, Carol P. *Diving Deep and Surfacing: Women Writers on Spiritual Quest.* 2nd ed. Boston: Beacon Press, 1986.

Dykeman, Wilma. "Appalachia in Context." In *An Appalachian Symposium: Essays Written in Honor of Cratis D. Williams,* ed. J. W. Williamson, 28–42. Boone, N.C.: Appalachian State University Press, 1977.

———. "Dollmaker a Credit to Appalachia." Film rev. of *The Dollmaker,* by Harriette Simpson Arnow. *Knoxville (Tennessee) News-Sentinel,* 27 May 1984, sec. C:2.

———. Letters to the author, 28 Feb. 1992 and 2 Dec. 1999.

———. *The Tall Woman.* New York: Holt, Rinehart and Winston, 1962; Newport, Tenn.: Wakestone, 1962; repr. New York: Avon, 1967.

"Dykeman: Writer Resents Regional Label." *Louisville Courier-Journal and Times,* 29 Apr. 1973.

Ethridge, Mark Foster. Papers. The Southern Historical Collection #3842. Wilson Library, University of North Carolina, Chapel Hill.

Gage, Jim. "Place in the Fiction of Wilma Dykeman's *The Tall Woman.*" *Iron Mountain Review* 5 (Spring 1989): 3–7.

————. "The 'Poetics of Space' in Wilma Dykeman's *The Tall Woman.*" In *The Poetics of Appalachian Space,* ed. Parks Lanier Jr., 67–80. Knoxville: University of Tennessee Press, 1991.

Marius, Richard. "The Rooted Heart and the Ranging Intellect: A Conversation." *Iron Mountain Review* 5 (Spring 1989): 8–13.

Miller, Danny. "A *MELUS* Interview: Wilma Dykeman." *MELUS* 9 (Winter 1982): 45–59.

Neufeld, Rob. "Choice Books." *Asheville (N.C.) Citizen-Times,* 15 Dec. 1991, 6L.

Rubin, Louis D., Jr., ed. *The Literary South.* Baton Rouge: Louisiana State University Press, 1979.

Stanback, Betty Anne. "Long-Suffering Lydia." Review of *The Tall Woman,* by Wilma Dykeman. *Greensboro (N.C.) Daily News,* 21 Oct. 1962.

Weatherford, Willis D. Papers. The Southern Historical Collection #3831. Wilson Library, University of North Carolina, Chapel Hill.

Welty, Eudora. "Place in Fiction." In *A Modern Southern Reader,* ed. Ben Forkner and Patrick Samway, 537–48. Atlanta: Peachtree, 1986.

O Beulah Land

The "Yaller Vision" of Jeremiah Catlett

JANE GENTRY VANCE

Mary Lee Settle's *O Beulah Land,* published in 1956, is the first novel she wrote of the Beulah Quintet. The historical order of the books runs from *Prisons,* set in seventeenth-century England during the Puritan Revolution; to *O Beulah Land,* set in Virginia and at Beulah, in what will become West Virginia, in the two decades before the American Revolution; to *Know Nothing,* set at Beulah in the decades before the Civil War; to *The Scapegoat,* set in Beulah Valley in 1912, when the union movement was beginning in the coalfields; to *The Killing Ground,* set in fictional Canona, West Virginia, on the Canona River, in the mid–twentieth century. The order in which Settle wrote the books is *O Beulah Land* (1956), *Know Nothing* (1960), *Prisons* (1973), *The Scapegoat* (1980), and finally *The Killing Ground* (1982). The completion of Settle's own "yaller vision," like Jeremiah Catlett's of Beulah (53), his salvation, his promised land, took her a full twenty-six years.

O Beulah Land, the crucial novel in the series, dramatizes the brief realization of the vision that begins in *Prisons* with the idealistic rhetoric of Johnny Church, a Leveller in Oliver Cromwell's New Model Army, and the ancestor of Captain Jonathan Lacey, the colonial militia captain who founds Beulah. The last three books of the Quintet dramatize the dissipation of Jonathan's and Jeremiah's vision of Beulah, so that all four of the

From *Iron Mountain Review* 7 (Spring 1991): 19–23. Reprinted by permission of the author and the publisher.

other books grow from this seminal, earliest novel. The Quintet comprises, and *O Beulah Land* epitomizes, a dramatic exploration, like no other in American literature, of exactly what America is, what our political, social, and religious roots are.

In *O Beulah Land* more than anywhere else in the Quintet, the writing, transparent and exact, seldom obtrudes into the reader's presence at critical historical events. *Prisons,* too, glistens with sustained intensity, but its range includes only the then-masculine world of ideology and power, while *O Beulah Land* dramatizes, in addition, a deeply imagined sense of the American wilderness and an account of how European civilization, with its religious, social, and gender dynamics, was brought to the western frontier. *O Beulah Land* takes us to the inside of the settlers' experience, gives it to us affectively, from the inside out, a view that has not been readily accessible to subsequent generations because even when the settlers were literate, they still had little time or energy to record their thoughts while they coped with the dangers of the wilderness. Also, our mythologizing of the westward movement, our making romantic heroes of pioneers like Daniel Boone and Morgan Morgan, and our viewing Christian white men's efforts to wrest the land from the heathen Indians as a prototype of the cosmic struggle between good and evil have prevented our imagining this phase of our history in terms of actual human event. Thus we have barred ourselves from as complete a knowledge as we could have of where we have been and of who we are.

Settle's historical fiction aims, then, to reacquire these lost experiences and to heal this crippling collective amnesia. In a 1984 *New York Times Book Review* article, "Recapturing the Past in Fiction," she writes that the task of such fiction is "to become contemporary," "to try to see, to hear, to share a passion." Painstaking, fully ingested research, she says, can carry the novelist "back to when the hates were new, the hopes alive, the prejudices merely contemporary fears" (36). In contrast to the historian whose job requires similar research, the fiction writer tries "to conjure out of the rescued fragments of forgotten time the historic memory that haunts us in dreams, in the residue of language, gesture and prejudice, traced to its genesis" (1). While history is necessarily defined by time, fiction "is timeless when it reaches the reality of a person, an act or a scene that transcends the words conveying it" (1) and places the empathetic reader at the very scene that shaped her or his own experience. Americans need this kind of fiction because, as Settle says, "in each American past . . . [there] is the generation that had to leave home. We inherited from it a sense of loss. . . . We seek a personal identity, and sometimes, with more luck than perseverance, when the memory has been truly evoked, we find it, a historic *déjà vu*. We have been there somehow and we are there again. It is a way of facing the old, cold passions, the fears, the notions that seemed once to be fact— things that can form nodules deep within the present as black as manganese" (1).

O Beulah Land, a series of these regained, deeply imagined scenes, gives back to us their lost truths. As in the fiction of the few other consummate historical novelists of the twentieth century (Mary Renault, Marguerite Yourcenar, and George Garrett), Settle's sensuous prose cuts and polishes those nodules, those moments of timelessness when the past rises up alive before the reader with the force of lived experience. Calliope, the muse of history, heard Settle's invocation as surely as she did Homer's and inspired her to re-member, to put back together again, the American experience of leaving behind the comforts of the known to make a home, a new place of belonging, in a formidable wilderness. Settle's subject, then, is that first and brightest American dream of a paradise of freedom and equality in the desert places, a new Eden of opportunity to all honest and hardworking people. The novel's epigraph from *The Great Gatsby* locates this dream:

> [Gatsby's] dream must have seemed so close that he could hardly fail to grasp it. He did not know that it was already behind him, somewhere back in that vast obscurity beyond the city, where the dark fields of the republic rolled on under the night.

Gatsby believes in the "orgiastic future" and yearns forward toward the dream when it is actually the missed opportunity of the American past: "So we beat on, boats against the current, borne back ceaselessly into the past."

Settle bears us back into the past in this key novel, dramatizing the brief flowering and tragic blighting of the dream of Beulah. In Settle's vision the dream fails because the new society cannot avoid contamination by the old European systems of class and authority. Despite the humane intentions of idealists like Jonathan Lacey and the schoolmaster-printer Jarcey Pentacost, and despite the ecstatic visions of mystics like Jeremiah Catlett, the old attitudes and prejudices do infiltrate the western settlements. But briefly, in Beulah's first two years (1763–65) as the diverse community struggles to survive, the old divisions that were Royalist and

Roundhead in England, and Tuckahoe and Cohee in eastern Virginia, are meaningless: each person is valued and respected for what he or she can contribute to the common good, regardless of family background or wealth. The Scotch-Irish family of Solomon McKarkle, the New Light family of Jeremiah Catlett and Hannah Newgate, along with the primitive Carvers and Cutwrights, and the German Dunkers, the Mittelburgers, co-operate with Jonathan and Jarcey to build a community in which all can flourish and be of use.

Jonathan's Tidewater wife, Sally Mason, whose limitations he cannot perceive while he is immersed in the blinding conventions of courtship, carries the contagion into Beulah when she arrives in 1765 with her slaves, her class consciousness, and her useless treasures. Johnny, finally realizing Sal's effect, later tells Jarcey: "We still look [to England] for the sensible virtues we've brought across the mountains. . . . What can we become out here? We may have brought the virtues, but we've brought a cancer, too" (249). Tragically, Sal is not the only carrier. Jonathan himself, despite his natural goodness and his democratic ideals, cannot be conscious of, much less control, the effect his own manners and carriage have on the resentful renegades of the frontier.

Doggo Cutwright, a rough young soldier who served in Braddock's Wars with Johnny, has come with him to Beulah, bringing his Indian wife. But as soon as Sal arrives and excites Doggo's deepest prejudices, he angrily takes his wife and brother and heads west into unprotected territory. "We don't hold with no Dutchmen and Neegurs" (258), his sister-in-law shrieks at Johnny when he asks them to stay. Doggo adds, "We'uns come out hyar to git away from ruffle shirts and Whigs, a-bringin their Neegurs and cups and saucers and fancy ways and settin up like back East. We'uns hain't got nuthin to do with sechlike." But even as he reasons with Doggo, Jonathan, sitting on his good horse, "didn't realize that the very look of him there, so at ease, only strengthened Doggo's hatred." When Jonathan asks about their children, whom they have left behind, the furious Doggo yells as he gallops away, "Ye try and make thim wildcats into Tuckahoes! Git out'n the way, Ruffle-Shirt" (259). Jonathan now understands that his Sal is a "mighty dangerous woman" (259).

Unbending Sal, who comes to the frontier from the Tidewater in 1765 after Jonathan has established the station and built their house, persists in calling the settlement by the classical name "Cicero," while Jonathan always calls it after Jeremiah's "yaller vision," Beulah. He and his common-law

wife Hannah settle there in 1756. Later, illiterate Jeremiah has Jarcey dip
into the Bible for guidance after Jonathan claims the valley, including
Jeremiah's stake. Jarcey comes up with Isaiah 62:4: "Thou shalt no more
be termed forsaken; neither shall thy land any more be termed desolate;
but thou shalt be called Hephzibah, and thy land Beulah, for the Lord de-
lighteth in thee, and thy land shall be married" (253). As God thus promised Canaan to the Israelites, so, as Jeremiah sees it, God promises him this
river valley Hannah had seen on her flight east. After Jeremiah has to kill
Squire Raglan to protect his land claim and his freedom, he heads west
with Hannah, back to the beautiful place she has told him about.

The popular New Light hymn echoes this promise of a land of peace and
plenty. Each of the four sections of the novel opens with an epigraph from
its chorus. "O Beulah Land, sweet Beulah Land, / As on thy highest mount
I stand" introduces the Prologue, in which we see for the first time the
Canona River valley that becomes Beulah. A fifty-two-page tour de force
set in August and September of 1755, this section dramatizes Hannah's escape from the Indians who captured her at Great Meadows, where she was
one of a dozen or so women taken along by the army for the soldiers' use.
At the end of her desperate run, Hannah stumbles onto Jeremiah's stake at
Goshen with its mineral spring (like the real White Sulphur Springs, West
Virginia), which later in the novel becomes the resort, Dunkard's Valley.
After Jeremiah nurses Hannah back to health, he decides God has sent her
to him to be his wife.

The next lines of the chorus ("I look away across the sea / Where mansions are prepared for me") introduce Book One (July 16, 1754–July 12,
1755), a flashback "across the sea" in which we learn of Hannah's early life
in London and of how she, Jarcey Pentacost, and Squire Raglan are deported
to America on the same ship. The section also includes a vividly realized
dramatization of British General Edward Braddock's ambush and defeat at
Great Meadows on July 12, 1755, by the French and Indians. Here we first
meet Jonathan Lacey, an officer under George Washington in Braddock's
army, as well as the hostile Doggo Cutwright and the pretentious Squire
Raglan, now the servant of Jonathan's English cousin Peregrine Cockburn,
who is killed in the battle. During this year, twenty-year-old Jonathan
marries sixteen-year-old Sally Mason, the belle of Alexandria.

Book Two (August 15, 1763–May 2, 1765) ("and view the shining
Glory Shore") opens with Jonathan's arrival from the frontier at Kregg's
Crossing of the James River, about eighty miles upriver, to register a

patent for the 5,000 acres of bottomland that will be Beulah. He wants
this fertile valley despite its situation west of the point where the rivers
flow back east for the easy transport of produce. In this longest section, in
which the potential for freedom and equality in Beulah is briefly realized,
we see Jonathan save Jarcey from mindless Indian haters who take offense
at his broadsides in defense of the Proclamation Line (1763). This section
also recounts Jonathan and Sal's arduous wagon train journey, with all their
household, across the Endless Mountains.

Book Three (March 16, 1769–July 20, 1774) ("My Heaven, my Home,
forevermore") covers the longest period of time, the years when Jonathan
attempts to create an inclusive community at Beulah. Here the cancer of
class prejudices and false manners takes its toll: Sal, proud in her disdain of
her daughter's marriage to Ezekiel Catlett, Hannah and Jeremiah's son, is
brutalized after the wedding by the Beulah Cohees tired of her uppity
ways. Finally, after a futile nine years, Jonathan gives up on the dream of
establishing his family on the frontier and takes Sal, broken and old at
thirty-five, back to the Tidewater. Ironically, her now-outmoded idea of
the *ton* will make her an anachronism there. While Jonathan is in the East,
Indians attack Beulah and kill Jeremiah and Hannah, whose descendants
nevertheless will inherit the valley just as Jeremiah saw in his vision. Beulah will flourish for more than a century, until the coal wars of 1912, and
both Jonathan's Tuckahoe blood and Jeremiah's Cohee blood will run in
the veins of its owners. But the seeds of ruinous evil also flourish in the
garden. Sal's favorite son, Peregrine, to satisfy his lust for Indian blood,
goes west to join the likes of Doggo Cutwright. Slavery is now established
at Beulah. This will lead to tragic consequences sixty years later during the
Civil War. Although honest and humane Jonathan has been elected to the
House of Burgesses, he has won in tandem with his true Tuckahoe brother-
in-law Brandon Crawford, who favors allowing power brokers in the East
to claim huge tracts of land on the newly opened frontier.

Crystalline as is the whole of *O Beulah Land* with inspiration and insight
transformed into lived events, still the jewel of the novel is the twenty-
three-page first chapter of the Prologue. This account of Hannah
Bridewell's frantic, six-week trek back east across the Endless Mountains,
in flight from the Indians who had captured her at Great Meadows, recreates the most dramatic component of the ever-popular Indian captivity
narratives, the actual escape. Such narratives, first popular in the seventeenth century in New England, remained so into the nineteenth century,

and were the forerunners of the stories of the Wild West, as well as of Gothic horror stories like Charles Brockden Brown's and Poe's. The ex-captives who told these tales were, of course, the lucky ones who managed to escape. Some of their stories were written for them by those more learned than they, often, especially in New England, by preachers, who laced the accounts with Providences, miraculous deliverances which rewarded constant faith, or dire calamities which punished moral waywardness.

Settle's Prologue takes us inside an Indian captivity story to make us experience effectively a white, London-born woman's desperate flight through the vast and lonely wilderness. The narratives themselves name but generally do not evoke the horror of situations like Hannah's. To regain the sensory and emotional realities of this lost experience, Settle, as she does throughout the Quintet, uses actual historical data to recreate the human reality, to bring the past into the present moment. Settle bases Hannah's flight most directly on that of Mary Draper Ingles, who at age twenty-three in 1755, the same year as Hannah's capture, was taken by Indians from her home on the New River, near Draper, Virginia, near what is now Pulaski. Ingles, whose story was written by her son, John Ingles, Sr., was kept by the Indians almost five months before she escaped, leaving with them by necessity her two older children. For forty-two days she desperately struggled, from Big Bone Lick on the Licking River in Kentucky, where the Indians had taken her to make salt (Ingles, 11), eastward back toward Virginia and her home.

Hannah's "forty days and forty nights in the wilderness of the Endless Mountains" (25) are much like Mary Ingles's. As Hannah follows a river we later know (in *Know Nothing*) as the Canona (like the real Kanawha), so Mary followed the Ohio and the Kanawha. As with Hannah, Ingles luckily must make this journey in late summer and into September when the streams are at their lowest, enabling each to cross many which would have stopped them at other seasons (Ingles, 13). Like Hannah, Mary Ingles and the old Dutch woman who was with her for part of the journey were

> woorn down by fateigue & starvation [and] wood have to pule themselves up by the srubs & bushes till they got to the top and to decend they wood slide all the way down. Under these defiqualteys and nothing to sustain nature but what they picked up in the woods such as black walnuts grapes papaws etc & very often so pushed with hunger that they wood dig up roots and eate that they knew nothing of. (Ingles, 13)

Just as Hannah left "a thin trail of linsey behind her in the selfish, high undergrowth" (5), so the "little clothing which [Mary] had started with was nearley or entierly worn out or dragged off of her by the Brush . . . [so] that she had become literalery naked and the weather growing cooler . . . all the chance she had for keeping herself from perishing at night was to hunt out in the eavening a hollow logg or tree and geather leaves & put in it and then crawl in amongst the leaves & lye" (Ingles, 15). *O Beulah Land* opens on Hannah, so frantic she literally does not know who she is (10), making a bed for herself, just as Ingles did, inside a hollow tree (3). And Jeremiah Catlett, when Hannah at last reaches his cabin at Goshen, feeds her (31) in the same careful way that Ingles's old neighbor, Adam Harmon, fed her when she reached his place on the New River (Ingles, 16–17). From such seeds, the whole experience, imagined by Settle from the inside out, grows and takes its shape, in words depth-charged with the truth of memory. Settle furnishes the mental and emotional substance that is implicit in John Ingles's account of the awful adventure he had heard his mother repeat many times.

Other details come from other actual captivities. Hannah Swarton, whose story Cotton Mather tells in *Christi Magnalia Americana,* found wild animal parts (a moose bladder and liver) and saved and ate them (Vaughn, 150), just as Hannah Bridewell does the bear's liver in *O Beulah Land* (17–18). Perhaps Settle took the name Hannah from Hannah Swarton and Hannah Dustan (Vaughn, 159), whose narrative also appears in Mather's compilation. But Settle's account of Hannah's escape takes us directly into the experience without the seventeenth-century interpolations of second-hand telling or of moralizing. We feel the physical and emotional realities of being totally alone in the wilderness, conveyed as they could not be by the escapees themselves, mainly women, many of whom were illiterate and did not know how to tell a story on paper, how to recreate the experience for readers.

Settle, on the other hand, knows how to make us feel the emptiness of the landscape and the isolation of the lone, defenseless woman running for her life, from the Ohio Valley to eastern West Virginia, with nothing to guide her except the sun. The first sentences of the novel place us with Hannah:

A single footprint lay alone. It seemed dropped from nowhere onto the underbrush between the black, muscular roots of the high tree which dominated the ragged, lonesome hollow. But a small hand, human, on a thin, rootlike white arm, wavered over the indent, fluttered the leaves, and the print was gone. (3)

Settle's language vivifies the scene with an animism that seems strange to us, removed as we are from any sense of a natural place unaffected by human interference. The footprint has a life of its own, a life-or-death significance, as it lies on the leaves. The tree is personified with its "muscular" roots, "dominating" the hollow. The disembodied hand, like the footprint, also has a life of its own, and in that wild place where nothing human lives, it must be designated "human" because most of the hands there belong to raccoons and possums. The "rootlike white arm" further blurs the distinction between the human and the wilderness world, making the human seem vegetative, and the vegetative, human. The sense of being alien in a neutral universe saturates these scenes of Hannah's flight.

The mindful life of the vegetation (the "hugging" laurel and the rhododendron roots "like the unkempt head of some insane giant" [5]) opposes itself, first, to Hannah's panicked flight from the west, and then, gradually, to her willful eastward march. The claw of hunger keeps her body and mind raw as she scavenges for fuel for her ordeal. She finds papaws, a few blackberries, even traps a squirrel with her bare hands and unconsciously eats it, fur and all (10). This necessity induces in her an animalism like that of the bear whose leavings she eats: the carcass of another bear whose foot got caught in a rock cleft.

> Its chest was nearly gone; its guts lay in the sun. Hannah ate until her head swam, the strong fat running down her skinny body—gorged her fill as the other had. . . . Then, full, her work finished, she began to drowse, drunk with meat, until the sun struck her sprawled body, and heated the blood on the littered rock. (17–18)

Settle demonstrates how thin the veneer of civilization is, how quickly a person reverts to the driven fulfillment of the few basic needs. The conventional Indian captivity narratives do not get down so stark a portrayal of this truth.

Moments of triumph and rest come to Hannah during this test of her will and intelligence as she "walked, stumbled, crawled automatically, hour after hour" (13). Along the Canona, Kanawha River, one scene etches itself in her mind and becomes the reason Beulah Valley, this site, is later home to her and her descendants:

> The bottomlands had run so long in strips between the hills and river that she stopped in her tracks at the sight of a deeper valley lying like an upturned hand between two hills across the river. The gentle place rested, with a creek like a lifeline running through it, as if God, sickened by the magnificence of the huge trees and the mountains, had lain down in mid-Creation, flung out His lovely hand, and gone to sleep awhile. . . . She stood with her arms crossed, measuring from a distance in her mind's eye, and frowned a little calculating frown. But the wide, calm river was between them; like Moses, she had to gaze from far off. (14)

Still personified, this hand-like landscape beckons kindly with God's own largesse. Hannah's memory of this beautiful valley brings her and Jeremiah Catlett back to it. Here Jonathan Lacey is to found Beulah, and the image of this valley becomes in the novel, as well as in the whole Quintet, an emblem for lost connections that determine the lives of the characters and their descendants.

O Beulah Land, like the other books of the Quintet, probes events of the American past by purging them of the generalizations and the mythifications of history. Through a deeply imagined poetry of body and place that never wavers from strenuous particularity, Settle takes us inside Hannah's journey across the Endless Mountains, on the march of Braddock's army to the Great Meadows, and to the settlement at Beulah in the 1760s and 1770s. Sounding for us the real voices of the people who think and speak in each of these places and circumstances, she takes us to the "nodules black as manganese" that she invokes in "Recapturing the Past in Fiction." With the immediacy of personal memory, she renders the all-but-lost experience of Jeremiah Catlett's "yaller vision": she dramatizes the forces and sentiments that made Beulah a brief Eden in the wilderness, as well as the ones that doomed it. Settle's fiction gives us back part of ourselves by realizing this loss, this failure of the dream, in the past of each American. She also sets the stage for the four rich novels that complete the Beulah Quintet, the truest vision that contemporary fiction offers of where Americans came from, of who we are.

Works Cited

Ingles, John, Sr. *The Story of Mary Draper Ingles and Son Thomas Ingles*. Ed. Roberta Ingles Steele and Andrew Lewis Ingles. Radford, Va.: Commonwealth Press, 1969.

Settle, Mary Lee. *O Beulah Land*. New York: Charles Scribner's Sons, 1987.

———. "Recapturing the Past in Fiction." *New York Times Book Review*, 12 Feb. 1984, 1, 36–37.

Vaughn, Alden T., and Edward W. Clark. *Puritans among the Indians: Accounts of Captivity and Redemption, 1676–1724*. Cambridge: Harvard University Press, 1981.

THE BEULAH/CANONA CONNECTION

Mary Lee Settle's Autobiographies

NANCY CAROL JOYNER

The foremost historical novelist of her generation, Mary Lee Settle is most renowned for her signal achievement, the Beulah Quintet. These five books take as their subject the times preceding the cataclysms of social upheaval and war from the British Civil War through American wars up to Vietnam. Published between 1956 and 1982, the books trace the descendants of the progenitor, Johnny Church, and are further connected through the characters' preservation of family heirlooms, and the author's effort to link one family's conflicts and coalitions with the American mythos.[1] "Sustaining the patterns and details of the whole Beulah Quintet," Settle writes, "was the most preoccupying and exhausting occupation I have ever demanded of myself."[2] She joins her critics in considering it her *magnum opus*. It richly deserves the critical scrutiny it has attracted.

The Beulah Quintet represents only a quarter of Settle's literary accomplishment, however. The other fifteen titles range widely in topic and form, from her National Book Award winner *Blood Tie* (1977), set in Turkey, to her most recent title, *I, Roger Williams* (2001), set in New England. She has also produced a second group of five novels that can be called the Canona Cycle. These novels, set in the Kanawha Valley of West Virginia, are *The Love Eaters* (1954), *The Kiss of Kin* (1955), *The Clam Shell* (1966), *Charley Bland* (1989), and the final novel of the Beulah Quintet, *The Killing Ground* (1982). This group is closely tied to significant events in Settle's own life, but it shares with the historical novels an emphasis on family clashes, the painful awareness of social class, and the struggle for individual autonomy. The subtitle of Brian Rosenberg's study of the Beulah novels, "The Price of Freedom," applies equally well to what George Garrett calls the "other Beulah writings."[3] Both cycles are searches for independence, whether personal or societal.

George Garrett, a long-time neighbor and literary champion of Mary Lee Settle, has noted three characteristics of Settle's writing that give her work "a singular coherence": accurate description of scenes; skillful evocation of a time, whether historical or contemporaneous to the writing; and presentation of a large number of well-developed and "dimensional" characters (17). I heartily concur with this assessment of Settle's technical strengths, but I wish to suggest that the basis for these accomplishments is her extraordinary use of autobiography in almost everything she has written. She mines from her own memories places, events, and people and then ships them to England in 1649, France in 1918, or Charleston, West Virginia, in 1980. The purpose of this essay is to demonstrate briefly that autobiographical elements evident in both the Beulah and Canona works constitute another factor that connects the two groups.

It can be argued that all writing is autobiographical, just as all autobiography is fiction, but Settle has combined her autobiography with historical research to an unusual degree. Also, Settle has a decidedly unorthodox view of autobiography. The extent and eccentricities of Settle's use of autobiographical elements are more apparent when her historical novels are considered in the context of her more directly autobiographical works.

A recent and noteworthy addition to Settle's canon is *Addie: A Memoir,* published in 1998, Settle's eightieth year. She wrote it in response to a request from her publisher for a memoir. True to both her predilection for historical novels and her independent if not downright eccentric attitude toward autobiography, she chose to write a "memoir" of her maternal grandmother. In the preface she explains, "An autobiography that begins with one's birth begins too late. . . . I was formed by eons of earthquake, and the rise of the mountains and the crushing of swamps into coal as surely as by timid human copulation."[4] Settle researched this book the way she researched her Beulah novels, consulting court records that disproved Addie's own account of her marriage. That Addie died in 1947, seven years before Settle published her first book, did not deter her from including a rich and illuminating account of her lengthy publishing career. Settle never has been a slave to chronological order.

This extraordinary literary biography is only the capstone of Settle's body of written material that deals with her methodology and rationale for her choice of subjects. Numerous articles and interviews address the same issues, as do the brief introductions in the uniform editions of the Mary Lee Settle Collection, recently published by the University of South Carolina Press. These materials are of special interest to the Settle scholar, for they not only enhance the reader's understanding of the fiction but also provide confirmation of the direct use of her autobiography.

Nowhere is this impulse toward autobiography more apparent than in the landscape of the Beulah series. In a 1984 essay for the Contemporary Authors Autobiography Series, Settle wrote that when she was ten years old her family moved from Florida back to her grandmother's home in Cedar Grove, West Virginia, to which various aunts and uncles had returned because of economic hard times. Although her family lived there for only a little more than a year, she wrote, "In my dreams, and in the Beulah Quintet, that house is 'home,' vortex and font at the same time."[5] Beulah Land is the fictional name for the Kanawha River Valley. The landscape of her historical novels is in fact the landscape of her childhood. Therefore, in large ways and small, the author's experiences inform the novels set in the distant past.

Settle claims that novels in the Beulah series are autobiographical in other ways as well. In an interview at Emory and Henry University in 1991, she responded to a question on autobiography by announcing that *Prisons*—the novel set in mid-seventeenth-century England—is her most autobiographical work. She admitted to calling that statement a "smart-alecky answer," but immediately went on to say that she has more "psychically in common" with Johnny Church, the protagonist of *Prisons*, than with any other character she has written about.[6] Elsewhere she reports that the book was conceived in 1968 and that her decision to pursue it was influenced by "present circumstances": the election of President Nixon, the antiwar riots in Chicago, the Soviet attack on Prague.[7] Brian Rosenberg has pointed out that "*Prisons* is her first book to be written in first person and the one most reliant on documentary evidence" (51).

Settle researched *O Beulah Land,* the novel set in late-eighteenth-century America, in the British Museum. In *Addie: A Memoir* she describes one day of her work there, when she succeeded in talking the person in charge into allowing her into the basement that housed artifacts of American Indians. In a sea chest she made a startling find:

[T]here were two large sea chests, piled high with round leather pieces tied to willow hoops that looked like the darning hoops that Addie used to use. They were as thin and frail as fine parchment; delicately painted—yellow and black and white and red—with designs in their centers. I picked one up, a yellow one with a painting of a tomahawk. A hank of blond hair fell nearly to the floor. (21)

She had picked up a scalp.

In *O Beulah Land* that personal experience is related in Captain Jonathan Lacey's warning to his young cousin against leaving a group of soldiers in Indian territory in 1754:

"There was a man today slipped off a little in the woods to relieve himself. . . . I heared something there and went and found him. These were Shawnees—must have been—small-scalped him. Their rings are neat—no more than five inches or thereabouts across. They paint up real pretty, once ye forget what they've been."[8]

Settle has said that she cannot write autobiography because, she says, "The minute I try to start it becomes fiction."[9] The opposite may also be true: the minute she starts historical fiction, it becomes autobiography.

Similarly, the novels of the Canona Cycle are both fictional and autobiographical. *The Love Eaters* (1954) focuses on an amateur theater group, and it can be surmised that it is based partially on Settle's apprenticeship at the Barter Theater in Abingdon, Virginia, in the summer of 1938. The novel, however, is set not in Abingdon but in Canona, and it is this book that introduces the circle of friends who reappear in her other Canona novels. Prominent are the Dodds and the Potters, members of the country club where much of the action takes place. Into this complacent society comes Hamilton Sacks, a viciously witty, gay, wheelchair-bound theater director accompanied by his mother, a long-suffering caretaker who lives a nomadic existence with her son. She is thrilled to be invited into a country club, so much better than the Rotary or Lions, she says (81). Settle has said that even when her parents complained of economic hardship they never dropped their country club membership (*Addie,* 186).

According to the author, *The Love Eaters* is an American adaptation of the Phaedra myth, with Selby, the recently discovered grown son of Jim Dodd, as the Hippolytus figure (Garrett, 86). The novel is therefore tragic in form, though the background of petty snobberies and embarrassments due to occasional drunkenness is predominantly satirical. The third-person omniscient point of view in this novel allows for the detached air appropriate to satire. Garrett reminds readers that Settle had written six unsuccessful plays before she began writing novels and attributes the presentational quality of this story of the Canona Thespians to that experience (86–87). This book first presents one of Settle's recurrent major themes: the corruptive influence of a classed society.

The Kiss of Kin (1955), the first novel written but the second one published, was originally conceived as a play. It is set at an old homeplace reminiscent of Addie's house in Cedar Grove, when the exceedingly dysfunctional family gathers to bury the matriarch, Anna Mary Passmore. The group includes both the numerous relatives resident in the house and several visiting family members. After the funeral Cousin Cadwallader, the lawyer, reads with some trepidation the will penned by the decedent's own hand. Upon hearing it, the family erupts in a fierce argument and threats of suits. In *Addie* Settle alludes to such an event at the reading of her grandmother's will, a document that ends, "This will may not please you all, but you will haft to put up with it" (211). Much of this novel is not based on the actual situation of the household; the relative who manages the house is presented as an extreme villain when the opposite seems to have been the case. Perhaps as a joke, Settle named that character Mary Lee.

"*The Clam Shell* is the closest thing to an autobiographical novel I ever wrote," Settle told Garrett in an interview (91). In *Addie* she explains that she turned it into fiction because she needed to reinterpret the traumatic experience she had lived through (211). This novel is a record of her first year as a student at Sweet Briar College, here called Nelson-Page. One evening a student from Charlottesville takes her out on a date and on the way back to the dorm attempts to rape her. She escapes and walks back ten miles to the dorm, arriving therefore after the rules required she be in. She was subsequently put on trial by the student senate and was convicted of coming in late, although she was convinced that, in spite of a medical exam proving the contrary, the college community believed she was guilty of sexual activity. In her introduction to the 1995 edition of the novel, she writes, "The central episodes of *The Clam Shell* are true: the joke turned appalling of the walk home from the car ride, the parody of a 'trial' by a jury of my peers, the interview between my mother and the college president."[10] She goes on to say, though, that by reviewing that trauma she came to realize that "out of that year was the opening of a clam shell of a mind in a world no longer feared, and the resolute passion to keep it open." The bare facts, she concludes, become finally a novel.

Although most of this first-person narration takes place away from Charleston, there are two chapters that are significant from both an autobiographical standpoint and a thematic one. The first chapter describes in rich detail a streetcar ride from the country club to her house, taking special note of some of the places she passes and the people she sees. The ride takes her and her friend Cincy from the hill where the wealthy live in columned mansions overlooking the river, to downtown, where there is a public park with tennis courts:

> I watch the figures moving with the ease I can never have. If I can't be Daisy, I want to be one of them, moving freely, not caring whether they go to high school or to the proving-ground parties, not even knowing the houses on the hill, to be one of them, or one of the others, but not on the streetcar, not in the middle, not so afraid. (38)

The narrator and her friend on the streetcar are in the middle between the upper and middle classes of Canona and also in transition between high school and college, uncertain about where they belong. It is a masterful description.

One other chapter in *The Clam Shell* is set in Canona. On Christmas Eve the narrator attends a late and somewhat drunken party at the club; the next day she goes with her family to Cedar Grove to be with her grandmother shortly after her uncle commits suicide there. Addie's prayer at the table, which she uses as a lecture—"don't let Bonnie's girl be c'rupted by being thrust into worldliness by her costly education"—is a close replica to a prayer she offers in the later book (166). Again, the details surrounding Settle's Uncle Babo's death are presented similarly in both books. This book stays very close to the truth, but it is transformed into art. As Settle maintains in *Addie,* "it is true beyond the facts, as a novel must be" (211).

In her introduction to the most recent of the Canona novels, *Charley Bland* (1989), Settle calls the book a coda to the Beulah series. More obviously it is a Canona Cycle fill-in, between *The Clam Shell* and *The Killing Ground.* The introduction, written for the Mary Lee Settle Collection edition from the University of South Carolina Press (1996), provides insights into the author's attitudes toward and habits of construction. It also makes a claim that the imaginary Canona is an amalgam of the West Virginia cities of Charleston, Morgantown, and Elkins, among others. In an earlier interview with Rosenberg in the Mary Lee Settle issue of *Iron Mountain Review,* she admits that this book is "the most thinly disguised autobiography" of her writing career, but she also asserts that Charley himself is a fictional character, as he "was lover, brother, most of the people I grew up with who didn't amount to a hill of beans, and one of my uncles."[11]

Although the eponymous character may be a blend of several men and the town he lives in an amalgam, the book is plainly autobiographical. Settle reports in her Contemporary Authors Autobiography Series essay that after the success of her first two novels, her marriage with Douglas Newton failed and she returned from London to Charleston. There, with the blessings of her mother and the country club group, she entered into a relationship with an eligible bachelor. "Three years later," she writes, "his mother, who needed him at home after his father died, decided to get rid of me, the *New York Times,* and the living room rug."[12] In the autobiographical essay, the introduction to the novel, and the novel itself, Settle quotes this sentence: "We don't knife people out of malice, we only knife people who get in our way."[13] She says this "sociopathic view of the world" cannot be softened, for it contributes significantly to the impetus for the scathing denunciation of the complacent comfort of the upper middle class.

The preceding summary encapsulates both the plot and the theme of *Charley Bland.* The first chapter, called "A Triangle of Stone," introduces the three principals: the unnamed narrator, Charley, and his mother. The novel follows the parabola of the affair between the younger couple, all with the approval of their parents. In the climactic chapter, "Fall into Winter," the narrator discovers she has been "hated out" when she takes her dog for a walk on the golf course and sees through a window a party going on at the club (136–41). Since she has not been invited, she assumes she does not know the people inside, but then she sees Charley come outside and light a cigarette. Literally outside looking in, she realizes she is no longer a member of the group. As the book ends, after the death of Charley's father and the raw conversation with his mother mentioned above, she buys a ticket for Turkey. The effect of the novel is to explore both the power of a closed social system and the weakness of the debonair mama's boy. It is chilling in its unromantic depiction of romantic love.

Although *Charley Bland* is the last of the Canona Cycle, its time frame of 1960–66 precedes the historical time of *The Killing Ground* (1982), which begins in 1978, goes back midway to 1960, and concludes in 1980. *The Killing Ground* is a spectacular conclusion to both the Canona cycle and the Beulah Quintet, for here the author makes explicit the connection between the two. In the brilliant first eight pages, the narrator, one Hannah McKarkle, sits in the Howard Johnson Motel of Canona, in the room closest to the site of the house where she grew up, and gazes at the confluence of two rivers. There she imagines an ancient killing ground (hence the title) and dreams of sacrifices in the sacred circle to placate the goddess, the grand mother Earth.[14] At this spot Hannah also imagines Johnny Church and Hannah Bridewell and "the lovely Lily," all characters from the Beulah books.

Through postmodern sleight of hand, Hannah McKarkle in this novel becomes the author of the Beulah Quintet. She has returned to Canona to give a lecture for a fundraiser for an art museum. With this tour de force Settle is able to conjoin the prominent characters of both cycles. Hannah is driven to her speaking engagement by four friends: Daisy, Ann Randolph, Kitty Puss, and Maria—all women who have appeared as young girls in the earlier Canona novels. And all have been romantically involved with Charley Bland.

In a scene reminiscent of *The Clam Shell,* Hannah traverses the same route from her house to the site of the lecture she is to give, but this time in a Cadillac instead of the trolley. She is introduced to the gathering at the old country club as the author of *Prisons, O Beulah Land,* and *Know Nothing,* who is in the process of writing *The Scapegoat.* Because Settle frequently switches narrative points of view, giving interior monologues to each of the friends, the reader learns that Hannah's return as successful author is greeted with resentment and surprise. Hannah's speech is designed to entertain rather than enlighten the audience, so she tells humorous stories about her research that Settle has previously recorded in interviews and essays. But Hannah does not keep the attention of the audience, for while she speaks a whisper is speeding around the room: Charley Bland has hanged himself. Hannah is hurried out of the room and begins the search she has come for, the reasons for her brother Johnny's death in a drunk tank eighteen years earlier.

This curious and self-conscious stylistic device is one that I have previously pointed out as evidence of postmodernism in Settle's work.[15] The convergence of author and protagonist is impossible to overlook, and I am unable to agree with Rosenberg, who notes this peculiarity but insists that it would be incorrect to think of Hannah as anything other than a "fictional construct" (127). Garrett calls this narrative procedure "astonishing, . . . a daring and risky choice but wonderfully efficient" (71, 72).

Settle herself admits only to "autobiographical bits and pieces" in *The Killing Ground*.[16] She defends her narrative strategy as just that, a device by which her narrator would reasonably know about the earlier books. In this extremely complex work, the device succeeds in providing a dramatic and objective focus to what otherwise might have devolved into an opaque interior monologue. Hannah, younger than Settle and more unsure of herself, wins the sympathy and interest of the reader as she searches for and finally discovers the answer to the questions that have inspired the writing of both cycles. If Hannah is a fictional construct as Rosenberg maintains, she is also an autobiographical construct. In this work fiction and autobiography merge in a unique way.

When the Beulah Quintet and Canona Cycle are considered together, as *The Killing Ground* demands that they must be, Settle's accomplishment becomes even more awesome. Through British and American military and political history covering more than three hundred years, through personal domestic and social history covering more than thirty years, Settle has held to her resolve to tell the truth. In the introduction to *Charley Bland,* the "coda" to the Beulah Quintet, Settle announces her purpose, to avoid the "verbosity and self pity" perpetrated by such writers as Thomas Wolfe ([ii]). Doing so means she must tell the truth about literal experience. As Emily Dickinson commands, however, Mary Lee Settle tells it "slant"—transmuting her autobiography into art.

Notes

1. The five novels are *Prisons* (1973), *O Beulah Land* (1955), *Know Nothing* (1960), *The Scapegoat* (1980), and *The Killing Ground* (1982). *Fight Night on a Sweet Saturday* (1960) was revised and included in *The Killing Ground.*

2. "The Search for Beulah Land," *Southern Review,* n.s., 24 (1988): 23.

3. See especially George Garrett, *Understanding Mary Lee Settle* (Columbia: University of South Carolina Press, 1988), and Brian Rosenberg, *Mary Lee Settle's Beulah Quintet: The Price of Freedom* (Baton Rouge: Louisiana State University Press, 1991).

4. Mary Lee Settle, *Addie: A Memoir* (Columbia: University of South Carolina Press, 1998), n.p.

5. Mary Lee Settle, "Mary Lee Settle," Contemporary Authors Autobiography Series (Detroit: Gale Research, 1984), 1:308.

6. Brian Rosenberg and Mary Lee Settle, "Wrestling with the Angel: A Conversation," *Iron Mountain Review* 7 (1991): 10.

7. Mary Lee Settle, "Recapturing the Past through Fiction," *New York Times Book Review,* 12 Feb. 1984, 36.

8. Mary Lee Settle, *O Beulah Land* (Columbia: University of South Carolina Press, 1995), 98.

9. Rosenberg and Settle, "Wrestling with the Angel," 10.

10. Settle, *The Clam Shell,* The Mary Lee Settle Collection (Columbia: University of South Carolina Press, 1995), [ii].

11. Rosenberg and Settle, "Wrestling with the Angel," 10.

12. Settle, "Mary Lee Settle," 316.

13. Settle, introduction to *Charley Bland* (Columbia: University of South Carolina Press, 1996), [ii].

14. Mary Lee Settle, *The Killing Ground* (New York: Bantam Books, 1982), 4.

15. Nancy Carol Joyner, "Cin Cin Nat I: Postmodern Appalachian Fiction," *Appalachian Heritage* 16 (1988): 19–25.

16. Rosenberg and Settle, "Wrestling with the Angel," 10.

THE APPALACHIAN HOMEPLACE AS
ONEIRIC HOUSE IN JIM WAYNE MILLER'S
The Mountains Have Come Closer

DON JOHNSON

The exploration of "felicitous space" undertaken by Gaston Bachelard in *The Poetics of Space* becomes especially poignant when applied to the Appalachian experience. In Appalachia the oneiric house is frequently a rotting cabin in a remote "holler" that loggers or coal miners have abandoned. More often than not only a foundation or decaying chimney remains to mark a homeplace, or, lacking these easily recognizable artifacts, only a bed of daffodils or a hardy apple tree that the careful observer can identify as evidence of earlier habitation. "Abandonment" is a luxury peculiar to rural America, owing quite simply to our culture's emphasis on mobility and to the vast amount of land available for habitation. A deserted cabin in the mountains of Tennessee is different in its essence, however, from the abandoned farm on the Great Plains or the hunter's shack up the canyon from the ghost town in Colorado. Because little productive, arable land as accessible as most old prairie homesteads tended to be lies fallow for extended periods, the farm on the plains is probably still being worked, even though the farmhouse might stand empty. And the hunter's shack sheltered a transient. Even the inhabitants of what is now the ghost town were transients, rootless seekers of fortune, their facades of permanance notwithstanding.

From *Iron Mountain Review* 4 (Spring 1998): 34–36. Reprinted by permission of the author and the publisher. The poems from *The Mountains Have Come Closer* are now included in *The Brier Poems* (Frankfort, Ky.: Gnomon Press, 1997) and are quoted here by permission of Gnomon Press.

For the people of the eastern mountains, a region continuously inhabited by descendants of the original white settlers for over two centuries, the mountain cabin is *homeplace,* and because of the circumstances described above, the effect of its abandonment is especially profound, having both personal and societal implications. Unlike the European, whose oneiric house might have been moved away from, might even have been demolished, the Appalachian can take no comfort in cultural evolution. The European's house might have been built on the ruins of four or five earlier cultures, a fact which argues not for impermanence but for continuity. Thus, when the European recreates the oneiric house in his reverie, his nostalgia, though poignant, is tempered by knowledge that the distance between past and present is almost wholly chronological.

When the Appalachian remembers the oneiric house, on the other hand, such reverie often carries with it a sense of deep loss and dislocation. It frequently engenders grief for the loss of "primal sympathy," but it also provokes a gnawing awareness of the renunciation of a way of life.

The Appalachian's obligation to reclaim his heritage through the recreation of the oneiric cabin is one of the basic themes of Jim Wayne Miller's *The Mountains Have Come Closer.* The volume might be read, in fact, as a Bachelardian manifesto (in the most positive sense of the term) applied to the Appalachian setting. In three of its key poems, "Abandoned," "Born Again," and the ultimate piece, the lengthy "Brier Sermon—'You Must Be Born Again,'" Miller insists that we "inhabit oneirically the house we were born in," that we can resurrect ourselves through the imaginative recreation of that house and the dreams we experienced in it.

A sense of loss pervades *The Mountains Have Come Closer,* a feeling of *homesickness* in the fullest meaning of the term. This feeling extends beyond the loss of childhood things and places to include the emotions one had in and about those places. In "Down Home," for example, Miller's speaker describes how he

> kept meeting feelings like old
> schoolmates, faces whose names he'd forgot.
> He came on feelings he could enter again
> only as a stranger might a house he'd once
> lived in; feelings like places changed almost
> beyond recognition: a once green pasture

field grown up in pines too thick ever to
enter again.
(28)

After noting that he could reclaim only some of those feelings, he laments
his inability to grasp others. He concludes by admitting that

                              he didn't live
here any longer. He was settled in a suburb,
north of himself.
(28)

The equation of home and self is made explicit here. Physical distance and
psychic distance are the same. Homesickness is longing generated by the
absence of familiar, comfortable surroundings, but it is also nostalgia for
the emotions we experienced in those environs and anxiety over the loss of
those emotions. "Not only our memories, but the things we have forgotten
are 'housed,'" says Bachelard (xxxiii). "Our soul is an abode. And by remembering 'houses' and 'rooms' we learn to 'abide' within ourselves. Now
everything becomes clear, the house images move in both directions: they
are in us as much as we are in them."

"Turn Your Radio On" reiterates the sense of disaffection and homesickness found in "Down Home" and defines as clearly as any piece in the volume the "right relation" between the land and those who live on it. In an
urban setting, Miller's alter ego finds it difficult to "hear his own thoughts."
They come only intermittently, through static, as if broadcast from a distant radio station. Struggling to maintain his equilibrium, he pores over
photographs from an old shoebox, focusing on an image of his grandparents
"sitting in splitbottom chairs" on the front porch of their mountain farm:

Weathered and home-made like the chairs they sat in, and like the house
and barn, so comfortably in place, they looked like one another.
Something about the way they sat spoke to him through his own
    thoughts

all the way from the mountains, like a powerful transmitter: this place
belongs to us, their faces said, we belong to it.
(22)

Having established the possibility for renewal in this unifying vision of his grandparents and their place, Miller's speaker explores in poem after poem his efforts to maintain contact with this physical and spiritual home. Most of these poems measure the distance he has come from the homeplace and record the losses he has incurred as a result of his journey; however, most hold out the possibility for bridging that distance, recouping the losses.

"Born Again" is Miller's most explicit statement of the method one uses to restore and maintain connections. The poem is almost a Bachelardian formula, its first three stanzas taking in turn the senses of hearing, touch, and sight.

Each sense translates perceptions, or imagined perceptions, into links with a mountain past. Sometimes "his whorled ear became a seashell / and he heard only correspondences: wind streaming / through the tops of trees was a far off waterfall," for example. A hunter's horn became the "baying of coonhounds," and all these imagined sounds take on a peculiar concreteness, "standing as solid as a bar on a ridge / in the clear air of afterstorm." At times, when his past is particularly elusive, he must content himself with objects (these too imagined) symbolic of that past: "a rusty hinge," "a plowpoint," "a bent nail." In even more difficult times, "his memory clouded" and he would have to wait until his "weather cleared," enabling him to "see some long lost day / as plainly as if it were a shiny quarter / . . . on the bottom of a pool," or a "tin-topped barn / in Sunday morning sunlight" (37).

The poem concludes with an affirmation of the memory's need "to be born again / and again / and again," the repetition affirming Bachelard's notion that "in reverberation, we find the real measure of the being of a poetic image. In this reverberation the poetic image will have a sonority of being" (xiii). While repetition alone can never ensure such "sonority," it serves in this case as an echoing reminder of the images already established, and of their effect on the poet.

Occasionally the speaker's perceptions of his loss overwhelm the imagination's ability to find solace in memory's recreations. "Abandoned" records such an occasion, when

> his mind flew black as a crow
> over hundreds of coves and hollers
> fallen silent since the people were

swept out like rafted logs on spring's
high water.
(46)

In those moments his "life would stand / empty as an *abandoned house* / in one
of those forgotten places" (italics mine). Here the symbol of cultural dislocation and dissolution collapses into the vehicle of the simile. The house is not
a structure from memory inhabited by spirits from the past. Instead, it becomes a metaphor for the life that seeks to incorporate those memories but at
this moment cannot. Bachelard writes that poetic images "give us back areas
of being, houses in which the human being's certainty of being is concentrated and, we have the impression that, by living in such images as these, in
images that are as stabilizing as these are, we could start a new life, a life that
would be our own, that would belong to us in our very depths" (33). In this
poem, however, the house image underscores the futility of some efforts to
found one's present and future on a remembered past.

During these periods of frustration, Miller's speaker

thought there was nothing left
but the life of a half-wild dog and
the shelter of a junked car turned
on its back in a ditch, half grown
over with honeysuckle.
(46)

The combined effect of these two images of the feral dog and the abandoned
car is especially powerful. One image represents the domestication settlers
brought to the mountains, the other the technology which carried those
settlers away. Both are, in this instance, being overtaken by wildness, a fact
which argues against Miller's attempts to reassert the past being seen as
simple primitivism or easy romanticism. The ideal he posits is one of nature
partially tamed by hard work and treated with more respect than rever-
ence. It is an ideal as old as Virgil's *Georgics,* in which man's works are also
constantly endangered by the relentless onslaught of the forces of nature.

"Abandoned" concludes with Miller's reiteration of the abandoned
house image he introduced in the poem's second section. Here the speaker's
life, during moments when his attempts to reintegrate himself with his
past are frustrated, is equated with

the house seen once in a
coalcamp in Tennessee: the second
story blown off in a storm so stairs
led up into the air and stopped.
(46)

Bachelard writes that "the space we love is unwilling to remain permanently enclosed. It deploys and appears to move elsewhere without difficulty; into other times, and on different planes of memory" (53). This observation is supported by a quotation from Jean Laroche's "Memoires d'été," which describes a house that is "Every morning recaptured in dream / Every evening abandoned / A house covered with dawn / Open to the winds of my youth" (54). Both the observation and its illustration expand upon an earlier assertion that "The well-rooted house likes to have a branch that is sensitive to the wind, or an attic that can hear the rustle of leaves" (52). But the house with which "Abandoned" concludes is not conversant with the winds which sweep over it. It has been ravaged by those winds, its psychic energy drawn off and dissipated, and left a truncated shell, an apt metaphor for the life of a poet cut off from his past, uncertain of his future.

The momentary disillusionment (the term should be taken in its most literal sense) of "Abandoned" lends credibility to Miller's case, arguing for a struggle toward reconciliation, not an easy, romantic return to nature. "Brier Sermon—'You Must Be Born Again'" emphatically declares, however, that the return can and *should* be made. Twelve pages long, the "Sermon" is by far the collection's most ambitious piece, and, standing at the end of the volume, it carries the most weight rhetorically. The poem is also the first piece directly attributed to "the Brier" that I have dealt with in this essay. "The Brier" is Miller's alter ego, the enlightened Appalachian who laments what is happening to the world that nurtured him. Although he is not clearly identified, he seems to be speaking in most of the other poems in the volume as well.

The Brier takes as his text "You must be born again," although he very quickly establishes another text which provides the image patterns to support the first. This is Christ's assertion that "In my father's house are many mansions," although Brier quotes only the introductory adverbial phrase, suggesting the complete idea but giving solid emphasis to *house,* which becomes synonymous with heritage. But while he is constantly expanding the cultural implications of his father's house and how his listeners must come home again, the reader never loses sight of the house as memory, a literal base from which all these extended meanings derive. In exhorting his "congregation" to "go home," Brier testifies to his own straying as an example of how the lost can find their way. He says,

> I left my father's house. Oh I was moving.
> But I noticed I wasn't getting anywhere.
> I was living in somebody else's house.
> I kept stepping out somebody else's door
> and the roads I travelled kept winding, twisting,
> had no beginning, had no end.
>
> My own house, heired to me by my foreparents,
> was right there all the time
> yours is too
> but I wasn't living in it. Well, I went home.
> And when I stepped out of my own front door
> when I knew where I was starting from
> I knew where I was going.
> The only road I could go was the road
> that started from my own front door.
> —In my father's house, that's what the Bible says.
> (56)

Bachelard explains the kind of dislocation Brier describes here by saying that "we reach a point where we begin to doubt that we ever lived where we lived. Our past is situated elsewhere, and both time and place are impregnated with a sense of unreality. It is as though we sojourned in a limbo of being" (59). Ironically, it is dreaming, firmly grounded in memory, that reestablishes reality.

It is difficult to quote individual passages from this poem without creating the impression of more or less straightforward polemic on Miller's part. Nothing could be further from the truth, however. "Brier Sermon" incorporates the major elements of a mountain camp meeting, but tempers them with humor, irony, and worldly wisdom. The poem as a whole amply illustrates the Brier's point that accepting one's past does not imply limiting one's future. Accepting foreparents does not mean one has to "think ridge-to-ridge, / the way they did. / You can think ocean to ocean."

Miller's strategy throughout the poem represents sophisticated "ocean-to-ocean" thinking. The Brier, like many lay people in rural America, is moved to preach, but he goes to a street corner in town on a Saturday morning, not to the church on Sunday. Across the street from the Green-stamp Redemption Store, he exhorts passersby to return to their father's house. The genius here lies in the poet's humanization of the ritual, his divesting both the father's house and the notion of rebirth of exclusively religious connotations and remythologizing them in terms of personal and cultural resurrection. By insisting on a return to the father's house Brier invites his listener to retrieve "the best part of yourself," the spirit. Being born again is

> like becoming a little child again
> but being grown up too.
> It's the best of both.
> It's being at home everywhere.
> It's living in your own house.
> (63)

The allusion in "becoming a little child again" illustrates how deftly Miller has turned the tables here. Just as conventional ministers take advantage of their congregations' shared experiences to reinforce the Christian message through parables and personal anecdotes, Miller's Brier depends upon his auditors' thorough knowledge of the Bible to intensify his unorthodox sermon. The result is not so much a secularization as it is a redirection of spirit. His listeners can transform the Christian concept of "my father's house" to the memory of a real place. They can then incorporate the idea of home as found in such hymns as "Softly and Tenderly, Jesus Is Calling," which invite the sinner to "Come home, come home," into an expanded context of memory as refuge. The process involves the transference of the two poles of the metaphor. In Miller's vision the house is an imagined, respiritualized hermitage very *like* the home offered in the traditional hymn or homily.

The Brier ends his discourse by blessing the nearly empty street corner where his listeners have stood. They have deserted him. He steps behind a motor home, and when it pulls away, he is gone. Again Miller anticipates and undercuts any criticism that his speaker is espousing an easy primitivism and advocating a life limited to well water and organically grown corn. Brier is a modern man, at home anywhere because the house of his father has become a living part of his imagination.

The Mountains Have Come Closer explores the implications of the loss of home for the rural Appalachian. Through his collection of poems Jim Wayne Miller demonstrates the universal application of Bachelard's *The Poetics of Space*. The Appalachian cabin, the homeplace, is undeniably Bachelard's oneiric house transplanted to the hollers of Tennessee and North Carolina. Abandoned literally or figuratively, it calls his reader back to inhabit it once more, and Miller says he can take possession of it again, in order to recreate the past and imagine the future. Whether that repossession is accomplished or not, the rotting cabin, the solitary chimney, and the green line of daffodils among the berry canes are haunting presences on the mountain landscape.

Works Cited

Bachelard, Gaston. *The Poetics of Space.* Trans. Maria Jolas. Boston: Beacon Press, 1969.

Miller, Jim Wayne. *The Mountains Have Come Closer.* Boone, N.C.: Appalachian Consortium Press, 1980. (Page references are to this edition.)

THE MECHANICAL METAPHOR

Machine and Tool Images in
The Mountains Have Come Closer

RICKY COX

Ours is a mechanical world. Even in old-time Appalachia, our lives roll by on steel wheels and radial tires. We go out to work in Fords and Toyotas, or farm with Massey-Fergusons. We stuff our woodstoves with the aid of a Homelite, and the soft summer air is alive with the raucous buzz of Weedeaters.

Useful things all, but not the stuff of poetry, at least not Appalachian poetry. Purist students of traditional Appalachia wring their hands and defame these as the very things that are destroying our culture. "They needn't be glorified in print; maybe if we ignore them they'll go away." They won't. As long as there is gas and money to buy it with, we will have our machines, and when they have inhaled their last gallon of hi-test and sipped their last quart of Quaker State we will have them still, cluttering yards and pasture fields, arranged like lawn furniture or concrete bird-baths. We don't know exactly why; we need a poet to tell us, I guess. We need a motorhead poet to explore this morbid fascination with dead machines, although I don't expect ever to see such a person, since greasy fingernails and laptop computers seem to be mutually exclusive. The wait

From *The Poetics of Appalachian Space*, ed. Parks Lanier Jr. (Knoxville: University of Tennessee Press, 1991), 50–57. Reprinted by permission of the author and the publisher.

is made easier by the appearance of the rare observer who sees machines as an integral part of Appalachia and employs the images related to them as a means of literary expression.

Jim Wayne Miller seems to understand our weakness for nuts and bolts, and his grasp, or at least acceptance of, this curious dependency shows itself often in *The Mountains Have Come Closer.* Machine and tool images are present throughout the book and, almost paradoxically, become increasingly stronger and more personalized as the poetry moves through three parts, becoming progressively more "Appalachian," or at least more tightly focused on Appalachian concerns, like outmigration and cultural identity.

"Part One: In the American Funhouse" is relatively general in content and focus. It is aptly titled, as it is American as opposed to Appalachian, universal rather than regional. Machine and tool images appear here, but are, for the most part, neutral, and not strongly identifiable as Appalachian. In the first selection, "Saturday Morning," Miller's house is a ship "plowing gently . . . through a moderate green sea of grass and wild onions" (3). A wonderful image, somehow soothing—as is this from the same selection: "In the garage I turn myself into a hammer. I drive two nails into the wall and hang awhile between them" (4). Cars, boats, and telephones appear in other pieces in Part One but are, most commonly, props—external to the omnipresent "I" who tells us of himself in all but one of the poems in this first of three parts.

"Part Two: You Must be Born Again" brings an abrupt change in point of view. The "I" of Part One has been supplanted by a ubiquitous "he," whom we come to know as the "Brier," a now, or onetime, displaced Appalachian man. A subtler change takes place in the use of machine and tool images as they become more internalized and serve at times as simile and metaphor for the Brier's thoughts and feelings, as he examines himself and his culture throughout Part Two and Part Three.

As these images move closer to the workings of heart and mind, they take on the attendant complexities and begin to reveal feelings about technology as friend or foe in Appalachia. While this question has been raised over and over, it is yet to be answered to everyone's satisfaction. Miller is not the first to experiment with it, as well-meaning romantics have consistently sought to protect primitive mountain society from the corrupting influences of labor-saving devices and machines. At the same time, industrial concerns and even government agencies have worked just as hard to introduce technology, and thus progress, into a region often thought of as economically and culturally underdeveloped in comparison with the rest of the eastern United States.

The literary exploration of this conflict has been a recurrent subtheme in Appalachian literature, with authors siding—by implication if not openly—with one faction or the other. Many seem to regard anything self-propelled as the motorized offspring of the Trojan Horse. No promachine examples come immediately to mind, but Harriette Arnow sets the two sides head to head in the characters of Gertie and Clovis Nevels. Gertie, the heroine of *The Dollmaker,* compels the reader to share her hatred and fear of machines, but her man, Clovis, an inveterate tinkerer, is no less believable as a mountaineer willing and eager to embrace modern industry and home conveniences.

Jim Wayne Miller takes one side, then the other, in Parts Two and Three of *The Mountains Have Come Closer.* The machine and tool images he uses in doing so might be considered with an eye toward the positive and negative implications of machines for life and work in the mountains. The contrast that emerges is interesting in its own right. But what these images may or may not tell us about the attitudes of the Brier or his creator, Jim Wayne Miller, is really not essential to the point I wish to make, which is that machine and tool images are effective as communicators of the so-called Appalachian experience. I look, then, at selected references to machines and tools in "Part Two: You Must Be Born Again" and in "Part Three: Brier Sermon" without trying to be inclusive, or even conclusive, about what is bad or good. My aim is only to point out these images, to recognize them as strong and familiar and therefore a valid part of Appalachian life and literature.

"Brier Visions" offers one of the first tool metaphors found in Part Two: "When he thought hard, his mind became a plowpoint digging in, turning a furrow in his brow" (26). While this is a striking image, it is not un-Appalachian in any sense, for plowing is quite acceptable in a romanticized Appalachia, especially when the plow is pulled by a horse. One may assume that this is the case, for the telltale "gee and haw" appear three lines later (26). The ax and plow handles mentioned in "Down Home" enjoy also this muscle-driven legitimacy (28). Images like these are soothing, almost passive, even though hard physical labor is involved. This sense of calm is shattered, however, in "Set Apart": "Always now he carried a pearl-handled grudge, / snub-nosed, heavy, holstered close to his heart" (34). Guns, too, are an accepted part of Appalachia, but the image is no longer one of peace. Remembrance of the dangerous feel of a handgun is unsettling, and so, too, are the lines, "He drove his mind so hard it sang like whining / wheels rolling high over gaps and gorges / or trestles of determination" (34). Here at last is a machine not chained by the physical limitations of its master, and it seems that Jim Wayne Miller has cast it in an unsympathetic role, hard, cold, unfeeling.

The trend is reversed, though, even before it is established, as the very next poem, "On the Wings of a Dove," offers machine images that are strongly positive. The Brier is relaxing, listening to Bill Monroe and the Bluegrass Boys:

> . . . his mind throbbed and hummed
> like pistons under the hood of a good truck
> hauling his thoughts over a long open highway,
> and the lights on the riverbank got in tune,
> his mind turned into a whining sawblade
> spinning so fast it grew invisible and quiet.
> (35)

I can understand this man. I know the hum and throb of pistons under the hood of a good truck and it is a good feeling; I have been under the spell of a whining sawblade.

Abruptly, the negative image reappears. Junked cars line the creeks in "Every Leaf a Mirror" and "Time swept past roaring like a tractortrailer, / leaving him hatless in a wake of fumes" (36). And then, back to the pleasant, pastoral aura of hand tools in "The Brier Breathing":

> breathing that sang
> easy rhythmical
> a crosscut saw in timber
> breathing short
> shallow
> strokes
> chopping corn
> hoeblade
> clacking in rocks.
> (38)

Within "Part Three: Brier Sermon," machine images find even more intense usage and are strongly polarized around the friend-or-foe dilemma.
"The Brier Losing Touch with His Traditions" is somewhat of an anomaly
in that it deals with machines as machines and bluntly confronts the question of tradition versus technology. Electric lathes and power drills come
away with reputations intact and so cast a tentative vote for acceptance of
modernizing influences. Turning but one page reveals yet another reversal.
The ugly junk car reappears in "Abandoned" (46), and "How America
Came to the Mountains" is fraught with frightening images of motorized
mayhem; the machine comes screaming into the garden:

> it sounded like a train whistle far off in the night.
> They felt it shake the ground as it came roaring.
> Then it was big trucks roaring down an interstate,
> a singing like a circle saw in oak,
> a roil of every kind of noise, factory
> whistles, cows bellowing, a caravan
> of camper trucks bearing down
> blowing their horns and playing loud tapedecks.
> (47)

This image of machines as a plague on Appalachia, though less strident or
awesome, is carried into "Brier Sermon—You Must Be Born Again," the last
selection in *The Mountains Have Come Closer*. Through the persona of the
Brier, Miller talks about boys "with their heads up under cars, / nothing
but their feet a-sticking out, / their hands mucking around in grease and
gears" (57). He is talking to motorheads, to me, reformed, yet still excited
by high-lift cams. The Brier as sidewalk evangelist begins to warm to his
subject, and chastizes the twin-exhaust sect of his transient congregation:

> And I think to myself
> I'd like to open up your heads
> just like you raise the hood or go into a gearbox.
> I'd like to re-wire your heads
> and gap your sparkplugs and re-set your timing.
> (57)

It's a shame that *Hot Rod* magazine doesn't have a poetry corner. These lines say something to people who have no use for poetry about roses. They shine like a new set of Keystones and kick in like a Holley with vacuum secondaries.

While few people who habitually crawl around under cars are likely to purchase copies of *The Mountains Have Come Closer,* I see something wholly positive in Jim Wayne Miller's use of machine and tool images in his poetry. The mere presence of machines and tools in Appalachian poetry is not proof of belonging within the culture. But the fact that these images are so effective in communicating a wide range of thoughts, feelings, and sensations is powerful testimony to the notion that experience of machines and tools is a part of that collective memory which is the essence of any distinctive culture. While the poet may leave to historians the task of evaluating cultural consequences, he is responsible to select images from his own experience that will strike familiar chords in the heart and mind of his reader. I have heard a circle saw singing in oak, and the throb of pistons is a cast iron heartbeat. And when I think hard, my mind becomes a plowpoint.

Kin and Kindness in Gurney Norman's

Kinfolks: The Wilgus Stories

DANNY L. MILLER

While reading an interview with Gurney Norman (conducted by Jerry Williamson) in a 1984 issue of *Appalachian Journal,* I came across a rather daunting and yet also heartening discussion between interviewer and interviewee regarding "English-professor-criticism." At that time Gurney expressed his appreciation for the literary critic. He told Williamson, "If I had energy to invest right now in nourishing anything other than my own work, it would go into pushing the criticism. If I had five hundred extra dollars, I would announce a five-hundred-dollar literary prize for the outstanding critical essay on whoever." Williamson seemed surprised, if not shocked: "You're telling me that a standard English-professor-piece of writing is useful to you?" To which Gurney replied, "Yeah, I really am. Maybe the word 'standard'—I don't know—but yeah, yeah, I definitely am [telling you that]." He went on to say how he was "helped in [his] appreciation of the uses of criticism by reading Annalucia Accardo's essay on *Divine Right's Trip*" and to praise her reading of the book as "most excellent." "My own book was illuminated for me," he said. "That's what criticism does. It's another intelligence being brought to bear on the same subject

Originally published in a slightly different form in *Iron Mountain Review* 8 (Spring 1997): 16–23. Reprinted by permission of the author and the publisher.

and the same material, and by the time the readers and the scholars and the authors are all chewing on the same thing all at the same time, it's like a tribal experience." Williamson was less kind: "Well, I must say your critique of English-professor-criticism sounds like a lucky experience. Maybe I'm harder on English professors as critics than I ought to be, but it seems that rather than making connections a lot of the time, professional literature critics tend to put a wall around what they're saying. Nobody can penetrate their jargon. They don't really seem at all concerned about making this or that piece of writing accessible to the people it was written for" (54–55).

Needless to say, this discussion was frightening for me as I prepared to write just such a piece of "English-professor-criticism" of Gurney's *Kinfolks: The Wilgus Stories.* While I agree with Jerry Williamson that much literary criticism is jargony and incomprehensible, I like to think, like Gurney, that it can be useful and "illuminating." I was likewise daunted because Gurney is a friend of mine, whom I have known and loved and admired for almost thirty years, and it is hard sometimes to write about the works of a friend, even when one's motive, as it should be, is to make a work more accessible to its readers. Reading the conversation noted above put the fear of God in me to write something that would be *illuminating* and *connecting* about *Kinfolks.* If I were submitting my essay to Gurney's hypothetical contest, I wondered, would it be judged a useful one?

But to return to the heartening part of the above discussion, as I prepared this essay I felt that Gurney was on my side as a critic. I did not feel completely intimidated. I teach a course in the short story at Northern Kentucky University, and as a teacher of this genre of fiction I have always stressed the *connections* between reader, writer, and text, the "reader response" approach. I begin each discussion of a story by asking the students to take a few minutes to write down what they would like to discuss about the story—what they found interesting, compelling, mysterious; what questions they have; what elements of the story they would like to focus on. We put these comments on the board, and I use them to direct the class discussion. I use this same method in my Appalachian literature course, in which I have often taught Gurney's *Kinfolks,* and many of my remarks have been influenced by student reactions to the book.

The title of this collection, *Kinfolks: The Wilgus Stories,* announces its two major subjects and themes: kinship and the relationships between members of a family—specifically, by the use of the Appalachian term "kinfolks," an

Appalachian family; and the focus on one particular person, Wilgus Collier. Unlike many other collections of short stories, these ten stories published together in 1977 are unified by this focus on subject and by a focal character. The stories can surely be read individually and each one analyzed separately, but they can also be read collectively as a kind of novel.

First of all, let's look at the subject of "kin"-ship in the stories. All of the stories of the collection are about family and family relationships. The clannishness of the Appalachian family has often been noted. Appalachian clannishness has been looked upon negatively, especially in terms of the feuds of the later nineteenth and early twentieth centuries, such as the famous Hatfield-McCoy feud. One person even referred to the Hatfield-McCoy feud in his review of *Kinfolks* (perhaps part of an "Appalachian" stereotyping): "Recalling the Hatfields and McCoys, the funny, astringent family 'troubles' are told with tough tenderness and a good ear for dialogue" (*Booklist*). But usually this devotion and loyalty to family is seen as a positive characteristic of the Appalachian people. As Loyal Jones says, for example, in his book *Appalachian Values:*

> Appalachian people are family-centered. Mountain people usually feel an obligation to family members and are more truly themselves when within the family circle. Family loyalty runs deep and wide and may extend to grandparents, uncles, aunts, nephews, nieces, cousins and even in-laws. . . . Families often take in relatives for extended periods, or even raise children of kin when there is death or sickness in the family. . . . Blood is thick in Appalachia. Two brothers were talking. One said, "You know, I've come to the conclusion that Uncle Luther is an S.O.B." The other said, "Yeah, he is, but he's our'n." (75)

The major interpretation placed on this clannishness is that "family is family" no matter what—"blood is thicker than water." Families protect and defend one another even if the members do not always agree with each other. Large extended families and a code of family loyalty have been depicted in many works of fiction about the Appalachian people, such as the Tussie clan in Jesse Stuart's *Taps for Private Tussie.* Likewise, there is the clannishness and "code of the hills," which prompts Brack Baldridge in James Still's *River of Earth* to declare that he cannot turn his freeloading relatives out of his house as long as there is a scrap of food to share with them.

The theme of family is introduced in the first story of *Kinfolks*, "Fat Monroe," which sets the stage and the serious-comic tone for the other stories that follow. In this story young Wilgus shows his fierce loyalty to and love of his family, specifically his parents, as he defends them against the mock attack on their honor by the cigar-chomping, practical joking Monroe Short. Monroe Short, "Fat Monroe" of the title, picks up the eight-year-old Wilgus as he hitchhikes a ride home from the movies. Fat Monroe is obviously having some fun with the boy as he teases Wilgus about his name, tells him about his several wives, and gives him a soggy cigar butt after offering him a fresh cigar, among other things. The situation gets somewhat more serious (and perhaps uglier—some of my students accuse Monroe of outright child abuse) when Monroe begins to tease Wilgus about his parents:

> "You know," said the fat man. "It seems to me like I've heard of Glen Collier. Ain't he that fishing worm salesman from over on Leather-wood?"
>
> Wilgus didn't have anything to say. . . .
>
> "If he don't sell fishing worms, what *does* he do? Talk to me now, Short Wilgus, let's get all this said while we've got the chance."
>
> "Daddy loads coal for the Harlowe brothers when there's work."
>
> "And your mommy? How does he treat your mommy?"
>
> "Daddy's real good to us," said Wilgus.
>
> "Well that ain't the way I heard it," said the fat man, and he clucked his tongue and shook his head knowingly. (6)

Wilgus is confused and angry as he is confronted by the somewhat sinister fat man:

> "What do you mean?" Wilgus asked.
>
> "Somebody told me your daddy drunk whiskey, played all his money away on cards, laid out on the weekends and that when he *would* come home . . ."
>
> "That's not so. My daddy's good."
>
> "How often does he beat your mommy up?"
>
> "My daddy's *good*."

"That ain't the way I heard it," said the fat man. "I heard he beat on you and was too sorry to work and that him and your mommy fit one another all the time, that they just fit and throwed things and rassled all over the floor. And that she went out with boy friends and he went out with girl friends and left you at the house all by yourself without anything to eat and no coal for the stove. Now me, I don't blame you for hating a man like that. If *my* daddy had ever treated me like that . . ." (6–7)

Wilgus is indignant and cries out in defense of his parents:

"None of that's so!" Wilgus cried. "I *like* my mommy and I *like* my daddy, and that's the last thing I'm going to say. And I'm going to tell him on you too if you don't hush."
"But *why,* Wilgus? *Why* do you like them? That's the point?"
"Because I just do," said Wilgus. "They're my mommy and daddy ain't they?"
"I don't know," said the fat man. "Are they?" (7)

After Monroe has said these ugly things about Wilgus's parents, Wilgus would like to hit him and is given his chance when Monroe appears to choke and orders Wilgus to hit him on the back. Wilgus begins tentatively to do so and then gains force as he releases all his pent-up anger at what Monroe has said and mercilessly beats him on the back.

When Monroe gets Wilgus to his house, the reader learns that Monroe and Glen, Wilgus's father, are old friends. Monroe laughingly tells Glen that Wilgus is "a pure-god wildcat" (8) and says, "You've raised you a tough 'un there now Glen, I declare you have" (9). Says Glen, "Aye god, don't I know it. . . . You've got to watch out for that Wilgus. He'll beat your ears off if you ain't careful. . . . He's my defender, that boy is" (9). Wilgus's love for his parents and his defense of them is thus the main theme of this first story, and an emphasis on love of family is continued throughout the collection.

In the stories that follow, Wilgus lives with his Collier grandparents in an extended Appalachian family setting, including aunts, uncles, and cousins. Wilgus's love for his family is clearly revealed in these stories, as well as family members' occasional difficulty in expressing love for one another. In the story "The Favor," for example, Wilgus loves his grand-mother so much that he cannot bring himself to tell her the awful news that her husband, Grandad Collier, is leaving her, the favor Grandad asks of young Wilgus. Instead, Wilgus decides that he will never face Grandma again so he won't have to tell her this news. But he cannot abandon her either, so he decides to build himself a cabin nearby and look out for her. He is saved from having to implement his plan by Grandad's unexpected return—he has decided not to leave after all.

Family is also the theme of "Home for the Weekend," one of the funni-est (and yet most serious) stories in the collection. This story, like several of the others, adds a new and realistic dimension to the family relationships among the Colliers. They obviously love each other, but they also love to fight with each other. As one reviewer stated, "Mr. Norman is especially good at writing about the high currents of feeling that perpetually anger and annoy close members of a family" (*New Yorker*). In "Home for the Weekend" everyone fights with everyone else, beginning with what may seem like trivial or insignificant things, such as which are better, Fords or Chevrolets, and escalating to more serious things, such as the consequences of strip mining or the role of John L. Lewis in the UMW. As the family members each remember old debts and call for payback, the tension grows. Grandma Collier starts crying and demands that all the money collected be given to her. She then says she plans to give the money to Wilgus for col-lege. Wilgus's family-centeredness is revealed in his first thoughts about what he will do with the money:

He'd buy watermelons with it. He'd host the entire family at a water-melon feast, outside in the yard. He'd jump in Delmer's Ford and run down to Godsey's store and get four of those big ripe melons just in from Georgia, and they would all gather in the yard and feast on them before they set out for their various destinations later in the day. (74)

"But," Wilgus realizes, "that was a romantic vision, and terribly timed. His relatives had no patience for any watermelon feast this Memorial Day" (74).

At the end of the story, however, the theme of acceptance and love of one's family, no matter what, is reiterated when Wilgus says he is going to use the money to treat his college friends to beers:

He would spend it on beer at the Paddock Club, share his windfall with his writer friends. And as they drank, he would tell them about his family in the hills, describe Memorial Day weekend with the clan. His friends might not believe the stories about his family, but still they would join him in a toast to their benefactors. "To the clan!" Wilgus would say, holding his glass aloft. And his pals would clink their glasses and drink together, and then say, "To the clan!" (74–75)

The reader of this story is perhaps left with the same kind of ironic and paradoxical attitude toward the Collier family as Wilgus seems to convey: are they a comic-strip feuding family to be made fun of by the more "sophisticated" (and "writerly") college students, or are they a loving and giving family to be admired and cheered?

The paradoxical nature of the relationships among the Collier clan—loving and fighting—is revealed in the aptly named story "The Fight," in which Wilgus's aunt Jenny and his Grandma Collier have an actual fistfight, ironically over who can take better care of ailing Grandad. In one of the most humorous scenes of the story Norman writes:

"I'll be glad to calm down," said Jenny. "And while I'm at it I'll just get my daddy and go. Come on, honey," and Jenny took a step toward Grandad.

"You come back here!" Grandma yelled, and she grabbed her daughter by the arm and spun her around. As she turned, Jenny screamed and closed her eyes and swung a big haymaker at Grandma. She only hit her on the shoulder but Grandma made a face like she was half-killed. Without a word Grandma lunged past [Wilgus] with both hands open, reaching for Jenny's hair. Jenny raised her own hands and the women collided heavily, twisted their hands into each other's hair and began to pull and squeal and stumble in an awkward dance around the room. As I [Wilgus] moved in to try to separate them, Grandma backed into the coal bucket and lost her balance. Letting go of Jenny's hair to try to catch herself, she stumbled over backwards and fell harshly to the floor, sending a tremor through the entire house. (50–51)

Jenny, of course, is horrified that she might really have hurt Grandma, and to Jenny's chagrin Grandad comes to Grandma's defense. Jenny insists on

Kin and Kindness in Gurney Norman's *Kinfolks*   147

leaving that afternoon, and Wilgus takes her to the bus station. On the way, Jenny confides to Wilgus that she has made a decision:

> "I've decided to quit worrying about people. I've decided to just let people alone from now on, let 'em get along any way they can and start paying attention to my own life for a change. It seems like, all my life, all I've done is worry about somebody besides myself, trying to do things for people whether they wanted me to or not. And it's never occurred to me that some people might resent that." (53)

Jenny's recognition gives the reader an insight into the basis for many of the fights among the Colliers, not their hatred of one another but their concern for each other, however it might be misconstrued or misapplied.

This theme of family fighting is continued in the last story of the collection, another humorous-serious one, the epistolary "A Correspondence." Wilgus is only briefly mentioned in this story as the means whereby Drucilla Cornett Toliver, living in Arizona, has become aware of her brother Luther back in Kentucky after forty or so years. The letters between Drucilla and Luther are paradigmatic of the family relationships between the Colliers. At first Drucilla and Luther are overjoyed to be reunited after so many years, but after only a few letters between them they begin to fight about who will move in with whom, about their religious/moral values, about which is better—the country or the city—and so on. They can't get along well enough to get together in the first place, let alone live together. But their memories of childhood and family bind them together even over the years and the distance.

In addition to centering on the Collier family and the theme of family relationships, all of the stories in *Kinfolks* are about the character Wilgus. Arranged chronologically, the stories follow Wilgus's growth and maturation from age eight through his early twenties. Throughout these stories the main role that Wilgus plays with his family is that of caregiver—defender, consoler, helper. It is a role that I sum up in the title of this essay as "kindness." It is Wilgus's kindness that defines him as a character, his unselfish concern for his family, individually and collectively. In many ways Wilgus's character is simple; in others, it is more complex. It is no wonder that Anji Hurt, one of my students in an Appalachian literature class in which we were discussing *Kinfolks,* predicted that Wilgus would one day need psychotherapy, a prediction which Anji was gratified to see proved true when Gurney read to our class some of his later Wilgus stories in which a middle-aged Wilgus does in fact undergo therapy. Anji's observation was that Wilgus gives so much and gets so little.

Wilgus is indeed the family caregiver and defender. As we have seen in "Fat Monroe," even as a child of eight Wilgus defends his parents' honor as decent people. In "The Favor" his chief desire as a child of ten or so is to protect his grandmother from hurt. Wilgus is likewise sensitive, caring, and protective of his aunt Jenny in "The Fight." He does not take sides in the fight between his aunt and his grandmother, but rather tries to act as arbitrator between them. After the fight, he drives Jenny to the bus station. Jenny is crying as they leave the house, and Wilgus narrates: "I was keyed up myself, wanting to talk. But I didn't want to impose a conversation on Jenny till she felt more like talking herself. I'd never seen her that upset before and I felt very protective toward her" (52). Jenny, like many others in the stories, does confide in Wilgus. She reveals to Wilgus her own loneliness since the death of her husband, and Wilgus and the readers understand that this loneliness is what has made her want to have Grandad come live with her in North Carolina, not her notion that Grandma isn't treating him well enough.

In "The Tail-End of Yesterday," Wilgus is the caregiver of his Grandad Collier. During most of the story Wilgus stays with his grandfather in the dying man's hospital room. When Delmer's turn comes to stay with his dying father, he is so frightened of his father's death that he can't do it: "Delmer turned pale and came very close to fainting" (65). But Wilgus stays and comforts his grandfather as the old man raves in his final moments about "Furniture! . . . History! Sweet-cold fire!" (66).

Wilgus is caregiver foremost in two stories, "The Revival" and "Maxine." A poignant companion piece to the earlier story "Night Ride," "The Revival" shows a thoroughly defeated Delmer suffering from the effects of a long drunk. Delmer is at his lowest point of physical and emotional defeat. Wilgus comes to his house, gets him to eat, bathes him, and gives him the hope (perhaps false) that his wife Pauline and the children, who have left him, will return on the next day. In addition to providing physical nourishment, Wilgus helps Delmer to feel better about himself. Similarly, Wilgus momentarily helps his cousin Maxine feel better about herself in the story "Maxine."

One of the saddest features of these two stories for me is that Delmer and Maxine both have such very low self-esteem and poor self-images. If

Wilgus is the caregiver, they are certainly in need of care. Even in the ear-lier story "Night Ride," Wilgus's uncle Delmer puts himself down and re-veals his low self-image. When Delmer and Wilgus talk on the slag heap, Wilgus asks Delmer about his meeting with Pauline. Delmer says, "Me and her might get married one of these days" (36). "Yeah," he tells Wilgus, "we didn't act like it much a while ago though, did we? . . . I've tried to tell her I'm a son of a bitch but she won't listen" (36). Wilgus tells Delmer, "You're not a son of a bitch" (36), but Delmer says, "Yes I am too" (36). In "The Revival" Pauline has left Delmer because of his drinking, and Delmer still sees himself as a loser. He admits to Wilgus that he's "bad off" (78) and says, "I guess you know I'm hell-bound, don't you? . . . My soul's blacker'n a piece of coal" (78). When Wilgus tries to get him to eat some-thing to make him feel better, Delmer says, "I don't *deserve* to feel no better" (79) and asserts that Pauline's leaving him is a punishment from God (81). He says that his children are "like little angels to [him]" (83), "But what have they got for a daddy but a damned old devil" (83). Wilgus tries to tell Delmer that he's "not a devil but a good man" (83). Delmer de-cides to sober up and try to do better as Wilgus goes to the phone to call "his aunt Pauline, and try to persuade her to come on home" (86).

Maxine has a similarly low self-image in the story "Maxine." Unable to get her pregnant daughter Cindy to leave her no-account husband Billy Dixon in Detroit, Maxine has returned home full of troubles and hopeless-ness. Wilgus tries to get her mind off her troubles by telling her about his own plans to go to California. When he kindly suggests that Maxine come with him, Maxine reveals her almost suicidal desperation and loneliness. Wilgus says he wants to see the Grand Canyon, but Maxine says, "Lord, honey, don't take me to no canyons. . . . If I's at a canyon I'd dive head first into the damn thing and be done with it" (103). Maxine feels that her life is passing her by—she'll soon be a grandmother and she's stuck in a holler in the middle of nowhere. She'd like to go on a killing spree:

> "I'd shoot Billy Dixon's ass plum off," said Maxine. "And then there's one or two on Bonnet Creek I'd like to kill. Kill me a couple of strip miners. Few sons of bitches over at the courthouse. When it was over I'd shoot myself. Blow my brains out with a big ol' .44." (103–4)

When they get to Maxine's house she tells Wilgus, "This place feels like the end of the world to me" (105). He tries to make Maxine think better about things, but when he tells her she's "wonderful," she thinks, "A left-over piece of shit is all I am" (106). To comfort Maxine, who is now drunk on Mogen David wine, Wilgus prepares her for bed and lies down with her, offering her physical comfort as Maxine dreams of making love with him and "riding away with Wilgus, headed west, somewhere" (107).

Gurney himself has spoken about the condition of loneliness and hopelessness among people today. In an interview in *Appalachian Journal,* discussing the nonlinear, fragmented style of much of his work (like *Divine Right's Trip* and "Crazy Quilt"), Gurney comments:

> The form reflects the times, I think, and the times seem pretty fragmented. In cultural terms, in North America, it is a time of *dis*-integration, and my characters are usually pretty disintegrated. And to seek integration is the quest. That's the impulse, the longing. For one individual person or for a community or a nation or finally a world to knit itself together again. (52)

He goes on to talk about the suffering of people everywhere:

> Boy, I mean people are so lonesome and in such pain. It's just outrageous. Here and there, I gather, there are happy homes and normal life going on, but boy, the untold millions of people living in "single-family" households—that means one poor bastard all alone smoking cigarettes and watching TV at midnight is what that means. It's an epidemic. I think about that a whole lot because that's a symptom of the loss of community. The *collapse* of culture. It's the collapse of all the old binding ties. It's an epidemic in Appalachia as much as it is in Chicago or anywhere else. (52–53)

Referring to his more recent writings, Gurney says, "To account for what it's like to live and struggle to hold on to your sanity in contemporary Appalachia is a central theme" (53), but this statement could just as easily refer to the earlier *Kinfolks.*

Why do these people, these Appalachian people particularly, like Delmer and Maxine (and even to a degree Wilgus, though here I'm thinking of the later Wilgus, not the Wilgus of *Kinfolks*), feel so badly about themselves? One reason, I think, is the economic condition of Appalachia, the blight imposed on the region, the "War on Poverty" mentality. It is not easy to see your once beautiful mountainous countryside turned into a dumping ground. It is not easy to become dependent on welfare assistance. It is not easy to be told repeatedly that you are poor, and therefore worthless; if you're told this often enough, you may begin to believe it and to *feel* worthless. Although not overtly "political," in many ways the *Kinfolks* stories show an awareness of the economic and social blight imposed upon the Appalachian region by the coal industry. The sovereignty of coal is alluded to throughout the stories.

In "Night Ride," for example, Wilgus and Delmer visit the slag heap:

Delmer stopped the car in front of a hillside that was on fire. It wasn't really a hillside burning. It was a slagheap big as a hill, steaming all over, and on fire in a hundred different places. . . . The great mound of burning slag was the refuse of several decades from one of the biggest industrial mines in Kentucky. (33)

In his hospital room, probably on his deathbed, Grandad Collier wonders, after his son Delmer has left the room, "Whose side was he on?" (65), an allusion to the miners' strikes and the song "Which Side Are You On?" In "Home for the Weekend," the family argues about deep mines versus strip mines, and Junior and Delmer argue about whether or not "John L. Lewis had any guts" (69). In "Maxine," as Wilgus drives Maxine home from the bus station, "The road through the Rock Creek Valley was paved but it was so narrow there was barely room for two cars to pass. Every few miles Wilgus had to ease the car half off the road to let a coal truck pass, twenty-ton empties, most of them, the drivers headed home after their last run to the loading ramps at Champion" (101). And Maxine would like to kill the strip miners. So even though these stories are not explicitly about the coal mining industry, the casual references to mining create an impression of the industry's debilitating and destructive effects on the region.

The stories of *Kinfolks* reveal Wilgus's maturation and initiation into adulthood, the continual quest for selfhood and wholeness. As one reviewer stated:

Unlike Norman's first novel, *Divine Right's Trip* . . . , a story of the American counterculture, *Kinfolks* is about growing up in the Kentucky coal country. However, it does resemble Norman's earlier work in its protagonist's gradual progress toward self-discovery. Only nine years old [*sic*] in the first story, Wilgus grows in understanding about himself, the complex personalities of his relatives, and his ties with them, until the concluding story, when, in his early twenties, he leaves Kentucky for Arizona, seeking adventure. However, even there he rents a room from an eastern Kentucky woman, unable to disconnect himself from the web of relationships that tie him to home and family. (*Choice*)

Wilgus's first initiation comes in the first story, "Fat Monroe," when he is confronted by a confusing and somewhat frightening experience and seems to learn something about the nature of adults, even seeing his father in a different light.

In "The Favor," too, he must try to handle a serious problem with maturity and, in fact, seems to do so. I would like to quote at length from an undergraduate student paper by one of the best students in my Appalachian literature class several years ago, Diane Stehle Dix:

> Several passages are key to this story, and it is in these passages that its theme can be discovered. As Wilgus watches his grandfather walk away, he feels, at first, overwhelmed by what he is facing, and his first reaction is to run the other way, as if running away will make it go away. When he later regains his breath, his next feeling is light-headedness and constrictions in his chest as he confronts his task. And finally, as Wilgus's breathing and heart slowly return to normal, the narrator says,
>
>> All along his spine, the purest sense of ease that he had ever known was flowing smoothly. . . . Wilgus felt something fresh inside him. Something was trying to occur to him. What was it? He didn't know. It was a feeling, a sense, that somehow this was it: everything he cared about was now at stake. In his hands. Up to him.
>> The question was whether or not he was up to it.
>> The glory was that he believed he was . . .
>> Suddenly his own mind awed him, he felt so powerful and so wise. . . . [I]f he could be quiet in this rare moment and give this force inside him room to grow, then all he cared about, all the things and people that he knew, would be delivered, safe, and life could then go on and on and on. (15–16)

This tale is one of maturation, and Wilgus, as revealed in these passages, rises to assume the tremendous responsibility which has been handed him; he convinces himself he can manage it. Wilgus the boy becomes Wilgus the young man.

The light tone of "The Favor" brings it to perfection. Gurney Norman's playfulness and sense of humor will not allow Wilgus's initiation tale to be a somber one for long. As soon as Wilgus resolves not to tell Grandma that Grandad has gone (reasoning that as long as she does not know, it has not really happened yet), then decides that he must also disappear (for his Grandma's sake, so she will *never* know), Norman indulges in the boy's celebration of himself. Wilgus rolls and tumbles joyfully in the lake, exhilarated with the responsible decisions he has made and his newfound sense of manhood.

The remainder of the story is quite humorous, and the reader delights in the way this "mature," sensible young man seriously carries out his plans, fully believing in them and their possibility. He decides that rather than running far away he ought to hide nearby so he can secretly "look in on" Grandma from time to time to make sure she is getting along well, as a responsible man should do. He furiously begins to build his house and imagines the way he will live. Of course, this is not funny to Wilgus at all, but an extremely serious matter, and it is the very seriousness with which he carries out his plan which makes it so amusing to the reader. The narrator explains, "Then for awhile he worked on his little rock dam. He'd started it earlier in the summer but hadn't got very far. Now in half an hour he did as much work as he'd done earlier in three or four days" (19). Earlier in the summer, the little dam was a boy's plaything; now, it must be completed because it is a man's resource for survival.

When Grandad Collier suddenly reappears, Wilgus returns to his subordinate status as a young boy, and the story is structured so that it ends by returning everything to its initial state, with one crucial exception. Although Wilgus tells his grandfather he has "just been playing" (20), he has proved to himself that he can think and work like a man. The narrator even calls him "a patient man" (21) at the end, and his maturation process has begun. Wilgus will never again be the same.

Diane's paper is an excellent discussion of Wilgus's maturation in this story, especially her reference to Wilgus's being called "a patient man" at the story's conclusion.

"Night Ride" is the most obvious initiation story, as Wilgus undergoes all the male rites of passage to adulthood—drinking, shooting, sexual discovery, and driving. It is this story, most probably, that some readers of *Kinfolks* find objectionable. In the Williamson interview mentioned earlier, Williamson told Gurney:

> I recently participated on a panel whose function it was to choose books, regional books, to pair with classical books for high school reading, a community reading program. One of the books I suggested was *Kinfolks* by Gurney Norman, because I thought there was no book nicer that addressed the whole theme of community, the values of community. So *Kinfolks* was dutifully read by some of the high school librarians and they said, no, we couldn't have this book because it's got some fornicating in it and some riding around in automobiles drinking whiskey in it and some other things that would be objectionable to our communities. And so they wouldn't allow that book. (56)

Gurney commented that the book had been banned in some parts of east Tennessee (56). "Night Ride" is also the story, I believe, that prompted one reviewer to declare: "The kinfolk bring up Wilgus in the good ol' boy tradition" (*Booklist*). Drinking, driving, and shooting guns may be part of the "good ol' boy" tradition, but, more importantly, "Night Ride" uses these masculine symbols to show Wilgus's initiation into manhood. As in "The Favor," Wilgus assumes responsibility in "Night Ride." After Uncle Delmer passes out, Wilgus drives them fifty miles back home. Some readers may see this as foolish and dangerous, but others know that Wilgus is mature enough and capable enough to drive the car home.

"Home for the Weekend" marks a further stage in Wilgus's initiation into adulthood—he begins to see his family more clearly (perhaps more objectively) with both their comic and pathetic aspects. Significantly, he has begun the process of separation from his family, both physically and emotionally, by going away to college, and he has begun to see himself as a writer. Wilgus continues this separation by heading for California after graduating from college. Whether this part of his initiation—his separation from his family, from his "roots," we might say—is good or bad, we can't really know, but in mythic terms it marks the beginning of the quest.

The journey/quest motif is important to Gurney. In *Kinfolks* his major character Wilgus just begins the separation process that had earlier been described in *Divine Right's Trip*. In an *Appalachian Journal* interview with Gurney, Beth Tashery Shannon commented on the "quest-tale" in *Divine*

Right's Trip and then said, "At the end of *Kinfolks,* too, Wilgus goes off traveling in an almost quest-like way" (20). Gurney replied:

> Ed McClanahan and I have often laughed at the fact that if it wasn't for automobiles and whiskey I wouldn't have anything to write about. So many of the stories in *Kinfolks* are about people in automobiles. I guess it's about wandering, or looking for a home. . . . That means home in a literal sense of a place on the ground, but it also means coming to rest inside one's mind, feeling at home with oneself after a long time of feeling split away from home and alienated from oneself. But it's also the ancient quest for higher consciousness and new knowledge. (20)

For Gurney, this quest "for higher consciousness and new knowledge" not only involves the forward movement outward and things looked for but also all of the things left behind. One's past is part of who one is and what one becomes.

Gurney is very aware of the uses and forces of the past; in the interview with Jerry Williamson, he stated: "It's been important to me to deal with the sadness and the sense of loss of the old life. The life of the grandparents" (53). In the story "Night Ride," for example, an underlying theme is Wilgus's uneasiness about his grandparents back home and their concern and love for him. As Mack Wiseman sings "The Old Folks at Home" on the radio, Wilgus thinks about his grandparents on the farm, possibly worrying about him and Delmer.

> As they rolled along Route 80 toward Hindman, Wilgus looked out the window at the people still working in their gardens in front of their homes along Troublesome Creek. . . . All the people still working after sundown made Wilgus think about his grandparents, who had probably worked through the evening in the garden back at the homeplace. . . . The picture in his mind of his grandmother and grandfather working alone in the last hours of daylight made Wilgus feel a little sad. (27)

As the ride with Delmer continues, Wilgus thinks about "the homeplace again, about how far he was away from it now, away from his grandma and grandad" (29). Additionally, Delmer and Wilgus talk about the Collier family and especially Wilgus's father Glen when they stop at a smoldering slag heap:

For the next hour, or two, or maybe even three, Delmer and Wilgus sat by the slag heap drinking and shooting the pistol at the little pools of fire winking at them in the darkness. And in the intervals between the great explosions of the gun they talked . . . about their family, about the old days among the Colliers on Trace Fork. They talked about their relatives who had died. Delmer asked Wilgus if he ever thought about his father much. (35)

Wilgus says he thinks about him, and Delmer tells Wilgus, "He sure was a good old boy. . . . He was the best one of us, that's for sure" (35).

In this same interview, Williamson asked Gurney about the need for storytellers in a society: "What is the good of a story? I'm serious" (59). In reply, Gurney discussed the shamanic role of the storyteller in the community and the shaman's *healing* function:

I was reading in some account about the way in which the shaman would treat mental illness in some of the primitive tribes on the western plains of North America. You have—let's say—someone in the tribe who's having a nervous breakdown, a psychological crisis. Well, then, it's time to call in the story-teller or the shaman, and the healing of the mentally ill person is brought about when the story-teller places the sick person on a bed in the lodge, and the family is summoned, and the community gathers and surrounds the sick person and focuses its energy upon the person who is lost and doesn't know where he is. (59)

In many ways this recalls the role of Wilgus for his uncle Delmer in "The Revival," and Wilgus, in fact, *is* the writer, the storyteller and healer. Gurney went on to discuss the importance of the past in the healing process:

and then the story-teller begins to tell the ancient story from the beginning, which means he tells the creation myth. Someone in the community must always be in the archetypal role of the story-teller . . . and he keeps telling the story until he comes down through time and begins to refer to known ancestors of this person, the great-grandfathers and grandmothers and then the grandparents. (59–60)

The storyteller continues to tell the sick person about his parents and then the sick person's own life, right on up to the time—"Yes, just here lately you haven't been feeling well, and you flew off in your mind." And the person is talked back from the lost place, psychologically, through this process, and that is the story-teller in a cultural role at its most archetypal. *That* is the function of story and of story-teller today. The story-teller opens the old channels of memory so that he has a renewing function to remind, or *re-mind,* to renew the mind of the listener or the audience, to make sure that the audience remains in continuity, in *continuous feeling association,* with what has gone before. (60)

"What has gone before" is what makes us what we are. Wilgus, in the stories in *Kinfolks,* is a young future-artist assimilating the forces of life around him, his family, his community.

Works Cited

Booklist, review of *Kinfolks: The Wilgus Stories,* by Gurney Norman, 15 June 1978, 1602.

Choice, review of *Kinfolks: The Wilgus Stories,* by Gurney Norman, May 1978, 401.

Dix, Diane Stehle. "Analysis of a Short Story by Gurney Norman." Unpublished paper written 25 Apr. 1989 for my Appalachian literature class at Northern Kentucky University.

Jones, Loyal. *Appalachian Values.* Ashland, Ky.: Jesse Stuart Foundation, 1994.

New Yorker, review of *Kinfolks: The Wilgus Stories,* by Gurney Norman, 5 Dec. 1977, 241.

Norman, Gurney. *Kinfolks: The Wilgus Stories.* Frankfort, Ky.: Gnomon Press, 1977.

Shannon, Beth Tashery. "An Interview with Gurney Norman." *Appalachian Journal* 6 (Autumn 1978): 16–28.

[Williamson, J. W.] "Interview with Gurney Norman." *Appalachian Journal* 12 (Fall 1984): 44–60.

"THE PRIMAL GROUND OF LIFE"

The Integration of Traditional and Countercultural Values in the Work of Gurney Norman

TIMOTHY J. DUNN

As it was for the rest of the country, 1960 proved a watershed year in the life of Kentucky writer Gurney Norman.[1] In Lexington, where Norman was completing work in creative writing at the University of Kentucky, civil rights activists were staging public protests and sit-ins at downtown lunch counters. At the same time, Norman's hometown of Hazard, Kentucky, was a center of labor controversy between coal mine operators and striking coal miners. In the spring of 1960, Norman was awarded Stanford University's prestigious Wallace Stegner Creative Writing Fellowship. He moved to the San Francisco Bay area, arriving soon after the student protests in downtown San Francisco of hearings by the House Un-American Activities Committee. At Stanford, Norman studied writing under writer and critic Malcolm Cowley and Irish short story writer Frank O'Connor. Cowley had lived among the American expatriate writers in Paris after World War I. The author of *Exile's Return* (1934), Cowley served as literary editor of the leftist-radical *New Republic* from 1929 to 1944. In the 1930s, he traveled to Norman's home region of eastern Kentucky with other prominent writers to observe conditions of striking coal miners who were

A version of this essay appeared in the *Journal of Kentucky Studies* 12 (Sept. 1995): 111–18. Reprinted by permission of the author and the publisher.

trying to unionize. In the 1950s, Cowley was Jack Kerouac's editor and champion at Viking Press, which published *On the Road* in 1957.

While at Stanford, Norman spent much of his time on Perry Lane, a short tree-lined street near the Stanford campus that was home to an eclectic community of graduate students, artists, writers, beats, and bohemians. The radicalization of American culture in the late fifties and early sixties included a renaissance in folk music and a renewed interest in bluegrass music and the music of labor and protest. Norman had anticipated some adjustment to Stanford, but found instead "a politicized atmosphere" that was familiar and welcoming in many ways. After Stanford, Norman served two years in the U.S. Army. In early 1964, he returned to Hazard to work as a reporter for the weekly *Hazard Herald* as President Lyndon Johnson's War on Poverty began. Two years later—in the tradition of Jack Kerouac, beat poet Gary Snyder, and other counterculture writers—he traveled to Oregon to work for the U.S. Forest Service as a fire lookout in the Mt. Hood area of the Cascade Mountains. In late 1967, Norman returned to the Perry Lane neighborhood and became involved in the Free University movement. In 1969, he worked as a reviewer and editor for *The Whole Earth Catalog,* "the counterculture's Bible." Norman's novel of the counterculture, *Divine Right's Trip,* was first published in *The Last Whole Earth Catalog* in 1971.

Norman's personal sojourn was set against a larger backdrop of cataclysmic change for the nation and the planet (or the Whole Earth, if you will). The 1960s saw the rise of antiwar protests, the burgeoning "green" movement, student activism, Eastern mysticism, psychedelic drugs, and a great deal of artistic experimentation that came to be understood generically (and ultimately self-consciously) as "the counterculture." A particular type of idealism fed this movement and sprang from it as well. Michael McClure recently said that these were a "new people . . . pro-nature, pro-consciousness, pro-liberty" (quoted in an advertisement for the boxed set of four compact discs from Fantasy Records entitled "Howls, Raps & Roars: Recordings from the San Francisco Poetry Renaissance," 106). At the time, the editors of *The Last Whole Earth Catalog* affirmed the belief in "the power of the individual to conduct his own education, find his own inspiration, shape his own environment, and share his adventures with whomever is interested" (Brand, 1). Even the troubles in coal country offered the opportunity for idealism in the form of community-centered activism on the grassroots level. In sum, there seemed to be a convergence of cultural forces and events, both at home in Kentucky and wherever the road took him, that confirmed and encouraged Norman's own innate idealism as it found its shape in his writing.

In Norman's work, idealism is a quality of the hero, characterized by a restlessness of spirit that leads to the journey, and by a compulsion to create or discover a place to which the spirit tends and from which it draws its sustenance. For Norman, that place is eastern Kentucky. In the late 1980s and early 1990s, Norman wrote and presented onscreen three documentary films in collaboration with filmmaker John Morgan for Kentucky Educational Television (KET). *Time on the River* and *From This Valley* explore the landscape and social history of the Kentucky and Big Sandy River valleys. *Wilderness Road* follows Daniel Boone's trail across the Appalachian Mountains through the Cumberland Gap to Kentucky. In Boone's time, rumors had spread through the settled parts of the Appalachian frontier of an Edenic land beyond the mountains to the west. Boone spent two years, 1769–71, exploring Kentucky and pronounced it "a second paradise." In his fiction, Norman celebrates the effort to create again the promise of what Daniel Boone first saw. In Norman's mind, heroism takes the form of engagement and commitment to place and to ideals associated with place.

Modern-day heroes do not, in Norman's fiction, discover Kentucky, but rediscover it and reclaim it and its potential. Norman quotes Joseph Campbell's *The Hero with a Thousand Faces* in one of the epigraphs for *Divine Right's Trip.* Campbell found that "[the] effect of the successful adventure of the hero is the unlocking and release again of the flow of life into the body of the world." The heroes of Norman's fiction return to their homes, seeing them anew and restoring the sum and substance of their potential in both a literal and spiritual sense, redeeming both the place and the heroes themselves. And Norman's work itself undertakes this project with the tools of Appalachian story and language, as he states in "When and What Is the Appalachian Region?": "The words also function as windows through which we may view the whole world as citizens of not just our local place or state or valley, but the very planet itself" (18). Norman's fiction, therefore, takes character, author, and reader through the processes of rediscovery and redemption to a new wholeness and integrity of identity, and serves as model for the larger redemptive project.

In *Divine Right's Trip,* Norman's unlikely hero Divine Right Davenport (D. R.) travels east with his girlfriend Estelle in his VW microbus, Urge, absorbing the "new consciousness" of the sixties. He learns and experiences a great deal that is worthwhile; but as his travels continue, he loses his sense of self and control of an older consciousness that would offer him a spiritual and emotional center. At the end of the novel, however, D. R. returns in Urge to Trace Fork, Kentucky, summoned to care for his father's brother Emmit, who is dying. The call for D. R. comes from God, as recounted in the section entitled "The Lord Works in Mysterious Ways":

> around eleven the phone rang and woke him up and when it turned out to be God Himself calling to summon D. R. to Kentucky, alertness spread through him like a rush. God was calling in the guise of Mrs. Godsey, Uncle Emmit's neighbor down in Finley County, but Divine Right had no doubt who it really was. Her high, nasal voice was certainly a strange one for such a weighty summons, but the Call was clear and unmistakable. (171)

At this point in the narrative, D. R.'s psyche is fragile. But without hesitation he tells Mrs. Godsey he'll come to Finley County immediately, and Mrs. Godsey observes that "it's sure a Christian act for you to come" (173). D. R.'s response to God's summons is one that embodies the heroic duty to which the epigraph by Campbell speaks. The instinctive immediacy of D. R.'s response also seems to speak to a level of enlightenment that is the goal of both traditional Christian belief and the Eastern-influenced consciousness of the sixties that D. R. discovered through his physical, spiritual, and psychedelic journeys. There is an implicit leap of faith that involves little intellectualization or examination. D. R. returns to Trace Fork, experiences an emotional breakdown, and then spends three days with his Uncle Emmit before the older man dies (222–34).

In spending those three days with his uncle, D. R. begins to discover and reclaim a sense of self that will serve as foundation for the work he will do for himself and his community. In a very important sense, he is reborn. After Emmit's passing, D. R. begins to build on that foundation. First, he helps dig Emmit's grave and, after the other gravediggers have left, he climbs into that hole in the family cemetery to feel Emmit's spirit and to remember his father, reconnecting to the earth and to his ancestors (237–40). Then he discovers "a vast, private joy" in planning and preparing the funeral with the help of Emmit's neighbors (242), and in connecting with the community and his family. Because of this joy, and because of the strength he draws from his new connections that makes it possible for him to create a new sense of self, D. R. decides to remain at Trace Fork in his uncle's home and to take on and expand Emmit's "scheme to save the world with rabbit shit" (255).

That scheme represents the convergence of sixties idealism and the possibilities of the rural landscape, as well as Norman's penchant for playfulness. Emmit has started to reclaim the landscape of his home, repairing the ravages caused by the strip mining endemic to the region. In a year's time, he has built a herd of rabbits from a single buck and two does. His neighbor Leonard tells D. R. that Emmit would occasionally eat a rabbit, but he kept them for the manure they produced. He spread that organic matter on the barren earth behind his barn and soon "he had redeemed a patch twenty by ten," big enough for a small garden (278–79). Emmit had also built a worm pit:

> He'd built it when he first got his rabbits, filled it with manure and stocked it with five thousand red worms he'd ordered through the mail. A year later there were so many worms in it he was scooping them out by the pitchfork full and planting them in the garden rows to go to work on the mulch of shit and hay. (280)

This is exactly the kind of scheme that the editors of *The Whole Earth Catalog* envisioned for the reclamation of the planet, and D. R. embraces it wholeheartedly. "Our purpose," he writes to his friend Anaheim Flash, "is soil redemption. Salvation! . . . we'll breed ten thousand rabbits and twenty million worms, and make this dead old hillside bloom" (284). By taking up what his uncle has left him, D. R. finds a new space and a new version of an old vision. He discovers in this new business he calls "the Magic Rabbit" an opportunity to renew "the flow of life" (to use Campbell's phrase), both in the literal sense of restoring the land and in the spiritual and personal sense of recovering his own individual power. Most importantly, D. R. reclaims a place in the world for himself, with connections to his ancestral past and to the community of friends and neighbors. In "The Land as Therapy," Harry Caudill has said that recovering and transforming the landscape "will provide a strong new bond between an American family and the vast rich continent their ancestors so precipitously cleared" (64). D. R.'s rabbit farm and his rediscovered sense of self establish a place, a context, for that new bond, both for D. R. himself and for others.

D. R.'s enthusiasm for the reclamation project and the strength and will he finds to carry that project through come from several sources, and all these come together at the end of the novel in D. R. and Estelle's wedding ceremony. Their hippie friends from California and local members of the Trace Fork community gather together to celebrate their marriage. It is at this point in the novel that we see the idealism and the values of both communities or cultures merge and become as one. As Jim Wayne Miller has put it, we see how "Appalachian values and customs parallel the freaked-out California counter-culture" ("Appalachian Literature," 87). The hippies and "the leather and denim freaks" of the counterculture espouse the value of doing their own weaving and making quilts, of having babies at home, and of ginseng as "the answer to about half of mankind's problems." The locals pass no judgment on the fact that these young people are coming back to what they might call "the old ways." Mrs. Thornton simply says, "I had all my younguns at home, tended by a granny-woman. Old Aunt Dicey Pace from Turkey Creek" (297). "Shoot," says Elmer the mailman. "My daddy picked 'sang for a living, when I was a boy. It's as native to these hills as it is to over yonder in China" (297–98). The identities of the two communities intermingle in a powerful utopian moment on D. R.'s family homeplace.

No comparable countercultural polemic informs Norman's collection of short stories entitled *Kinfolks: The Wilgus Stories,* at least not explicitly. Wilgus Collier does not go off on the literal journey of heroic self-actualization that Divine Right Davenport does. But the Wilgus stories are just as concerned with "the flow of life" and with the sense of self as *Divine Right's Trip.* There is an implicit idealistic belief in the power of the individual and a celebration of that individual's potential in the world. In addition, there is a need for movement and a need for return in *Kinfolks* as in the earlier novel.

Kinfolks actually begins with a return, a return to Trace Fork, home of D. R. and home to Wilgus Collier and his family. In "Fat Monroe," eight-year-old Wilgus is trying to get home after having seen the Saturday matinee. He is picked up by "a big fat man" in "a dusty pickup" (1–2) who, after the boy settles in, asks Wilgus his name. When Wilgus gives it, the man pretends to hear "Monroe Short" (3), and this begins an exchange in which the man raises questions about Wilgus's name, age, marital status, family history, and parents' reputations as upstanding people (4–7). In short, Wilgus's identity is called into question. The man's remarks about his parents get the boy so upset that when the man starts coughing and tells Wilgus to pound him on the back, Wilgus willingly does so, over and over, getting so carried away that "with both hands he beat the fat man with all his might" (8). When Fat Monroe's truck finally stops in front of the Collier homeplace, Wilgus is so disoriented he barely recognizes his own father when he sees him:

> Wilgus' father looked strange without a shirt on. It was strange to see him in the daytime without coal dust on his face. He was clean and shaved, and he'd got a haircut somewhere that day. His father looked so different that in some ways Wilgus didn't recognize him. The light refracting off the windshield seemed to curve him. (9)

By the end of this first story of the collection, Wilgus's perspective has been challenged and the world is no longer simple. However, one thing is clear: he has a duty to his family. In the last sentence of "Fat Monroe," he runs to find his mother (9).

In the next story, "The Favor," Wilgus is two or three years older and his parents have died. Wilgus lives with his grandparents. The favor of the title refers to a request of his grandfather: the old man says he is leaving his wife, leaving the county and even the state, and he wants Wilgus to take that message to his grandmother. He hands Wilgus one hundred dollars to give to her. After the grandfather walks away toward the railroad, Wilgus flees into the woods and across the fields to a little creek where he can find some peace of mind. Here, Wilgus begins to get a sense of his power and responsibility:

> He felt his heart regain its calm and easy rhythm. All along his spine, the purest sense of ease that he had ever known was flowing smoothly.
>
> Lying there, feeling the rock beneath him, hearing the water flowing past his head . . . Wilgus felt something fresh inside him. Something was trying to occur to him. What was it? He didn't know. It was a feeling, a sense, that somehow that was it: everything he cared about was now at stake. In his hands. Up to him.
>
> The question was whether or not he was up to it.
>
> The glory was that he believed he was.

Wilgus was amazed that such a feeling was growing inside him. Suddenly his own mind awed him, he felt so powerful and so wise. (15)

Wilgus finds he has the power to keep his grandmother in the dark about her husband's flight. In fact, if he doesn't tell his grandmother, it's as if it never happened. Wilgus decides to live on the farm at the creek near his grandmother so he can care for her. He begins to make a place for a cabin beside the creek, clearing away underbrush and carrying stones for a foundation and a chimney. He begins, in fact, what D. R. Davenport has begun at the end of *Divine Right's Trip:* he begins to create a space for himself where he can do the most good. This is how his grandfather finds him upon the older man's return. His grandfather has decided to return, and Wilgus could do him a favor and not tell his grandmother that he left. It seems almost as if Wilgus brought the man back. It's a power that the boy doesn't understand, but he doesn't mind because he feels that "just knowing that one day he would know was quite enough for now" (21).

For the rest of the collection, the pattern of departure and return evolves as Wilgus's sense of his own power and identity develop. In "Night Ride," at age thirteen, he learns to drive and takes his drunken uncle Delmer home. As he grows older, Wilgus becomes the family's source of stability and permanence, holding things together, comforting the weak and the sick, tending to the dying. Wilgus is not as animated or as brash as D. R., but in his own level-headed, almost serene manner, he is just as idealistic: he recognizes the goodness around him and recognizes his own responsibility for nurturing that goodness. As Wilgus's world fragments more and more, he understands and acts upon his understanding of his own role in that world.

Recognition often is coupled with a particular and resonant part of the Appalachian landscape of eastern Kentucky. In "Night Ride," Wilgus and his uncle visit the burning slag heap where Wilgus's father, Glen Collier, piled slate when he worked for the Blue Diamond mine. "The slate we dug," says Delmer, "went on that very pile yonder. It was on fire then and there it is, still yet burning. That's something to think about" (34). The permanence of the pile is connected with Wilgus's memory of his father and, by extension, his sense of connection with the land and with his family. In "The Fight," Wilgus is driving his Aunt Jenny to the bus station after a terrible fight with her mother, Wilgus's grandmother, when they stop on the top of Black Mountain:

On a clear day you can see for miles . . . across the tip of southwest Virginia, into Tennessee. . . . Up where we were there was plenty of daylight left, but in the enormous valley below, Black Mountain's shadow was spreading rapidly across the rows of smaller hills, and here and there patches of evening mist were beginning to form and rise. Jenny gazed into the distance, and as she did, for the first time that day I had the feeling she was relaxing a little. The flesh around her mouth loosened, and she looked instantly younger for it. Her breathing became slow and even. (52–53)

In places like Black Mountain, the slag heap, Wilgus's cabin site in the woods, his grandparents' home, the kitchen where his grandmother cooks, the bedroom where his grandfather is dying, Wilgus and his family draw the peace and strength they need to do better. Family is often a source of torment, but it is also a source of real goodness, a goodness that keeps drawing its members back. Norman has stated that he and his friends and colleagues from the region understand the landscape of Appalachia "as a homeplace, and write about it, and read about it, and then, at least in my own case, travel around it restlessly, visiting the old places that remain, seeking out our family" ("Where and What," 17). Here again the author, his characters, and his readers find themselves coming to the material of Norman's texts with the same impulses and the same mission.

At the end of the story "Maxine," Wilgus leaves for the west. His cousin Maxine says she's afraid she'll never see him again: "Maxine made her remark jokingly but Wilgus was serious when he answered. 'No,' he said. 'I'm coming back'" (102). The collection ends before he returns, but in *Kinfolks'* final story "A Correspondence," Wilgus reunites his landlady in Phoenix with her longlost brother in Kentucky. The brother is ready to roam and the sister ready to return, resulting in discord between the two. Their correspondence ends in a fractious "we just as well forget the whole thing" from Luther and a curt "Suit yourself" from Drucilla (118–19). But it is difficult to believe that is the end of it when Wilgus Collier is staying in Drucilla's upstairs apartment. Norman has said that Wilgus's departure from Kentucky at the end of *Kinfolks* marks the beginning of a stage in his life in which "he can learn to regard all of his culture as a family and begin to function as an artist in ways that may help restore some of the sense of unity that has been lost" (Norman interview with William Grant, 37). In Norman's fiction, the processes of disintegration lead, inevitably, it seems, to rediscovery, reclamation, and ultimately reintegration of self and community.

The last two words of *Kinfolks*—"Suit yourself"—touch upon the theme of individualism in the stories. The characters create a sense of self and build their worlds around this sense to satisfy their needs. But these same characters inevitably come to an understanding of the world that is communal as well as individual. They understand and act upon the recognition that connections to our immediate and ancestral places are integral components of our identity. "Home is our refuge and strength," Norman has said, "a place we love, and want to protect and nourish, even as it nourishes us" ("Where and What," 18). Characters like D. R. and Wilgus are healers and caretakers who seek to renew the "connection with the primal ground of life" (interview with Grant, 38). They are young idealists who work to restore the health and integrity of their families and communities and to reclaim the optimism of the region. In *Divine Right's Trip* and *Kinfolks,* Norman expresses his utopian visions, shaped by his native culture of the eastern Kentucky mountains, the counterculture of California, and the social movements of the 1960s. Jim Wayne Miller has said that "Norman is traditional in the true sense of the word. . . . His traditionalism is not static, but dynamic" ("Living Into the Land," 69). Informed by their travels and their times, rediscovery of tradition offers life and cohesion and value to Norman, D. R., Wilgus, their friends and families, and to the readership that takes their lives and lessons to heart.

Note

1. Biographical discussion in the first three paragraphs is based on a personal interview with Norman, 24 Feb. 1994.

Works Cited

Advertisement for "Howls, Raps and Roars: Recordings from the San Francisco Poetry Renaissance." *Fantasy Catalog* 1994, Fantasy, Inc., Berkeley, Calif., Classic and Original Blues and Jazz Recordings. 106.

Brand, Stewart, et al., eds. *The Last Whole Earth Catalog.* Menlo Park, Calif.: Portola Institute, 1971.

Caudill, Harry. "The Land as Therapy." In *A Gathering at the Forks: Fifteen Years of the Hindman School Appalachian Writers Workshop,* ed. George Ella Lyon, Jim Wayne Miller, and Gurney Norman. Wise, Va.: Vision, 1993.

Miller, Jim Wayne. "Appalachian Literature." *Appalachian Journal* 5 (Autumn 1977): 82–91.

———. "Living into the Land." *Hemlocks and Balsams* 9 (1988–89): 59–73.

Norman, Gurney. "A Conversation with Gurney Norman." With Anne Johnson. Appalshop, 1991.

———. *Divine Right's Trip: A Novel of the Counterculture.* Frankfort, Ky.: Gnomon, 1971.

———. "From This Valley." Dir. John Morgan. Kentucky Network (KET), 1989.

———. Interview with William E. Grant. *Adena* 3 (Fall 1978): 26–44.

———. *Kinfolks: The Wilgus Stories.* Frankfort, Ky.: Gnomon, 1977.

———. Personal interview. 24 Feb. 1994.

———. "Time on the River." Dir. John Morgan. Kentucky Network (KET), 1987.

———. "Where and What Is the Appalachian Region?" *Mountaineer Times* 9 (Spring 1994): 16–18.

———. "Wilderness Road." Dir. John Morgan. Kentucky Network (KET), 1991.

"Roving Pickets 1961–65." Dir. Anne Lewis Johnson with Buck Maggard. Appalshop/Headwaters, 1991. Gurney Norman, humanities adviser.

John Ehle and Appalachian Fiction

LESLIE BANNER

In the pantheon of American myth, two figures hold undisputed sway: the cowboy and the Southern Appalachian mountaineer. These two are the acknowledged icons of our national identity because they are associated with America's two great frontiers: the western plains and the eastern wilderness of Appalachia. Forever alive in the popular imagination, the cowboy and the mountaineer embody the quintessential characteristics of the American experience: rugged individualism, ready violence, and a special connection to space and time that forever tells the one to keep moving westward, ahead of fences and preachers and schoolmarms, while telling the other to stay where he is, locked in the isolated mountain fastness that protects his independence from revenue agents, missionaries, and scribbling tourists on horseback.

I won't attempt to trace the mythologizing of the cowboy here, but I would like to review briefly the development of the figure of the mountaineer in American literature in order to demonstrate just what it is that John Ehle has done to counteract the widespread debasement of one of our most important representative American types.

The Southern Appalachian mountaineer burst into the consciousness of the American public in 1884 with the publication of a volume of short stories, *In the Tennessee Mountains,* by Mary Noailles Murfree. The book was phenomenally successful, going through eighteen editions in three years,

Originally published in a slightly different form in *Iron Mountain Review* 3 (Spring 1987): 12–19. Reprinted by permission of the author and the publisher.

and today most critics and historians would agree with Henry D. Shapiro that the credit for convincing America that Southern Appalachia was "a strange land inhabited by a peculiar people" should go to Murfree.[1] Some forty years later, in the first major sociological study of the mountain people, *The Southern Highlander and His Homeland,* John C. Campbell found it necessary to warn his readers that the Southern Appalachian region was, at that time (1921), "a land about which, perhaps, more things are known that are not true than of any part of our country."[2]

Campbell was responding to the need for public recognition that Appalachia's population comprised a diverse people who needed more from the rest of America than "revenooers," blueback spellers, and socially acceptable forms of religion. Campbell knew that scores of missionaries had come into the mountains to "do good," their concept of doing good based on the mountaineer they knew primarily from the fiction of Mary Noailles Murfree and her followers in local color fiction.[3] Campbell was concerned with presenting an accurate picture of the real Southern mountaineers so that something could be done for *them* as opposed to the corncob-pipe-smoking, still-stoking stereotype America believed in. To counteract the image Murfree created, Campbell packed his excellent volume with an impressive array of charts, tables, and photographs, statistical breakdowns of the population, learned descriptions of geography and mores—in short, with the concentrate of a lifetime of devoted work in the field and scholarly research—an amount of ammunition that is a tribute to the imaginative powers of Mary Noailles Murfree, the little lady from Nashville, Tennessee.

Yet to be fair to Murfree, her literary Southern mountaineer was not entirely wrong. Incomplete, surface, limited, non-differentiated—but not wrong, for prior to the coming of the coal mines and lumber camps, the First World War, TVA and the Great Smoky Mountains National Park, the people of the Southern highlands had more in common with each other than with the inhabitants of those areas of their individual states lying outside the mountain region. They did possess a homogeneity within Appalachia that made true the composite picture presented by Murfree and numerous other touring writers in that this picture acknowledged the existence of a group of mountain people distinguished by certain traits related to their environment.

Thus, if no one mountaineer born of woman ever said "you'ens," "we uns," and "bodacious" in the same sentence; carried on a fifty-year-old feud; married a fourteen-year-old girl; fathered fifteen tow-headed children and one "eejit"; brewed blockade liquor, plowed an incline cornfield, got saved at camp meeting by the circuit rider, and all this while sitting motionless on a rail fence—well, no matter: sometime, somewhere, some mountaineer did one or more of these things, and with the possible exception of feuding, he was as likely to do them in Carolina as in Tennessee, or Southwest Virginia, or anywhere else in the Southern Appalachian chain.

It is worth noting that this prototypical mountaineer, so firmly established in the consciousness of all succeeding generations of American writers and readers, was based on Murfree's observations of the mountain people of the Great Smoky Mountains country of East Tennessee and Western North Carolina. Remarkably, she completely characterized this mountaineer in her first volume of stories and established certain literary conventions as well, conventions that are still observed today. The most important of these is her use of the landscape, not as a geographic reality, but rather as something with which to conjure atmosphere and to explain character. In Mary Murfree's stories and novels, the Appalachian wilderness is largely impressionistic; as one critic has said, "Her wild scenery is Alpine in ruggedness; its distinctiveness lies in the vivid painting that makes Chilhowie, Big Injun, or T'other Mounting a mysterious force brooding over and dominating the human figures."[4] Mary Murfree was not bent on botanical discovery. Instead, she contributed to Appalachian fiction the important concept of the mountains as a vital psychological force in the lives of the mountaineers. Interestingly, she most often communicated this idea as a reflection in the faces of the people. Typical is her description of a mountain man in her story, "A-Playin' of Old Sledge at the Settlemint." Budd Wray's expression is one "of settled melancholy . . . very usual with these mountaineers, reflected, perhaps, from the indefinable tinge of sadness that rests upon the Alleghany [sic] wilds, that hovers about the purpling mountain-tops, that broods over the silent woods, that sounds in the voice of the singing waters."[5]

Murfree's environmental impact statement is vague, only suggestive of the idea that the identity of the mountaineer is in some essential way affected by the presence of the mountains.[6] But it is recognizable as the beginnings of a concept which later, more sophisticated laborers in the field of Appalachian studies would transmute into the gold of sociological and economic explication. And for all subsequent Appalachian fiction her romantic, impressionistic use of the landscape established the first prerequisite of characterization: that in some important and mysterious way, the mountains dwell in the mountaineers.

By creating a lush, romantic landscape, Murfree also was able to imply the existence of an Appalachian Eden wilderness, an idea she coupled with her pervading emphasis on the remoteness of the land and the people from the rest of America. Although the president of Berea College, William Goodell Frost, did not until 1899 capture this notion of space as time once and for all by designating the Southern mountaineers as "our contemporary ancestors,"[7] Murfree had amply illustrated fifteen years before that the prototypical American frontiersman survived in a land that time forgot.

So pervasive was this idea that even in a highly regarded factual study of Western North Carolina—*Our Southern Highlanders* by Horace Kephart—the author took an unabashedly romantic attitude toward his subject. "The Southern highlands themselves are a mysterious realm," he pointed out in 1913, and the mountaineers are "creatures of environment." Among these people he expected to "realize the past in the present, seeing with my own eyes what life must have been to my pioneer ancestors of a century or two ago." But his "chief interest," he admits, was at first "that mysterious beckoning hinterland," "that superb wilderness," "an Eden still unpeopled and unspoiled."[8] It is little wonder that this image has lingered into the present day; it is a favorite American idea, tied closely to our most cherished notions of national origin and identity.

Only one other writer made a significant contribution to the creation of the mountaineer legend. John Fox Jr., Bluegrass native, author of such best-selling novels as *The Little Shepherd of Kingdom Come* (1903) and *The Trail of the Lonesome Pine* (1908), shifted the emphasis of the mountaineer's literary portrait. As one critic has said, "[Fox] usher[ed] in an era of uncouth, belligerent feudists to replace in popular concept Miss Murfree's gentle, garrulous women and lackadaisical rail-sitters."[9] John Fox became the most widely read interpreter of the mountaineers during the 1890s and 1900s, and to him must go the credit for popularizing the feud story.

He came by it honestly. Young, adventurous, with a newspaper background and a timely knack for the genteel literary formula, John Fox moved to Big Stone Gap, Virginia, in 1886, and walked smack into the Black Patch wars, an eruption of violent family feuds in the border counties of eastern Kentucky, southwestern Virginia, and West Virginia, that reached a crescendo in 1903 when the governor-elect of Kentucky was shot down on the statehouse steps. Such goings-on could hardly escape national attention. The *New York Times* reported the Kentucky feuds extensively from 1901 to 1905, and "descriptions of feuding in Appalachia," one historian notes, "began to transcend the anecdotal."[10] Reasons for the excessive virulence and number of these feuds in this time and place are various. The 1916 U.S. census shows that homicide rates in the mining counties of Virginia and Kentucky were higher than for anywhere else in Appalachia, leading John Campbell to point out that anyone

> familiar . . . with conditions existing in and about new mining communities . . . need feel no hesitation in calling attention to the likelihood of violence when a people who are unprepared for industrial conditions and who hold still to some of the standards of a past age, are thrust into the congested life of a modern mining development. The increase of moonshining in such regions . . . should also be considered as a contributing cause of other crimes. (116–18)

Interestingly, Fox had come to Southwest Virginia to join his family in their mining and engineering ventures. It is ironic to think that the feud violence which Fox witnessed, recorded, romanticized, and eventually participated in by joining a vigilante group at Big Stone Gap in 1890 probably owed quite a lot to the presence of entrepreneurial outsiders like himself and his family.

Although Fox made his home in Big Stone Gap from 1890 until his death in 1919 and was genuinely fond of the mountain people, his literary portrait of the mountaineer not only reinforced Murfree's picture of an ignorant, quaint, and backward people living in a distant world and time, but also, and more importantly, emphasized a view of them as bloodstained across an impassable gulf. It was the strength of this false image that mountain people themselves deplored. John C. Campbell quotes from a letter written to him by an outraged highlander around 1920: "I want to say that in all the feuds and in all the moonshining only a bare remnant of the population were engaged notwithstanding what any yellow journal, parson, or novel-writer may have said. I mean for 'yellow' to apply to all of them" (104n).

But such protests published by Campbell and others had little influence on the popular imagination in which the mountaineers of the Great Smokies, the Blue Ridge, the Ozarks, and the Cumberlands had merged into one violent regional type and class. "To be sure," Horace Kephart wrote, in Miss Murfree's novels, as in those of John Fox, Jr. . . . we do meet characters more genial than feudists and illicit distillers; none the less [*sic*], when we have closed the book, who is it that stands out clearest as type and pattern of the mountaineer? Is it not he of the long rifle and peremptory challenge? (12–13)

By the time Kephart revised *Our Southern Highlanders* in 1922, World War I had come and gone, and life had begun changing for the inhabitants of the South's mountain fastness although portrayals of them in literature had not. The ubiquity of the picturesque originals of conventional literary Appalachia did not wane with the coming of the modern era. Serious authors and hacks alike have continued to visit Appalachia and to write fiction in which they reproduce the mountaineers created by Mary Noailles Murfree and John Fox Jr. The longevity of this stereotype has been reinforced by its continuation in such pop culture forms as television programs like *The Beverly Hillbillies,* cartoon strips such as *Li'l Abner* and *Snuffy Smith,* and a tourist industry that has made of the mountain people expert self-parodists in the interest of economic gain—from the *Hatfields and McCoys* outdoor drama in Beckley, West Virginia, to the billboards and trained bears of Maggie Valley.

If the persistence of the stereotype has created a relatively harmless industry for Appalachia, it has nonetheless created a problem for those who would write a serious literature about the mountain people. On the one hand are the expectations of the reading public, as literary historian Cratis Williams observed after an extensive survey of Appalachian fiction up to 1960:

> writers who have attempted to present a literary mountaineer based on any type of real mountaineer other than the one [Mary Murfree] selected have met with an indifferent popular success. Only those whose mountaineers fit at least approximately the patterns she cut for the Tennessee covites have succeeded in satisfying American readers that they were presenting mountaineers at all.[11]

On the other hand are the literary critics and book reviewers who by now ought to know better. In vain, however, did I seek a book review of Lee Smith's highly praised *Oral History* (1983) which would explain or even notice that the novel is a pastiche of every major strain in Appala-

chian fiction for the past one hundred years. In 1981, critic William Slavick explained the puzzling failure of DuBose Heyward to write an acceptable novel about the mountain people by *blaming the subjects,* whom he
described as "a group of characters whose lives are so barren and repressed
and who are so inarticulate that only crabbed gestures or allegorical role-
playing reveal at all what their experience means to them."[12] If we follow
out this line of reasoning, the credit for Heyward's classic success *Porgy*
should probably go to the residents of Catfish Row. Even at the University
of Tennessee, a scholar has observed that

> the southern mountaineers do not inspire individualized fictional treat-
> ments as do their kinsmen the poor whites. . . . [The] mountaineers . . .
> have achieved identity as a social group and in a circumscribed environ-
> ment. Their culture, like that of all arrested groups, is static, a fact
> about all such groups which limits their usefulness to fiction.[13]

Unfortunately, the American public and American critics have remained more than a bit fuzzy about the fact that there has developed a serious literary tradition of Appalachia, and that this genre is related to but
not the same thing as the local color fiction created by Murfree and Fox.
This serious literature is written by natives of Appalachia and can in general be described as a realistic literature having two veins, naturalistic and
romantic. Especially distinguished in depicting the struggles of a brave
people doomed by environment and economic circumstance have been
Kentucky writers such as Harriette Arnow, James Still, Elizabeth Madox
Roberts, and, with a strong touch of the primitive and comic, Jesse Stuart.
From Tennessee and Southwest Virginia, I would name Anne Wetzel Armstrong, and from North Carolina, John Foster West. Fewer writers, however, have been successful in creating an Appalachian literature of any
stature in the romantic vein—one in which the figure of the mountaineer
appears, emergent from the great Southern wilderness, triumphant and
profoundly American. I can name only two who have created such a portrait with the depth and breadth that a series of interlocking novels and
frequently poetic diction can bring to the subject, and those two are
Thomas Wolfe and John Ehle.

John Ehle's way of telling the story of the mountain people defies those
critics who have conceived of Appalachia as a confining topic for the novelist. With the single exception of *The Winter People,* Ehle sketches the

history of the mountaineers as a chronicle not of an isolated and backward population but of a people who have been participants in their own times. In *The Land Breakers,* his characters are pioneers, not mountaineers, winning America from the Appalachian wilderness. In *The Journey of August King* (set in 1810), the post–Revolutionary War population may have been born and reared in the mountains, but Ehle's focus is less on their characteristics as "mountaineers" than on their involvement with the growing national evil of slavery. Fifty years later, in *Time of Drums,* his mountain families are fully engaged in the Civil War and the issue of a central government's power over its citizens; a dozen years or so after that, in *The Road,* they are constructing a railroad from Old Fort to the Swannanoa Gap, opening up their section of Appalachia to greater opportunities in trade and an expanded tourist industry. Flouting literary convention, Ehle does not write about a reluctant lost world being broken into by outsiders; instead, he shows the mountain people determined to reach out for whatever improvements contemporary America has to offer. When some of those improvements prove illusory, he reminds us that the mountain folk were touched by the Great Depression just as were the city folk—while Asheville "rocked and shivered" from the economic onslaught, in the surrounding mountains belts were tightened and it was a case of make do or do without "in every barn and house and field in Yancey County." Ehle's point of view on the crash is different from that of Thomas Wolfe, who concentrated on the catastrophe to those who had been corrupted by newfangled ways of making money. In *Lion on the Hearth,* mountaineer storekeeper Caleb King is thoroughly disgusted by the spectacle of Asheville's fall: "This, as he analyzed it, was the return on the lazy notion that a man can work only with paper and be productive. He had never believed it."[14]

The effect of America's move away from a rural economy on the dynamics of family life is beautifully depicted in *Last One Home,* in which the growing differences between generations living in and around Asheville have less to do with anything peculiarly Appalachian than with the acceleration of the nation's economy after the First World War. The incongruities during the period are poignantly realized when Enid King, a cobbler and farmer, travels from the surrounding mountains to visit his grandson in the Asheville city hospital where Enid's old-fashioned ways are a matter for amusement and the word "mountaineer" a term of ridicule to the younger generation of city dwellers. Contrasts throughout the country between rural and urban cultures were still sharply defined in the

1920s and '30s, and the children of the Jazz Age were more distant from their parents' experience than any generation before or since. This is not to say that *Last One Home*—or any of Ehle's other Western North Carolina–based fiction—isn't thoroughly grounded in Appalachia. But whatever the period he depicts, Ehle's mountaineers are not "our contemporary ancestors," and so his approach to what is termed regional fiction is neither a limited nor a limiting one. Though he writes knowledgeably about a particular time and place, his books open outward on human nature and on American life. Unlike so many who have written about mountaineers, he never conveys to his readers any sense of excursion among a strange kind.

Perhaps this idea of a special American resonance in Ehle's work was lurking at the fringes of reviewer Ivan Gold's consciousness when he wrote in the *New York Times Book Review* that Ehle had "staked a serious, quiet claim to this profoundly American territory."[15] Gold did not explain precisely what he meant; perhaps it seemed self-evident to him that Appalachia, the Appalachia most familiar in our literature, has come to be perceived generally as a sort of original America, source and pattern of our national identity. Paradoxically, the novel about which he made this comment, *The Winter People,* is the only one of Ehle's novels to emphasize the common literary conception of an Appalachia cut off from the rest of the nation. Very likely the success of this novel owes something to its use of the more traditional Appalachian fiction elements: the bear hunt, the feud, the sense of being trapped by geography in another time, one of fur-bearing trappers on horseback, the rest of America merely an irrelevant echo of outlanders. This is a familiar world the American reading public is prepared to enter, but not without reservation, for it is, after all, the locale of a population group for whom the regrettable term "mountain white" was coined. Against the odds, however, Ehle works an unlikely magic: like Margaret Mitchell, who turned the reading population of New York City against damn Yankees virtually overnight, he makes it possible for his readers to identify fully with his protagonists. Part of the explanation lies in the fact that the mountain people he portrays are not poor whites—they form a recognizably prosperous middle class. But what is more, they are not unheroic because of it; they remain clearly the inheritors of the American wilderness despite being careful builders of a civilization. Ehle identifies as belonging to the mountaineers those ethnic characteristics which Americans most like to consider uniquely their own, as a people, invented by them for the sake of a new land. The true American is an independent part of his country and lives his life close to the land. He is proud, and the measure of his worth lies not in his lineage but in what he himself chooses to do or not to do. Just so the Appalachian mountaineers, who have never been more appealingly presented than in the staunch homeliness of Ehle's mountaineers' creed, which reads in part:

> We work with the rocky land. . . . We track wild animals. We fish the streams. . . . We do not say sir to anybody . . . [but] should a fence be broken, we will help mend it. . . . We love our country, whatever it is, wherever it is; we know where it starts out from. We sell timber. We make whiskey. . . . We build with stone and logs we own already. . . . We have strong, fast dogs, surprised by petting. We shoot accurately. . . . We do not steal. We do not rape. We abhor mistreatment of anybody. We never forget any mistreatment of ourselves. . . . We welcome strangers, but we do not imitate them.[16]

This personal statement of identity is bound up in how a people live where they live, and it does not occur in *The Winter People,* a book which perhaps best illustrates it, but in *Last One Home,* a novel about so-called "civilized" mountaineers and how they live in their part of what once was their town.

Although Ehle's work contradicts the popular conception of the mountain people as our contemporary ancestors, he does follow Mary Murfree's literary insight—and, incidentally, Thomas Wolfe's—that the mountains and the mountaineers are inextricably part of one another. Throughout his seven mountain novels the theme appears, gradually acquiring a mystic element. In *The Journey of August King,* Ehle contends that a mountain is a living presence that must and will take a man into itself:

> A creek is an artery of a mountain. . . . [T]he water cleanses the body, permits the earth to breathe deep inside itself. . . . It seeps through it and breathes into it, and in this way the mountain lives. . . . The mountain is a living creature of dirt and rock and water and trees and bushes and vines . . . and animals, too, which take the water into their bodies and so become a part of the life of . . . a place. All beasts, even all men, must. It is wonderfully simple, yet complex.[17]

There are echoes here of Mary Murfree's descriptions of the Tennessee mountaineers as inseparable correspondents of the landscape, even of her

"T'other Mounting," which seems to have an evil will of its own. Ehle's representation of the mountains as influential creatures imaginatively points out the impact of surroundings on character, especially when a character is sensitive to those surroundings. In *The Winter People* this theme reappears, now artistically transformed. The landscape has become a poetic evocation of the psychological moment, and the concept of the place in the person has been distilled into the concentrated image of a culture shaped intensively by geography. *The Winter People*'s setting might almost be described as stylized—a land-locked mountain valley whose timeless peace is shattered by the arrival of a clockmaker, the winter landscape a spare and powerful haiku: "she saw a man moving through her deadened woods . . . where

limbs fell at random . . .
trunks tilted like named corpses,
their black arms scraping."[18]

A few pages further on the landscape becomes more recognizably Appalachian, "shimmering in the sunlight, with now and then a wand of smoke rising from a cabin . . . black hulks of mountains, big, brooding mysteries, with mist rising from them, from their crannies and warts and bleeding branches and streams, like hot breath" (19). It is not, however, the familiar beauty and lostness of the place which Ehle invokes, but rather, its cruelty: the cold that freezes a herd of cattle to the ground; the hunger among wolves and people; the prudent seasonal preparations—two or three graves dug ahead, covered with bearskins staked at the four paws. In the outlands it is the time of the Great Depression, but in Western North Carolina, near the Tennessee border, it is the time of winter, an isolating, hard-living time. As Mr. Samuel King once said, "My great-grandfather never would have come here to settle if he'd knowed about all this meanness" (73).

In *The Winter People*, the place itself is a participant in death. Not only has Ehle informed us of the meanness of the season in the countryside, but he indicates that the season has a psychological effect as well: "Any other time he probably wouldn't have died, if the water were warmer," Wayland says. "I don't know about water," Collie replies, "but I know I wouldn't have helped drown anybody except in the wintertime" (196). Beyond the reality of the temperature of the water and Collie's depression, is Wayland's perception now that the landscape expresses its sympathies not with the accused nor with the victim, but with the act itself:

> The sunset . . . cast a red glow over the woods, over the community all
> about. . . . Near his feet the snow melted into red water. The red blood
> of the earth seeped away. The snow and trampled ground were sopped in
> it; wherever he trod, blood was left, he noticed. That was the way the
> earth was now, and was its promise. (187)

Ehle apprehends poetically the intertwining of human event and lowering,
ancient countryside. What other American landscape of the 1930s could so
rightly support the Campbells, "a group of horsemen . . . dressed in furs . . .
moving in a world of their own interests . . . content to wait for an act of
destiny to relate them to others" (17)? Where else might a mild-mannered
craftsman from Philadelphia, in order to win acceptance into the community, be required not to join the Kiwanis Club but rather to confront a
black bear, "popping his teeth" (104)? Only where the winter streams are
so cold they take a man's breath would a woman be likely to find herself responsible for drowning her healthy, vigorous lover. Only where frontier
customs linger of necessity would she lay out his body for burial herself, in
front of the community. Only where the law seldom comes would she find
herself the final source of justice. Living like an outcast at the edge of a
wood with her illegitimate child, walking out of the forest to proclaim her
sin before the eyes of a hostile community, sacrificing herself in an act of
Biblical justice, Collie Wright is as intimately and inseparably a part of her
unique American setting as was Nathaniel Hawthorne's Hester Prynne.

   Balancing this dour mountain world is Ehle's accompanying portrayal
of a warmly domestic culture. Indeed, all of his novels about the North
Carolina mountaineers characteristically depend on the minute knowledge
of cultural details with which he recreates the mountaineers' past lives.
Thus, the narrative structure of an Ehle novel is built around incidents of
ordinary living: the getting of food, the cooking and eating of it; matters
of courtship, of childbirth, of death. That this signal quality of domesticity infuses all of Ehle's books set in Western North Carolina is a point
which should be remarked because five of the seven novels contain events
of sudden, shocking violence. Yet this violence, so often presented in Appalachian fiction as a concomitant of the lives of mountaineers, occurs in
Ehle's work as a regrettable and unforeseen event. Far from being a part of
everyday life in the hills as John Fox Jr. had implied, such violence is considered disruptive of the mountaineers' efforts at maintaining the precarious balance of civilization on the edge of a wilderness. In addition to being

a family tragedy, the sudden death of Cole Campbell poses a threat to the entire community. Ehle's emphasis throughout the narrative falls on the ordinary, civilized nature of the people involved, people who are committed to an orderly way of life. In Harristown bodies don't just turn up daily and get casually carted off to mortuaries, written off as another result of controversy over a still. This is not a conveniently ignored happenstance in one of the last remaining pockets of the American wilderness; this is a domestic catastrophe, a point Ehle makes by devoting some twenty pages to the disposition of the body itself, from the time of its discovery, to its recovery by Drury Campbell. And the grief of this father must be faced, for though Drury Campbell is a hunter, the killer of 246 bears, he weeps as readily at the loss of "his youngest and best" as any other man. When Collie visits the Campbell compound, Ehle provides all of the standard popular appurtenances of an Appalachian patriarch—the hulking, leather-clad, armed mountain men, the log cabins, the hunting dogs, the furs. Truly, Drury Campbell, patriarch and feudal lord of this Appalachian clan, is the very personification of Horace Kephart's favorite—he of the long rifle and peremptory challenge. The conversation, however, is a homely reminiscence of Cole Campbell's baby years:

> "Cole stood here at the table next to my elbow to eat his meals. He was three, or maybe he was younger. Harmon, how old was he?"
>
> "I don't know, Papa, would you think to ask her about Cole's dying, Papa?"
>
> . . . "I remember it now just as clear as if it was yesterday," Drury said, beaming with pleasure. . . . "Applesauce I remember he liked—with the inside portion of a biscuit—" (243–44)

He of the long rifle and peremptory challenge? These mountaineers, like any other civilized people, live primarily domestic lives, care most of all about their families.

Delving into our national philosophic history, the great Harvard historian Perry Miller once stated that American writers have posed as the essential problem of American identity the "irreconcilable opposition between Nature and civilization." Pointing out that this idea has been current in our literature from Cooper to Faulkner and beyond, Miller concludes that "We are all heirs of Natty Bumpo"—that "the American . . . cherishes in his innermost being the impulse to reject completely the gospel of civilization, in order to guard with resolution the savagery of his heart."[19] Certain figures, representative of this spirit in our national ethos, have arisen in the pantheon of American types, among whom we can surely place the Southern Appalachian mountaineer. Indeed, critic Malcolm Cowley has noted that the mountaineer's native habitat—"a crazy-roofed cabin not far from a corn liquor still"—is one of the "registered trademarks" of American literature.[20]

The good side of this stereotype that was created for the mountaineer— what we might call the profoundly American side—has always been represented as the anachronistic survival of our national frontier spirit, embodied in a figure whom the march of civilization has passed by. John Ehle has revised this figure into the mainstream of American life, lending dignity and character to one of the most persistent stereotypes in popular American culture. In the process he has given us a revitalized American hero and a renewed sense of our uniquely American identity. Heir to both Benjamin Franklin and Natty Bumppo, John Ehle's mountaineer stands proudly, with one foot in the forest and one in civilization, doing business as usual in his savage heart.

Notes

1. Henry D. Shapiro, *Appalachia on Our Mind: The Southern Mountains and Mountaineers in the American Consciousness, 1870–1920* (Chapel Hill: University of North Carolina Press, 1978), 18. Shapiro cites (3) and later turns a phrase on the title of an 1873 article by Will Wallace Harney in *Lippincott's Magazine* describing a trip through the Cumberland Mountains, "A Strange Land and Peculiar People."

2. John C. Campbell, *The Southern Highlander and His Homeland* (New York: Russell Sage Foundation, 1921), xxi.

3. Shapiro writes of the Protestant Home Missionary Movement into Appalachia in the late nineteenth century: "For the first decades of benevolent work in Appalachia . . . the short stories of Mary Noailles Murfree's *In the Tennessee Mountains* (1884) remained the principal text used to understand the peculiarities of mountain life" (xv).

4. Claude Mitchell Simpson, *The Local Colorists: American Short Stories, 1857–1900* (New York: Harper, 1960), 204.

5. Mary Noailles Murfree, "A-Playin' of Old Sledge at the Settlemint," in *In the Tennessee Mountains* (Knoxville: University of Tennessee Press, 1970), 90.

6. Nathalia Wright in her introduction to the Tennesseana Edition of *In the Tennessee Mountains* (cited above), notes that Murfree's implication that "the mountaineers and the mountains [are] by nature inseparable . . . may be her most significant achievement" (xxxiii).

7. William Goodell Frost, "Our Contemporary Ancestors in the Southern Mountains," *Atlantic Monthly* 83 (March 1899): 311–19.

8. Horace Kephart, *Our Southern Highlanders* (New York: Outing Publishing, 1913), 13, 19, 29–30, 50.

9. Isabella D. Harris, "The Southern Mountaineer in American Fiction, 1824–1910" (PhD diss., Duke University, 1948), 3.

10. Shapiro, 278n; 105.

11. Cratis Williams, "The Southern Mountaineer in Fact and Fiction" (PhD diss., New York University, 1961), 666.

12. William H. Slavick, *DuBose Heyward* (Boston: Twayne Publishers, 1981), 90.

13. Wright, xxxii–xxxiii.

14. John Ehle, *Lion on the Hearth* (New York: Harper and Brothers, 1961), 41.

15. Ivan Gold, "Mountain People," review of *The Winter People,* by John Ehle, *New York Times Book Review,* 9 May 1982, 13.

16. John Ehle, *Last One Home* (New York: Harper and Row, 1984), 117.

17. John Ehle, *The Journey of August King* (New York: Harper and Row, 1971), 1–2.

18. John Ehle, *The Winter People* (New York: Harper and Row, 1982), 1; hereafter cited parenthetically in the text.

19. Perry Miller, "The Romantic Dilemma in American Nationalism and the Concept of Nature" (originally published in the *Harvard Theological Review* 48 [October 1955]: 239–53), in *Nature's Nation* (Cambridge: Belknap Press of Harvard University Press, 1967), 199; 207.

20. Malcolm Cowley, "Three Cycles of Myth in American Writing," in *A Many-Windowed House: Collected Essays on American Writers and American Writing* (Carbondale and Edwardsville: Southern Illinois University Press, 1970), 235–37.

THE POWER OF LANGUAGE IN LEE SMITH'S
Oral History

CORINNE DALE

"There's two things I like to do better than anything else in this world, even at my age—and one of them is talk. You all can guess what the other one is" (Smith, 233). This is the voice of Sally in Lee Smith's most complex novel, *Oral History,* a novel told over a hundred-year period from thirteen different points of view. The multiple narrators in *Oral History,* most of whom live in or near Hoot Owl Holler in the North Carolina mountains, demonstrate Smith's extraordinary ear for dialect, especially for the speech patterns of the Appalachian mountain people. These distinctive voices reveal personality and create irony and humor. More important, they also define and thus produce individual experience.

Sally's comment suggests the importance of language in this novel; in fact, as Anne Goodwyn Jones has observed, all of Smith's novels are about language (255). Moreover, Sally's humorous connection of body language and verbal language broadens our concept of discourse. While literary critics debate the relationship of anatomy to language, Smith shows that sex, the language of anatomy, is intimately connected to verbal discourse. In *Oral History,* sexual anxiety is linguistic anxiety, alienating patriarchal discourse and silencing the mother tongue. But Sally empowers herself sexually and linguistically and thus constructs a revisionary narrative based on the authenticity of her own experience.

From the *Southern Quarterly: A Journal of the Arts in the South* 28 (Winter 1990): 21–34. Reprinted by permission of the author and the publisher.

The characters who are most alienated in Smith's novels are those most dependent on written language and thus most limited by figurative symbolic language. Symbolic language is the ordinary discourse learned, according to Lacanian theory, at the Oedipal stage of separation from the mother. Symbolic discourse overrides, but never fully represses, a primal and prelogical discourse, the rhythmic sounds heard in the womb by the fetus and in the mother's lap by the pre-Oedipal infant and termed the "semiotic" by Julia Kristeva in *La Révolution du Langage Poétique.*

Smith explores the relationship of linguistic repression and alienation—a problem that has absorbed French feminist critics; she also shows that patriarchal culture promotes this inhibited and inhibiting symbolic discourse—a fact that American feminists stress. Thus, Smith demonstrates the alienating nature of patriarchal language, probing both its anatomical and its cultural roots.

The recollections that make up *Oral History* are framed by the visit of Jennifer, a descendant of the Cantrell family who comes to tape the Cantrell ghost for her college history project. The ghost obligingly makes primal and prelogical (and thus to Jennifer scary) noises and the narrative voices seem to drift on the wind as Jennifer sits on the steps waiting. But Jennifer is incapable of hearing the true stories, for her perceptions of reality are shaped by symbolic language—specifically the prefabricated linguistic patterns of freshman prose.

As a student at the university, Jennifer is indoctrinated in the academic father speech, an elevated form of symbolic discourse formally taught to replace the vernacular (Gilbert and Gubar, 251–71). Jennifer's self-conscious reactions to such clichés as the "salt of the earth. . . . Please pass the salt of the earth" (16) indicate her condescension to the vernacular and her affected reliance on metaphors. Jennifer's most characteristic phrase is "[things] resemble nothing so much as." And although she writes in a journal, a form of literature that is often associated with women's private and unpublished writings, Jennifer chooses her words carefully for her reader: her professor and future husband. Her journal, a hilarious parody of freshman prose, lacks a sense of immediacy and authenticity: she transforms her own first-person experience into written third-person "Impressions" that "leave one with the aftertaste of judgment in his or her mouth" (18).

Moreover, these judgments are in error. Defining her relatives in terms of pastoral stereotypes, Jennifer misjudges what she sees and what happens to her. "I shall descend now, to be with them as they go about their evening chores" (20), she writes, literally condescending to her relatives, only to find that no one is doing chores after all. For Jennifer, the holler is "so peaceful" (15) and "wonderful"; the people are "so sweet, so simple, so kind" (16). At the end of the novel, when her cousin Al kisses her brutally, destroying her notions of simplicity and peace, she can accommodate that shocking experience simply by flipping the cliché: "Crude jokes and animal instincts—it's the other side of the pastoral coin" (284).

The strained metaphors and binary oppositions of Jennifer's academic father speech thus alienate her from experience so that her perception—her reality finally—is not the reality of her mountain kinfolk. The two chapters on Richard Burlage, Jennifer's grandfather who visits first as a young schoolteacher and later as a photographer, further develop this theme of linguistic alienation through the academic father speech.

Richard is the most alienated of the narrators; he is also the one who acknowledges his alienation and comes to the mountains with the expressed purpose of finding a more meaningful—that is, a more engaged—life. Richard is aware of his own alienation, connects it to decadence and modernism, and purposefully sets out as a rural schoolteacher in search of the primitive, especially the natural religious impulse, which he feels has been stifled by his own Episcopal Church.

As a wealthy Virginian educated in Latin, French, history, literature, and ukulele at the University of Virginia, Richard speaks the academic father speech, which corresponds with the speech of genteel southerners. Significantly, Richard and Jennifer both give us a journal rather than the interior monologues of the other characters; they are both immersed in the written language. Richard has admitted the truth of his brother's words: "Your tendency is to catalogue a thing to death" (99). Nevertheless, he is determined to keep a "valid record" and to find "coherence" (97). Again like Jennifer, Richard tends to perceive everything in terms of something else. And his metaphors are usually drawn from his university studies: an old mountain woman becomes an "old priestess of the realm of Lethe" (105); the train is a "medieval monster" (107). The quotation marks that litter Richard's section as well as his parenthetical comments, "unknown angst (I like that phrase!)" (121), further demonstrate his self-consciousness, his distance from experience.

That Richard is aware of his own alienation does not allow him to escape it: language defines experience. As we have seen in Jennifer's chapters, Richard's perceptions, guided by the father speech, are in error. He fantasizes that a country woman whose face is turned away is a lovely lady with a Grecian nose, but in truth she is birthmarked and walleyed. And his vision of Dory, the daughter of a bootlegger, as a shepherdess out of Christopher Marlowe's poem "The Passionate Shepherd to His Love" is surely ridiculous.

In the mountains, however, Richard begins to change. What happens, in fact, is that his own father speech is challenged and almost overwhelmed, as a comical episode in the schoolroom demonstrates. Wishing to impress the supervisor with his ability to teach "the sentence" to the mountain children by exploiting their own interests, Richard writes on the board, "The home run . . . ." When the boy completes the sentence by adding the word "away" (117–18), the vernacular has triumphed over the father speech, revealing the limitations of Richard's linguistic perceptions and the resilience of the mountain dialect.

Richard's sexual relationship with Dory almost saves him from his linguistic alienation. With Dory, Richard experiences transcendent moments of true communication: "We spoke so easily . . . even our vastly different manners of speech seemed to meet and blend together into some single tongue we share" (129). He begins to focus on life rather than on his own verbal reactions to it: "for once—for possibly the first time in my life—*I found myself at a loss for words!*" (145). He recognizes that Dory has awakened him to sensory experience—"yes!! *Bringing me to my senses!* For this is exactly what she has done" (156). Eventually, he loses control, ejaculating both sexually and verbally—"!!!!!!!!" (147). His loss of controlled verbal expression accompanies passion, a heightened participation in experience: "For once I am living my life rather than watching it pass in review" (154).

But Richard cannot so easily relinquish verbal and sexual control. At one point, Richard gives his pen as a present to Dory, but she throws it back at him, having no use for the tools of the written language. And Richard takes it up again. Anxious about the impropriety of their affair, Richard writes down a list of pros and cons for continuing to meet Dory in secret, reducing his relationship with Dory to the binary oppositions of the father speech. His last con reveals what an empty exercise this list has been: "Her father and brothers would kill me" (136). After making love with Dory, Richard's journal entry echoes his relaxed state: written with no controlling punctuation, "these sentences just run on" (159). Yet the fact remains that Richard is still writing, even as Dory's father and brothers converge threateningly on the schoolroom where he and Dory have been making love.

Richard's flirtation with the rural church runs a parallel course: he is attracted to spiritual passion but ultimately cannot give up control. He cannot stop noticing the grammatical errors in the sermon. Even as he impulsively responds to an altar call, Richard observes his own behavior. Most tellingly, he is fascinated by the glossolalia that he witnesses among the Freewill Followers, but cannot himself be inspired to speak in tongues. This babbling in unknown languages, which are completely out of the control of the speakers, is an unlearned god tongue, a language that communicates pure feeling, bypassing symbolic discourse.

Later, Richard asserts his belief in this "mountain God who traffics not in words and acts but in the heart" (162), yet he has not truly been converted. The habits of the father tongue are too strong; "that old muddled syntax again!" (160) reasserts itself. Immediately after pledging allegiance to the god of the heart, Richard resolves to take Dory home to Virginia with him, but, fatally, writes her a note asking her to join him on the train as he leaves the mountains. Of course, the note never reaches Dory— Richard's literary education should have warned him that love notes never do reach the intended—and Richard leaves without her.

Richard fails because he fears loss of control, especially sexual passion. His sexual anxiety is expressed in his linguistic anxiety, his reliance on the father speech. Its formulas give him a perspective on life, a buffer between the event and his experience of it. Only when Richard's sexual defenses are downed by Dory does his symbolic discourse give way to the semiotic. But Richard cannot live in a state of sexual and linguistic abandonment. When Richard returns, years later, he is more alienated than ever, as the elevated language of his second chapter title suggests, "Richard Burlage Discourses Upon the Circumstances Concerning His Collection of Appalachian Photographs, c. 1934."

He has become a photographer, even more distanced from experience than he was as a writer. No longer lacking self-confidence, he now thinks of himself as a mature artist, and he has a philosophy of photography and life itself—that a frame can "illumine and enlarge one's vision rather than limit it" (223). Nevertheless, Richard's fatuous diction reveals that frames do limit: his purpose now is to "capture" (a word he repeats three times) the mountain culture. He "frames" everything and "entitles" his pictures: his photo of the Smith hotel, where he once lived, becomes "Whorehouse, c. Hard Times." But Richard cannot frame (enclose, lay blame on) or entitle (take possession of) Dory. When he tries to capture her in the frame of her doorway, her image does not show up in the photograph. Still, Richard does have moments of illumination: when a mountain man shatters the rearview mirror on Richard's car, suddenly the vision is "like a prism, in all truth." The shattered mirror shows him a view of life that is "all different, all new" (228) and colored the green of life instead of the black and white of his photographs.

Richard's experience with glossolalia, his string of exclamation points, and the shattered mirror suggest that pure experience, pure feeling, is inarticulate and that true vision is incoherent. For the most part, Richard, like Jennifer, is alienated; he is "sentenced" by academic father speech. Smith does not suggest, however, that formal education is the cause of Richard's alienation nor that only intellectuals are alienated. *Oral History* combats the notion that the vernacular is synonymous with the genuine discourse of the mother tongue as is often supposed (Gilbert and Gubar, 252–53). Instead, Smith shows that vernacular discourse is formalized just as educated speech is.

The chapter devoted to Jink, Dory's young brother, demonstrates that the oral tradition of the mountains is not the antithesis of the written father tongue. Nor is it the cure for alienation. Smith has been praised for evoking the "rootedness of mountain folk culture" (Jones, 254) and for celebrating the immediacy of oral language (Jones, 268–70). But Smith shows here that just what solidifies that folk culture can be damaging and that the vernacular is a form of symbolic discourse that can be just as alienating as the father tongue of southern gentility. In fact, the mountain culture has its own father speech, its own language of manhood.

In Jink, Richard has recognized a potential worth cultivating. And Jink has tried hard to learn the academic father tongue that Richard has sought to teach him. Richard's sentiment and poetry seem to offer Jink an escape by giving him access to abstract ideas (Jones, 270), but Jink's natural voice is original and concrete and surely more promising. Jink vacillates between the hackneyed academic father speech as he observes "rosy-finger dawn" (187) and the vernacular, which he keeps correcting, "they wasn't no—any—stars" (187). Jink's appreciation of the sunrise shows his sensitivity, an appreciation which he can express with a metaphor that is neither a cliché nor an echo of another poet: the sunrise looked "like a big old electric light-bulb set right on the top of the Mountain" (188).

Jink likes to sit in the crotch of a tree—he calls it the "mother-seat"—and say a word-spell he has made up. He is certain that if he can get the whole long piece right, he will be able to fly. Sadly, though, this child who yearns to fly must leave the mother-seat and the mystical and poetic mother tongue; he will be grounded by the father speech of his own culture. His perceptions will be shaped by that symbolic discourse, which is a language of violence, misogyny, and sexual anxiety.

The father speech of the mountain men in *Oral History* serves to separate men from women just as academic father speech originally served to differentiate men from women, being limited almost entirely to men until the nineteenth century. Just as the teaching of Latin and Greek once constituted a male initiation ritual in boys' schools, as Walter Ong has shown (Gilbert and Gubar, 243), learning the father speech of the mountains is part of Jink's initiation into manhood—the hog-killing, where he will "stand up and be a man" (187). Jink begins playing with the children; he shouts that he is "Home free!" (191), but he is nevertheless dragged off to the hog-killing, where the men force him to witness and to participate by gutting hogs and eating the cracklings, drinking moonshine, and listening to dirty songs and stories. Although Jink is initially nauseated and frightened by all this manplay, he comes to laugh at Paris Blankenskip's bawdy story about a witch and to join in the songs, which focus on female genitalia and brutal sex.

The academic father speech, such as Richard uses, promotes distorting visions of shepherdesses and goddesses. The father speech of the mountain culture, which Jink learns, is more direct in its brutalizing of female sexuality: "If ever I marry in this wide world, it'll be for love, not riches. Catch a little girl about five feet high and fuck her through the britches" (195). Such linguistic rape reveals fear of sexuality, an anxiety that demands distance—sexual love becomes rape of a little girl, further distanced by her clothing. In other songs, the woman is reduced to genitalia: a woman's "ring-a-ding-a-doo" is described in graphic detail but detached from any female body.

Gilbert and Gubar note Ong's contention that there is actually no true father speech since all language is referential to the mother, and conclude that anxiety about the primacy of the mother underlies the misogyny of much patriarchal language (263). Certainly the symbolic discourses of Richard Burlage and of the mountain men express their anxiety about femininity. As a part of an initiation ritual, the language of patriarchy subjugates the feminine, sexually and linguistically. Thus, Jink must repudiate words like "pretty" that seem somehow feminine and that naturally come to his mind. Bloody, drunk, and brutal, Jink has unwillingly become a man. His child's voice, a poetic, mystical voice that responded authentically to experience, has been silenced.

Another mountain man, Little Luther Wade, partly avoids indoctrination into the father tongue and the macho culture of the mountain. It is Little Luther who sings the dirty songs at the hog-killing; he also relies on misogynist expressions from the father speech of the mountains: "cold as a bitch" (171) and "cold as a witch's tit" (173). Little Luther, though, is not considered a whole man. As a cripple, he is exempt from some of the expectations of his gender. Little Luther's special status frees him to marry Dory even though she is pregnant by Richard. Little Luther does not have to kill Richard—though he is tempted—as another mountain man would. Perhaps this half status as a man explains why and how he writes songs that are genuine and individual responses to his experiences. At times, his voice is so pure that it seems to come out of the air and the mountains themselves, a genuine and unedited discourse that comes naturally.

As we have seen, Smith's characters express themselves genuinely at times—especially in moments of passion—speaking with inarticulate or uncontrolled voices that disrupt the orderly flow of symbolic language. The French feminist critics argue that this primal semiotic discourse is the source of genuine expression. As these critics have stressed, women are objectified by symbolic language—they are the "other," the inferior side of the binary oppositions developed in the effort of the child to separate from the mother. Also, as American and British critics emphasize, women are the "other" in patriarchal institutions, which are often structured to separate men from women. Thus, semiotic discourse is especially valuable for women, who are particularly alienated from the symbolic language of the patriarchal society.

In Smith's novel, semiotic discourse is particularly accessible to the mountain women, who are more likely than other characters to express themselves in genuine and primary voices. Unlike Jennifer, the women of Appalachia are not educated in the academic father speech. And unlike Jink, they are not initiated into the macho culture of the mountains. Nevertheless, the sexual anxiety that informs symbolic discourse and the patriarchal culture affects women as well as men. At the end of chapter 1, when Jennifer sits on the steps listening for the voices in the wind that she cannot hear, she is not alone. Next to her sits Ora Mae, an uneducated mountain woman, untroubled by any father speech but not free to respond naturally in her mother tongue either. Ora Mae hears the voices; she knows the future, and has the gift of healing, though she refuses to use it. The sort of woman whose intuitive powers might be labeled witchcraft, Ora Mae represses her own sexuality and muffles her own voice. Like Richard's, Ora Mae's linguistic repression is connected to fear of sexual passion. Ora Mae's anxiety, though, is expressed in tightly controlled vernacular.

Courted by Paris Blankenship, whose outstanding feature is his talent for talking, Ora Mae refuses to marry him or to leave the mountains with him, even though escaping the mountains is her secret desire and even though she loves Paris. When Ora Mae recalls a moment of passion with him, she loses control of her sentences, abandoning her usual terse style: "but I laid there just as still while he kept kissing me on my shoulders and my breasts and my belly, every damn place, I laid there just as still while he did it, and every kiss burned like fire on my skin, I can feel them kisses yet if I've got a mind to. Which I don't" (215). The last sentence reasserts her usual firm self-control and reinstates her customary laconic voice. Ora Mae scorns the others for being so "mealy-mouthed" and especially Dory, who in addition seems to be constantly pregnant.

Ora Mae's sexual memory, which causes her sentences to run on out of control, reminds us of Richard's journal entry in which he records his sexual experience with Dory: his sentences run on also. These episodes demonstrate a major theme in the novel—sexual passion makes us let go; recklessly we immerse ourselves in the moment. Richard recognizes this immersion in experience as a miracle, but ultimately he cannot relinquish control. For Ora Mae also, such passion threatens her sense of control. She will not risk passion; she will not leave the mountains with her lover, even though she feels the mountains have "closed up in a circle around me" (208), because inaction and control are safer. It is Ora Mae who fails to deliver Richard's note to Dory. Ora Mae rationalizes that she is protecting Dory, but her silence about the note eventually destroys Dory. Ora Mae thus "sentences" herself and Dory to a life of sexual and linguistic repression.

Ora Mae's feelings escape her tight linguistic control again at the funeral of Pearl, Dory's daughter, who has dared to leave the mountains and to choose love over security. Confronted with Pearl's failure—she has abandoned her lover and died in childbirth—Ora Mae expresses her despair in a genuine voice, "the awfulest low sad wail. . . . It sounded like something right out of the burying ground, some rising up of age and pain" (277). This primal wail voices Ora Mae's authentic feelings.

As Smith has shown, this sort of genuine voice is rare. Furthermore, if it is not silenced, like Jink's voice, it is usually inarticulate—Ora Mae's wail. In *Oral History,* many women characters are silent: their voices are heard, if at all, from the mouths of others who tell their stories for them. Pricey Jane is said to hum to her children the wordless songs of love that she remembers from her own mother. The mother tongue, described by Hélène Cixous in *La Jeune Née,* is "the first voice of love which all women preserve alive" (Moi, 114), but Pricey Jane is killed by poisoned milk and the infant Dory is sickened by the milk from Pricey Jane's breast—certainly an ironic way to silence the mother tongue. Later, Dory's homespun phrases contrast with Richard's alienated father speech, but Dory too is silenced—she finally commits suicide—because of Richard's betrayal.

Though inarticulate, the semiotic voice is powerful, as Smith shows in her portrayal of Red Emmy the witch. Originally, Smith wrote a section of the novel from Red Emmy's point of view—but this section was deleted on the advice of Smith's editor at Putnam (Arnold, 254). Thus, Red Emmy has no section of the novel to narrate, and she communicates by looks rather than by speech when she is described by Granny Younger. She never defends herself verbally; her communcation with Almarine has been strictly sexual, at least as Granny Younger presents them. But as a mad woman, both angry and insane, she avenges herself by cursing the Cantrells, and in death she makes herself heard: banging, crashing, creaking the rocking chair and laughing wildly.

This is the secret language of witches, a powerful and disruptive voice that has been feared and muffled through the ages. The mystical semiotic voice has been considered the voice of divine truth; it may be the voice of psychosis as Terry Eagleton insists (190). Perhaps it is both. In any case, it is a primal voice that the community suppresses.

Like Pricey Jane and Dory, Red Emmy is naturally sexual and fruitful. As a woman of sexual power, however, she is feared and persecuted by the community, including the women, who believe that she is a witch and the devil's lover. A voluptuous, redheaded mountain woman, Red Emmy is neither modest nor chaste. She exposes her naked breasts to a stranger when he comes upon her bathing, and she refuses to tie down her flaming hair. Almarine Cantrell believes that she has bewitched him with her sexuality, that she is exhausting him by "riding him" at night—the usual sexually charged complaint against witches, which betrays a fear of female sexuality. To save himself, Almarine throws her out of the house, though she is pregnant with their child. Later, rumors have it that she has murdered the baby and become a prostitute.

Red Emmy's discourse is picked up by the tape recorder, ensuring Jennifer an A on her history project and propelling her toward marriage to her professor. The rocking chair becomes the center of Ghostland, a theme park that is eventually built in Hoot Owl Holler. The Cantrell curse, then, is based on the repudiation and exploitation of female sexuality. Nevertheless, Red Emmy is linguistically as well as sexually powerful. She cannot be silenced, not even by death itself.

Gilbert and Gubar identify a female literary tradition that transforms "a female dream of linguistic witchcraft into other visions of female verbal power" (246). *Oral History* is part of this tradition. Red Emmy is linguistically powerful: through her curse, she transforms reality, constructing an alternative history of Hoot Owl Holler that challenges the patriarchal versions of Richard and of the mountain men. But Red Emmy's linguistic power is malevolent: she destroys innocent women and children; perhaps her own murdered baby is among them. And finally, Red Emmy's voice is inarticulate: the semiotic is prelogical and thus communication is problematic.

Eagleton notes that the semiotic operates within the symbolic order of conventional language as a marginal and challenging discourse (190). In *Oral History,* Sally speaks with this sort of subversive yet wholly positive voice. Sally re-envisions narrative by relying on the authority of her own experience—that is, she connects to primal feelings, especially her own sexuality, and she also is comfortable within the patriarchal culture. Thus, she accommodates both the sexual and the intellectual, the primal and the cultural. Appropriately, only Sally is able to name the curse and thus to escape it: "every one of them [are] all eat up with wanting something they haven't got" (235).

Sally has suffered from passion; like Red Emmy, she was abandoned by her lover when she was pregnant. Sally has also suffered from repression: she married a man who "didn't believe in talking to women and he never said one word, just roll over and go to sleep" (234). But Sally escaped this sexual and linguistic silencing. Her second husband, Roy, is a tireless lover who likes to hear her talk, even while they are making love. And Sally's two favorite things, talk and sex, show that she has reconciled the language of the body with the language of the mind.

Sally further shows that she understands the linguistic failures that have destroyed those around her. She recognizes the inauthenticity of Pearl's talking "in the breathy way she'd taken up since she had gone to college and gotten so arty" (262). When Pearl describes her boyfriend as looking like a Greek god, Sally comments, "This didn't tell me a thing" (272). Sally also knows the danger of linguistic power when language becomes a way of repressing others or of silencing oneself. She describes two kinds of unhappy families: the kind in which everybody yells at each other and the kind in which "nobody has got anything to say to anybody else" (236).

Understanding these linguistic power plays, Sally repudiates traditional linguistic patterns: she hates poems and rejects narrative with its beginnings, middles, and endings. Although her husband Roy is a telephone lineman who "has to believe in connections" (253), Sally refuses to find meanings or to make the tale coherent. Besides resisting formulas, Sally subverts her own formulations by starting her tale several times, observing that it is hard, even impossible, to find the beginning. Sally tells her story to entertain Roy, who has a cast on his leg. The narrative is hurried along by the approach of dinner; in fact, she tells part of it while she is preparing a pot roast, and she ends the story when dinner is ready. Thus, Sally rebelliously invents an alternative narrative that is responsive and responsible to her own experience.

As fond as she is of talking, though, Sally recognizes that some experiences, particularly women's experiences, defy linguistic definition: "There is something about a baby's pull on your nipple that puts you in mind of a man, but it is entirely different from that—it's different from everything else. And there's a lot of things, like that . . . you can't explain" (266). Smith observes elsewhere that Sally's voice is "diluted," that compared to other characters who lived in an earlier time, "she just hasn't got the narrative feel because she doesn't have the words" (Arnold, 246). Nevertheless, Sally emerges as the most positive voice in the novel, partly because she can accept the limitations of her symbolic language without accepting limitations on experience. Smith admits that Sally has "a grand passion" for her husband (Arnold, 247).

Sally demonstrates that genuine feeling and authentic language—so elusive to Smith's characters—are possible. All of the characters in *Oral History* experience moments of true feeling and natural expression when their primal voices come through. Often these semiotic voices escape the sentence, violating conventions of punctuation and syntax. Often they are inarticulate: wails, creaks, hums, curses, speaking in tongues, and !!!!!!!! Nonrepresentational and nonsymbolic, this semiotic language is immediate. It does not set up a linguistic buffer between experience and expression.

Sally's triumph, though, transcends these inarticulate voices. She reconstitutes symbolic language through the semiotic voice, constructing an alternative, and thus subversive, narrative that may properly be called the mother tongue. This is, of course, exactly what Smith herself does in constructing the novel *Oral History*. Like Sally's tale within the tale, there is no one beginning, middle, and ending but instead overlapping and sometimes conflicting testimonies. We cannot even be sure there is a witch to curse the Cantrells; isn't Red Emmy instead a misunderstood and persecuted woman? But then what do we make of the crashing and laughing recorded by Jennifer's tape recorder? Speaking about *Oral History*, Smith observed, "[Y]ou never *finally* know exactly the way it was. I guess I see some sort of central mystery at the center of the past, of any past, that you can't, no matter what a good attempt you make at understanding how it was, you never can quite get at" (Arnold, 246).

Like Sally, Smith herself accepts the limitations of her narrative attempt to elicit the past. All we can be sure of is the perspective of the different narrators, and what their language tells about their anxieties and their triumphs. As Sally would say, "Life is a mystery and that's a fact" (275).

Works Cited

Arnold, Edwin T. "An Interview with Lee Smith." *Appalachian Journal* 11 (Spring 1984): 240–54.

Eagleton, Terry. *Literary Theory*. Minneapolis: University of Minnesota Press, 1983.

Gilbert, Sandra M., and Susan Gubar. *The War of the Words*. Vol. 1 of *No Man's Land: The Place of the Woman Writer in the Twentieth Century*. 3 vols. New Haven, Conn.: Yale University Press, 1988.

Jones, Anne Goodwyn. "The World of Lee Smith." In *Women Writers of the Contemporary South*, ed. Peggy Whitman Prenshaw, 249–72. Jackson: University Press of Mississippi, 1984.

Kristeva, Julia. *La Révolution du Langage Poétique*. Paris: Seuil, 1974.

Moi, Toril. *Sexual/Textual Politics: Feminist Literary Theory*. New York: Methuen, 1985.

Smith, Lee. *Oral History*. New York: Putnam, 1983.

A New, Authoritative Voice

Fair and Tender Ladies

DOROTHY COMBS HILL

The Music That Breathes

The seed for *Fair and Tender Ladies*[1] was sown when Lee Smith bought a packet of letters for seventy-five cents at a yard sale and found the letters to contain a woman's whole life in correspondence to her sister. It occurred to Smith that if the writer of the letters "had a chance to be educated and not have five children she might have really been a writer of some note."[2] Smith creates the redheaded Ivy Rowe as her letter writer. Although Ivy writes to many different people, the most significant letters are to her beautiful silvery sister, Silvaney.

A brain fever damages Silvaney's mind; the murder of her twin brother, Babe, destroys it. A do-gooder, meddling in mountain culture, has Silvaney institutionalized. She is placed in a home for lunatics, where she dies in the flu epidemic after World War I. The twins appear to symbolize two sides of the unsocialized self necessary for imagination but displaced, and really at risk, in society. By refusing to believe Silvaney is dead, continuing to write her, Ivy apparently keeps that side of herself alive—"my lost one, my heart" (*Fair,* 120).

Originally published in a slightly different form in *Lee Smith,* ed. Frank Day. Twayne United States Authors Series (New York: Macmillan, 1992), 103–20. Reprinted by permission of the author and the publisher.

Until her own death, Ivy never stops writing Silvaney; she will not abandon her, not ever. In effect, through Ivy's refusal to let Silvaney go, Smith rescues that part of the female spirit imaged (and imaged as damaged) in Crystal, Lily, Dory, Pearl, and Fay. This primal she, silver-haired like one "fotched up on the moon," is now the muse, a mountain sylph, the internal self, a wood spirit, forever running wild and free: "I will tell you of my Family now and she will be first, I love Silvaney the bestest, you see. Silvaney is so pretty, she is the sweetest. . . . She takes after a Princess in a story, Silvaney does" (*Fair,* 17).

> She scares easy, sometimes she will put her apron up over her head and start in crying and other times she will get to laghing and she cant stop, you have to pour a gourdfull of water down over her face. . . . Silvaney is bigger and oldern me, but it is like we are the same sometimes it is like we are one. We have slept in the same bed all of our lives and done everything as one. I am smart thogh I go to school when I can and try to better myself and teach Silvaney but she cant learn. . . . We put black-eye susans and Queen Annes lace in our hair. (*Fair,* 17)

As with *Oral History,* Smith used research on Appalachia (which she published at the back of the book) for this epistolary novel that "spans four generations, three wars (Ivy's grandson goes to Vietnam), the gradual, sad loss of a way of life, and the entire range of human experience. It is a novel about Appalachia, family, forgiveness, love and the resilience of the spirit."[3]

Those critics who expressed disappointment that *Family Linen* did not measure up to the "myth-laden, haunted lushness of a Black Rock, a Hoot Owl Holler" fell under Smith's spell once more as, "drunk on the language of Appalachia," *Fair and Tender Ladies* renders the mythic present and the present mythic.[4] Smith pushes harder than she ever has in her fictive work to find mythic resolution for the tensions that fuel her fictive impulse. Her success is measurable in the ways in which *Fair and Tender Ladies* reconciles female and male, female and female, body and mind, collective and individual, mother and lover. Above all, *Fair and Tender Ladies* brings together art and love—"the music that breathes"—the function of the storytelling of Aphrodite as analyzed by linguistic anthropologist Paul Friedrich in his exploration of changing narratives of women in the circum-Mediterranean over the last several thousand years.[5] Aphrodite is a liminal (from *limen,* threshold) figure who reconciles opposites. Not only does she inspire love, longing, and poetry, but she combines intelligence, motherhood, and sensuality. In his book *The Meaning of Aphrodite*, Friedrich cautions that Aphrodite is already constrained by patriarchy in the Golden Age of Greece, by which time even a relatively active woman is considered dangerous. But Friedrich points out that Old Irish mythology, which predates Greek, conserves the sex and love goddesses of earlier mythology, and thus conserves the active woman as sacred. (Given that myth undergirds all societies, it is no surprise that in ancient Celtic culture women could be warriors and could own property.) Smith may be peculiarly situated to recover these lost contents insofar as bits and pieces of Old Irish mythology persist in Appalachian mountain lore and language. (She told me in conversation that she could not find heroic roles for women until she returned to her Appalachian mountain material.) Whatever strings of the lyre this artist plucks, the fact remains that Lee Smith breathes into this novel the complex lyricism of a woman's life while giving it the dignity and durability of collective language—that is, rendering it mythic. On its release the novel was variously described as "a mixture of lyricism and sexual boldness that might have been sung into being"[6] and "as true to life as the high sweet sound of mountain music in a gathering dusk."[7]

Oral History was the turning point wherein Smith began to write her way out of social constraints and patriarchal imagination. Being locked-in produced fictions such as her short story "I Dream of Horses," in which she chronicles the loss of female mythology with concomitant loss of the understanding of female psychology. In *Oral History*, she lifted the problems of her female protagonists out of isolated selves and began to make them public and collective. She tapped or recreated (it matters not which) "the secret stream, below ground, of our classical heritage of symbolic communication."[8] Golden Dory must be sacrificed for the Secret Wound— the split between culture and nature, male and female, body and soul— ultimately, the split between sacred and sexual. Society actually splits Dory in this novel—separating her body and soul—finally turning her into the quintessential female by severing her head from her body. She could not do this to herself spiritually, as had Brooke and Crystal, so she allows society's machine to do it for her physically by placing her head on the train track. In that sense, she fulfills the patriarchal imagination. The same culture turns the Victor of *Oral History* into the quintessential male, a head with no body. He is the voice of abstraction in the library, whiling away his hours with disembodied ideas on flat pages with no golden Dorys to trouble his cognitive renderings.

Fair and Tender Ladies is not as shackled by the patriarchal imagination as *Oral History,* nor has it the need of the earlier novel to break those shackles. This is partly because Smith accomplished that imaginative work in the writing of *Oral History.* Now Smith is ready to create a persona like Ivy Rowe who is the writer of this epistolary novel, an alter ego who is glad to burst those bonds—glad she is "ruint" by her illegitimate pregnancy because being "ruint" frees her from those bonds. Moreover, Ivy the writer will not allow Silvaney, the potential victim in a long line of victims, to be victimized. By her own act of writing, she keeps Silvaney alive. But in refusing to allow Silvaney to die, Ivy does not keep her in pastness. Her attachment to Silvaney is not nostalgic; she does not relive the times they had. Rather, though Silvaney dies, she remains with Ivy spiritually. Here is the overlap with Mary Magdalene's message about Jesus. Physically, he is gone; but, spiritually, he returns and extends the relationship. So does Silvaney help Ivy cope with the present by being a voice, a presence she can turn to. Ivy writes to Silvaney about the present and the future. She keeps Silvaney alive and Silvaney keeps her alive—not by cutting her off from the present, but by spiritually remaining with Ivy in it.

Smith's redemptive spirit helps her accomplish an enormous feat of integration as she returns to her territory—the mountains and the conflict—and finally writes her way to another end, one that no longer demands the spiritual death of the female or her collusion in her own spiritual paralysis and death. Smith, the writer, has imagined her way out of the accepted social construction. She has made that other end available for females and collectively compelling. She has given us an authoritative voice that breathes another story back into the music of the world.

THE AUTHORIAL VOICE

In Smith's earlier fiction, the silencing (*Black Mountain Breakdown*), ignoring ("Saint Paul," "The Seven Deadly Sins," "I Dream of Horses"), and even removal of the actual female is imaged time and again, and when the root cause is traced, it leads back to mythic cultural foundations. The removal of the actual female is imaged in Smith's short story "Not Pictured" when another of her golden women, the lovely Lily, is put away in a mental hospital. Lily's name evokes both Judeo-Christian and non-Judeo-Christian mythology and thus her removal alludes to erasure of women in received myth. Lily echoes the name of Lilith—the powerful, sexual, sacred female who was exiled thus "put away" in Judeo-Christian mythology. Numerous other sacred sexual female figures, as well as the key symbols associated with them, were also expunged from positive imagery—for instance, the Baltic Sun Maiden and her apple, and "the pomegranate and lily of the Ishtars" (Friedrich, 75). Only the rose of the Indo-European dawn goddess remained attached to the sacred sexual female (the Baltic Sun Maiden's apple having been confiscated to effect The Fall), but we lost the goddess and her symbol, the rose, drifted toward the virginal as that became the only sacred sexual female figure. Additionally, the early Sidonians worshiped a sensuous Astarte (or Asherah?) "depicted as a naked woman in the prime of her years, often with emphasis on the erotic zones. The lily that she held symbolized her charm, the serpent her fecundity" (Friedrich, 18).

In the desecration of both the apple of the Baltic Sun Maiden and the serpent of Astarte, and in the reassigning of the lily, we witness the same phenomenon, the root cause: the defiling of women and the symbols of their power. Arguably, had Mary Magdalene's role been foregrounded in Christian narratives, then Easter symbolism need not have so obliterated female, in exchange for male transcendent, regenerative power. For it is Magdalene who comes to the tomb while it is still dark the third day after the crucifixion, the sexual woman in the dark, just before dawning. It is Magdalene who sees the angels, Magdalene to whom Christ first appears and gives the charge of telling the disciples that he is not dead, but risen. This sacred task goes to Magdalene—the sacred, sexual, active female—who asks the man she believes to be the gardener to tell her where they have taken the body of her lord and "I will take him away" (John 20:15). The active female, she will go and get him. It is Magdalene whose name Jesus calls and she who recognizes his voice and identifies him as "Rabboni" (teacher). It is Magdalene who sees and conveys, and thus gives transcendent birth, not just to flesh but to spirit. It is she who brings the message that spirit is here, with us. It does not die with common death. Ivy understands the truth that Mary Magdalene communicated and applies it to those dearest to her. She keeps the spirit of her sister Silvaney alive, a binding love that does not separate Ivy from life but rejuvenates, gives it rebirth.

Christian iconography has not recognized the goddess of the dawn, who brings forth the resurrected sun, but Christ did. And Lee Smith, who gets the point and treats it with humor, puts Mary Magdalene in *Fair and Tender Ladies,* but she is not the active sexual female who is honored by Christ outside the tomb. For the active sexual female is not honored in Christian iconography; rather, she is dishonored. In *Fair and Tender Ladies* she is diminished, "little," and in a pink dress, not full and red (*Fair,* 257).

The whole cultural drift, as Friedrich argues in *The Meaning of Aphrodite,* toward the demonization, marginalization, and severance of powerful and benevolent images of women in the history of mythic storytelling in the circum-Mediterranean is sadly apparent in the case of Lilith, whose name Lily—the woman who is "put away" in Smith's short story "Not Pictured"—echoes. Lilith was

> probably well known to the Hebrews, although she is mentioned only once (Isaiah 34:14). She becomes much more important in the Talmudic and even more in the Kabbalistic period. By this time she is often nude, sexually aggressive, a child-killer, liminal, very red (lips, hair, robe), and the procreatress of a whole race of demons. In some ways, but only some, the medieval Hebrews distinguished sharply between two aspects of sensuousness (roughly Eve versus Lilith) that had been fused in Cybele, Astarte, and even some of the Greek Aphrodites. This distinction corresponds roughly to the one in many contemporary cultures between a wife and a whore (i.e., *either* a wife *or* a whore). . . . Some variant of the Babylonian goddess was seen by the authors of Revelation 17 as a woman with whom the kings of the earth had fornicated "and the inhabitants of the earth have been made drunk with the wine of her fornication. . . . A woman upon a scarlet-colored beast, full of the names of blasphemy, having seven heads and ten horns . . . arrayed in purple and scarlet color, and decked with gold and precious stones and pearls, and having a golden cup in her hand full of abominations and the filthiness of her fornication." (Friedrich, 213)

Ivy Rowe's is the healing, authorial voice *both* telling and writing a new story, inserting her story into the canon as well as speaking the mother tongue. Growing up in the mountains, Ivy *writes* in mountain dialect, thus providing a bridge between the lyrical oral and the codified written. Her first rhapsodic letters are set against no standard English that would tarnish and diminish their magic power. Some readers and critics expressed disappointment that her language became more standardized over time, but that may simply be a part of Ivy's learning to live both lyrically and realistically in the world. Ivy Rowe is born around the turn of the century, the time of the first Almarine's manhood. Her life spans both world wars and Vietnam, but the mythic past is also present. When Ivy and Honey Breeding—both exactly the same size, like Red Emmy and Almarine as well as Dory and Richard of *Oral History*—make love on a mountaintop and in a cave, Ivy asserts that "Whitebear Whittington lives yet up on Hell Mountain. . . . He lives there now I tell you and he is wild, wild. He runs through the night with his eyes on fire and no one can take him, yet he will sleep of a day as peaceful as a lullaby" (*Fair*, 315).

We are as far back in time as Red Emmy (Ivy, too, is redheaded), as humankind's earliest religious stirrings, when the goddess of the hearth sat and talked all night with the cave bear, the "earliest animal master."[9] According to Joseph Campbell, the cave-bear sanctuaries date from ca. 200,000 to 25,000 B.C. (*Primitive*, 395), putting us back in time before the diminishment and eventual defilement of the naked goddess and her replacement by men in magical costumes.[10] So in some sense we jump the gap jumped in *Oral History*, going all the way back to an imagined time before the devolution of the female image occurred, before Inanna, Sumerian Queen of Earth and Heaven, became the whore of Babylon.

But the sacred-sexual figure of Ivy, bridging as she does the present and the mythic past, heals this split. Smith seems again, by *Fair and Tender Ladies*, to associate caves with female sexuality. The first time Ivy is kissed—by her future husband, Oakley Fox—is when as a girl she has entered a cave in a timid exploration (*Fair*, 59). She goes back to stand at the cave mouth after his death.

Furthermore, Ivy has a mind, but it is not a disembodied mind. Even though she is a reader and a writer, she is not a "disembodied voice in the library"; the book is epistolary, woman's immanent thought and art. Ivy refuses all the lures and rewards of the dominant culture, including a Boston education and European travel, and chooses to stay in her beloved mountains. She refuses to be condemned by polite culture: pregnant and unmarried, she is glad to be "ruint" because it makes her free. She refuses to be condemned by the church, closing her mind to the hellfire-and-brimstone preacher Brother Garnie, who tells her that she is Babylon's "whore and an abomination" (*Fair*, 251). And Ivy never abandons Silvaney, that part of the female self that is all shimmering, vulnerable light and tenderness, who, because society is so cruel to it, must be hidden in the silvery part of the imagination. Silvaney's name evokes woodland spirits—the maenads and satyrs, wilderness companions of Bacchus, who abandoned themselves in sheer ecstasy to the joys of wine and dance. *Satyr and Maenad,* a portion of a Roman frieze at New York's Metropolitan Museum of Art, is a paean to wild joy worthy of Silvaney herself.[11]

Ivy writes Silvaney, even after Silvaney is dead. As Smith's writing becomes more healing, she gives wounded women each other; she gives them sisters who bring self-repair. Ivy goes the final step and takes this damaged and beloved figure inside as part of herself, part of her psychic core, and refuses to allow her to die. Society kills her, but the point now becomes quite different from Smith's earlier novels, in which the woman had needed to learn to admit that death existed but also that she need not be complicitous in societal murder. When society has killed something so valuable, the point is for women, humans, to keep it alive, even if only in the imagination. Ivy refuses to admit that Silvaney is dead, even after her brother Victor—the second Victor in Smith's fiction who is a voice for cynicism and negation—throws Silvaney's death in her face. Here, by refusing to admit her death, Ivy stands up to this Victor and keeps Silvaney alive, hence making that part of women's lives durable. Ivy has what Crystal Spangler lacked: a collective voice, a stubborn will, and a self-determination remade daily. Having made women's lives and their pain durable and collective—that is, mythic—in *Fair and Tender Ladies,* Smith can allow them imaginative flight.

APHRODITE AND DEMETER

> Perhaps some future titan of the novel or epic will create a full synthesis of the meanings of Demeter and Aphrodite that will recapture the archaic synthetic imagery of the early Mayans and Indo-Europeans. Perhaps, also, we can hope for a future that will recognize, accept, and encourage the deep and natural connections between sexuality and motherliness-maternity. The split between them should be healed in the world view, or by the religion, by the system of ideas, whatever it is called, that connects our concrete lives with the awesome powers beyond our control. (Friedrich, 191)

With *Fair and Tender Ladies* we come to the fulfillment of Smith's long fictive exploration of the problem of female development. Ivy Rowe, whose name promises order without destruction of nature, embodies female victory over the social forces, externally inflicted and internally realized, that would destroy her. This novel stands in direct counterpoise to *Black Mountain Breakdown,* with *Oral History*'s sacrificial offering of Dory the mediating link. Arguably, *Fair and Tender Ladies* solves what Friedrich sees as the greatest single problem in female psychological development: the disjunction of sex-sensuousness and maternity-motherliness or, as he argues it is embodied, the separation of Aphrodite and Demeter (Friedrich, 187–88). Dory had embodied Aphrodite and Demeter, and Dory died. She found herself in the same position as Anna Karenina in more ways than one: "Anna Karenina certainly houses the two complexes [Aphrodite and Demeter] within herself, but it is precisely the conflicts they engender that lead to her suicide" (Friedrich, 183). When we recall the cat, Anna Karen, in Smith's first novel, we see that this was always a preoccupation: "It's named for a Russian lady Mama told me about who got killed when a train ran over her," Susan explains to Gregory, adding, "That's how much you know about anything." Understandably, this makes Gregory mad and he stalks off, the cat going after him. "I liked that cat a whole lot more after I knew about the Russian lady and the train," Susan muses, "I wondered why she didn't run when she saw that train coming at her."[12]

The lady did not run because she had internalized the split. Friedrich traces the disjunction of these emotional complexes—sex-sensuousness and maternity-motherliness—as far back as Inanna: "One decisive fact is that Inanna is never maternal, and that procreation and generation are patronized by various important mother goddesses, with whom she should not be confused. . . . The sharp dichotomization between sexuality and maternity anticipates at the very outset of this study a basic issue" (Friedrich, 14). Friedrich sees Aphrodite as a synthesis: she is not only the most sensual and powerful but the most motherly of the four queens of heaven—Hera, Athena, Aphrodite, and Artemis. But in his analysis her motherliness and maternity are relegated to secondary status, and "the symbolic conflicts between this and sexuality/sensuousness" keep her from filling what he refers to as an "emotional gap" in the Greek pantheon (Friedrich, 150). Friedrich sees Demeter as standing for the mother-child bond, especially the bond between mother and daughter:

> It is the Greek Demeter, the loving, nurturing, grieving mother, who alone can be said to epitomize the tenderness and loyalty between

mother and daughter, which reaches a sort of acme during the daughter's later childhood and early adolescence—precisely when Persephone [the daughter] was raped. [Demeter] stands for motherliness just as Aphrodite stands for sensuousness, and in each case the meaning is partly Greek and partly universal. (Friedrich, 158)

But Friedrich goes on to note that the filling of the "emotional gap" by Demeter still leaves a lacuna in integrated female psychology. The dichotomy between erotic and maternal remains (and now we are back to Smith's first novel, *The Last Day the Dogbushes Bloomed*), even when all the queens of heaven are explored: "Both Aphrodite and Athena lack a mother (in some sense), but one incarnates sexuality while the other is a- or antisexual. Artemis is antisexual but is maximally identified with her mother (and in earlier myth was very much a mother figure herself). It is striking that nowhere, even when we add Demeter-Persephone, is a strong mother tie combined with strongly positive sexuality" (Friedrich, 160). In surveying "myth, religion, and high literature" Friedrich finds the dissociation of sex-sensuousness and maternity-motherliness a barrier against "a more general image of the artistically creative woman" (182, 190). The separation of emotional complexes that no doubt derive from the same source prevents a woman from being understood or from understanding herself.[13]

SYNTHESIS

Ivy Rowe walks out of this conflict and establishes a different option, another ending. Society and its cultural imagings continue to be destructive of her self, but she is not. Ivy constitutes a synthesis of Aphrodite and Demeter, incorporating both in her person and in her life. She balances these impulses and refuses the prescriptions of patriarchy—shame, self-disgust—by staying close to her mountain roots, her womanly life. She is, to borrow Friedrich's words, "at once maternal, sororal, and erotic" (46), intelligent and proud.

With Honey Breeding, a beekeeper whose name and occupation suggest a union of male and female, of sweet sexuality and equality between honey men and candy women, we have come as far from the rape of Susan and of Crystal as possible. Like Ivy Rowe's, Honey Breeding's name also means a union of nature and culture. Smith has given us a new sex god and sex goddess, and we like them. As male and female get closer together, they become more alike in size and in essence. In fact, Honey Breeding becomes like Aphrodite: "He is not a big man, Silvaney. . . . He is skinny, wiry, with pale thick curly gold hair on his forehead and thick gold eyebrows that nearabout grow together, and hair all over him like spun gold on his folded forearms. . . . [He] did not seem quite real. He seemed more like a woods creature fetched up somehow from the forest, created out of fancy, on a whim" (*Fair,* 214).[14]

As the forty-year-old mother of five children, Ivy surrenders to sensuality with Honey Breeding. Like Joline B. Newhouse of Smith's short story "Between the Lines," with her memory of Marcel Wilkes in the "holy Woods," Ivy never regrets this affair. She feels it brings her back to life, gives her her "soul back," and renews her relationship with her husband. But, as with Joline, there is some struggle with the idea of punishment, of inflicting suffering on children. Joline struggles but finally refuses to believe that her son's birth defect is a result of her "sin." But when Ivy comes down from the mountain to find that her next-to-youngest daughter, LuIda, is dead, apparently from an attack of appendicitis (*Fair,* 250), Ivy says that "a part of me died with her" (243) and, further, "I know LuIda's dying is all my fault and if I had not run off with Honey Breeding it would not have happened, LuIda would be alive today, playing down at the creek from Maudy. . . . I wish it was me instead" (244).

Ivy does not receive Joline's consolation, but Ivy nonetheless never repudiates the joy of her time with Honey Breeding, nor does she put herself in the way of any trains. The anxiety of the disjunction, however, is not erased, for the death of LuIda encodes the conflict between sex-sensuousness and maternity-motherliness. But men, too, are not free from this disjunction. As characters, Ivy's uncle Revel Rowe, her lover Franklin Ransom, and even Honey Breeding are subjected to stereotyping in which "a large number of women in many cultures dichotomize men just as sharply into what is a mirror image of the lover versus the mother, into the sensuous (and relatively irresponsible) male lover versus the positive and nurturing father-husband" (Friedrich, 188). Honey's configuration as liminal and a divinity, however, may take him beyond such categories.

The interlude with Honey Breeding is necessary for Ivy to feel alive enough to give life to her children. It is a moment of sacred sex, of healing

the Secret Wound. This moment intersects with a timeless realm and be-
stows, at least temporarily, divinity. It seems to be an encounter with the
divine and thus beyond the categories of social stereotypes.

IVY'S FAMILY

Ivy's first letters show a strong identification with the mother. Like Pricey
Jane, Ivy observes the effects of a hard life on her mother, who becomes
"hard as a rocky-clift, and her eyes burns out in her head" (*Fair,* 27). "My
momma was young and so pretty when she come riding up Sugar Fork, but
she does not look pretty now, she looks awful, like her face is hanted, she
has had too much on her" (15). She also writes lovingly of Granny Rowe,
who "chews tobaccy and spits in the fire" (21). The fact that "Granny
Rowe is my antie I think not my granny relly" (21) does not diminish the
fact that Ivy remembers Granny's wisdom and advice throughout her life,
and even thinks she sees her, walking up ahead, at times of trouble.

Women's relationships with women are much more fully developed in
Fair and Tender Ladies than in Smith's other novels. They are teaching,
talking to, telling stories about, and connecting to other women. Granny's
sister, Tennessee, is a sort of Aphrodite-gone-to-seed who exposes herself to
men. Ivy also loves the old sisters, Gaynelle and Virgie Cline, who arrive
on "Old Christmas! for this is when they used to come every year, January
5 like clockwork and stay up all nigt and drink coffee and tell storys with
Daddy, they did it when he was not but a child living here with his own
momma and daddy and his sister Vicey and brother Revel. Daddy allus
said it seemed to him that they were old ladys then, so dont nobody know
how old they migt be now" (*Fair,* 33). It is the Cline sisters who tell the
mythic story of Whitebear Whittington. Later, with Honey Breeding, Ivy
says she is "starved for stories," stories told by wise, craggy, and sometimes
tender old women.

Ivy also has tender regard for her father, whom she mostly knows as
lying on a "pallet" with a heart condition but remembers as healthy, saying
to her: *"Farming is pretty work . . . Now Ivy, this is how spring tastes. This is the
taste of spring"* (*Fair* 42, 177). In fact, there is healing in the father-male
image in *Fair and Tender Ladies,* partly signified by Ivy's father's name,
John Arthur. This is the third time the name Arthur appears in Smith's
fiction. As Jean Markale traces in *Women of the Celts,* the legendary Arthur

"is a mocked and cuckolded king whose wife Guinevere (Gwenhwyfar in Welsh, meaning 'white shadow') symbolizes true sovereignty according to Celtic belief; but she is often taken away from him by her lovers and it is not unreasonable to wonder whether Arthur is a later, patriarchal transformation of an ancient bear goddess." (The postulated root of Celtic **arto-* yields "bear" and "Arthur.")[15]

I realize that all the associations here cannot be disentangled within the scope of this study. What I do wish to point out is how Smith's imagination, and particularly her linguistic sense, restlessly returns to root sources of cultural constructs that have to do with white/black, female/male, and human/animal. If the name Arthur does come from perhaps an animal and perhaps a female deity, then all the boundaries drawn by patriarchal constructions—reified in heroic tales of such semihistorical figures as Arthur—are breached.

What is important in *Fair and Tender Ladies* is that linguistic possibilities merge with imaginative contents, and within Smith's own naming and image system enormous reconciliation has occurred. A far cry from the sick fantasy figure of Smith's first novel, *The Last Day the Dogbushes Bloomed,* the Arthur of *Fair and Tender Ladies* is a tender and sensual man who teaches his daughter how spring tastes and how pretty farming is. He is sick, but what ails him is his heart—perhaps the best we can hope for of the patriarch at this stage of Smith's work. And the figure that fires the imagination in *Fair and Tender Ladies* is not the perverse Little Arthur but a healthy animal—the wild Whitebear Whittington, who runs through the night with his eyes on fire, and no one can take him. Through Ivy's healthy imagination, the father and the animal are held in tension, reconciled and redeemed. I am suggesting that one reason this feels so satisfying is that Smith's unerring linguistic sense has rediscovered an ancient connection.

To bridge domains further, Whitebear lives up on Hell Mountain. (Hell fire probably stands for internal creative fire in the first place.) As much as King Dog, who comes down from the mountaintop with his twelve disciples to surround Susan in the healing vision of Smith's first novel, the image of Whitebear Whittington, running Hell Mountain at night, redeems darkness, fire, and even hell. John Arthur's red hair and his lying in front of the fire while his heart hurts suggest both a kinship with the bear and the possible source of his heart trouble. Now Smith, who refused to turn her back on Little Arthur in her first novel, nurses an Arthur neither perverse like Little

Arthur nor trivialized like the Arthur of *Family Linen* (who marries a nurse). This third Arthur is a worthy man whose suffering hurts his daughter and hurts us as well. John Arthur bears the Secret Wound (as does Crystal's father)—that iconography for the split between nature and culture, between matter and spirit, which Smith is trying to heal.

Although the father in *The Last Day the Dogbushes Bloomed* is not king in the way that the King Dog is, John Arthur of *Fair and Tender Ladies* may well be the bear. We can learn something about the imagination if we remember, as James Joyce in *Ulysses* reminds every English literature student, that "dog" is "god" spelled backwards. As Smith matured as a writer, her early crude playfulness with language—imaged in Susan's spellings and Brooke's crossword puzzles and practiced in "King Dog"—has developed into the ability to cast a spell as well as to discover those ancient crossroads where words—and meanings and categories usually held as oppositional—really do intersect, making it possible for us to remake the world. Reversal and sarcasm are liberating, but they do not heal like the slow and painful digging for forgotten connections.

MATERNAL INSTINCTS

Ivy likes the mothering duties she has as one of many children ("The next leastest has to watch out for the leastest ones, and I loved to do that" [*Fair,* 19]), and she becomes a mother herself at about age eighteen. Mothering, or at least a choice of love that leads to mothering, is what she chooses instead of going to Boston with Miss Torrington to "fulfill her potential."

Instead, Ivy stays in Majestic, Virginia. That very night, she has intercourse with Lonnie Rash. She does not love Lonnie Rash and does not pretend, even to herself, that she does. They are incompatible; he can neither read nor write, and Ivy is smart and knows it. He is simply the first male to whom she feels erotically drawn. Smith acknowledges the need to address the purely erotic, but she sees it for what it is. Even though Ivy is "ruint" she never thinks of marrying this boy who is eventually killed in World War I. When Lonnie leaves to join the army, Ivy stands on the river bridge and watches the water in "little eddies, little whirlpools." "Well, I thought, that's that, and with him gone it was like my whole self came rushing back to me again and I looked at the water and thought, Oh I *do* want to go to Boston, I do want to go after all!" (*Fair,* 119). Her next thought is particularly interesting in light of our discussion of emotional disjunction: "And I recalled Miss Torringtons letter, how she said that there are kinds and kinds of love and that sometimes we confuse them being only mortal as we are, and how she said that she would never be other than my good true friend if I would reconsider coming" (119).

Just as she is writing Miss Torrington to tell her she will come to Boston, Ivy discovers her pregnancy, does not go to Boston, and winds up going to Diamond to live with her eldest sister, Beulah, who has delivered an illegitimate son and named him John Arthur, just after their father's death. "Granny Rowe says that sometimes it happens like that, one spirrit goes and a nother one comes direckly" (*Fair*, 50). Ivy goes to live with Beulah and her husband, Curtis (who finally marries Beulah against his mother's wishes), in Diamond Mining's company town. Beulah is bitter about her past, her womanhood, her childbearing, and her red hair: "Dont you *ever*, Beulah said, I mean *ever* Ivy Rowe, call old Granny over here with all her crazy old ideas. I wont have it. I will not. Beulah laid in the bed with her red hair splayed out on the pillow like a sunset. She is very beautiful. *I will not forget, she said, how we lived on Sugar Fork, how I bore that one*—she pointed at John Arthur, playing with a pan on the floor—*by myself on a cornhusk tick and cut the cord myself with the hatchet*" (134).

But Ivy's experience is different. Granny Rowe shows up just at the time Ivy's baby, Joli, is to be born: "Then Beulah popped up and said, Why that is ridiculous, Granny! You know nobody can tell exactly when a baby is coming, especially a first baby" (*Fair*, 143). "But Granny laughed, and in the dark you could see her pipe shine red [note the repetition of the color red] when she pulled on it. *It's the full moon, honey, she said. Just look at it*" (143).

Ivy's memory of the birth is lyrical, reversing Susan's fear and shame of the blood bucket:

The blood smell was not so bad. It was sweet some way, it was not like anything else in the world, and now it will always be mixed up in my mind somehow with the moonlight and my baby, for then Granny handed her to me. I held her close by my side and looked at the moonlight on closest star [quilt]. . . . *This is important, I want to remember this, it is all so important, this is happening to me.* And I am so glad to write it down lest I forget. I lay there real still while the moonlight slowly crossed my quilt, and listened to a hoot owl off in the woods, and little

Joli breathing, and—come morning—the long sweet whistle of the train. (*Fair,* 149)

The train no longer causes death; its sweet whistle we hear. And the woman herself—bleeding and red—has through Ivy's birthing and Smith's writing been redeemed. Ivy retains a special love for her firstborn all through her life, writing her in 1945: "And you can rest assured that there never was a daughter in this wide world that brought more joy to her mother's heart" (*Fair,* 268). Not only is Ivy happy to have Joli, but she is glad she is "ruint" because it saves her from wasting time trying to do everything exactly right (164).

After Ivy marries Oakley Fox and moves back up to the family farm at Sugar Fork, she bears twin sons, Bill and Danny Ray (born on Christmas Eve, 1929), and daughters LuIda (1935) and Maudy (1936). Apparently Joli was born in 1918. Now Ivy feels the drain of mothering, for that is also a truth of mothering, as Smith reminds us:

Silvaney, I have been caught up for so long in a great soft darkness, a blackness so deep and so soft that you can fall in there and get comfortable and never know you are falling in at all, and never land, just keep on falling. I wonder now if this is what happened to Momma. . . . I am so tired. . . . Maudy is the prettiest little baby I have ever had, but when she sucks it is like she is sucking the life right out of me. (*Fair,* 195)

Ivy is thirty-seven when she writes this; she will not feel alive again for three more years, not until Honey Breeding, the erotic who brings her to life again: "It is like I've had an electric shock. So now I am so much alive, I am tingling. I believe I know how you felt, Silvaney. For the first time, I know. I am on fire. I can feel it running through my veins and out my fingers" (*Fair,* 210).

Ivy's venture into the wild, from its beginning in the springhouse, restores her joy in the world: "And I love it here! Honeysuckle vines have grown up all over the bushes along the path, and wild white roses all down the steps. . . . It is like another world" (*Fair,* 213). What Honey Breeding does is make Ivy recognize that she is a queen: "Then he grabbled . . . down in the bag . . . and came up with the Queen" (215). Then he fashions Ivy a crown of starflowers. When she protests that she is too old to be a princess, he says "then you look like a Queen" (230). But what of her relationship with her family?

And yet you know that I love Oakley. He is my life. I love this farm, and these children, and Oakley, with all my heart. But there is something about a man that is *too good* which will drive you crazy. . . . It makes you want to dance in the thunderstorm. . . . For a long time I thought I was old. . . .

But now I am on fire. (*Fair,* 210)

Ivy's erotic love for Honey Breeding enables her to return to the farm, the family, and the children and love them with all her heart, for her heart is then larger. That is precisely what great, ecstatic, imaginative love does, according to Smith:

You know Silvaney, it is a funny thing, but that time I ran off with Honey Breeding helped not hurt, with me and Oakley. He has been *new* for me ever since, some way, and me for him, and even though I am way too old now to think on such things, I blush to say they come to mind often, they do! I am always ready for Oakley to lay me down. Back when I was lost in darkness, it was not so. For when you are caught so far down, you can not imagine the sun, or see a ray of sunshine any place. (*Fair,* 269–70)

Honey and Ivy's passion creates light, and she brings this light home. Her capacity for mothering has broadened, as has her need for selfhood. Ivy mothers children other than her own in the course of the novel. She takes in Violet Gayheart's retarded daughter, Martha, and Joli's son, David, after Joli's divorce. But in her old age, more than anything else, she wants to be alone. Ivy is a mother, but she is not defined by motherhood.

CONCLUSION

In her essay "From Shadow to Substance: The Empowerment of the Artist Figure in Lee Smith's Fiction," Katherine Kearns traces throughout Smith's fiction the ambivalence about the dual roles of artist and mother.[16] Ivy's demurral that "I never became a writer atall. Instead I have loved, and loved, and loved" (*Fair,* 315) testifies to the conflict but suggests a solution, for Ivy is a writer. Roz Kaveney, reviewing *Oral History, Family Linen,* and *Fair and Tender Ladies,* also points to the solution: "If Lee Smith has a weakness as a writer, it is that she writes at her best when she writes out of love" (Kaveney, 803). If Smith writes at her best when she writes out of love, then the writing and the love nourish each other. As with maternal-motherliness and sex-sensuousness, the disjunction between maternal-motherliness and art-artist is false.

Not only is Smith's reconciliation of male-female rich, vast, and broad in *Fair and Tender Ladies,* but so is her reconciliation of female-female. One of the most interesting things to trace in Smith's fiction is the development of this character who is Brooke, Lily, Crystal, Dory, Pearl, and then Fay, and who finally reaches a kind of culmination in Silvaney, or rather in Ivy's preservation of Silvaney. In her various guises she is an essential part of the female psyche. First self-consciously shallowed, then catatonic, then irreparably—by biology and society—maimed, this female core in Silvaney is again irreparably maimed, but she is saved through a woman's remembrance, through female honoring of the female. In Silvaney this female core is finally internalized.

Ivy burns the letters to Silvaney at the end of the novel, saying that the letters did not matter, "it was the writing of them that signified" (*Fair,* 313). The connection between Ivy and Silvaney is mutually redemptive, and it is a process, not an artifact. Each saves, preserves, and allows for the existence of the other and for "female creativity as a necessary and sufficient condition" (Friedrich, 117).

Fair and Tender Ladies validates a woman's life and strength. It validates the woman-woman connection and women's stories. It promises hope. Its last line, "O, I was young then and I walked in my body like a Queen," is a benediction for every woman's life. Above all, it valorizes women's grief, and their ability to withstand it by sharing it. And they will not stop, not even for God himself.[17]

Notes

1. *Fair and Tender Ladies* (New York: G. P. Putnam's Sons, 1988); hereafter cited in text.
2. Ken Ringle, "Lee Smith at Home with Her Muse," *Washington Post,* 4 Dec. 1988, F6.
3. Vicki Covington, "Hail to Lee Smith and Ivy Rowe and the Courage to Write," *Atlanta Journal and Constitution,* 25 Sept. 1988, 11.
4. Roz Kaveney, "In the South," *Times Literary Supplement,* 21–27 July 1989, 803; hereafter cited in text.
5. Paul Friedrich, *The Meaning of Aphrodite* (Chicago: University of Chicago Press, 1978), 220; hereafter cited in text.
6. *Newsweek,* 31 Oct. 1988, 72H.

7. W. P. Kinsella, "Left behind on Blue Star Mountain," review of *Fair and Tender Ladies*, *New York Times Book Review*, 18 Sept. 1988, 9.

8. Joseph Campbell, *Creative Mythology* (New York: Penguin, 1976), 109.

9. Joseph Campbell, *Primitive Mythology* (New York: Penguin, 1987), 349; hereafter cited in text.

10. According to Diane Ackerman, "We like to think that we are finely evolved creatures, in suit-and-tie or pantyhose-and-chemise, who live many millennia and mental detours away from the cave, but that's not something our bodies are convinced of" (*A Natural History of the Senses* [New York: Random House, 1990], xxvii).

11. Yet further corroborative proof of a drift towards desacralizing female joy may lodge in the etymology and definition of *maenad* and *satyr*, the female and male ecstatic followers of Bacchus and Dionysus. Interest in Silvaney and the complex she embodies, particularly her name's evocation of *sylvan*, led me to explore these terms. I was taken aback when each dictionary definition of *maenad* led fairly quickly to "madwoman," whereas the first definition for *satyr* seemed to be "wilderness god" or "sylvan deity." *Webster's New Twentieth Century Dictionary Unabridged Second Edition* (Prentice Hall, 1983), for example, gives meanings of *maenad* as (adj.) "raving, frantic" and (noun) "a madwoman." Then the definition moves to "in Greek and Roman mythology, a priestess of Bacchus." Interesting to our study here is that the first quotation in the *Oxford Dictionary of English Etymology*, edited by C. T. Onions, links the maenad to Mary Magdalene in a quote from T. Robinson's 1620 work, *Mary Magdalene:* "The maenads, Bacchus frantick priestes . . . " The *Webster's* cited above first identifies *satyr* as "satyr, companion, sylvan god usually represented as part animal . . . fond of riotous merriment and lechery." Full chronological examination of these words and the history of their definitions with cultural implications is beyond the scope of this study, but etymology shows *maenad* to be derived from the Greek *mainas*, literally "madwoman." *Satyr* is derived from the Greek *satyros*, meaning a satyr, companion, sylvan god. *A Compact Edition of the Oxford English Dictionary* (Oxford University Press, 1971) stretches the mythological definition of *satyr* as "one of a class of woodland gods or demons, in form partly human and partly bestial, supposed to be companions of Bacchus." It is interesting that *satyr* moves toward the animal kingdom, whereas the Greek root of *maenad* also gives *spirit* and *mind*. So could one be led to believe that, in the throes of ecstasy, he's likely to become an animal (and a bit demonic at that), whereas she's in danger of losing her mind?

12. *The Last Day the Dogbushes Bloomed* (New York: Harper and Row, 1968), 9.

13. According to Patricia Monaghan, "All these apparent contradictions cease to be problematical, however, if one extends the 'three persons in one god' concept to this trinity of Sumerian divinities. They've seen that the mother, the lover, and the sister were all aspects of a single grand figure: the queen of heaven" (*The Book of Goddesses and Heroines* [New York: Dutton, 1981], 150).

14. Regarding the split between sex and language I discuss in chapter 3 of *Lee Smith* (when Crystal is raped), note:

At a deeper level there is an association between gold, honey, speech and sexual fluids, as we find in Slavic (especially gold/honey) and Indic (gold/semen). As for gold/speech, the entire phrase "speech sweeter than honey" is . . . one of the relatively complex syntactic units that we can reconstruct with complete confidence for Proto-Indo-European because of point-for-point correspondences between the strings of words in Greek, Celtic, (Old Irish), Anatolian, and yet other languages. . . . Gold and its semantic cognates in speech, honey, and semen therefore symbolize the yet deeper Aphrodite values of procreation, verbal creation, and so forth. There are more strands to this skein, but I think what

I have singled out so far should suggest the richness and complexity of the supposedly "simple" epithet "golden." (Friedrich, 79)

15. Jean Markale, *Women of the Celts,* trans. A. Mygind, C. Hauch, and P. Henry (Rochester, Vt.: Inner Traditions, 1986), 92–93.

16. In *Writing the Woman Artist,* ed. Suzanne W. Jones (Philadelphia: University of Pennsylvania Press, 1991), 175–95.

17. The epigraph to *Fair and Tender Ladies,* Kathryn Stripling Byer's poem "Weep-Willow," collected in *Wildwood Flower* (Baton Rouge: Louisiana State University Press, 1992), includes the lines "but she'd not stop, / no, not for God Himself."

"WHERE'S LOVE?"

The Overheard Quest in the Stories of Jo Carson

ROBERT J. HIGGS

Grace is a recurring theme in the stories of Jo Carson. The idea of grace is announced in the prologue of *Stories I Ain't Told Nobody Yet:*

Willis Comfort did not outlive
as many enemies as he hoped to.
I know because I was one of 'em.
I do not plan to do to his grave
what he swore he'd do to mine.

Grace or dying, one got Willis;
I hope it was the grace.
See, grace don't always come
on the wings of a dove
or as a thief in the night
or however it's supposed to.

Originally published in a different form in *Iron Mountain Review* 14 (Summer 1998): 9–18. Reprinted by permission of the author and the publisher. Excerpts from *Stories I Ain't Told Nobody Yet* by Jo Carson © 1989 by Jo Carson. Reprinted by permission of Scholastic Inc. "Waltz Across Texas," words and music by Talmadge Tubb. Copyright 1965 by Ernest Tubb Music. All rights reserved. International copyright secured. Used with permission.

Sometimes it comes like a two-by-four
to the side of the head
and folks don't live through it.
(3)

To some of Carson's more desperate characters, teaching lessons to others
by violence appears an option, however unwise or unproductive. In
"Maybe," a sad but often funny story of a triangle about love and marriage,
Harry and Dessa, whom Harry calls "Maybe" for her indecisiveness about
getting married, live together for fourteen years in what qualifies as a
common-law marriage. Harry, though, wants another kind of marriage.
"Common law," he says. "Well, hell, it's embarrassing to have waited so
long that the state of Virginia decided for you" (*The Last of the "Waltz Across
Texas" and Other Stories,* 63). Harry then tells what happened when he went
the route of the ordinary kind of marriage:

> Now, I did go and marry Brenda and I guess that's a reason to get pretty
> mad, but I asked Dessa first and I asked a hell of a lot in fourteen years,
> if you count it once a month, it's an awful lot and I was asking more
> than that early on. Say two hundred times. A man gets turned down
> two hundred times, he's got the right to change something. Now,
> Dessa's gonna tell you she lived with me all those years and she did.
> And she's gonna tell you that I got a wild hair and went down to
> Nashville and met Brenda and married her. And I did. But it wasn't a
> wild hair. I told her I was gonna do it and she didn't budge an inch. And
> then, she's gonna tell you I brought Brenda back home and was throw-
> ing her out. I guess I was, but why the hell did she wait till then to tell
> me something? "You bastard," she said. "I love you!" and then she shot
> me. (65)

Dessa could have killed Harry but instead shot him in the leg, explaining her reasons as follows:

> I had thought I might kill Harry if he really came back with a different
> wife, but Sunshine pointed out that no man was worth spending the
> rest of your life in jail over so I wasn't going to do anything until they

stood together right there in front of me—but I hadn't planned for the sight of them. I couldn't stand not to do something. I shot Harry because I wanted him to have to look down that gun and see me holding it. I wanted him to get scared. I wanted him to think about fourteen years and to regret this new wife even if it was just for a second. Harry is not the sort of man who comes up with regret by himself. (64)

Much as in the case of the Grandmother in Flannery O'Connor's "A Good Man Is Hard to Find," Harry might have been a good common-law husband if Dessa had threatened to shoot him every minute of their fourteen-year common-law marriage; or, from poor Harry's point of view, he might have been a good common-law husband if Dessa just once had said, maybe even ten years into their relationship, "I love you, you bastard." There is the strong implication here that love, at least in some cases, needs confirmation by the tongue.

The following brief masterpiece of comedy by Carson will give some idea of the precariousness of marriage and divorce and just about everything else in the imperfect world inhabited by her speakers:

I was born three months before I's due,
then I turned around
and got pneumonia
and then when I was nine,
I had leukemia.
I did.
I fell off'en a horse
and broke my neck
and lived.
And I went to war.
And since then,
I've wrecked two cars
and walked away,
clipped the wings off an airplane
landin' it,
and run out of a house afire.
I wiped out on a motorcycle
doin' about a hundred.

I been married full four times,
middle two liked to 'a killed me.

The fourth one's doin' alright so far,
except she keeps a-tellin' me
to be careful,
that I'm gettin' old.
(*Stories*, 74)

If second marriage represents, in the words of Dr. Samuel Johnson, the triumph of hope over experience, the speaker here exemplifies the continuing triumph of hope—which apparently culminates in that highest object of hope, true love, if wife number four doesn't say too much about her husband's age.

The pearl of great price in Carson's stories is usually not marriage for the sake of marriage but love itself, which often hangs in the balance as it does between Ralph and Nancy, husband and wife in the superb short story "The Last of the 'Waltz Across Texas.'" After another drinking binge, Ralph has returned to Nancy at their home near the intersection of Highways 19 and 23 to try one more time to make up.

> Ralph came slowly to his feet as Nancy approached and with a grace that is sometimes a gift to the desperate, he took Nancy in his arms and began to dance.
> "What the . . ."
> "Wait," he told her, "One, two, three, a waltz . . ."
> "Ralph!"
> "Please, dance with me."
> Nancy knew the song. She had loved it when Ernest Tubb first sang it on the radio, she had loved it when Ralph stepped down from the band and asked her to dance, she had cried to it in the last three days, Ernest Tubb singing it again on the record as she danced alone to find out how it felt.
> Ralph sang it.

> *When we dance together my world's in disguise,*
> *It's a fairy land tale that comes true.*

And when you look at me with those stars in your eyes
I could waltz across Texas with you.

"Don't," she begged, "you just make it harder." She tried to stop dancing but Ralph used the moment to turn and begin again in a new direction.

"I'm trying my damndest to make it so hard you won't," he whispered. Nancy stopped again but Ralph held her tighter and began the second verse.

My heartaches and troubles are just come and gone
The moment that you come into view.

Nancy danced and she began to cry.

And with your hand in mine, dear, I could dance on and on,
I could waltz across Texas with you.

Ralph held her, they stopped dancing.

Waltz across Texas with you in my arms,
Waltz across Texas with you,
Like a storybook ending I'm lost in your charms
And I could waltz across Texas with you. (125–26)

Carson's characters stand in need of love from one another, a fact of which they are usually keenly aware.

The love quest in Carson's stories is often desperate and takes several forms. Episodes are often humorous and even hilarious, but the blurb on the book's cover errs, I believe, when it refers to *The Last of the "Waltz Across Texas" and Other Stories* as "a comedy of survival." I don't mean to devalue the humor in Carson's pieces by this statement or humor in general. I agree with Johan Huizinga that the playful, in which I would also include the humorous, is of a higher order than the serious because the playful can be serious but the serious can't be playful. Humor, though, is a tool or a technique or a tone, the emotional attitude of the author toward a subject, but it is not precisely the subject itself, though it may tell us more about a region or a people than any other approach available to a writer.

Carson's characters and the people behind her voices do not set out merely to survive or endure but to prevail, and what they want to prevail in is the elusive thing called love, preferably with marriage but if necessary without it. Carson's characters will do anything for love or in the name of love: chain cars to furniture as in "Free Will" to preserve a marriage; shoot, maim, and murder; or even steal the dead as in "Splitshin." One of the grieving characters in this story is named Love so that at one point we have this question concerning his whereabouts after he disappears following the death of his brother Hascel: "Where's Love?" This question, viewed broadly and philosophically, is the major one in the fiction of Jo Carson; or put another way, in a phrase or idea that also appears frequently in her work, "Where is the good place?" Her people do not always succeed in finding such a place, but their quest is worthy of our attention. One section in *Stories* is entitled "Relationships," but that is what all Jo's pieces and stories are about: community and kin, marriage and divorce, and relationships with nature and God.

Carson's characters do not try to tell us with precision what love is, but whatever it is, it is something they seek, lament when lost, and seek to find again. Carson is not so much interested in love as a glorious abstraction that creates the music of the spheres and the beauty of the morning and evening star as in how it plays out in the ordinary houses, bars, and trailer camps in Appalachia, how it works out along Highways 19 and 23. Instead of serenely encircling the cosmos like Emerson's Oversoul, love in Carson's work is intertwined with death at ground level, eros and thanatos, like strands of DNA, each making the other meaningful, each redeeming the other in a very real sense.

In Carson's universe the only place we do see love is in the lives of ordinary people in their humble homes, communities, and places of work. Carson proceeds on the principle of *multum in parvo*, much in little. She does not so much offer splendid examples of love from the cosmos, great art and classical music as human illustrations of it in the everyday world, vignettes, snatches of conversations overheard, glimpses gained from the corner of one's eye.

What, then, are some of the features of love that we infer from what we overhear in Carson? Basic to love is learning to give and receive, as we note in selection number three from *Stories*.

I spent the first years of my life
sittin' on what we called splinter benches
'cause we were too poor for store-bought furniture.
You scooted, you got splinters.
My mama used to cry
'cause she wanted a bed with a real mattress
for Grandma Lynn to die on.
Turned out Grandma Lynn didn't need it.
She died mid-sentence at the women's circle.
But the first money I ever earned
I got Mama a store-bought mattress.
Daddy bought her two straight-back chairs
so she and him could sit proper at the table.
It was her birthday.
I never seen anybody since
made so happy by a gift.
(7)

As we have always known, love is seen as patience, long-suffering, and sacrifice, not to be confused with beauty, law, or wealth. Every case is different, though, so that long-suffering in one case may not be a good example of love in another. Love is also principle, standing for what is right, finding one's backbone and feeling it, as in the case of June Bug in "Hunting Husbands." It is close to duty but not synonymous with it. Duty means service and love means sacrifice, though sometimes both become so much a part of a particular "habit of being," to use a term of O'Connor's, that it becomes difficult to distinguish one from the other, as in the case of the speaker's mother in the following:

It was a Saturday and my mother was cooking.
She always cooked on Saturday
for us and for her bachelor brother
who came by on Sunday afternoon
and got his casseroles for the week.
None of them used tuna fish, mushrooms, peas . . .
there was a list of things he wouldn't eat.
We were not allowed to be so picky.

By Sunday they'd be frozen.
All he had to do was keep them frozen
and put them in the oven one at a time.
His were labeled, he knew what he was going to eat.
For herself, she looked into the frozen layers
and tried to remember.
I don't know why she did it.
He was perfectly capable of doing
anything else he set his mind to.
He could have learned to cook.

This Saturday
she was up to her elbows again in family and food.
I heard her in the kitchen. "No," she said.
After a moment: "I'm honored, but no thanks."
Another moment: "No, thank you, no, no, no."
I asked who she was talking to. She said,
"I'm practicing my speech for the circle,
they are planning to ask me to be president."

I thought she was very silly practicing
her public speaking with a series of emphatic no's
as she stacked casseroles in her freezer.
"No!" to the macaroni and cheese and tomatoes.
"No!" to the broccoli in concentrated celery soup.
"No. No. No."

It was twenty years before I understood
she was trying to learn how to say it.
(11–12)

What, for Carson's characters, is love's nemesis? Pretty much the same
as always for all of us. For the most part, they like to have money around.
Many of them know, though, that the problem is not the dollar but the
love of it, which corporations all too often in her stories have put ahead of
the welfare of employees. Carson's characters thus are quick to go on strike,
not simply to be striking but to obtain decent wages and working conditions and to achieve justice, as the female narrator explains in *The Last of*

the "Waltz Across Texas" at the opening of the short story "The Governor," which deals with a coal strike in Virginia.

> Everybody on our side was wearing the same colors, men, women, younguns, everybody who supported the strike. It surprised me who came down to the picket line. There is a woman on our block who doesn't ever give anything to that charity where somebody they talked into it— me—goes door to door and asks for money. Easter Seals or something. She won't even buy a chocolate bar to support the high school band and she ended up sitting down at the picket line. I know some people did it just to get arrested but I don't care. Maybe she has diabetes and can't eat chocolate. She sat down and got carried off to the bus. The bus was awful and hot and they'd make you sit there an extra hour or two with no water or anything just so you got good and miserable but people still did it even after they started imposing fines for civil disobedience.
>
> I loved that part of it. Solidarity. Like Poland. (35)

The "Governor" in this story is not the governor of Virginia but a three-foot rattlesnake, expert at giving shoe shine inspections of state law enforcement officers called in to keep the strike from becoming violent, a skillful touch of humor to leaven a serious endeavor with literally explosive possibilities.

Love of great ideas like liberty, equality, and justice is just as prevalent in Carson's work as the quest for romantic love and the search for the perfect mate. Indeed they have much in common. Life at work affects life at home and vice versa. Wherever injustice prevails, pain and trouble abound, as the speaker in the following reveals after being "terminated" from a local corporation apparently seeking to downsize.

> For the next person who pats me on the back
> to say a rotten deal, a crying shame,
> or some other easy whitewash
> that does not say what happened
> I have some new words: try injustice,
> say abuse out loud.
> And to those who will not look at me
> because somehow fired and failed
> are too close together,

bend over this barrel, friend,
your turn is likely to be next.
And for all who've never thought to ask it,
a question I never thought to ask till now:
who decided money is more valuable than people,
and why did all the rest of us agree to work that way?
(67)

Seeking justice in groups, getting involved in what Sherwood Anderson called the "gang spirit" in order to improve the quality of the lives of ordinary people, is one matter. Taking justice into one's own hands and in effect playing God, no matter how deplorable the situation, is another. In the short story "Sweet Rage" the situation is not just deplorable but hopeless from the outset. Here rage takes the form of a character, as in a medieval morality play, as the mother Pearl takes it upon herself to beat some sense into the head of her son-in-law Bobby, who repeatedly abuses her pregnant daughter Crystal, threatening the life of the seven-month-old child Crystal is carrying. Crystal, though, defends her abusive husband, saying that Bobby will be fine as soon as he sobers up, which Pearl knows he will never do any more than her own ex-husband did. She says to Crystal:

> "It doesn't get better, it just gets worse."
> "But I love Bobby."
> "You can love him to death, you know, it's just you that dies of it."
> (86)

Taking matters into her own hands, Pearl, to protect her grandchild, smashes Bobby's skull with a Civil War cannonball her grandmother Opal had given to her. In rescuing her grandchild, though, she loses a daughter, who in turn feels the same murderous rage against Pearl that had driven Pearl to her horrific act. Though the word "love" is used throughout "Sweet Rage," the story is more about self-deception, blind love, and blind rage, one as deplorable as the other. Crystal can't see the truth about Bobby, and Pearl can't see the truth about herself. Rage, like Bobby's drunkenness, is to be avoided both at home and on the road.

"Sweet Rage" is the least subtle of Carson's stories about an unsubtle, recurring theme in her work, domestic abuse, usually spurred on by alcohol. Fortunately, Carson presents a third alternative which perhaps requires more courage than either patient endurance of abuse on the one hand or murder on the other. The voice in "I cannot remember all the times he hit me" from *Stories* could be that of Pearl of "Sweet Rage" before the rage consumes her. It is, though, a wiser voice directed to all women who might come in contact with the speaker's ex-husband. It is both a caveat and a homily.

I want to post this in ladies' rooms,
write it on the tags of women's underwear,
write it on coupons to go in Tampax packages,
because my ex-husband will want to marry again
and there is no tattoo where he can't see it
to tell the next woman who might fall in love with him.
After six months, maybe a year,
he will start with a slap you can brush off.
Leave when he slaps you.
When he begins to call you cunt and whore
and threatens to kill you if you try to go
it will almost be like teasing but it is not.
Keep two sets of car keys for yourself.
Take your children with you when you go.
If he is throwing things, he is drinking.
If he is drunk enough he cannot catch you.
A punch in the breast hurts worse than a punch in the jaw.
A hit with an object does more damage than a hit with a fist
unless he is so drunk he picks up a broom instead of a poker.
If you pick up the poker, he will try to get it.
If he gets it, he will hit you with it.
He probably will not kill you because you will pass out,
and then, he is all the sudden sorry and he stops.
When he says he will not hit you again
as he drives you to the hospital,
both of you in tears and you in pain,
you have stayed much too long already.
Tell the people at the hospital the truth
no matter how much you think you love him.
Do not say you fell down stairs
no matter how much he swears he loves you.

He does love you, he loves you hurt (and he will hit you) again.
(52–53)

Clearly, there are times when the love of truth ought to surpass the love of
spouse.

All types of the love quest in Carson's stories relate to one kind, really,
the search for the good place, not utopia—which means no place—but
eutopos, the good place, the object of eternal quest in literature. Where is the
good place? It is, to answer in a circular fashion, a place where love exists,
where, to draw on composite features noted above, family members live
without fear of abuse by hand or tongue from other members, where individual differences are not only tolerated but respected and even encouraged, where families live peacefully with other families in a community of
mutual trust, without regard to race or marital status, where the air doesn't
smell and where the water is not filled with strange tastes, and where nature is seen as ally and teacher. The several references to the earth and the
love of the earth in these selections show Carson at odds with the plastic,
dehumanized love, and close to that of Walt Whitman in Section 5 of
"Song of Myself." Whitman saw love as a kelson of creation running not
just through the upper levels of the great chain of being but through every
bit of it, through "limitless . . . leaves stiff or drooping in the fields, / And
brown ants in the little wells beneath them, / And mossy scabs of the
worm fence, heap'd stones, elder, mullein and poke-weed." One of Carson's
voices in *Stories* describes the good place in Appalachia this way:

I grew up here,
I have lived here,
worked here,
and I have made
all my decisions
about here and for here,
and in those many moments
I have kept my family together
and in health,
I have lived in harmony and good union
with my friends and neighbors
and I have kept
a piece of earth

in working order.
I am proud of that.
(65)

Like many other American authors, Carson makes effective use of "the sermon." In the closing selection of "Stories," the preacher or speaker is still alive but imagines the consequences of being dead and forgotten. Whatever else we may think a good place to be, it is, we learn here, not worth much without remembrance of things past, without knowledge of what Whitman called our "embryons and go-befores," the knowledge that connects the generations, the love that overcomes death itself—or could if properly embraced. The speaker is a mother addressing her child.

I am asking you to come back home
before you lose the chance of seein' me alive.
You already missed your daddy.
You missed your uncle Howard.
You missed Luciel.
I kept them and I buried them.
You showed up for the funerals.
Funerals are the easy part.
. . . .
I'd rather you come back now and got my stories.
I've got whole lives of stories that belong to you.
I could fill you up with stories,
stories I ain't told nobody yet,
stories with your name, your blood in them.

Ain't nobody gonna hear them if you don't
and you ain't gonna hear them unless you get back home.

When I am dead, it will not matter
how hard you press your ear to the ground.
(93)

I know I cannot improve on the last two lines, and I do not intend to try, but would merely like to add to them for purposes of the theme of this essay. We also hear, I think, the mother saying, "You can watch reruns of movies and TV programs, things you see, until you're blue in the face, but you won't be able to re-hear what I've got to tell you until you hear my stories once. That is what I would love for you to do if you care enough to do it. The burden of loving back, though, is upon you."

Works Cited

Carson, Jo. *The Last of the "Waltz Across Texas" and Other Stories.* Frankfort, Ky.: Gnomon, 1993.

————. *Stories I Ain't Told Nobody Yet.* New York: Orchard Books, 1989; paperback ed., New York: Theatre Communications Group, 1991. (All citations are of the paperback edition.)

O'Connor, Flannery. *A Good Man Is Hard to Find and Other Stories.* San Diego: Harcourt Brace Jovanovich, 1983.

————. *Mystery and Manners.* Ed. Sally and Robert Fitzgerald. New York: Noonday Press, 1970.

Whitman, Walt. *Complete Poetry and Selected Prose.* Ed. James E. Miller. Boston: Houghton Mifflin, 1959.

FAMILY JOURNEYS IN JO CARSON'S *Daytrips*

ANITA J. TURPIN

Vena, Dolie, Lonnie, May, Anita—when I was a young girl growing up in eastern Kentucky, it often took my mother five tries to get my name right. The names of her four sisters were stuck in her head in front of mine and she had to go through them to get to me. I wasn't particularly bothered by it at the time, and now I see the multiple naming as a comforting symbol of family interconnections, an auditory thread connecting me to the generation of women ahead of me.

In Jo Carson's autobiographical play, *Daytrips,* Pat's mother Irene and her grandmother Rose also call Pat the names of older female relatives. However, with Irene and Rose, the confusion indicates more than a head full of names; it indicates a merging of actual identities, a merging of present and past in an indistinguishable mix.

Daytrips takes a universal problem—how to care for aging parents and grandparents, especially when one of them is stricken with Alzheimer's—and explores that problem in a personal and regional context, the region being eastern Tennessee. *Daytrips* becomes, consequently, a multifaceted play about loss of identity—loss of individual identity due to the ravages of aging and disease, and loss of regional identity due to the passage of time.

Daytrips first appeared in 1988 as a workshop production of the Johnson City, Tennessee, Road Company and Virginia Polytechnic Institute and State University. The national premiere of the play came in September 1989 at the Los Angeles Theatre Center. Also in 1989, Carson and *Daytrips* received the Joseph Kesselring Award for Best Play by an Unknown Writer. The Hartford (Connecticut) Stage Company produced *Daytrips* in

March 1990, and the play appeared in New York City in October 1990 at the Women's Project and Productions.

Structurally, *Daytrips* breaks with realistic theatrical conventions of both characters and staging. Those structural innovations align Carson with a distinguished group of twentieth-century dramatists, including Eugene O'Neill, Tennessee Williams, and Brian Friel, all three of whom have used innovations to "stage" the inner lives of their characters. O'Neill's 1928 Pulitzer Prize–winning *Strange Interlude* became both a critical and commercial success, in spite of its lengthy nine acts. O'Neill intersperses the realistic stage dialogue with "interludes" in which the characters use asides to reveal their thoughts to the audience. Williams frames *The Glass Menagerie* (1944) with opening and closing monologues, in which Tom Wingfield provides background information for the audience. In the opening monologue, Tom reveals that he is both the narrator and a character, and that the play comes from his memory. Almost five decades later, Brian Friel's *Dancing at Lughnasa* (1990) would use a similar technique: a grown-up Michael provides a narrative perspective for the events unfolding on the stage, events that took place when Michael was seven and living with his mother and her four unmarried sisters in the small rural village of Ballybeg, Ireland. An earlier Friel play would recreate the O'Neill *Strange Interlude* strategy of revealing the inner thoughts of the characters. Friel's first theatrical success, *Philadelphia, Here I Come!* (1966), puts on stage the Private and Public selves of twenty-five-year-old Irish lad Gareth O'Donnell. The play takes place on the evening before Gar is scheduled to emigrate from his home of Ballybeg to Philadelphia. As his final hours in his homeland pass, Gar says his public good-byes while his inner self reveals the tumult of emotions he is experiencing, from excitement to fear to sadness to bitterness.

Jo Carson's *Daytrips* uses a combination of techniques of Friel, Williams, and O'Neill. Carson's play presents three generations of women played by four actors. One actor plays Rose, mother to Irene and grandmother to Pat. Rose is not afflicted with Alzheimer's, but she is old enough to be cranky and set in her ways, and she converses fairly regularly with the ghost of her dead daughter, Helen. A second actor plays the dual role of Irene and Ree, two versions of Pat's mother. The healthier Irene has occasional lucid moments, but by the beginning of the play's "present," Irene has been almost completely absorbed by the Alzheimer's victim Ree. Two actors who play Pat the narrator and Pat the character complete the cast. In a 1997 interview, Carson explains that the split Pat is necessary because the narrator has an emotional distance from the events that the character Pat does not have (Arnow, 34). In addition to representing the distanced Pat, the narrator occasionally plays the role of minor characters, such as a pharmacist at Revco or Rose's sister Bee. By having the narrator deliver the lines of all the secondary characters, Carson keeps a tight focus on the intimate family unit of women.

The staged events take place in what Carson calls "memory time, not linear time" (*Daytrips*, 57). Consequently, she says, the "staging should be part literal, part metaphor," meaning that a sofa can be a sofa, or a sofa can be a car when the characters go off on a daytrip (ibid.). The play makes sudden and frequent shifts in time with very little in the way of explanation through the dialogue of the characters, and while those shifts accurately represent the fractured state of mind of both Irene and Rose, Carson's use of what she calls "memory time" could have resulted in a confusing and frustrating plot. To add coherence, Carson employs a number of unifying devices in the play: the five "daytrips," the source of the title; three dreams Pat has in which she kills Ree and Rose; a series of stories about Ree's Alzheimer's incidents; and a series of stories about other Alzheimer's victims. Carson skillfully weaves together the separate devices in a layered structure. For example, a daytrip leads into a dream followed by the recounting of a Ree Alzheimer's incident and then a story of another Alzheimer's victim. The unifying devices do not always appear in the same order, but the overall structure welds them into a coherent whole, with natural, seamless transitions from one device to the next.

Of the unifying devices, the most obvious are the daytrips in the car. On most of the trips, Pat and Ree go to Rose's house to take her to Kingsport to the grocery store and occasionally to the drugstore. However, one of the daytrips deviates from the usual. An old photograph Pat finds in Rose's closet results in a daytrip to Kyles Ford, where Rose grew up and where Irene was born. The three of them—Pat, Rose, and Ree—have some difficulty finding their destination because the familiar landmarks are gone, both literally and in the faded minds of the two older women. But eventually they get to the site of the house Rose grew up in and the nearby field where Rose's parents are buried. Pat wants to get out of the car to visit the graves of her great-grandparents, but Rose adamantly forbids it, declaring, "You're not gonna pay respects to a man that was that mean" (12). The daytrip to Kyles Ford reveals Rose's unhappiness growing up there and her determination to escape, an escape that came in the form of Floyd Cusick, her schoolteacher. As they sit in the car near the graves, Rose tells Pat about eloping with Floyd and then moving "as far as they could afford to go which was a half mile away" (13).

Later in the Kyles Ford daytrip, the three visit the home of Rose's sister, Bee, where apparently Pat has never been before. Rose refuses to get out of the car here also, but Bee climbs in for a visit with Rose. During their conversation, Bee tries to give Rose some souse. Rose turns her nose up at the offer with a terse, "I don't like it. And I left here 60 years ago so I wouldn't have to eat no more of it" (25). Bee presents a poignant dramatic foil to Rose. On the one hand, Bee appears to be in better physical condition, hale and hearty enough to be able to make her own souse from a neighbor's donated hog's head. But she clearly lives an isolated and presumably lonely life in her "weatherbeaten little farmhouse" (24), and her connections with her sister Rose appear to be intermittent at best. Her world inside the farmhouse has shrunk to the kitchen, where she has even moved her bed (24). The scene with Bee illustrates what Rose's life might have been had she remained in Kyles Ford. In Kingsport, Rose's fear of strangers keeps her mostly inside her house behind triple locks on the door, but she has neighbors next door and periodic visits from her daughter and granddaughter, and, as the Narrator points out in the final line of the scene, in Kingsport, Rose "doesn't have to cook or eat souse meat" (26).

The last daytrip of the play focuses on Irene and provides a compelling, if brief, glimpse into the past. In this daytrip, a reluctant teenaged Pat accompanies Irene on a visit to Rose's. In the car, Irene urges Pat to visit her grandmother more often because Rose is lonely and because she is family—they share the same blood. The vision of a vital, healthy "mother" Irene near the end of the play sharpens the sadness of Ree's current condition. The scene also reinforces the responsibility of one family member toward another, as Irene tells a sullen Pat, "We're all she's got" (37). As audience members, we realize the unspoken words that must be a constant refrain in the adult Pat's head: "I'm all they've got."

The most striking of the unifying devices are Pat's three dreams, which she describes to the audience as scenes of Rose and Ree dying, with the active assistance of Pat. Spaced throughout the play, the dreams incorporate three of the four basic elements of the universe: water in the first dream; air in the second dream; and fire in the third and final dream. At the beginning of the recounting of the third dream, the narrator explains to the audience: "There is no earth dream. Maybe earth is left for the real dying" (55).

In the first dream, Pat "leads" Rose and Ree into the waters of Watauga Lake, a lake in eastern Tennessee, allowing them to walk until they drown, while she stands on the shore and does nothing to save them. In the second dream, Pat lies in bed between Rose and Ree. She smothers first Rose and then Ree with a pillow. In the third and final dream, which ends the play, Pat sets the house on fire with Rose and Ree in it, leaving them there to die as she gets into her car and heads home. This dream ending underscores the "real" ending of the play, which happens just prior to the dream scene. In the "real" ending, Rose tries to shoot Pat, who is spending the night at Rose's house. Pat disarms her grandmother, locks her in the house, and goes out to the car to sleep the rest of the night. The fact that the play then ends with the imagined deaths of Rose and Ree brings home both the pain and the honesty of Carson's approach.

This honesty also characterizes the presentation of Ree's condition, which seems to worsen during the play. We see the Alzheimer's become more intense through Ree's actions on stage, and we also realize it through a series of four stories about Ree's "incidents." In the first, Ree sits down in the middle of the road and refuses to move. In the second, Ree disappears and is later found in a tree in someone's backyard, scared and confused. The third incident occurs when Ree gets upset with Pat during one of the daytrips to Kingsport and tries to get out of the car while it is going sixty-five miles per hour. The final incident happens in the grocery store during one of the daytrips, when Ree attacks Rose, apparently believing that Rose is a threat to Pat. Consequently, Pat refuses to take Ree or Rose along with her to the grocery anymore; instead, she goes by herself, leaving the two of them at Rose's house, a risky solution and not one Pat could safely use very often. We get the sense that Ree's public outings are going to become increasingly rare.

The recounting of Ree's Alzheimer's incidents becomes more foreboding by the juxtaposition of the five stories of other victims of Alzheimer's. Each story focuses on the helplessness and increasing hopelessness of the caretakers. The first story Pat hears on the radio: a woman gets lost for a week in a storage area of a big-city department store after her husband drops her off for her weekly appointment at the in-store beauty salon. Pat reads the second story in a newspaper article about a middle-aged man who kills his mother and himself with a gun; because he does not want to be a bother to anyone, he meticulously cleans up after shooting his mother, and then prepares everything so that the emergency workers who arrive after he shoots himself will not have to do anything but turn on the hose to wash away the blood. The third Alzheimer's story comes from Pat's friend, whose mother has been in a nursing home for eight years, gradually and inexorably curling into a fetal position. The friend's father died caring for his wife. A newspaper again provides the fourth story, the account of a failed murder-suicide. A son takes his mother out of a nursing home and attempts to kill both of them through carbon monoxide poisoning. The mother dies, but the son survives and is then charged with murder. The fifth and final story comes from an acquaintance of Pat's who calls her. The acquaintance is the former director of an Alzheimer's unit at a nursing home. She tells Pat about a woman who allows her husband to starve to death after he has endured twelve years of suffering with Alzheimer's. The starvation takes three months, during which time the husband cries and gestures for food. While none of the stories could be called pleasant, this last story seems to bleed a new level of desperation.

As the five Alzheimer's stories evidence, *Daytrips* resonates with complex questions about family and duty. The play leaves the situation of Rose, Ree, and Pat unresolved, just as Jo Carson's real-life situation was unresolved when the play premiered. Carson and her father shared the responsibility of caring for her mother, an Alzheimer victim, for eight years in the 1980s. Eventually, they were forced to place her mother in a nursing home, where she died in January of 1995. In an interview before the Los Angeles opening of *Daytrips* in 1990, Carson reveals: "I came to think of myself as my mother's jailer. . . . As my mother's care-keeping got harder and harder, I figured I'd make something out of it, so I started keeping notes. You say these things out loud and it helps. And short of saying them out loud, you write them down. . . . Basically what the play talks about is how I began to question what the real duty to my mother was—because I would not want to live through what my mother was living through" (Mitchell, 56). From Carson's notes came the eventual play *Daytrips,* in which Carson allies herself with a community of sufferers by including the stories of other Alzheimer's caregivers.

The storytelling aspect of the play resulted in mixed reviews from theater critics. Reviews expressing reservations about *Daytrips* have most often chided it for lack of drama, complaining that the play remains too narrative in structure. But other reviews laud the strengths of the play, notably its mixture of pain and laughter. To these reviewers, the structure becomes an organic part of the play's message. In his review of the Los Angeles production, Dan Sullivan writes:

> Yes, there are rules about constructing a play. But the great rule—as Jo Carson clearly realizes in "Daytrips," at the Los Angeles Theatre Center— is to be true to the experience that inspired the play.

Find your shape *there,* and you'll produce something original. "Day-trips" is just that. I can't remember a play with a more painful subject. Yet the subject is looked at with composure and even humor, everything implied by a word we don't hear much these days: *acceptance.* (1)

Carson's technique of combining storytelling with more conventional dramatic scenes of characters interacting in the present can, of course, be traced all the way back to classical Greek tragedy, in which the audience was helped toward a catharsis by being asked to imagine the horrific events being *told* to them by characters on stage. In other words, by having to create its own images of Medea slaying her young sons, or Oedipus blinding himself, the audience becomes a full participant in the ritual act. Carson's use of stories calls for the same participatory act from her audience.

As Sullivan indicates, one of the strengths of *Daytrips* lies in its blend of tragic and comic. Ree has a running joke about her brain turning to jelly. This "joke" receives a macabre underscoring in the scene with Bee's souse, which Pat, the narrator, describes for the audience as "a big platter of brown jellied glob that filled the room with a smell reminiscent of canned dog food" (25). Rose's and Ree's confusion about the identity of Pat provides a rich vein of both pain and humor throughout the play. Identities merge without warning. The first instance of a merged identity occurs in line two of the play, when Ree calls Pat "Olivia." Olivia was Rose's sister; Helen was Irene's sister. Rose often calls Pat "Helen," and sometimes she and Ree argue about whether Pat is "Olivia" or "Helen," both ignoring Pat's insistence that she is neither. This confusion of name and identity highlights the way we keep our ghosts alive through memory, and the myriad ways family members hurt each other. It becomes clear in the play that Rose loved Helen more than she did Irene, and that she always wished that Irene had died instead of Helen. The fact that Rose keeps Helen "alive" through her ghostly visits reminds Irene constantly of her mother's preference for Helen. By making her characters so real that it is difficult at times to like them, Carson forces a harsher confrontation with the concept of family and duty. Rose does not even have the excuse of Alzheimer's for her cruelty. After a confrontation about Ree's condition early in the play, Ree says to Pat, "I can't go away just because you want me to" (16). Nor could Irene be the one to die just because Rose wanted it that way. But clearly Rose's attitude never stopped Irene from making the daytrips to visit her; the awareness of familial duty seeped into Pat as the years passed. Pat may have dreams of ridding herself of both of them, but her patience and loyalty remain consistent throughout the play. She responds to Rose and Ree with remarkable tolerance and good humor, generated by a very real love for the two women. The audience gleans this love through observing Pat's actions, but it is also revealed explicitly by Pat when she tells us about the second dream. The dream ends with the following: "I sit in the bed, in the half dark of city nights, of bedrooms when someone is confused or ill and the bathroom light stays on, the half dark of dreams, and I hold their hands and I cry because I loved them and they are gone" (46).

Writing a play about incurable disease must be a tricky business. How does a playwright maintain an unflinching honesty and still keep the audience from turning away in disgust or fear, or both? A number of contemporary playwrights have accepted the challenge, including two Pulitzer Prize–winning writers from the 1990s. The Pulitzer Prize of 1993 went to Part I of Tony Kushner's brilliant two-part play about AIDS, *Angels in America,* and Margaret Edson's *Wit,* about women dying of cancer, won the 1999 Pulitzer. The works of both Kushner and Edson reflect the understanding expressed by Brian Friel in "Theatre of Hope and Despair," an article he wrote in 1967. According to Friel, the dramatist must create works that make the audience "recognize that even in confusion and disillusion, strength and courage can exist, and that out of them can come a redemption of the human spirit" (17). Carson's character Pat quietly embodies that strength and courage, and, we must assume, so does the dramatist Jo Carson. *Daytrips* offers a multidimensional portrait of pain and frustration, leavened by love and laughter—the product of personal experience milled through the mind of a gifted storyteller.

Works Cited

Arnow, Pat. "The Wealth of Story: A Conversation." *Iron Mountain Review* 14 (Summer 1998): 31–37.

Carson, Jo. *Daytrips.* New York: Dramatists Play Service, 1991.

Friel, Brian. "Theatre of Hope and Despair." *Critic* 26 (Aug.–Sept. 1967): 13–17.

Mitchell, Sean. "Eavesdropper Jo Carson Spins a Personal Story." *American Theatre* (Jan. 1990): 56–57.

Sullivan, Dan. "'Daytrips' to the Rhythm of a Disease." Review. *Los Angeles Times,* 26 Sept. 1989, Calendar Part 6, p. 1. http://web.lexis-nexis.com/universe.

Points of Kinship

Community and Allusion in Fred Chappell's Midquest

JOHN LANG

To view Fred Chappell as principally a "regional" writer is to overlook the varied communities on which he draws and with which he identifies himself, especially in his greatest poetic achievement to date, *Midquest.* Those communities include not only the author's relationships with his wife, Susan, with other members of his family, and with the local storekeeper Virgil Campbell, but also his larger social-political identity as an American citizen in the twentieth century. Moreover, through *Midquest's* literary and philosophical allusions, Chappell creates a series of wide-ranging communities, from the poet-friends to whom he addresses several epistolary poems to the broader literary tradition implicit in his extensive use of Dante and other writers. By organizing each of *Midquest's* four volumes around one of the elements the pre-Socratics believed to be fundamental to life, Chappell also identifies himself with a philosophical community that enables him to probe the origin and nature of human existence, particularly the relationship between mind and matter, body and spirit. Throughout *Midquest,* Chappell repeatedly weaves the personal and the "widely representative" (x). His allusions and themes link the local and the national, the regional and the universal.

From *Dream Garden: The Poetic Vision of Fred Chappell,* ed. Patrick Bizarro (Baton Rouge: Louisiana State University Press, 1997), 97–117. Reprinted in this abridged version by permission of the author and the publisher.

Such interconnections are evident from the very beginning of *Midquest,* whose first volume, *River,* takes its epigraph from *Moby-Dick.* Chappell opens his book not with the markedly regional but with the placelessly personal and the directly allusive. "The River Awakening in the Sea" sets the self in relation to the beloved in a bedroom that could be anywhere. No doubt this generalized location is meant to reinforce the poet's status as a representative figure. Like Whitman's persona in *Song of Myself,* "Ole Fred" is intended to be a modern Everyman in his search for love, community, and spiritual renewal. Yet this initial poem, like the first and last poem in each of *Midquest'*s four volumes, is addressed to the poet's wife, Susan. Susan also appears in at least one other of the eleven poems in each volume. Fred's marriage to Susan is thus the principal relationship in *Midquest,* a relationship that provides the poet with one crucial experience of community.

But Susan is not simply Fred's wife. In the larger Dantean structure of the poem, she is also his Beatrice. Similarly, marriage itself becomes one of *Midquest'*s central metaphors, as it testifies to the union—often a difficult one—of distinct personalities or qualities. *Midquest* depicts not only Fred's marriage to Susan but also his grandparents' and parents' marriages. In addition, Chappell describes life itself as originating at the moment "when void and atom married" (41). And the nearly impenetrable *"marriage / vow* joints" of "Firewood" (67) lead the poet to reflect that

> when man and nature
> got married they agreed never to divorce although
> they knew they could never be happy & would have only
> the one child Art who would bring mostly grief
> to them both.
> (72)

These repeated references to marriage remind the reader that the search for love and the desire for order and harmony are central to *Midquest,* a book in which the concept of marriage has the kind of significance it attains in Kierkegaard's *Either/Or* and Wendell Berry's *The Country of Marriage.*

Family ties other than marriage are also extremely important in *Midquest,* as is evident in the many poems devoted to the poet's grandparents and parents. Some of Chappell's liveliest, most entertaining writing results from his portraits of these people and from the distinctive voices he creates for them. Certainly, these portraits reinforce a number of *Midquest'*s distinctively regional elements, especially in their description of the difficulties of surviving on a hardscrabble mountain farm. Yet even before Fred's grandparents first appear in the third and fourth poems of *River,* Chappell has already invoked the name of Dante in the book's second poem, "Birthday 35: Diary Entry." That poem also alludes to Plato, St. Francis, and Kierkegaard, thus establishing the philosophical and religious nature of the poet's quest. Moreover, "Birthday 35: Diary Entry" also introduces the first of Chappell's many allusions to other American writers—in this case, the waste land vision of T. S. Eliot and his Prufrock (7). Like Eliot's various personae, Ole Fred seeks to escape the spiritual desolation of contemporary life, its emotional aridity and lack of connections. The quest for love and community as a means of defining the self is crucial to the thematic structure of *Midquest.* For Chappell, genuine selfhood exists only in and through relationships to something outside the self. As he remarks in *Midquest*'s opening poem, "Everyone begins slowly to reach toward another" (1). In many respects an autobiographical poem, *Midquest* rejects the intensely private confessional mode of much American poetry of the 1960s and 1970s.

It is Fred's grandmother, first introduced in the third poem in *River,* who emphasizes the role family plays in defining the individual and who urges her young grandson not to forget his roots: "'It's dirt you rose from, dirt you'll bury in'" (12). Yet as she reveals to the boy the comic catalogue of the family's black sheep, Chappell draws not only upon the tall-tale tradition of his native Appalachia but also upon such literary ancestors as Mark Twain. The glass eye of Aunt Paregoric Annie is an heirloom from chapter 53 of *Roughing It.* Similarly, when young Fred's grandfather orders the boy to clean the family's well in *River*'s fourth poem, Chappell depicts the experience as a version of the archetypal descent into the Underworld, with its imagery of death and resurrection. "Jonah, Joseph, Lazarus, / Were you delivered so?" the adult poet asks (16). Although he has plumbed the well's depths, he is unable to communicate whatever it was he discovered there. Echoing Bottom in Shakespeare's *A Midsummer Night's Dream,* he can only conclude inconclusively: "I could not say what I had found. / I cannot say my dream" (16). Such allusions are typical of Chappell's artistic strategy in *Midquest.* Only rarely are they obtrusive. Instead, they work together to suggest the underlying unity of human experience despite differences of place and time.

Virgil Campbell, the local storekeeper, is the character in *Midquest* "who is supposed to give to the whole its specifically regional, its Appalachian, context" (x). Yet even in "Dead Soldiers," the first poem devoted to Virgil (*River* VI), Chappell inserts a literary allusion. While Virgil shoots at the empty whiskey jars that a flood has liberated from his basement, Chappell notes the "load on load of bottles rumbling out" (27). The phrase echoes Frost's "load on load of apples coming in" in "After Apple-Picking." Moreover, the reader's introduction to Virgil is preceded by *River*'s most explicitly philosophical poem, "Susan Bathing," a single-sentence, stream-of-consciousness, free-verse meditation addressed to Susan. In style and content, "Susan Bathing" has none of the simplicity and directness of "Dead Soldiers." Yet in his juxtaposition of these two poems, Chappell again harmonizes apparent opposites and indicates the inclusiveness of his poetic vision.

"Susan Bathing" also reinforces the connection between the particular and the universal in its movement from Fred's personal relationship with Susan to more general questions about physical beauty and humanity's responses to it. The poem begins and ends with the word "you," thereby affirming Fred's tie to Susan. But Fred's consciousness also moves freely through time, invoking "a Renaissance poet's wish, to be the pleasing / showerhead touching you with a hundred streaming fingers" (18). From this sensual response to Susan's presence the poet moves on to establish her identity as an emissary of the divine. Not only does he conjoin his praise of Susan with Gabriel's annunciation to Mary, "Ave, plena gratia" (20), but he also depicts Susan both as divine intermediary and as *deus absconditus.* When Susan's body vanishes in the steam from the shower, the poet declares, in lines reminiscent of Donne's anguished prose,

> Why do you go away? where do you go? will you
> again return from behind the spiritual mists & acquaint again
> my senses? or are you for good ascended into ideal spaces & rely upon
> my hurt memory to limn your shape my heart starves to join, do not
> so scar my will I plead you, for my will is stricken and contort,
> its own most effort has fouled & burst it & only intercession from
> without can restore it . . .
> (21)

Although Susan's allegorical function remains subordinate to the poet's personal relationship with her, Susan reminds Fred of the powerful claims of both body and soul, the physical and the spiritual. In response to her,

the poet gives voice to "speechpraise," for "unattending beauty is danger &
mortal sin" (19). Praise becomes Chappell's "instrument of unclosing and
rising toward light" (19), a light that brings spiritual illumination, "for
once the mind prepares to praise & garbs / in worshipful robe it enlarges to
plenitude" (19). "Susan Bathing," like *Midquest* as a whole, moves toward
an affirmation of love: marital love, love of family and friends, love of nature, love of language and literature, love of God. As Chappell writes near
the end of this poem,

> it is praise, love is praise, Susan, of what is, and if it be prisoned
> in low earth it shall bound in high air saying like howitzers its
> name and if it be scurried to & fro over cold waste of skies yet
> shall it touch with all its names blade root stone roof . . .
> . . . nowhere would you escape it.
> (23–24)

Chappell's credo here echoes that of St. Paul in Romans 8:38–39.

The interpenetration of the distinctively regional and the extraregional
that I have been tracing in *Midquest*'s first half-dozen poems recurs
throughout the volume. From the firmly established network of relationships with Susan, with his grandparents and parents, and with other members of the mountain community like Virgil Campbell, Chappell reaches
out to affirm his literary kinship with writers both inside and outside the
region, writers both living and dead, European as well as American.
Midquest is anything but insular or provincial. Just as the book's sense of
place involves both the mountains and a broader natural landscape suggested by Chappell's use of the four elements, so the literary communities
in *Midquest* build upon both the local and the global.

Each of the four separately published volumes that compose the book,
for example, bears its own epigraph. Two of those epigraphs, the first and
the last, come from American writers: Melville and Hawthorne in *River*
and *Earthsleep,* respectively. The other two are drawn from European writers:
René Char and Dante in *Bloodfire* and *Wind Mountain*. The epigraph from
Melville includes the apt statement, "Meditation and water are wedded for
ever" (xiii). The lines from Char, "This is the hour when windows escape /
houses to catch fire at the end of the / world where our world is going to
dawn" (53), are equally appropriate both to the natural element emphasized in Chappell's second volume and to *Midquest*'s theme of regeneration.

Moreover, Chappell's incorporation of a modern French poet who uses symbolist techniques is especially apt in a volume in which Rimbaud is a central figure. Char may also appear in *Midquest* because of his fascination with Heraclitus, one of the major pre-Socratic philosophers. The stanza from the *Inferno,* Canto V, quoted both in Italian and in English translation, that appears as the epigraph to *Wind Mountain* extends the series of allusions to Dante that began in *Midquest*'s second poem. The stanza reappears, the wording of its second line slightly altered, in *Wind Mountain*'s seventh poem. Dante might be said to be the guardian spirit or the muse of the whole of *Midquest,* but he is an especially effective source of *Wind Mountain*'s epigraph because of the traditional association of wind with the divine, whether the breath of God by which Adam was created out of the dust or the mighty wind of the Holy Spirit's descent at Pentecost. Similarly, the epigraph in *Earthsleep,* taken from the final paragraph of Hawthorne's "The Haunted Mind," not only returns the reader to the American literary tradition that Chappell so ably represents but also introduces the imagery of sleep and dream, death and the passage to eternity that pervades this final volume. Hawthorne's prose portrays the spirit wandering "without wonder or dismay. So calm . . . so undisturbed, as if among familiar things" at the moment of death (143). The serenity of this passage sets a tone that Chappell repeatedly invokes in *Earthsleep* as he attempts to reconcile himself and his readers to the fact of mortality. Yet death remains problematic in the final volume of *Midquest.* For both Chappell and Hawthorne, the human mind is "haunted." In the words of the sentence from Hawthorne's sketch that immediately precedes the passage Chappell cites, "You emerge from mystery, pass through a vicissitude that you can but imperfectly control, and are borne onward to another mystery."

As has already been indicated, Dante is the single author whose work is most significant to the architecture and the thematic development of Chappell's poem. Even Virgil Campbell, the most "specifically regional" figure in the book, functions also within the larger literary structure Chappell gives to *Midquest* through his extensive use of Dante. After all, Campbell's first name is that of Dante's guide in the *Inferno* and the *Purgatorio,* although Chappell's Virgil represents a homespun oral tradition, not the highly refined literary tradition of the author of the *Aeneid.* Dante's Virgil embodies the best that human reason, unaided by divine grace, can achieve in the realm of moral virtue. Campbell, in contrast, embodies the earthier values of food, drink, sexual desire, and comic storytelling. Yet both Virgils are artist-figures. And the Roman Virgil who celebrates humanity's ties to the earth in the *Georgics* clearly anticipates Chappell's insistence throughout *Midquest* on the value of the physical world that Virgil Campbell represents.

Nevertheless, in keeping with the structure of *The Divine Comedy,* Campbell is not Fred's ultimate guide. Susan is the Beatrice of *Midquest,* to whom the poet turns in the book's last two poems. Thus, after Fred visits Campbell's grave in the sixth poem of *Earthsleep,* the seventh poem opens appropriately with lines from Canto XXX of the *Purgatorio,* the canto in Dante's epic in which Beatrice appears and Virgil vanishes, and one of several cantos Dante devotes to his visit to the Earthly Paradise. Yet Chappell's own seventh poem, "How to Build the Earthly Paradise: Letter to George Garrett," continues to focus on the physical world whose spokesperson Campbell has been. Moreover, Chappell asks near the end of that poem,

> what if it's true already? and
> we have but to touch out to see it
> among our amidst.
> (177)

These lines recall the poet's earlier references to his waking with Susan "in the dew-fired earliest morning of the world" (51) and to their feeling the wind and rain advancing "out of the green isles / of Eden" (94). For those whose vision is cleansed by love, Chappell implies, paradise is here and now. But the love that Susan embodies is both human and divine love, "the love that moves the sun and other stars" (187), as Chappell translates the closing line of Dante's *Paradiso* in his own final poem.

Chappell's use of Dante involves more, however, than the poet's quest for spiritual renewal, more than his depiction of Virgil Campbell and Susan as spiritual guides. At times, for instance, usually for comic effect, Chappell employs the terza rima of Dante's original, as in "My Grandfather Gets Doused" (*River* VII) and "In Parte Ove Non E Che Luca" (*Wind Mountain* VII). The former recounts the conversion of Old Fred's grandfather from Methodist to "hard-believer / Baptist" (30) and contains such humorously inventive rhymes as moues/ooze/bruise (30) and Methodist/pissed/exhibitionist (31). The latter poem, whose title is taken from the final line of Canto IV in the *Inferno,* draws heavily on Dante's description of the damned in Hell's Second Circle, home of the carnal. The punishment of the lustful is described in Canto V of Dante's masterpiece, and better than half of Chappell's poem simply paraphrases its Italian original. The reader has been prepared for this descent into the Dantean underworld by the reference to Paolo and Francesca near the end of the preceding poem (120), where the allusion appears in the context of a tall tale narrated by Fred's father. But what surprises and delights the reader of *Wind Mountain*'s seventh poem is Chappell's daring updating of Dante's cast of sinners. It includes not only Casanova and Lord Byron but even, in Dantean fashion, one of the poet's contemporaries—James Dickey. In fact, Chappell devotes more lines to the castigation of Dickey's vices than he does to those of either of the other sinners. Moreover, at the end of this poem, Fred glimpses "the round form, the red face / Of Virgil Campbell" (123), who is then asked to explain *his* presence in the Second Circle.

The ensuing poem, "Three Sheets to the Wind: Virgil Campbell Confesses," is one of the funniest in all of *Midquest,* a book filled with a humor all too rare in contemporary American poetry. Chappell creates here a set of circumstances entirely appropriate to Virgil's character while drawing upon the humor of physical discomfort that was the stock-in-trade of George Washington Harris's Sut Lovingood. In fact, Virgil's plea, *"Feet don't fail me now"* (126), as he attempts to escape from the scene of his illicit lovemaking, comes directly from Sut's mouth. Thus, Chappell once again embeds Virgil *both* in the literary and folk traditions of the mountain South *and* in the wider Western literary tradition represented by Dante.

While Dante is the author whose work is fundamental to *Midquest,* Chappell fills his book with dozens of allusions to other writers. The Old Southwest humor that shaped not only George Washington Harris but also Mark Twain appears at various points. "My Father's Hurricane" (*Wind Mountain* VI), for instance, draws upon Twain's account of the Washoe Zephyr in chapter 21 of *Roughing It.* And Fred's term "Old Hoss," used to address "Uncle Body" (114), derives from Sut's nickname for Harris. But Chappell also incorporates in *Midquest* a series of four epistolary poems that call attention to contemporary southern writers who are personal friends of the poet. In addition, *Wind Mountain* includes a playlet, "Hallowind," in which Fred converses with Reynolds Price. Taken together, these five poems define yet another of *Midquest*'s many literary communities while providing insight into some of Chappell's major poetic concerns. In their epistolary structure, furthermore, these poems re-emphasize Chappell's refusal to be trapped within the isolated self, the personal ego.

The first of these poems, "Science Fiction Water Letter to Guy Lillian" (*River* IX), details the literary failings of much science fiction writing: its abstractness, its underdeveloped sense of the past, of history; its disregard of saints and heroic suffering; its departure from myth. Written in thirteen-syllable lines, the poem also contains Old Fred's excerpt from his own science fiction novel-in-progress, an excerpt that offers one of *Midquest*'s many myths of origin, in this case a myth of language's origin. Such creation myths attest to Chappell's desire to probe the mystery of creativity in all its forms, a desire that may in part explain his use of the pre-Socratic philosophers in *Midquest*. Fred's novel presents a wildly improbable account of the primeval relationship between word and thing, an account that nevertheless affirms the transformative power of words as the human imagination interacts with the physical world. That novel also reinforces the poet's earlier pronouncement, "Fresh wonders clamor for language" (40), a statement Chappell makes to criticize the loss of the objective world, the realm of nature, in much modern literature. According to Chappell, this retreat into the subjective self, this detachment from nature,

> is a fashionable oddity left over from
> the '90s (Wilde, Mallarmé, & Co.). Marvell
> or Donne or Vaughan wouldn't let such opportunities
> rot on the stalk; . . .
>   they had senses
> alive apart from their egos, and took delight in
> every new page of Natural Theology.
> (40)

Sharing Eliot's diagnosis of the modern "dissociation of sensibility," these lines also echo the concerns raised in Emerson's "Blight," with its insistence that human beings recover a right relation to nature.

The other poetic epistles in *Midquest* raise additional literary concerns that help define the diverse communities in which Chappell situates himself. In "Rimbaud Fire Letter to Jim Applewhite" (*Bloodfire* II), Chappell recounts his youthful infatuation with Rimbaud and Baudelaire, an attraction that led the young Chappell to practice such derangement of the senses that eventually he was expelled from Duke, where he had first met fellow poet Applewhite. Quoting in French from Rimbaud's poems "Barbare," "Comédie de la soif," and "Le Dormeur du val," Old Fred acknowledges his debt to his predecessor's craftmanship while recognizing the self-destructive elements in Rimbaud's life. After returning to Canton from Duke, Fred "watched the mountains until the mountains touched / My mind and partly tore away my fire-red / Vision of a universe besmirched" (60–61).

But the mountains were not alone in helping the poet reorient his life. He also started the concordance to Samuel Johnson that became his MA thesis and began reading "folks like Pope" (61), whose rationalism one can well imagine as a partial antidote to Rimbaud. Chappell concludes this letter with the playful valediction, "Yours for terror and symbolism," but the discussion of literary symbolism in "Hallowind," together with Chappell's own poetic practices in some of his work, reveals the continuing influence of Rimbaud, whose relationship with Verlaine had also served as a point of departure for Chappell's second novel, *The Inkling.*

"Burning the Frankenstein Monster: Elegiac Letter to Richard Dillard" (85) returns in part to the realm of science fiction introduced in the first of *Midquest*'s epistolary poems. Chappell's point of departure in this poem is not Mary Shelley's prophetic novel but the film version of *Frankenstein* starring Boris Karloff. It is from the film, not the book, that the poet draws his description of the monster's fate. The story of Frankenstein and his creation, as Chappell recognizes, is both a version of the Prometheus legend and a cautionary tale about "the will made totally single," the "tortured, transcendent-striving will" (85). To image that will, Chappell quotes Virgil's description of the newly blinded cyclops Polyphemus in the *Aeneid* (III, 658): *"Monstrum horrendum, informe, ingens, cui lumen ademptum"* (85). The line is one Chappell had used as his epigraph to *The Inkling,* and here, as there, it suggests the blindness of the self's desire to dictate the conditions of its existence.

In this poem, then, Chappell unites the figures of Polyphemus, Prometheus, and Frankenstein as he meditates on the hapless monster's destruction. His allusion to Virgil is followed by others to Rimbaud and Percy Bysshe Shelley, to the horror films of twentieth-century popular culture, and to the apocalypses of modern politics:

Why must poor Karloff be born out of fire, and die, fire-fearing,
    In the fire? Is he truly our dream of Promethean man?
Does he warn us of terrible births from atomic furnaces, atomic
    Centuries, shambling in pain from the rose-scented past?
Having been burned and then drowned, reversing the fate of Shelley,

> The lame monster brings back upon us the inverted weight
> Of the romantic period. Whose children we are, but disinherit,
>   Stranded in decades when all is flame and nothing but flame.
> (85)

The misguided deification of the will, the desire for omnipotence combined with the assumption of omniscience, is a tendency that Chappell's allusions discover throughout human history. Frankenstein and his creation, like Lear, "are bound to a wheel of crazed fire" (87), and the poem's closing image of "the hilltop mill ... always burning" (87) recalls not only Canton's polluting paper mill but also Blake's "dark Satanic mills" of reason unilluminated by the imagination.

By evoking sympathy for Frankenstein's creation, Chappell achieves several poignant moments in this poem. Recalling the monster's first glimpse of light, for example, the poet inquires:

> What wouldn't *we* give to undergo in our latter years the virgin
>   Onslaught of light? To be born again into light,
> To be raised from the grave.
> (85)

> Faith calls to faith, but our faith must be earned from terror, consummate
>   Love must be thirsted for, light must be wholly desired.
> (87)

Ultimately, this poem testifies to the responsibilities imposed by the power to create. Frankenstein is held accountable by and for the "son" whom he fathers, just as modern science bears the responsibility for its inventions—and each of us for the lives we invent for ourselves.

Midquest's final epistolary poem, "How to Build the Earthly Paradise," is addressed to George Garrett (*Earthsleep* VII). Its thirteen nine-line stanzas are all end-stopped, a device that reinforces the poem's building-block structure as Chappell lists the materials needed for this project: stone, sand, earth, the dead, water, air, plants, animals, people, "the troubadour atoms / dancing / full" (176). The precision of these stanzas' appearance on the page gives the reader confidence in Chappell as builder (a poet is a *maker*) and successfully prepares for the imagery of rebirth in the poem's closing lines:

          New
     now you
see me a new man, unshucked from
my soiled hide, I'm coming belchlike out of
the cave.
(177)

This cave recalls both Plato's famous allegory in *The Republic* and the dwelling of the Cyclops to whom Chappell alludes in "Burning the Franken-stein Monster." That the poet has grown by this point in his quest is clear. Yet Chappell forestalls any mystical heightening of this moment by using the self-deflating simile "belchlike."

Almost as important as the varied literary communities with which the poet identifies is the community of metaphysical speculation represented by the pre-Socratics and the many other philosophers and religious thinkers to whom Chappell refers or alludes. As has already been noted, each of *Midquest*'s separate volumes revolves around one of the four elements that pre-Socratic philosophers such as Thales, Anaximenes, and Empedocles believed to be the origin of all existing things. Chappell's decision to use these four substances—earth, air, fire, and water—in this fashion reflects his commitment to exploring the elemental, to investigating what is fundamental to human existence. In *Midquest,* as in his early poem "A Transcendental Idealist Dreams in Springtime" (*The World Between the Eyes,* 6), Chappell implicitly rejects the abstraction of Plato's world of Ideal Forms, returning for his key concepts to the earlier naturalistic phase of Greek philosophy. And Chappell also challenges the spirit of abstraction in modern philosophy, from Descartes on. The Emerson of *Nature,* for instance, distinguishing between the Me and the not-Me, relegates his body to the category of the not-Me. Chappell's creation of "Uncle Body," whom he jovially addresses in both "The Autumn Bleat of the Weathervane Trombone" (*Wind Mountain* V) and "The Peaceable Kingdom of Emerald Windows" (*Earthsleep* IV), seems to derive from the poet's impatience with the loss of the Creation, whether in Platonic idealism, Cartesian idealism, Emersonian Transcendentalism, or Protestant fundamentalism, with their tendency to denigrate the physical world.

The diverse communities in *Midquest* are ultimately unbounded in either space or time. From the intimacy of his marriage to Susan and the bonds of familial love, the poet reaches out toward a community of the moral and philosophical and literary imagination and toward communion with all creation. Although the mountains of North Carolina and the people who live there are central to Chappell's poetic vision in *Midquest,* it is the poet's interweaving of the particulars of his region with materials drawn from outside Appalachia that creates the book's distinctive resonance. *Midquest* belongs primarily not to Appalachian or Southern literature but to the larger Western literary tradition. The book's astonishing variety of poetic forms, its range of literary and musical and philosophical allusions, its blending of lyrical and narrative and meditative verse, and its social-political concerns all demonstrate the breadth of Chappell's sensibility. Nor is that breadth of mind and imagination a characteristic of *Midquest* alone. It is evident as well in the short stories of *Moments of Light* (1980) and in the poems of *Castle Tzingal* (1984) and *First and Last Words* (1989). But *Midquest* remains Chappell's masterpiece, a book that deserves wider recognition as one of the greatest achievements in contemporary American poetry.

Works Cited

Fred Chappell. *Midquest: A Poem.* Baton Rouge: Louisiana State University Press, 1981.

————. *The World Between the Eyes: Poems.* Baton Rouge: Louisiana State University Press, 1971.

22

FRED CHAPPELL'S URN OF MEMORY

I Am One of You Forever

HILBERT CAMPBELL

Ah, happy, happy boughs! that cannot shed
  Your leaves, nor ever bid the Spring adieu;
And, happy melodist, unwearied,
  Forever piping songs forever new.

—*Keats, "Ode on a Grecian Urn"*

Fred Chappell's 1985 novel *I Am One of You Forever* should certainly come in the future to be acknowledged as a classic of American literature. For this is a book by a master storyteller and humorist, absolutely in control of his language and of the nuances of charged moments and telling gestures. But it is likewise a magical book, suggestive of the miraculous, the mysterious, and the transcendent in our lives and in our world. Shining through this entertaining story of family farm life in the early 1940s, of zany visiting relatives, of tall tales and practical jokes, is a persistent aura of rich suggestiveness of the transformations and transfigurations that characterize our waking and sleeping hours, our lives and deaths. Something like a kaleidoscope or a many-faceted gem, the book seems to undergo its own transformations in meaning or tone as it is approached from slightly different angles. Ultimately, Chappell is exploring here the very nature of that most puzzling of transformations, the alchemy by which the human imagination turns life into art.

The title *I Am One of You Forever* is not only an affirmation but also the answer to an implied question, the urgency of which is underlined by the last sentence of the novel, in which the spectral figure of the dead foster

From the *Southern Literary Journal* 25 (Spring 1993). Copyright © 1993 by the Department of English of the University of North Carolina at Chapel Hill. Used by permission of the University of North Carolina Press.

brother, Johnson Gibbs, demands of the narrator Jess, *"Well, Jess, are you one of us or not?"* Chappell here summons up all the powers of his creative imagination to grapple once more with one of the preoccupations of his work, the problem of recapturing—or even knowing—one's past in some way that is meaningful to the present, of asserting that we are not eternally strangers to that which may have gone before.

Chappell's tribute to his Appalachian boyhood is developed not only by telling some marvelous stories about it but also by simultaneously exploring the possibility and nature of storytelling itself, the magical process by which the imagination can transform life and memory to the timeless realm of art. Reminiscent of Keats's "Ode on a Grecian Urn," *I Am One of You Forever* is Chappell's urn of cherished memories, of recollections of the "bright happy days" (21) that in art will never fade or pass away, the only realm in which it is possible to be "one of you forever."

The thirteen stories in *I Am One of You Forever,* loosely arranged as a novel, are told by Jess, a boy of nine to twelve years old in the early 1940s, as filtered through the memories of an adult narrator. Jess relates these stories of his boyhood family vividly, affectionately, and humorously. There is Joe Robert, the fun-loving and practical-joking father; Johnson Gibbs, the beloved "adopted" older brother; the sterner and more practical yet respected and admired grandmother; and the mother, a paler presence in Jess's narrations but nevertheless in some subtle way the center who lovingly and tolerantly holds the family structure together. About half the book is devoted to accounts of the various "wandering aunts and uncles" who "showed up to break the monotony of a mountain farm life" (119). A collection of eccentrics and black sheep, they both demonstrate the essential tolerance of the mountain family for its crazies and become a source of endless fascination to Jess, for whom they assume legendary proportions and serve as the main stimuli for his developing curiosity about various adult subjects, including death, sex, and the imagined excitement of the outside world. It is largely in the context of family rather than community that Jess develops his own identity, but it is both an extended family (with grandmother, uncles, and aunts) and a family that can accommodate those who are not blood kin, such as Johnson Gibbs.

Uncle Luden, the wastrel and n'er-do-well, a drinker and womanizer of heroic proportions just back from California, seems to Jess to embody not just the Prodigal Son but likewise Santa Claus, Gene Autry, the Fourth of July, and indeed all of the splendor, wickedness, and forbidden knowledge that exist outside his isolated and protected childhood existence. The "famous," "fabled," and "legendary" beard of Uncle Gurton absorbs Jess's curiosity and imagination so completely that he eventually sees in its billowing vastness "a birchbark canoe with two painted Cherokee Indians," a mermaid, and even "a damn big white whale" (59). Uncle Runkin, physically nondescript but truly of monumental proportions in the extent to which he spends his life brooding upon and preparing for its end, becomes the stimulus for Jess's own first serious—and highly imaginative and visionary—speculations about death. Through the visit of his grandmother's cousin, Aunt Samantha Barefoot, Jess learns more about his grandmother than he has ever known before and also is struck for the first time with a realization of time and history when he has a "sudden vision of my family lined up in a single file that stretched backward in time to Noah" (170).

The book consists of ten stories numbered in sequence, with three other italicized sections placed at the beginning, exact middle, and end. My purpose in what follows is to analyze briefly some of the methods and structures by which Chappell accomplishes his ends in *I Am One of You Forever*: first, by calling attention to some different levels of "magic" with which he infuses his narrative; second, by identifying some subtle structuring devices that he had used also, in more obvious ways, in his earlier book of poems, *Midquest* (1981); then, by speculating briefly on the nature and function of the three "framing" italicized sections of the book, necessary to understanding the scope of his vision; and, finally, by returning, as one must, to the question *"Are you one of us or not?"*

The magic of *I Am One of You Forever* is at least threefold. First, the world of the child's receptive imagination is one of an easy and comfortable coexistence of the real and the fantastic, the natural and the supernatural, the ordinary and the legendary—a world perceived as constantly undergoing fascinating transformations and transfigurations. Uncle Gurton's beard transforms itself into a threatening upheaval of all the elements. Nature can suddenly be transformed into something utterly foreign and overwhelming, as in the summer storm of "The Change of Heart," which breeds "storm angels," lifts Jess, his father, and Johnson Gibbs "thrashing in midair," and makes of them momentarily "men transfigured" (72). The World War is a threatening, transforming element, creating in Jess's formerly carefree mind a fear "that not even the steadfast mountains themselves were safe and unmoving, that the foundations of the earth were shaken and the connections between the stars become frail as cobweb" (92). Time itself is a mysterious force that transforms everything.

A second kind of magic is that by which the past is transformed in memory. The past does not exist except in memory, where it not only fades with time but likewise undergoes a constant transformation because of later experience, emotion, and the persistent reshaping of the past in which we engage in order to make sense of the present. But if the past does not exist, cannot be recaptured, and is only faultily or selectively remembered, it does nevertheless intrude itself insistently upon our conscious and un-conscious beings and provides whatever material we have for the shaping, imagining, conjuring, dreaming, and creating that we do in the attempt to impose some order or meaning on our present existence. Chappell's adher-ence to the notion that the past, if recaptured at all, must be imagined, created, or even dreamed is even more plainly evident in his 1989 novel, *Brighten the Corner Where You Are,* in which Jess, again the narrator, is ap-parently at home in bed asleep and dreaming all day while his father, Joe Robert, goes through the adventures that he is narrating.

It is a similarly imagined world that Chappell is exploring in *I Am One of You Forever,* a world of "The Good Time," a dream of midsummer in which the "bright happy days darted past us like minnows," a time when "it seems we were laughing and joking from one hour to the next" (21). As remem-bered, the father Joe Robert and the young man Johnson Gibbs become playmates and co-conspirators of the ten-year-old Jess in subverting the discipline, authority, and practicality of the family matriarch, the grand-mother. The several eccentric uncles and one aunt who visit to break the monotony of farm life take on in memory an even more exaggerated di-mension of the legendary stature by which they impressed themselves on the imagination of the boy.

The ultimate magic, however, is the transformation of life to art, the ability of the human imagination to shape the raw materials of a shifting, always-disappearing, and time-bound existence to the realm of the perma-nent and the unchanging. Chappell explores this phenomenon primarily in "The Storytellers." Uncle Zeno, the consummate storyteller, hardly seems present at all except as a voice. Stories seem to pass through him "like the orange glow through an oil-lamp chimney" (103); he "lived in a different but contiguous sphere that touched our world only by means of a sort of metaphysical courtesy" (102–3). Like Homer before him, he is leaving "no trace in the world" (107). Unlike the ineffective storytellers of the novel, such as the father and Johnson Gibbs, he calls absolutely no attention to himself, answers no questions, nor indeed leaves room for any. In a humorous, fanciful way, Chappell has Jess conclude that "Uncle Zeno's stories so thoroughly absorbed the characters he spoke of that they took leave of the everyday world and just went off to inhabit his narratives. . . . Homer and Uncle Zeno did not merely describe the world, they used it up" (113). Jess even naively assumes that his father may fade away before his very eyes because Uncle Zeno has begun a story with Joe Robert as the main character. But of course Jess is right; stories do "use up" reality, absorb it, replace it. They are what remain.

Chappell provides another example of "art in the making" in the story of the old man who inhabits the fishing shack in "The Wish." He has lost everything and is now barely existing in a sort of limbo at the outer edges of the living world. As he relates to Jess and Joe Robert the story of incredible sorrow, loss, and betrayal that have been his life, "He spoke all this in a dreamy nostalgic voice warm with fondness, as if he had been recounting the biography of a close friend. It seemed that the old man liked the shape his life had made in his mind; it was like an antique statue of a goddess, beautiful in its ruined lineaments" (164). The "shape his life had made in his mind" is the transformation wrought by the creative imagination; it has already replaced whatever "reality" it is based on.

I Am One of You Forever shares some thematic, tonal, and structural similarities with Chappell's earlier volume of poems, *Midquest.* Both include reminiscences of a rural Appalachian boyhood by a middle-aged man, and parts of each work share a humorous, "tall tale" quality, with the same freewheeling mix of reality and fantasy. There are likewise some interesting parallels in form between the two works, and to note the subtle presence in the novel of some structuring devices that had been employed in much more obvious ways in *Midquest* can aid in understanding the shape and purpose of *I Am One of You Forever.*

Midquest is made up of the forty-four poems from four previously published smaller volumes: *River, Bloodfire, Wind Mountain,* and *Earthsleep.* As their names suggest, each cycle of eleven poems focuses on one of the four classical elements: water, fire, air, and earth. In the middle of each cycle (with some minor variation) stands a sixth poem dealing with a favorite character of Chappell's, Virgil Campbell, a poem that represents a kind of three-dimensional center of the cycle, because Chappell arranges the poems so that "The first poem is mirrored by the last, the second by the next to last, and so on inward" (ix). The "center," then, is not just the middle part of a linear structure, but the heart of a structure resembling a set of nested boxes.

An emphasis on the four elements and an arrangement based on them is present also, if much less obviously than in *Midquest,* in *I Am One of You Forever.* Many of its stories focus primarily on one of the elements, including "The Wish" (water), "The Change of Heart" (air), and "The Maker of One Coffin" (earth). Some of the characters are repeatedly associated with one of the four elements. Johnson Gibbs, for example, is associated throughout with fire. The nocturnal and phenomenal spread of Uncle Gurton's beard through the house, in one of the central fantasies of the book, is described by using images not only of both the flood and the fire that might suddenly overwhelm an Appalachian farmhouse at night but of air and earth as well, as if to emphasize the marvelous event as something that represents an upheaval of all the elements.

The avowed "nested box" arrangement of each cycle of poems in *Midquest* is also present, if less strictly or formally, in *I Am One of You Forever,* with similarities or contrasts of various kinds linking loosely the first story with the tenth, the second with the ninth, and so on. For example, stories one and ten focus on the grandmother, stories four and seven pair Jess's visions of the creatures of the storm-charged air and of the creatures of the bowels of the earth, and stories three and eight share the scary fantasies that children "seize upon . . . to be frightened of" (135). Each story about the visit of a strange uncle or aunt is paired in the same fashion with a story about the immediate family, and so on.

To note this "nested box" feature of the structure of the novel adds significance to the italicized section "The Telegram," which is positioned at the exact middle of the book and which is nightmarishly vivid in its accounts of the myriad and amazing transformations in substance, shape, and size that the telegram undergoes in the eyes and emotions of the family members. Similar to the *Midquest* structures, this "agonizing rite" of the family's being forced to come to terms with Johnson Gibbs's death not only is the middle part of the book but becomes the central core or "heart" of the structure. Such a prominent positioning of this shattering experience is the best indication that Chappell is writing not just about "The Good Time" but also of sorrow and loss, although, characteristically, he will approach serious subjects obliquely and provide some "distancing" through the use of humor, dreams, or other devices. As Dabney Stuart is introduction to *The Fred Chappell Reader,* Chappell understands psyche's way of turning its attention aside from events of disaster and grief to scenes and activities obliquely attached to them. Too direct a memory numbs; the indirect route makes us able to continue the trip. It's a compromise struck between facing reality head on and trying to evade it altogether" (xiii).

Dreams are one of the common ways we revisit the past, and fantasy, vision, and dream are part of the fabric of the entire book. In fact, the dream provides perhaps the closest analogy for Jess's entire account, with its vividness, its constant suggestion of transformation and transfiguration, and its seamless merging of the magical and the supernatural with the "real" world. But the three italicized sections, "The Overspill," "The Telegram," and "Helen," go even further in their surreal qualities that suggest an actual dream state. Although not devoid of humor, they are also the sections in which serious matters are the most likely to be raised or suggested. Furthermore, in "The Overspill" at the beginning and in "Helen" at the end, Chappell suggestively places his story in the broader context of several of the universals, legends, and archetypes of our common human experience: birth, rebirth, the heroic, our longing for the ideal, and death.

"The Overspill," standing first in the novel, tells an apparently simple story of Jess's father's ambition to drain, clear, and plant a new garden spot and to bridge a small stream to provide easier access to the newly claimed land. All this is to provide a pleasing surprise for Jess's mother upon her return from a visit to California. Just as the mother returns, however, the paper mill above opens its floodgates, and all is utterly ruined and destroyed. The section ends with the family clinging together in the face of their disappointment.

The springtime setting of "The Overspill" is heavy with the elements of earth and water and rife with suggestions of fertility, rebirth, and growth. The father's "heroic" struggles to tame and reclaim the land are suggestive both of the difficulty of the agricultural life and of the young boy's perception of his father as "hero," which is echoed in various "epic" touches later in the book, including the battle of near-Homeric proportions that takes place between the father and Johnson Gibbs. The dominant theme of family love and cohesiveness, especially in times of difficulty or disaster, is here foreshadowed. Finally, the tear on the mother's cheek that magically expands to take in all three of them is suggestive also of procreation, of the founding of a family: the father and mother come together, and the small creature that is their offspring *"began to swim clumsily toward my parents"* inside a watery sac suggestive of the womb.

If "The Overspill" is suggestive of fertility, rebirth, and heroic effort, the concluding italicized "Helen" section, in stark contrast, takes place in a barren winter setting suggestive of stasis, inactivity, and death. Although difficult to interpret, it certainly must represent the disjointed nightmare of an older Jess, dreaming of family members now most likely dead, still worriedly preoccupied with the question of whether he is the "stranger," whether he is "one of them" or not. The landscape where Jess "seemed" to be in a hunting cabin with Uncle Luden, Johnson Gibbs, and his father is blanketed with heavy snow. Earth and water, the elements so prodigally present in "The Overspill," are here absent and have been replaced, if less obviously, by air and fire. The three men are ghostlike presences who do almost nothing; we hear them say nothing except for the mumbling they do in their sleep. The mostly nighttime setting remains essentially colorless, soundless, and motionless.

After hearing each of the three utter what sounds like the word "Helen" in their sleep, Jess becomes even more worried that they share some secret, see some vision, that he cannot share. Then he too glimpses a face, *"familiar to me, I fancied, if I could remember something long ago and in a distant place"* (182). He is *"disturbed most of all by the unplaceable familiarity of the vision"* (183). Perhaps Helen is Helen of Troy—who figures earlier in the story as part of Jess's father's inept retelling of the *Iliad*—an archetype of our shared longing for the ideal that consistently eludes us in this transitory life but that might be possible in art. The nightmare ends, and the dreamer undoubtedly awakes, when the figure of the dead soldier and foster brother Johnson Gibbs looms in "harsh light," "blackly burning," to demand of Jess in a "deep and hollow" voice, *"Well, Jess, are you one of us or not?"*

This "burning" question with which the novel ends suggests more than one interpretation, although all are ways of asking "Who am I?" The most likely meaning might be "Are you still one of the family?" or maybe "One of the plain country folks?" Given that the others present at the hunting cabin are his father, Johnson Gibbs, and Uncle Luden, who have been Jess's principal male role models in the story, the question could mean "Have you become a man?" Or, given the novel's inclination to expand suggestively to universals, it might mean "Are you one of the human race, sharing the common experiences of sorrow and loss?" Also, since this section is probably Jess's dream of the dead, the question might even mean "Are you one of the dead?" in the sense of "Have you faced your own mortality?" Finally, standing as the last words in the book, the question could mean "Have you succeeded in your effort to show that 'I am one of you forever'?"

Thus, *I Am One of You Forever* is not simply about "The Good Time" but also about its inevitable loss and the question of whether any meaningful connection with the past can be made. It remains doubtful that the assertion of the title convinces us that we can go home again, or at least that we can go all the way home again.[1] After all, the question with which the novel ends apparently retains considerable urgency. The surer sense of *I Am One of You Forever* is that, in these stories, the transitory existence of the boy and his family has taken on a permanent existence in the realm of art. The novelist Clyde Edgerton, in a recent remark about Chappell's art, puts the matter directly and succinctly: "'I Am One of You Forever' is . . . about storytelling up against death—both always forever and forever neck and neck down the home stretch, in constant war like brightness and darkness, good and evil" (84–85). Chappell's creative imagination, through the magic of storytelling, has molded here his everlasting and unchanging urn of memory in a shape that is indeed pleasing to him and to us.

Note

1. Fred Hobson remarks, in his perceptive discussion of *I Am One of You Forever,* that "one cannot altogether will himself back into the world where he came from. . . . That is precisely what Chappell attempts in his book . . . to will himself back—but . . . neither can he go back all the way" (91). Hobson's understanding of the novel is quite compatible with my own; and I am indebted to his discussion in ways not specifically documentable for helping me clarify my own assumptions about the novel.

Works Cited

Chappell, Fred. *I Am One of You Forever.* Baton Rouge: Louisiana State University Press, 1985.

———. Preface to *Midquest: A Poem.* Baton Rouge: Louisiana State University Press, 1981.

Edgerton, Clyde, et al. "Tributes to Fred Chappell." *Pembroke Magazine* 23 (1991): 77–92.

Hobson, Fred. *The Southern Writer in the Postmodern World.* Athens: University of Georgia Press, 1991.

Stuart, Dabney. "'What's Artichokes?': An Introduction to the Work of Fred Chappell." In *The Fred Chappell Reader,* xi–xx. New York: St. Martin's, 1987.

23

COMING OUT FROM UNDER CALVINISM

Religious Motifs in Robert Morgan's Poetry

JOHN LANG

Raised in a household in which his mother was a Southern Baptist and his father a member of the Pentecostal Holiness movement, Robert Morgan experienced, at a particularly impressionable age, what he has called in an essay on William Cullen Bryant "the terror and exclusions of Calvinism" (56). In an interview with Suzanne Booker in *Carolina Quarterly* he remarked, "For me just becoming a writer, becoming a poet, necessitated a kind of distance from the fundamentalistic Baptist doctrine that I grew up with. . . . And I think this is true not only of me but of many American poets, going all the way back to Emerson and Thoreau and Whitman— coming out from under Calvinism" (22). Morgan might have named additional American writers, of course, most notably, perhaps, Hawthorne, Dickinson, and the Faulkner of *Light in August*. Yet, if "emerging from the rapt gloom of fundamentalism into the wide natural daylight" is one powerful impulse in Morgan's poetry (qtd. in Quillen, 50), an even more significant impulse is his celebration of the motif of resurrection, of rebirth, a motif central to the Christian tradition in which he was raised. "The central figure of our culture is the promise of rebirth," he declares in "The Cubist of Memory" (192), and in "Poetry and Revival," "All tropes are variations on the figure of resurrection" (77). Morgan's loving attention

From *Shenandoah* 42 (Summer 1992): 46–60. Reprinted by permission of the author and the publisher. The poetry of Robert Morgan is reprinted here by permission of its author.

to the physical world, his self-proclaimed role in "The Transfigured Body" as "the elohist of topsoil" (35), is meant to counteract the otherworldliness of much Protestant fundamentalism. But he also seeks to affirm nature's and humanity's capacity for rebirth—physical regeneration within nature, moral and spiritual renewal within the human community.

With few exceptions, the poems in Morgan's first three collections—*Zirconia Poems* (1969), the chapbook *The Voice in the Crosshairs* (1971), and *Red Owl* (1972)—contain little material of an explicitly religious nature. When such material does appear, it largely reflects the poet's negative reaction to the religious experiences of his childhood, as in "Prayer Meeting" *(ZP)* and "Church Pews" *(RO)*. *Land Diving* (1976), the poet's fourth volume, includes many more poems with explicitly religious subjects, in part because in this book Morgan was beginning to draw more heavily on his own and his family's past. The wrathful God he encountered in the Calvinism of his childhood reappears in several of these poems, most notably in "Signs" and "Face." The poem that precedes "Face" is entitled "After Church," and it too reflects the young Morgan's discomfort with many of the emotions generated by the church services he attended. In response to the fear of mortality and of divine judgment aroused by the preacher, the poet meditates on the "permanence [that] flared in the pine / grove." "[S]un fell nondenominationally," he adds. "Even the black coverts of laurel / and bleached pastures said / something comforting."

This movement toward nature as a means not only of consolation but of revelation recurs throughout Morgan's poetry. In the manner of his Puritan and Transcendentalist predecessors, Morgan in "The Transfigured Body" looks to nature for "the promise of signs and wonders" (31). He has acknowledged the powerful impression made upon him by his reading of Emerson's essays, especially Emerson's "sense of nature as dial of the spirit" (letter to the author, 10 Feb. 1991).

Like the unorthodox Emily Dickinson, Morgan prefers to celebrate divinity out-of-doors, not in the institution of the church or in doctrinal statements. Certainly the term *signs* in the poem of that title is meant to suggest, by ironic contrast, the larger typological tradition to which Morgan belongs. In *Land Diving* such poems as "Affliction," "Double Springs," "Easter Algae," and "Ice Worm" clearly participate in that tradition. "Affliction," for instance, describes the continuing impact of the chestnut blight, a curse in nature whose effects might be said to parallel those of the biblical Fall. New shoots, Morgan notes, continue to emerge, "thrive until the age of saplings, then / blossom and die." The poem's closing lines make explicit the connection between the human and the natural worlds:

Like us straining to ascend,
immortal
only in dirt.

This longing to ascend appears, paradoxically, in a volume entitled *Land Diving*. Its presence here attests to the dual movement that defines Morgan's world view. He remains enough of a Calvinist to see the world as fallen or broken; yet he rejects both the otherworldliness and the emphasis on human depravity found in much Protestant fundamentalism. For Morgan, human spirituality is rooted in the soil, and the natural objects he depicts often share this human thrust toward rebirth. Their powers of resurrection parallel humanity's own, as in "Easter Algae," a poem that celebrates what Morgan calls "the old impossible blessedness" visible in creation. Sacred and secular renewals coincide here—though ultimately, it seems to me, Morgan seeks to transcend the very dichotomy implicit in the terms "sacred" and "secular."

"Nature is the symbol of spirit," Emerson proclaimed. For Morgan, too, the temporal mirrors and reveals the eternal. Thus, to cultivate the natural world is not to cut oneself off from the divine but to immerse oneself in it. Morgan takes seriously—more seriously than does much of the Protestant fundamentalism that he knew as a child—the doctrines of creation and incarnation. This attitude accounts, I believe, for Morgan's repeated use of images of dirt, earth, mud, and manure. Body and soul are not at war in Morgan's poetry; instead, the body is the instrument, through the senses, of the soul's spiritual awakening. As the title of the final poem in *Land Diving* affirms, the poet is "Paradise's Fool," living in an Eden of wonders often overlooked. The poet's impulse, then, as he records it in "Midnight Sun," is to "strike into the long night of need / a rank garden, an eden." That eden is to be established within the temporal world, in part through a Blakean cleansing of the doors of perception. Many of Morgan's poems, in their celebration of natural phenomena, echo Blake's credo that "every thing that lives is holy."

Morgan has called *Land Diving* the pivotal volume in his career because of the new possibilities it opened up for him both in subject matter and in poetic form. During the period of its composition he was involved in what

JOHN LANG ✒ 264

he has described as "a new coming to terms with the rhetoric of the New Testament which I had forgotten since childhood," and he has identified hymns, "readings from the Bible and the fine rhetoric of pulpit and prayer" as among the most important influences on his sense of language, its rhythms and diction and imagery (Booker, 17, 18). In addition to immersing himself in a new reading of Scripture during this time, Morgan was also studying both Christopher Smart's *Jubilate Agno* and the religious poetry of Geoffrey Hill. Out of these new and renewed influences came not only *Land Diving* but *Trunk & Thicket* (1978).

About the latter volume Morgan said to Booker, "I wanted to get a new cultural and historical richness and density in my work. . . . At the same time I wanted to recover some of the incantatory power of 'prophesying' as I'd heard it as a child" (19). That recovery is most apparent in the book's third and final section, entitled "Mockingbird," in which imperatives resembling biblical injunctions predominate.

That section is preceded, however, by a prose Part II that bears the title "Homecoming." The word refers to the annual gatherings, now discontinued, of present and past members of the church Morgan's family helped to found. The poet's account of this ritual reunion is interspersed with information about the various doctrinal disputes that divided the congregation. Here again Morgan emphasizes the sectarianism and intolerance, the "exclusions" of that church's religion. The vindictiveness bred by such schisms is underscored by the poet's portrait of the man who rose during service one Sunday to declare "that in a vision it had been revealed to him my Uncle Robert's death in Europe had been sent as punishment for family sins." Such an attitude helps explain Morgan's negative reaction to the services depicted in "Prayer Meeting," "Church Pews" and "After Church." More important, though, the sectarian disputes described in "Homecoming" help prepare the reader to receive what might be called the "new commandments" set forth in "Mockingbird."

The "good news" Morgan proclaims in this poem directs his readers away from ecclesiastical institutions and toward nature. Yet his diction is suffused with religious terminology. "Believe in the immaculate / conception of matter from energy" is the first of these major pronouncements. Others include:

Interpret literally the eros of detail,
the saints of wind and water.

Keep the covenant
with bottomlands . . .

. . . Say the statute of
limitations has run out on original
sin.

. . . Reject the dryhides and
take the holy dance.

The flood of language in "Mockingbird" attests to the energy of the poet's vision. Once again, in the image of "the church's talon in the night sky," Morgan expresses his estrangement from the institutional Christianity he encountered as a child. Here, too, he rejects Calvinism's emphasis on human depravity, a rejection that has led William Harmon to characterize Morgan's work as "Pelagian," after the fifth-century theologian Pelagius, whose denial of original sin was attacked by St. Augustine and condemned as heresy in the year 416. While Morgan does not ignore evil in either nature or humanity, he does seek to counteract the near obsession with human sinfulness in some varieties of Christian fundamentalism. In this poem he seeks to bridge as well the presumed gap between this world and the next, time and eternity. "Know time as / magnification," he writes, for "Being is fed by time as by / oxygen."

Yet despite his distrust of many of the tenets and practices of Protestant fundamentalism—as evident, for example, in his reference to "the sermon as firedrill"—Morgan recommends the ecstatic sensibility. "Take the holy dance," he urges. Moreover, he affirms the sense of mystery that underlies all religious consciousness. "See entities beyond / nomination," he declares, a statement that insists on the limits of language, that bears witness to the reality and the significance of the ineffable. "Mountains speak in tongues. . . . / . . . The absent god leaves the forest / and tundra soaked in divinity." And thus Morgan advises the reader to be "in congregation / with mist and rock," to "Play with matches, / correspondences," presumably correspondences between the natural and human worlds and between the realms of matter and spirit. "Where is the man who / would not kill to be reborn," the poet asks, announcing the major theme of "Mockingbird" and of many of Morgan's subsequent poems: the theme of rebirth, of metamorphosis.

If *Trunk & Thicket* is the volume in which Morgan's prophetic, incantatory voice is most audible, his next four collections of poems—*Groundwork* (1979), *Bronze Age* (1981), *At the Edge of the Orchard Country* (1987), and *Sigodlin* (1990)—continue to address the issues he raises there and in his preceding books. A number of the poems in those volumes extend, for instance, his portrait of the religious practices and beliefs he experienced as a child: such poems as "Death Crown" and "Baptism of Fire" in *Groundwork,* "Earache" in *Bronze Age,* and "Baptizing Trough" in *Sigodlin.* At times, as in "Death Crown," he seems to adopt the stance of objective informant. Typically, however, Morgan's response to these experiences is tinged with irony, as is evident in his use of the word "trough" and in his character sketch of the contentious Gondan in "Baptism of Fire."

Consider in this regard "The Gift of Tongues" (from *Orchard Country),* which reveals most fully the young Morgan's discomfort at the Pentecostal religion practiced by his father:

The whole church got hot and vivid
with the rush of unhuman chatter
above the congregation
and I saw my father looking at
the altar as though electrocuted.
It was a voice I'd never heard
but knew as from other centuries.
It was the voice of awful fire.
"What's he saying?" Ronald hissed
and jabbed my arm. "Probably Hebrew."
The preacher called out another
hymn, and the glissade came again,
high syllables not from my father's
lips but elsewhere, the flare of
higher language, sentences of light.
And we sang and sang again, but
no one rose as if from sleep to
be interpreter, explain the writing
on the air that still shone there like
blindness. None volunteered a gloss
or translation or receiver
of the message. My hands hurt

when pulled from the pew's varnish
they'd gripped and sweated so. Later,
standing under the high and plain-
sung pines on the mountain I clenched
my jaws like pliers, holding in
and savoring the gift of silence.

Such a poem, with its carefully balanced contrast of title and closing
phrase, reflects the largely negative emotions Morgan felt at such religious
services when a child. As he comments in his interview with Booker,

> When young, I remember being extremely frightened of [my father]
> and others speaking in tongues, shouting, and I remember being espe-
> cially terrified of the phrase "baptism by fire." It sounded too much like
> Hell to me. And I was often afraid the Rapture would come and I'd be
> left with the sinners and the moon turned to blood. . . . But mostly I re-
> member the great relief when the service was over, and we could go
> back out into the sunlight and the sweet breeze among the pines. . . .
> How friendly the stars seemed over the dark mountains after the sweat
> of a prayermeeting. (15)

In "Heaven" from *Sigodlin,* Morgan also expresses skepticism about traditional Christian views of the after-life, though his initial tone is clearly
one of regret.

And yet I don't want not to believe in,
little as I can, the big whoosh of souls
upward at the Rapture, when clay and ocean,
dust and pit, yield up their dead, when all

elements reassemble into the forms
of the living from the eight winds and flung
petals of the compass. And I won't assume,
much as I've known it certain all along,

that I'll never see Grandma again, nor
Uncle Vol with his fabulations,
nor see Uncle Robert plain with no scar

from earth and the bomber explosions.

I don't want to think how empty and cold
the sky is, how distant the family,
but of winged seeds blown from a milkweed field
in the opalescent smokes of early

winter ascending toward heaven's blue,
each self orchestrated in one aria
of river and light. And those behind the blue
are watching even now us on the long way.

Here the poet both acknowledges and resists his doubts. The unlikelihood of Christ's Second Coming, with its general resurrection, is underscored by the phrase "big whoosh of souls." Yet the poet inclines toward a species of agnosticism, however intense, rather than outright disbelief.

Through the first four stanzas "Heaven" is built on negatives—and on denials of denial: "And yet I don't want not to believe in," "And I won't assume," and "I don't want to think." Shifting to what the poet does want to think in the middle of stanza four, the poem changes from its predominantly optative mood to the indicative. Its closing sentence, preceded by the great beauty of the natural images in lines 15–19, stands in sharp opposition to the earlier skepticism: "And those behind the blue / are watching even now us on the long way." The conviction of that claim is somewhat diminished, however, by the poet's deliberately awkward syntax, his unidiomatic phrasing. Nevertheless, Morgan's poem, in its structuring of its ideas, clearly reverses the pattern common to many of Dickinson's religious poems. Whereas Dickinson often begins with certitude ("I know that He exists"; "This World is not Conclusion") and moves toward radical doubt, Morgan begins "Heaven" with skeptical detachment and moves toward what he has called "the triumph of aspiration and hope over ordinary skepticism" (letter to the author, 31 Mar. 1991).

That for Morgan one of poetry's principal functions is to adumbrate the possibilities of rebirth is apparent both in his poems themselves and in his remarks in various essays and interviews. "Most great poems," he has said in his essay on Bryant, "touch somehow the figure of resurrection" (56). Frequently, that movement towards rebirth and transformation involves descent into a pit of some kind and re-emergence from it. This motif is present in "Zircon Pit" (from *Groundwork*) and in "Potato Hole" (from *Orchard Country*), both poems in which the poet himself is the central figure. In the latter poem he states, "I'll rise with the first shoots / of Lazarus green."

These poems of human rebirth are complemented by similar poems involving creatures from the natural world—for example, "Wallowing" and "Den Tree" (from *Groundwork*). The former describes, in lovingly detailed, sensuous language, a horse's "emery submersion salving / harness galls and currying off sweat," a wallowing from which the horse arises "pure and free / as if new-born in the depression." The latter poem describes a bear's hibernation but looks toward the animal's spring awakening, when "He will hear that lovesong [a dove's] / lighting his new hunger."

Similar transformations also occur when human beings and nature interact, as in "Man and Machine" (from *Orchard Country*), in which the poet's cousin Luther plows all night, becoming a mythic figure of renewal. The resurrection motif is most prominent here in Morgan's concluding statement, the poem's only single-sentence line: "And by morning the fields were new." A variant of this motif likewise appears in "Hay Scuttle," although here the movement does not involve descent into a depression in the ground but a return to the barn's floor. That descent is imaged in ways characteristic of Morgan's commitment to the earth: "Only way out to the sun is down, / through the exquisite filth."

In all these poems immersion in the physical world is necessary and illuminating, even purifying. As Roger Jones observes, "[Morgan's] poetry provides proof that spiritual and metaphysical moorings are to be found first, and most powerfully, in the ground itself" (218). In opposition to the lesson taught by the Protestant fundamentalism of Morgan's youth—"how little this world had to do / with the next except as staging ground" (*Orchard Country*, 59)—the poet stresses the importance of "land diving," of "groundwork," of recognizing that, here and now, we dwell "at the edge of the orchard country," to cite just three of his books' titles.

In fact, Morgan's choice of the phrase "elohist of topsoil" to describe his function as a poet is doubly significant in this connection. Not only does that phrase emphasize the spiritual potential of the material world; it also indicates Morgan's rejection of Calvinist exclusivity in religious matters. In biblical criticism, the term "elohist" contrasts with the term "yahwist," each derived from a different Hebrew name for God. The word "Elohim" is the more inclusive of the two terms, for it refers to God in God's role as creator and ruler of all humanity, whereas the name "Yahweh" refers to the

God who enters into a covenant with a chosen people, the Israelites. It is not the elect but the entire creation for which Morgan chooses to speak.

In the vicinity of Eden, then, Morgan sets out to read the "signs and wonders" that surround him. Like the pioneer settler of "Feather Bed" (from *Orchard Country*) he is drawn "back / over the hills and piedmont and tidewater, / across the troubled Atlantic and centuries / toward a white immaculate garden," an image of primordial innocence and unity. That mythic garden is an important symbol in a number of his poems. More often, however, Morgan discovers spiritual presences and possibilities in the commonplace, the close-at-hand rather than the more remote realms of mythic gardens. He examines what one poem in *Orchard Country* calls "the scripture / of signs" (9) in such unlikely places and objects as manure piles, lightning bugs, and his aunt Florrie's parlor, as well as in such natural phenomena as Brownian motion and inertia.

Morgan's poems insist that such interpretation of "the written character of all creation"—a phrase used twice in the poem "Jutaculla Rock" (from *Orchard Country*)—is one major responsibility of human beings. Yet he acknowledges the difficulty of this interpretive process "without / a key to its [creation's] whorls and wisps / of scripture." Moreover, in "Writing Spider" (from *Sigodlin*), he warns against the extreme subjectivity to which that process can lead. But what he calls "a lifetime's work" remains: the demand that we "read" the world's manifold objects, name them, and accept responsibility for our naming.

The readings embodied in Morgan's poems typically emphasize the mystery and plentitude of existence. Amidst even the inanimate dust of "Brownian Motion" (from *Orchard Country*), Morgan discerns a universe of endless vitality:

> The air is an aquarium where
> every mote spins wild
> and prisms the morning light.
> Lint climbs sparkling on
> convection's fountain,
> and magnetic storms boil away
> like gnats bumped by molecules.
> Every breath swarms
> the clear spores, ion seethe,

magnified in playful flight.
Look at the dust panic
off a fingertip. Each
particle is an opal angel
too small to see but in the glare
of this annunciation.

In a poem like this one Morgan's scientific training and interests complement his poetic vision. Rather than seeing science and religion as foes,
after the fashion of much of fundamentalist Christianity, Morgan employs
the perspectives of both to convey the wonder of creation. In fact, he speaks
of "the counterpoint and harmony of the scientific and the spiritual," not of
their antagonism, and he notes that "some of the true mystics of the century are the physicists" (letter to the author, 10 Feb. 1991). In "Brownian
Motion" Morgan combines careful scientific observation with the insight
of a visionary like Blake. Morgan's poems often create a Brownian motion
of their own, as they become annunciations of a power in nature that radi-
ates supernatural light.

Another good example of this quality in Morgan's work occurs in
"Lightning Bug," the poem that follows "Brownian Motion" in *At the Edge
of the Orchard Country* and the poem that gives the collection its title:

Carat of the first radiance,
you navigate like a creature
of the deep. I wish I could read
your morse across the night yard.
Your body is a piece of star
but your head is obscure. What small
photography! What instrument
panel is on? You are winnowed
through the hanging gardens of night.
Your noctilucent syllables
sing in the millenium of
the southern night with star-talking
dew, like the thinker sending nous
into the outerstillness from
the edge of the orchard country.

The profusion of metaphors here, the care the poet has given to rhythm and phrasing and sound effects, the suggestiveness of the diction as it echoes and alludes to the Bible and classical culture, the poet's appropriation of the American tradition of reading nature symbolically—all contribute to the strength and beauty of this poem. The poet longs to interpret the insect's apparent message, a message that is linked to the process of illumination, and perhaps to the *fiat lux* of Genesis 1:3. The insect is not only *addressed* in this poem, its "noctilucent syllables / sing . . . / . . . with star-talking / dew." Here we encounter not a Calvinist Outer Dark, where sinners weep and gnash their teeth, but an "outerstillness" of immense tranquility. Moreover, Morgan's reference to "the thinker sending nous" into that outerstillness, while punning on the word *news,* recalls a long philosophical and religious tradition for which the Greek word *nous,* literally meaning mind or intelligence, also suggested the Mind that gave rise to the universe. Although Morgan does not capitalize the word *thinker* in this poem, he seems to invite a theological reading of that figure's identity.

Ultimately, Morgan's poetry strives to be, in a phrase that occurs in the title poem of his collection *Sigodlin,* "true to spirit level." "I can't imagine poetry without some sense of worlds beyond the merely physical," he said in an interview with William Harmon in the *Iron Mountain Review;* "perhaps poetry is the unifier, seeing at once the spiritual and the physical" (16).

The word *sigodlin,* as it is used in the Appalachian region, means out of plumb, askew, and thus captures Morgan's sense of living in a flawed, fallen world. But Morgan locates human beings in far greater proximity to Eden than did his Calvinist ancestors. For the Morgan of the poem "Sigodlin," the impulse to uprightness in a broken world reflects humanity's "love of geometry's power to say / . . . / the power whose center is everywhere." According to St. Augustine, that power (which he described as a circle whose center is everywhere and circumference nowhere) was God. For American readers, Augustine's definition of God is perhaps most readily available in the opening paragraph of Emerson's essay "Circles," an essay with which Morgan is most certainly familiar.

"The power whose center is everywhere." Surely this conception of divinity fuels Robert Morgan's imagination, intensifying its exploration of nature. Though he rejects the otherworldly religion of his youth, he continues to affirm humanity's spiritual potential, as two final paired poems in *Sigodlin* will help to demonstrate. These two poems, "Inertia" and "Stretching," appear initially to focus on physical phenomena. In both poems, however, Morgan evokes the spiritual. "There is such a languor to matter," the former begins. But as the poem progresses Morgan challenges "the reverie of substance, the / immobility and dream of / the body's authority" by describing such inertia as seeming "reluctant as a bear to wake / from the immanence and ponder." Morgan's poems, I would argue, are largely exercises in just such awakening to thought, to wonder, to what he calls in "Stretching" "the savor of being." In "the sweet mobility of used / muscle," Morgan writes in the latter poem, "you are more than you remembered." This recovery of an enlarged identity once more reveals the underlying motif of rebirth and renewal in Morgan's poetry. Despite their initial focus on the physical, both poems reflect their author's assumption that "the major subject of poetry is the recovery of spiritual desire" ("Asylum of the Real," 90).

Morgan "comes out from under Calvinism," then, by distancing himself from the otherworldliness of much fundamentalist Christianity, from its wrathful God, and from its vision of a depraved humanity of which only an elect few will be saved. He retains, however, the sense of wonder and mystery so integral to authentic religious consciousness. Like Blake he discovers "Eternity in an hour"—"in the millennium of / the southern night," as he puts it in "Lightning Bug." Among the various "powers" Morgan associates with poetry—the power of naming, of remembering, and of honoring the dead—the one he calls "perhaps the most important of all" is "the power of praise." "And all praise ultimately is praise of God," he writes, "whatever the names and terms we use" (letter to the author, 10 Feb. 1991). In addition to that power of praise, his poems repeatedly emphasize both the need for and the experience of rebirth, of resurrection, and they thus reinforce the Christian tradition's principal metaphor and promise. To read Robert Morgan is to stand again "at the edge of the orchard country," to gaze upon and move towards what he calls in the final lines of "Land Bridge" (from *Sigodlin*) with its provocative concluding pun,

> . . . the tip of some unfolding
> giant land of our new being,
> the bridge to the original
> now buried beyond the littoral.

Works Cited

Booker, Suzanne. "A Conversation with Robert Morgan." *Carolina Quarterly* 37.3 (1985): 13–22.

Harmon, William. "Robert Morgan's Pelagian Georgics: Twelve Essays." *Parnassus* 9 (Fall/Winter 1981): 5–30.

Harmon, William, and Robert Morgan. "Imagination, Memory, and Region: A Conversation." *Iron Mountain Review* 6 (1990): 11–16.

Jones, Roger D. "Robert Morgan." In *American Poets since World War II: Third Series,* ed. R. S. Gwynn. *Dictionary of Literary Biography* vol. 120. Detroit: Gale, 1992.

Morgan, Robert. "Asylum of the Real." *Mississippi Review* 19 (1991): 90–91.

———. *At the Edge of Orchard Country.* Middletown, Conn.: Wesleyan University Press, 1987.

———. "Bryant's Solitary Glimpse of Paradise." In *Under Open Sky: Poets on William Cullen Bryant,* ed. Norbert Krapf. New York: Fordham University Press, 1986.

———. "The Cubist of Memory." In *The Generation of 2000: Contemporary American Poets,* ed. William Heyen. Princeton: Ontario Review Press, 1984.

———. *Groundwork.* Frankfort, Ky.: Gnomon Press, 1979.

———. *Land Diving.* Baton Rouge: Louisiana State University Press, 1976.

———. Letters to John Lang, dated 10 Feb. 1991 and 31 Mar. 1991.

———. "Poetry and Revival." *Bluefish* 3/4 (Fall 1984/Spring 1985): 75–78.

———. *Red Owl.* New York: Norton, 1972.

———. *Sigodlin.* Middletown, Conn.: Wesleyan University Press, 1990.

———. "The Transfigured Body: Notes on Poetry from a Journal." *The Small Farm* 3 (March 1976): 31–39.

———. *Trunk & Thicket.* Fort Collins, Colo.: L'Epervier Press, 1978.

———. *Zirconia Poems.* Northwood Narrows, N.H.: Lillabulero Press, 1969.

Quillen, Rita. *Looking for Native Ground: Contemporary Appalachian Poetry.* Boone, N.C.: Appalachian Consortium Press, 1989.

Robert Morgan's Mountain Voice and Lucid Prose

CECELIA CONWAY

For more than thirty years, from *Zirconia Poems* (1969) to his musical collection *Topsoil Road* (November 2000), Robert Morgan has given us vivid poetry that sparkles like a rainbow crystal in spring water. Like Thomas Wolfe, Morgan left the North Carolina mountains early for university life. He graduated from UNC–Chapel Hill in 1965 and earned an MFA at UNC-Greensboro, where he became friends with his teacher Fred Chappell, later the poet laureate of North Carolina. In 1971, Morgan began teaching at Cornell University. During three decades as a teacher and an accomplished poet, Morgan developed certain themes and innovative artistic strategies that would persist when he returned to writing fiction in 1984. In his book *Good Measure* (1993), the reflective essays, interviews, and notes on poetry provide the artistic and intellectual context for his writing.[1]

One story Morgan often tells is of a journalist who wondered, "How did you get from Appalachia to Cornell—to the Ivy League? For practically speaking, you can't get there from here."[2] Morgan's journey beyond the mountains is inspiring. But even though he has been outposted in the Ivy League, Robert Morgan, like Thomas Wolfe before him, looked homeward. His writing, primarily set in western Carolina, enables us "to see the wilderness better" and to explore and dream wildernesses we "would never

Originally published in a different form in *Appalachian Journal: A Regional Studies Review* 29 (Fall 2001–Winter 2002): 180–99. Copyright © 2002 by *Appalachian Journal* and Appalachian State University.

otherwise know."[3] *Green River,* his 1990 collection of new and selected poems, bears the name of the waters that meander near Zirconia, North Carolina, where Morgan was raised among storytellers and churchgoers in the Blue Ridge mountains. Morgan's writings lead us deep into the frontier that shows the relationship between landscape outside and landscape inside.

After Morgan started to teach in upstate New York, as he has explained, he returned to and has "continued to live" in the mountains of his North Carolina homeland in "the imagination, in the geography and landscape of language."[4] Perhaps he felt less homesick during the snowy winters of the frozen Finger Lakes region when he wrote poems about spring drawing close to the Blue Ridge. Only after he left the mountains and the farm work he had been happy to escape did he become a serious student of Appalachia and begin to read all the county histories of the region. He later became friends with Appalachian writers and scholars such as Jim Wayne Miller, Loyal Jones, Gurney Norman, and Jeff Daniel Marion. Besides visiting on Green River, Morgan sometimes teaches at the Hindman Settlement School Writers' Workshop on the forks of Troublesome Creek in Kentucky. He continues to read local histories, botanical and geological studies, folklore, and novels about the mountains. His study of the region provides historical context and scientific detail for his mountain experience.

Indeed, the wellspring of Morgan's art has remained his mountain homeplace. Morgan's ancestors came to the Southern Appalachian mountain region from Wales during the eighteenth century. In 1840, his maternal great-great-grandfather cleared new ground on what remains the family homeplace today. Morgan grew up on his family's one-horse farm with no truck or tractor, and on the day before he left for college, at sixteen, he plowed the late bean field. He knows the traditional farm life and unmechanized labor he writes about. From the ground where some Morgans mined zircon gems, Robert Morgan has found the resources for sparkling mountain literature that recreates, in poetry and fiction, an agrarian Southern Appalachia of the turn of the twentieth century, its history back to settlement, and its diverse path into the ever-changing present.

At Cornell, Morgan began to reconnect with his childhood memories and the family and regional stories of his mother, his grandfather, and especially his "rememberer" father. While living in a university community of writers, he began to understand poetry as "voice" and "telling sentences" and tried to remember exactly how his "great aunts had spoken, and the smells of old houses heated by cooking stoves and fireplaces."[5] Morgan's early poems "had seemed to be spoken against the silence of all eternity," but in the collection *Land Diving*, "they began to sound like someone talking on a given afternoon."[6] Morgan's fascination with mountain voices would eventually propel him from poetry toward the freer spaces of stories and novels filled with strong narrative progression.

During the mid-1970s, Morgan's interest in narrative poetry turned toward "rhymed forms and balladic horror and compression."[7] A decade later, the author would apply to his fiction what he had learned from traditional ballad forms. From his first collection, *The Blue Valleys*,[8] Morgan's provocative stories maintain the narrative thrust and compression of ballads by leaping and lingering mentally if not physically. But unlike ballads, these stories include flashbacks that create intense psychological and philosophical depth. Later he would incorporate the laconic dialogue of mountain ballads and speech. The development of his mountain voices helped him move from eloquent, well-crafted short stories to lucid novels, and from conversation to full-voiced female protagonists.

Morgan's writing rests on the bedrock of his insider and outsider perspectives. His imaginative perspective is that of the "lucid" dreamer—the creative dreamer who remains participant, keen witness, and director at once. Both Morgan's knowledge of mountain ways and his expanding modernist perspective on literature and art (much of which he acquired outside the region) have shaped his fiction. A comparison of early short stories and later fiction demonstrates the growth of Robert Morgan's mountain voice and lucid fiction: his innovative outsider scholarly strategies become increasingly enhanced by an insider perspective and by well-crafted, traditional tale-telling. His vivid sensory descriptions and startling comparisons, inventive philosophical precision, narrative complexity (including flashbacks), and psychological depth find enough space in tale-telling and fiction to allow his characters to grapple, more fully than in his poems, with nature, work, and eventually intimacy. The characters' mountain voices increasingly explore the ritual of work and disclose the complexities of intimacy and its language.

The Blue Valleys—THE PRISONER

Based on a family remembrance, "A Brightness, New and Welcoming" introduces Morgan's first collection of short stories. In this poetic parable, a spring symbolizes the theme of the beauty of nature, its resources, and its reassurances. A spring had appeared in the poem "Blue Ridge":

> Here a spring has first choice,
> the first gathering of moisture, a . . .
> feeding out evenly
> far from the sweet thrusting
>
> . . . .
> At the farthest boundary of
> the ocean's magnet
> water gathers itself from
> the dirt speaking cold and clear.[9]

The author's precise, poetic language always enlivens his short stories. This introductory story emphasizes the welcoming brightness the mountain spring provides. Water is the source of life and no water is purer than spring water. The "vicious stench" of the Civil War prison camp and the awful, "muddy" well water drive the imagination of wounded North Carolina prisoner Powell to the spring in the hollow of his Blue Valley home. The author reminds us that the cool spring water, which runs along the roots of the poplar tree, enticed Powell to buy the land when he moved up into North Carolina and remains mesmerizing on the hottest July days. The spring "tasted of quartz rock deep under the mountains. Sometimes when he found a specially brilliant crystal he would place it in the spring to sparkle for all to see. Spring water was touched by all the mineral wealth it had passed through, the gold and rubies, silver and emeralds in the deep veins. The water was a cold rainbow on the tongue."[10] The spring as a source of life and image of the imagination is a rainbow of promise for the prisoner. This symbol returns intensely at the end of the story.

The Southern prisoners use little vernacular. A spoken sentence of hospitality initiates the story as the prisoner is ironically offered "muddy water." But never more than a line or two of dialogue appears, and usually rendered without dialect. As a result of his wounds and illness, prisoner Powell is almost voiceless. Nonetheless, his meditations, like his imaginary visits to the spring, bring the resonance and philosophical depth of Morgan's poetry to his fiction.

The only sentences of dramatic, vernacular language are the half-dozen that enliven the character of Powell's wife Louise. Her letter, replete with phonetic spelling, begins, "Dear husbun John, it raned all thrue the fall, but I saved most of the corn. The babye wannt come till March" (8). Powell deserts the battle—despite seeing other deserters hanged along the roadside for going home at Christmas—to return to Louise as promised for planting season. Startled, his wife says, "I thought you was an outlier. . . . I prayed you would come, now that it's corn planting time" (9). Her voice introduces themes of planting, birth, harvest, and intimacy that will emerge more fully in later works. In some ways, Louise echoes the speech of Morgan's great-aunts and foreshadows the mountain voices that will evoke the well-developed women protagonists of the later novels.

Most of the story intercuts the prisoner's gruesome, painful present and his often pleasant memories of home. The realistic time shifts of his feverish mind set a pattern typical of Morgan's suspenseful storytelling. From his prison camp cot, the wounded soldier transports himself in his mind to the cot in the laurels by the spring where he hid out at home during planting time. When Louise would visit him at night, Powell was never "so happy and so scared at once" (9). By honoring his promise to return home to plant, he has respected the land, procreated, and provided for his family. In his dark hour, he finally finds comfort in remembering the ritual of planting and harvest: "He kept thinking of the row of sunflowers . . . , and they were huge and bright, though he remembered them as black—bright and black" (19). By witnessing the huge, bright blossoming of the sunflowers, he appreciates the seeds he sowed on earth for his family—"the row of sunflowers he had planted" (19).

The sunflowers are also like blossoms of poetic inspiration and fictional creation. Morgan has acknowledged his "obsession with finding absolute structures in language that mirror the everlastingness of natural process."[11] At the end of this story, the multiple connotations of the mountain spring provide another natural structure as entrancing as the sunflowers. The eight sections of the narrative reflect two cycles through the seasons of two years—the actual duration of the events of the story: "The higher he got the newer were the leaves on the trees. On the mountain the grass was green but shorter. He was climbing back into early spring" (20). Amidst all the pain, loss, and death witnessed, the questor takes comfort in the everlastingness of the seasons, and perhaps finds hope for human rebirth in nature's annual renewal.

The cold mountain spring resonates with the seasonal spring of nature's rebirth and the spring in the step of a prisoner climbing to a mountain home: "the clear water thrust up from under the poplar roots and dimpled the surface like wrinkled silk. . . . The tart cold taste seemed to come from the deepest part of the mountain, from the beginning of the world" (21). The "tart" thrusting from the deepest imagination and the silky beauty of life merge the resources of nature and the rebirth of the seasons in the path taken by the questor.

The Mountains Won't Remember Us—THE STONEMASON

In the second collection of short stories, *The Mountains Won't Remember Us* (1992), Morgan returns eloquently to the theme of man's relationships with nature. Morgan's early encounters with the King James version of the New Testament and his later appreciation of Emerson, whose every sentence he describes as "a work of art in itself," influence his clean, poetic prose style.[12] Morgan uses their pristine echoes to transform New England Calvinistic, spiritual autobiography into modern philosophic, self-reflective meditations on nature and language as texts that reflect spirit.

"Poinsett's Bridge" was selected for *New Stories from the South* (1991) and began Morgan's publishing relationship with Algonquin. The meditations in this story introduce another of Morgan's major themes—the folk knowledge and value of hard work. The natural "brightness" of the mountain spring that draws the mind of the prisoner who faces death in the earlier story becomes here the "shiny" hammer (22), a craftsman's tool that guides and stabilizes the mason through work. In "Brightness," remembrance transports the prisoner from his agony and approaching death. Psychologically he soothes himself with meditation upon the spring, intimacy in the laurels, and blooming sunflowers. In "Poinsett's Bridge," the stonemason, threatened by robbers, entrances himself with the sacraments and rituals of work—with how man crafts natural resources. This second collection expands the mountain (occupational) folklore and the mountain voice of each protagonist.

Morgan's mountain life experiences provide wise, insider context and perspective for his keen (outsider) Ivy League scholarly knowledge. He further develops mountain voices in their storytelling context, and some of Morgan's stories are also "speakerly texts"[13]—traditional mountain taletelling intended to be heard. In this first story of the collection, also based on a family remembrance of a regional tale, Morgan's storytelling includes an audience that helps create a conversational style and tone. The first line establishes the context when the accomplished stonemason addresses his boy as "Son." As in "Brightness," the wife, despite a limited role, adds intimacy to the work of the story: "But it was a kind of fate, too, and even Clara didn't try to stop me. She complained, as a woman will . . . [but] she [also] give me a buckeye to put in my pocket for luck. She didn't normally hold to such things, but I guess she was as worried as I was" (6–7). Clara's gift shows her understanding of the necessity of work and craftsmanship to her husband's identity and sense of calling as a stonemason.

In this story, the young man works the rock resources of nature with growing competence. Through apprenticeship as well as experience, the speaker becomes skillful and self-confident, establishes his identity as a mason, and bonds with other men to create the handsome, useful, clean-lined bridge. In clashes with his boss, the stonemason learns to use the details, skills, and discipline of his work to stabilize his anger and reassure his confidence. Ultimately, as in many of the stories, the value of the work lies not in the money earned, but in the experience and craftsmanship gained, "seeing the ceremony," as Clara observes, reclaiming the speaker's "shiny" mason's hammer, and the story told.

Thus, in his second collection of stories, Morgan continues to develop his narrative strategies. He again creates suspense by cutting between the present threat of robbery and descriptive past meditation. He has mastered a thoughtful and sympathetic point of view by developing a mountain voice that gives the main character control of the entire narrative. Influenced by Eudora Welty, Morgan uses a vernacular signature rather than extensive dialect to enliven his Southern voices. His work demonstrates an understanding of folkways including stonework and the weather, as well as storytelling.

Clara's sensitivity to her husband and her understanding of his craftsmanship extend her mountain voice and character, as prefigured by Louise in "Brightness," and lead toward other important women in this second collection of stories. Several extended pieces have female protagonists—including "Frog Level," "Martha Sue," and the exceptional, concluding story, "The Mountains Won't Remember Us," which brings alive the remarkable voice of Uncle Robert's fiancée and transforms Morgan's fiction.

The Mountains Won't Remember Us — THE FIANCÉE

Morgan's dramatic turn of voice comes in this second collection with the concluding and title story, "The Mountains Won't Remember Us" (1989).

Morgan for the first time writes a novella told from a woman's point of view. In an early poem about his influential Uncle Robert, who died in World War II, Morgan writes:

> It was hinted I was "marked" somehow,
> not only by your name, but in some way
> unexplained was actually you. Aunts and cousins
> claimed we favored and
>
> . . . .
> I had the high-arched "'Levi foot'
> like you, and your quick laugh,"
>
> . . . .
> . . . I inherited
> your Testament with its boards of carved cedar,
> and the box of arrowheads you picked
> from the dust of the bottomlands on Sunday afternoons,
> like seeds and teeth of giants.[14]

Uncle Robert is the sacrificed lamb of the poem "Family Bible" whose blood is lost in battle on behalf of the extended family, young Robert, and others who come after.[15]

After vast research with documents and oral histories of Air Corps crew members, Morgan explained that he felt "hung up on runways and flight plans." He decided to turn the story over to an elderly woman who had been Uncle Robert's young fiancée when he died. Earlier, in *The Blue Valleys* collection, Morgan had experimented with the voice of this woman in "The Lost State of Franklin." This title serves as a metaphor for her loss in love and life. After rereading Thomas Wolfe's novella *Web of Earth* in the spring of 2000, Robert Morgan observed that the story, based on a visit by Wolfe's mother, sounded somewhat like his own mother's voice. He also said that the work had influenced him more than he had realized when he read it thirty years before. No doubt this influence, reflected in the fiancée, includes the impressive voice of an elderly and thoughtful female protagonist. After Morgan began to hear the elderly fiancée's voice reminiscing about her early love, he totally revised and re-created the story. A female protagonist gives Morgan's writing new psychological complexity in a novella many considered his best fiction at that time.

Morgan has spoken of the early and extensive influence of *Look Homeward, Angel* upon him. The questing artist and the poetic lines of Wolfe's epigraph must have caught Morgan's attention: " . . . a stone, a leaf, an un-found door. . . . O lost, and by the wind grieved, ghost, come back again." Indeed, dialogue with a ghost helps the fiancée find her voice in Morgan's "The Mountains Won't Remember Us." Facing challenging and realistic fears, the fiancée confronts the specter of the lost Robert, dead more than four decades. She speaks up dramatically and moves beyond Eugene—Wolfe's lone questor "grandiose in his introversion"—who remains forever a stranger engulfed in loneliness. Morgan's fiancée faces self-doubts and lets go of her loneliness.[16] The mountains won't remember the fiancée who becomes a woman, but we readers do: we hear her voice and her story. Through the mason we appreciate the stone of nature, and through the prisoner we acknowledge the lovely fragility of a sunflower in the passing seasons. With the fiancée, we may find a door to converse with a ghost, free the voiceless prisoner, let go of loneliness and fear, reach out to another, and come home to ourselves.

Morgan has also spoken of the artistic discipline required to maintain a character's voice and of the scary need to "erase oneself" to hear the voice of any character. This shape shifting entails the ability to enter the conscious-ness of another and return to the self.[17] In the early 1970s, Morgan said, "The poet must be in the crow's nest and boiler room at once, and not only at the helm. . . . I want a periscopic reach, to stay on the ground yet see from above."[18] This lucid, shape-shifting process becomes especially in-tense when crossing the gender barrier and genuinely hearing the voice of a woman. In fact, Morgan has said that the shift was so alarming and thrilling that he probably worked twice as hard on the story. Women nar-rators seem to have offered Morgan various masks to explore feelings in transition and intimacy in detail. Morgan has also spoken of authors as "ac-tors." At readings, for example, they perform and direct the scripts they have written. And Morgan has spoken of the delight of leaving one's ego and voice behind to genuinely explore another character's voice and script her journey. With women narrators from Uncle Robert's fiancée onward, Morgan's insightful witness to diverse women seems to have found voices that become masks of inspiration and freedom.[19]

The Hinterlands — PETAL

In *The Hinterlands: A Mountain Tale in Three Parts* (1994), the longer tales and the format of a cycle of tales inspire longer conversational cadences and the move from short stories toward a novel.[20] With the voice of the pioneer narrator Petal in "The Trace" (written in 1991), Morgan creates a more fully developed female protagonist.

The cycle of tales also expands the groundwork for Morgan's best fiction, for the writer apprentices himself further, through memory and attention, to traditional storytelling. He emphasizes family and regional legends, folktales, ghost stories, nature lore, and other folkways. His mother paid close attention to nature and plants, and his father remembered and recounted sometimes gruesome historical stories. His grandfather told the children horrifying bedtime tales of ghosts, snakes overtaking the hearth, and panthers chasing and clawing after early settlers.

The three tales of this cycle have traditional roots and are told by three generations of speakers who settle near Green River, North Carolina, and down the mountain toward the moonshine wilderness of Dark Corner, South Carolina. Petal's tale, set in 1772, is based on the ballad of Billy Holsclaw. In the second tale, Morgan weaves regional tall tales and legends into the story of Solomon Jones, who married the sister of Morgan's maternal great-great-grandmother. Morgan fills the third story of David Richards's 1845 road building with rumored cave-ins, and the author lets his imagination run wild with a regional panther tale heard as a child. Each tale echoes and varies themes of wilderness adventure and courtship with motifs of weather, panthers, and sometimes threatening humans.

Within *The Hinterlands,* Morgan's conversational storytelling technique also evolves with greater complexity in the narrator Petal. Her long, serious tale focuses on the theme of intimacy introduced by the earlier female narrators Louise in "Brightness" and Clara in "Poinsett's Bridge." The author has observed that women make exceptionally good storytellers because they notice details—from the floral wallpaper and the pork roast to the gossip of a holiday party—and especially because, unlike many of his male characters, women are quite willing to talk about their relationships and feelings.

With Petal, the influence of Wolfe's *Web of Earth* appears again in a strong elderly woman's reflective mountain voice and in her tale-telling awareness of child listeners, whom she directly addresses. Her monologue incorporates the effect of dialogue by repeating her grandchildren's question about her courtship:

> The first time I seen your Grandpa? Why, it was the year everybody was talking about going to Watauga and the Holston. Then every

young girl dreamed of running off to the West. They thought if they could just get there and start over, everything would be perfect, or near about. That's the way girls dream. It was the wilderness of the West they was studying on. (3)

The speaker thus characterizes herself as an adventurous girl and teaches the grandchildren of their heritage. Her comments about her courtship place an intimate relationship at the center of the extended tale.

Petal adds the wisdom of her now elderly perspective to the romance of young folks: "Of course, you could change yourself right where you are through hard work and determination. But there ain't much romance in hard work. . . . It's over the horizon, in back of beyond, where things will be different, and better" (3–4). Petal's novella-length tale gives room to expand the detailed folklore, mountain voice (not dialect), and storytelling from a woman's point of view.

The title of Petal's tale, "The Trace," symbolizes the path to the romantic wilderness, and its promise of settlement links the three generations of tale tellers. After Petal's tale of the trace, Solomon Richards tells the hilarious, true story of blazing "The Road" in 1816 by using the folk wisdom of grabbing the tail of a pig. Then in 1845—in the third tale, "The Turnpike"—David Richards tells of being chased by Old Trifoot the Panther. In these two tall tales, each energetic and savvy boy narrator blazes a trail headlong up the path to his sweetheart. One is pulled up the mountain by the hungry sow Sue headed for the feeding trough and the other is chased to near nakedness as he flings off clothes to distract the panther. Whether these tall tales reflect more the challenge of the trail or the challenge of romance, they certainly capture the humor of the journeys.

In the expanded format of this cycle of tales, Morgan continues to dramatize adventure but further reveals the sweep of national history through local events; he apprentices himself to traditional folk performances and folkways as well as to written learning; and he extends the distinctive mountain voice, with vernacular signatures, more conversationally and creates sustained storytelling that includes a stream-of-consciousness monologue to extend the psychological dimensions of the character—this time a female.

In addition to the romance of the trace and courtship, Petal's story returns to the realistic theme of women's work. With clear, vivid language, Morgan focuses on the consequences of romance and the special work only women perform—childbirth. The intense hardships and significance of childbirth are painfully and graphically described in all of Morgan's novels. The author says the question he is asked most often is how, as a man, can he write these scenes. He attributes his realism to attending Lamaze classes and being present for the birth of his two daughters. Then he gleefully explains that all the rest is just made up!

The account of Petal's childbirth experience heightens suspense because the heroine is alone. She, like the other narrators of this cycle of tales, is also beset by a panther—a "painter" that comes clawing at the chimney after her. With this crisis, Morgan reaches out to the skepticism of modernists and tempers Petal's spirituality with modern realism: "What do you mean, did I pray? Of course, I prayed. But I didn't have no time for lengthy prayers. I knowed I had to help myself, and I got on with it. I had to fight" (79). Petal concludes this story by saying, "And yet, at the worst moment, they was this solid thing down there that put a deep, sweet feeling inside the awful pain that was working out through me" (81). The author honors Petal's willingness to labor on behalf of her child and join this age-old tradition of women's work.

Later, by quoting scripture, Morgan deepens this theme in *Gap Creek.* The power and precision of language help Julie redefine her "pain" and "hurt" during childbirth with the more dignified and Biblical term "sorrow": "Sorrow was about understanding, about a long time passing" (283). By recognizing this work as her special "labor," Julie thinks of childbirth "as work and not as pain. I had a mountain of work ahead of me" (283–84). Julie becomes aware of her connection to "an endless chain" of face-to-face women "all the way to the end of time" (284). That Petal and other women protagonists suffer alone during childbirth emphasizes that birthing a child is the mother's experience only.

Petal also earnestly discusses the personal challenges of romance and intimacy, without the humorous distance maintained by the two male narrators in *The Hinterlands.* Like many of Morgan's early male characters, Petal's husband (Grandpa) has red-faced sensitivity but little voice; he is often inaudible. But Petal likes his laugh, and a "big old feller blushing like a kid" moves her heart. She says, "It shows their liveliness and their sensitiveness" (6). Many times Morgan's women protagonists have to read the minds of their uncommunicative men. Fiction offers great opportunity for mind reading to be accurate; the author knows the characters he creates. Morgan is sensitive to his men as well as his women characters.

Whereas in life we are often jolted up against the uncertain meaning of a lover's unexpected act or comment, in these novels the women's intuition and insight into the men's behavior and silences usually prove accurate. Although we learn from Petal that Grandpa is sometimes guardedly reticent, he proves sensitive as well as lively.

SILENCES OF MORGAN'S MEN

Morgan's male characters are interesting in their struggle to find a voice. Some readers have fretted that the husbands in the early novels are spoiled. These men occasionally threaten violence and often do not recognize or speak about the strength and personal beauty of their wives. Many are competent and skillful on the frontier, but they are typically shy and inarticulate. Prisoner Powell is feverishly voiceless, and the stonemason is often choked with anger.

Likewise, Grandpa's silences cause trouble. In *The Hinterlands* Petal's story ends with the discovery that her husband did not take her to the blue mountains of Watauga after all. He allows her to remain homesick even though they live close to her parents' home. Because of his inarticulate fear that she might leave him for not taking her into the wilderness where she dreamed of starting a new life, the trick got away from him, and he deceived her for years. Petal's husband never hears or understands the pain he caused her or articulates the tremendous fear that motivated his deceit. Speaking his fear and hearing Petal's concerns would have helped him and invited her forgiveness.

Morgan's men in the later, longer works are vulnerable, but with the support of the women, they sometimes come to express their fears and angers, curb impulsive behavior, grow more sensitive, and genuinely relate to others. In *Gap Creek,* for example, after lashing out at his wife for being conned, Hank at last comes up to bed to Julie. When he finally reaches out to hold her, he surprises her not with an apology or a sweet or longing word, but with "I got fired." This bad news helps explain his vicious behavior earlier that day. The point at which he begins to change and mature in this search for voice is when he finally speaks this secret. Hank admits he had been fired for hitting a "rawhider" foreman and probably will not be rehired (267). He takes the risk to trust, begins to let go of his guilt, and assumes responsibility.

Even though the grandchildren probably do not fully understand the dangers of male silences or the relationship between their grandparents, Petal explains that she has told this tale of intimacy so they will remember it after she is gone: "Your Grandpa's gone and he can't tell you. He always had trouble speaking his affections anyway, though he could charm anybody in a friendly way" (149). But despite this reticence, Grandpa does find an expressive way to make a symbolic peace offering. The morning after Petal reconnects with him, Grandpa brings her a witch hazel branch. This last bloom of winter is a reminder that, after winter, spring will return to their relationship as well as to the year. For Morgan, the "wilderness was a poem, and poems had the splendor and mystery and perhaps the danger of the wilderness."[21] With this gift of the witch hazel branch, Grandpa communicates his affections powerfully without words by offering a poem of the wilderness.

In addition to Morgan's inarticulate but interesting male characters, he creates certain other mature men—fathers and brothers—who appreciate women. In *This Rock* (2001) Morgan offers for the first time a male protagonist and his most ambitious handling of point of view. The tongue-tied Muir wants to be a preacher and searches to find his own voice. His prayers, like Hank's but more extensive, are eloquent and surprisingly modern. Muir struggles in harsh conflict with his moonshine-running brother Moody, whose soulful voice we hear in two letters. For readers who admire Morgan's female narrators, the engaging voice of the boys' mother, Ginny, the protagonist of *The Truest Pleasure,* helps to ground the work. Morgan has continued to develop male characters who seek to move beyond silence, and his novel *Brave Enemies* (2003) offers the full-voiced female narrator Josie and his most complex and compelling male narrator to date—the preacher John Trethman.

MORGAN'S FULL-VOICED WOMEN NARRATORS

Petal in *The Hinterland,* like the fiancée in "The Mountains Won't Remember Us," is a complex female protagonist. After her husband's betrayal and its serious consequences are unearthed, Petal eventually seeks reconnection. She says: "Now a touch speaks far beyond any words, children. A touch is a little thing, but at the right time it's like a current pours through. People ain't whole unless they're connected, and a touch is the first and true sign of that connection" (147). Morgan identifies the importance of touch to connection, emotional intimacy, and wholeness. The connection of touch prefigures the important theme of sensuality in later novels as crucial communication between people. Couples often survive the external crises they encounter and internal crises they create when they connect physically and emotionally through work and sexuality. Sharing an appreciation of nature and the seasons, storytelling, craftsmanship, other folkways, and the discipline of work helps focus identities, encourage communication, and create community.

If many of the males in Morgan's fiction fail to express their feelings or to understand the women, the author clearly celebrates the women with considerable nuance and realism. Morgan brings to life mountain women, gives them different voices, and appreciatively reveals their dignity amidst the exhausting work and dailiness of their lives. By shifting to this female protagonist in *The Hinterlands*, the author expanded the theme of intimacy to sometimes overshadow external doubts or suspense and has thus altered the narrative pattern of threat and meditation.

Morgan comes into his own especially in the later and longer works after he shape shifts and begins writing convincingly and fully from a woman's point of view. He uses the space to stretch out afforded by a novel to maintain a keen sense of traditional tale-telling. With a sensitive understanding of his protagonists, he lets the women take over the storytelling in the next two novels. While grappling with farm work and life, the female narrators in *The Truest Pleasure* (1995) and *Gap Creek* (1999) become as well dramatized as their tales. In *The Truest Pleasure* Morgan creates the full mountain voice of the eloquent and well-read protagonist Ginny.

After experiencing the new freedom and confidence of the fiancée who became a modern woman, Morgan turned to rewriting *The Truest Pleasure*. He worked on the novel for more than a decade, making the final revisions in 1992–93. Morgan dropped the extensive dialect and third-person point of view and created Ginny—and thus reframed, dramatized, and narrated the story from this poetic woman's heart.[22]

Ginny's mountain voice is always present even when the storytelling context is not. Sometimes the stories are too personal for a tale-telling audience; the readers become the audience of the narrator's personal and confidential quest. In *The Truest Pleasure*, based on the lives of his paternal grandparents and inspired by the storytelling of his grandfather and father, Morgan continues the family saga already introduced in certain short stories and tales.

The articulate Ginny, an avid reader, grows heartened by the expressiveness of the Holiness church. Morgan offers one of the few realistic and sympathetic presentations of Pentecostal religion in American fiction. The novel is filled with the "white hot" language and folkways of preaching, prayer, and singing. At the same time, the spiritual and everyday conflicts also reach out to modern readers. The Cedar Springs arbor service begins with the words "The Spirit speaks first through music" and the lining out of the hymn "Revive Us Again." Ginny notices that all is the same and yet changed and sweetened by music:

> The lantern light was still the same, and the people the same, and the smell of pine resin was still the same. But it was changed too. . . . I thought how time was more intense and sweetened by music. I felt closer to people. They were still the same but I saw them different and better. I had on my same white blouse, but it begun to glow in the lantern light like pearls or opals. (4)

Her pearly glow signals her illumination by the spirit. The preacher says that what is so sweet "is the fellowship of time with eternity. It is the communion of flesh with spirit; it is this world rubbing up against the next" (5). After Ginny feels intensified and sweetened by music and the outpouring of spirit for the first time, the preacher says, "Through you has flowed the sweet honey from the rock and in your mouth is the light of stars" (8). Early on, after the meteor shower fireworks and the couple's laconic engagement, Ginny describes Tom as "always a little flushed. It made him look more alive than others. He worked in the sun and was always a little sunburned. . . . He felt warm as a stove. It was like his face give off a kind of light" (53). His spirited glow, bright as the shooting stars, parallels her love for him.

Through Ginny's husband, Morgan also faces head-on the readers' potential resistance to the religious subject matter. Tom is the son of the prisoner in "A Brightness" who dreams of the spring on the homeplace. Tom, who grew up fatherless and too poor to attend school long enough to learn to read well, finds Ginny's expressive faith an embarrassment. Their struggles to achieve intimacy in spite of this conflict form the novel's exploration of marriage. As ever, the challenge is how to be responsive and intimate with the other and also remain true to oneself.

Like the couple in *Gap Creek,* Ginny and her husband dramatize the vulnerability created by self-expression. The couple's disagreements are filled with painful silences and withdrawals. Tom is taciturn. Although Ginny is eloquent, she is stubborn and, when angry, often silences herself—especially from remarking on Tom's good qualities. The readers hear Ginny's intimate and self-reflective story in much greater detail than any of her family do.

Despite their difficulties, work is one of the ways Ginny and Tom connect with each other. Ginny speaks of identity through work: "Sometimes I work because I can't stand not to be doing something, because I don't know where to look or where to put my hands. Other times I'll get so interested in a job I can't think of anything else. It will be like I forget I am me, and just think of the job, of what my hands is doing. That's when I feel the best" (16). In *The Truest Pleasure,* the author gives Ginny identity and relief from self-scrutiny through the roles of unselfconscious work. The results of her work—except for the labor of childbirth—are not usually tangible or beautiful like the stonemason's but serviceable and consumable.

After harsh conflicts with Tom and the loss of her third baby, Ginny recovers enough to figure out that "the best way to show . . . friendship with Tom was to help in the fields," and so, she says, "that hot summer I pitched in like a field hand. It was what needed to be done, and it was what I needed to do. If you sweat enough it will cleanse you. . . . I didn't wear shoes, and it felt like the dirt itself healed me. The hot ground drawed the poisons and ill will through the soles of my feet" (170). The work helps her regain her health, identity, and relationship with Tom.

One close reader of Morgan considers the male narrators, with their stories of fractured time, more postmodern than the women. Certainly the women protagonists are not conventional, for they present diverse perspectives frequently silenced before the 1960s. Despite the numerous novels over the centuries with women narrators, many—like ballads—end in unnatural death, and all too few convincingly portray a woman's likely motivations or her life beyond courtship.

The narrative of *The Truest Pleasure,* like that of "The Mountains Won't Remember Us," does not unfold in strict chronological order. After Ginny's courtship with Tom begins, for example, there is a seamless flashback to a time when Ginny's monthly periods have not started. This scene is too private to have introduced the novel. When Uncle's whiskey remedies do not work, Ginny's father calmly takes the motherless daughter to an Indian doctor. There she receives a potion, a secret name, and encouragement to shape shift into a pigeon. The cure does bring on her "monthlies" and foreshadows the time much later when she is in horrendous labor with her third baby: "I thought of a pigeon high above the valley looking down on hot wilting weeds and conniptions of heat boiling the air. I said my secret name over and over. It sounded cool and green as the perfume bottle" (147).

With the meditations on the green perfume bottle as well as the river from Sunset Rock, the narrator reintroduces the meditations of the early short stories—like the relief from the mountain spring in "Brightness." Ginny thinks:

> I figured if I could think about the perfume it would keep my mind off the pain. Light hit half the bottle and it looked like an emerald with a fire inside. . . . It was like a liquor or extract of the deep pools on the river. . . . I imagined the bottle held a soothing drug, some kind of green opiate. . . . I wanted to reach out and touch it like a piece of green Christmas candy. It was lit from inside and I wanted to taste it with my fingers. (146–47)

After Ginny's third baby dies, the sun moves off the bottle of perfume: "It was the color of a very dark emerald, sleeping in the shadows" (148). Just as Ginny had been "pearly" when illuminated by the spirit and Tom aglow with spirited love, so the green bottle had been illuminated as Ginny awaited the spirit of the baby. But with death, the emerald bottle darkened into sleep.

Ginny, like the author, has also learned to shape shift into another entity. Like the pigeon, the totem inspired by the Indian healer, she flies high and free into the cool and can see the horizon. She finds vision as well as relief from the immediate pain. Postmodern literature does not simply deconstruct the past but makes way for new and diverse voices. When a man can shape shift effectively into diverse women characters, we have come a long way in the American multivalent, postcolonial conversation.

Perhaps the most innovative aspect of these novels is Morgan's sensitivity to women's spirituality. In *The Wilderness Within: American Women Writers and Spiritual Quest*, Kristina Groover observes that women's ways are grounded in earth and body as well as in the spirit and do not distance or sever the world of spirituality from sensuality.[23] Readers may appreciate the female spirituality in *The Truest Pleasure*, when working the earth with

Tom heals Ginny, and especially when Ginny says: "As we loved, I . . . felt I was right and in the right place, even as I did at the revival services. And I thought how the thrill of loving was almost the same as communion with the Spirit and the thrill of solitude by the river, but I didn't understand how it could be. It was a mystery" (130).

The poet Denise Levertov declared *The Truest Pleasure* "a masterpiece." Indeed, Ginny and the novel are both masterpieces of language, point of view, and mountain voice that address stunningly the hardest themes of intimacy and spirit. With good measure in the novel, Morgan lucidly and generously draws, accurately narrates, and intensely dramatizes the full coming of age and mountain voice of the woman teller as well as her tale.

Morgan's caretaker quest amidst ancient rhymes from the mountain spring to new frontiers offers a rainbow in *The Truest Pleasure* that forecasts *Gap Creek* (1999). Fred Chappell called *Gap Creek* the work of a master, and the novel received the Southern Book Critics Circle Award for 2000. Oprah Winfrey expanded Morgan's national reputation by selecting *Gap Creek* for her Book Club.

In the internationally best-selling novel, after a horrendous year in Gap Creek, South Carolina, Hank and Julie head back for home in the North Carolina mountains. Both the female and the male character have grown. Despite her astonishing but stripped-down, focused, mountain voice, Julie has learned to state her reticence and speak beyond it. Though often stymied, Hank has sometimes spoken his feelings, cared for their endangered baby, and learned to converse with a contentious drinking man like Timmy Gosnell. Pregnant in the promise of spring, the couple journeys up the mountain path—perhaps toward the genuine intimacy and playfulness of call and response.

Morgan has always worn the title "Appalachian" writer with pride and sometimes refers to the Ithaca mountain region as northern Appalachia. Morgan is now nationally recognized because of his mountain voice. The *New York Times Book Review* described his prose in *Gap Creek* as sentences that "burn with the raw, lonesome pathos of Hank Williams' best songs."[24] Morgan has carried mountain life—inside and out—to new frontiers.

Even if the mountains won't remember us, Robert Morgan helps us remember them lucidly. The author has created an imaginative cultural geography of Dark Corner and Gap Creek, South Carolina, and of Green River, the Blue Valleys, the Blue Ridges, and the Sunny Peaks of North

Carolina. By revisiting his mountain homeplace, Robert Morgan prepares us for new journeys and reminds us that, at any time, You can go home again—through the starlit wilderness of his imagination.

Notes

1. Sections of this paper were presented at the American Folklore Society and South Atlantic Modern Language Association annual meetings and at the Jerry Williamson Symposium, Appalachian State University, Fall 2000.

2. Robert Morgan, "You Can't Get There from Here," *Appalachian Journal* 8 (Winter 2001): 222. Unless otherwise noted, quotations are drawn from author's interviews and videos of Robert Morgan, Fall 2000.

3. Robert Morgan, "Nature is a Stranger Yet," *The Jordan Lectures, 1998–1999* (Salem, Va.: Roanoke College Department of English), 31.

4. "Nature is a Stranger Yet," 28.

5. Robert Morgan, *Good Measure: Essays, Interviews, and Notes on Poetry* (Baton Rouge: Louisiana State University Press, 1993), 9, 135.

6. *Good Measure*, 9–10.

7. Ibid., 10.

8. Robert Morgan, *The Blue Valleys* (Atlanta: Peachtree Publishers, 1989).

9. Robert Morgan, *Groundwork* (Frankfort, Ky.: Gnomon Press, 1979), 2.

10. *The Blue Valleys*, "A Brightness, New and Welcoming," 4.

11. Robert Morgan, "The Transfigured Body: Notes from a Journal," *Good Measure*, 109.

12. "Nature is a Stranger Yet," 38.

13. As Henry Louis Gates explains in *The Signifying Monkey: A Theory of African-American Literary Criticism* (New York: Oxford University Press, 1988), a "speakerly text" is "a text whose rhetoric strategy is designed to represent an oral literary tradition, designed to "produce the illusion of oral narration'" (181). For example, in *Their Eyes Were Watching God*, Zora Neale Hurston's "two-speech communities" shift between her "'literate' narrator's voice and a highly idiomatic black voice" (203).

14. Robert Morgan, *At the Edge of the Orchard Country* (Middletown, Conn.: Wesleyan University Press, 1987), 44–47.

15. Robert Morgan, *Topsoil Road* (Baton Rouge: Louisiana State University Press, 2000), 26.

16. These passages of the fiancée's imaginary dialogue are as dramatic as the best two-chair Gestalt work, and both serve as the basis for therapeutic change.

17. Shape shifting, like "the heart of the shaman's journey" in Native American as well as Celtic cultures, is "the ability to send one's own consciousness into the consciousness of another entity—whether it be the wind, a hawk, or an entire landscape, either in this world or the other world—and return to one's own self" (*Fire in the Head: Shamanism and The Celtic Spirit* [San Francisco: Harper, 1993], 29).

18. *Good Measure*, 116–17.

19. Jung believed every person has a masculine (*animus*/spirit) and a feminine (*anima*/soul or psyche) aspect, and wholeness requires developing both. In these wonderful, diverse women protagonists, Jung might have seen masks and testaments of Morgan's inspiring *anima*.

20. Quotations are from the John F. Blair paperback, 1999.

21. "Nature is a Stranger Yet," 31.

22. In *The Mountains Won't Remember Us*, "Martha Sue" is told by the mother of Ginny, narrator of *The Truest Pleasure*. The protagonist Martha Sue speaks in the vernacular and concludes her deathbed tale by emphasizing the impossibility of ever reconciling her differences with her husband.

After the author removed the 75-page "Martha Sue" section, he sent the manuscript of *The Truest Pleasure* to Algonquin Books. Editor Shannon Ravenel left Robert Morgan on his own to cut the 550-page manuscript to a 350-page novel.

Ginny, late in life, revises her mother's reflections by saying, "Suddenly I saw all the things I had hated about Tom I could just as well have loved. Maybe that was me seeing through other eyes. Maybe Locke was right about me refusing to accept Tom's gifts. I saw what fools we had both been. All our quarreling had been such a waste" (329). The author has Ginny reflect further on her husband, "But it would have been impossible for Tom to have changed. I thought of his shoes by the hearth and fresh tears come to my eyes. The saddest thing of all was I saw that people couldn't be any way but what they are. Even when doing right they are apt to be doing something else wrong" (329).

23. Kristina Groover, *The Wilderness Within* (Fayetteville: University of Arkansas Press, 1999), 9.

24. Dwight Garner, "This Old House," review of *Gap Creek* by Robert Morgan, *New York Times Book Review*, 10 Oct. 1999, sect. 7, p. 10.

Class and Identity in Denise Giardina's *Storming Heaven*

TERRY EASTON

When novelist Denise Giardina states in a letter to the *New York Times* that Appalachia has always been distinctly "other" in the American imagination, she captures in a single sentence a concept that has produced over the last one hundred years or so a seemingly unfettered amount of discourse both from within and beyond Appalachia (21). For Giardina, Appalachian "otherness" rests on the belief that Appalachians are solely responsible for their poverty, that they are "simple throwbacks to the past, inhabitants of a land time forgot, lazy and shiftless, quick-tempered and ready to grab a gun to settle differences." In what appears to be a response to the "culture of poverty" theory espoused since the 1960s, Giardina's larger aim in her letter to the *New York Times* is to demonstrate that Appalachians themselves are not responsible for their poverty. Rather, Giardina asserts that the myths and stereotypes of Appalachians mask an economic structure that functions precisely to create poverty and injustice in Appalachia. In her letter to the *Times* and in interviews, Giardina contends that absentee corporate ownership of Appalachia exploits both the people and natural resources of the region. In her fictional and nonfictional writings, Giardina demonstrates that, from the late nineteenth century and continuing into the contemporary period, Appalachians have encountered economic forces well beyond their own control.[1] Historically, of course, Appalachia has

Originally published in a slightly different form in *Journal of Appalachian Studies* 6 (Spring/Fall 2000): 151–60. Reprinted by permission of the author and the publisher.

been "rich" in mineral resources and yet many of its people are among the poorest of the poor in the United States.

In this essay I offer examples of how Giardina's 1987 novel *Storming Heaven* can be used to think about the class situation that was produced in central Appalachia during the turn to industrial coal mining in the region. What comes out of this type of textual analysis is a kind of literary criticism enabling us to understand various aspects of the socioeconomic history of central Appalachia. Moreover, viewing *Storming Heaven* through a class-based lens provides an opportunity to use a historical novel to better understand working people's struggles for justice in a decidedly unjust place and period. Through her fictional depiction of the region and its people, Giardina not only illuminates working people's lives and struggles for justice but also makes it necessary for readers to question the stereotypes of the Appalachian "other."

Published in 1987, *Storming Heaven* traces the economic and cultural transformation of southern West Virginia and eastern Kentucky from 1890 to about 1923. Told in mixed rotation by four narrators, the novel allows readers to view the events of the novel from a variety of perspectives. The narrators include C. J. Marcum, a sympathetic, though cautious man seeking justice for miners and their families; Rosa Angelelli, an Italian immigrant who cleans the home of a coal company boss and experiences overwhelming pain and loss after her four sons die laboring in the mines; Rondal Lloyd, a miner and union organizer; and Carrie Bishop, a local nurse whose narrative connects families, events, and themes in *Storming Heaven.*

One way of moving toward a class-inflected analysis of *Storming Heaven* is to examine the setting for familial relationships. The families experience, in a multitude of ways, pain and loss from the openly repressive and covertly ideological forms of power created during the industrialization of central Appalachia. At a purely structural level, Antonio Gramsci's notions of "civil society" (ideological and hegemonic forms of power and consent) and "political society" (overtly repressive physical forms of power and consent) help to explain the forms of power cultivated in coal mining camps during industrialization (12). At the level of "political society," for example, historians have recorded how the mine-guard system, more specifically the Baldwin-Felts guards employed by coal companies, created in coal mining camps and communities a system of repression that restricted the civil rights of miners and their families. Curtis Seltzer offers a vivid portrait of the conditions in coal camps when he contends that they were a "total institution," a place where, in many camps, the concept of "public sector" did not exist in the way we think of it today. "The company, rather than the government," Seltzer reports, "decided how much attention would be paid to environmental protection, public health, and community services" (20).

At the level of what Gramsci calls "civil society," cultural theorists and historians report that coal companies brought with them a determination to alter the habits of miners and their families. The development of specific kinds of schools, churches, and recreational activities, for example, shifted local ways of thinking in Appalachia. John Gaventa, in his study of the development of power and its relationship to acquiescence and rebellion in Appalachia, coins the phrase "mobilization of bias" to explain the conjunction between absentee corporate coal camp owners and local middle-class elites as they mobilized their efforts to control miners and their families in coal camps and coal communities. Gaventa writes that "[w]hether by 'moulding' in the socialization institutions, or by 'choice' from amongst the alternatives presented to him in the power situation, the effect upon the mountaineer was the same: a shaping and influencing away from his 'stock' to participation in the ways and values of the new order" (68). Gaventa's analysis of the power structure in Appalachian coal camps and coal communities goes a long way in describing and helping to explain the situation that developed in the closing years of the nineteenth century and the first quarter of the twentieth century in central Appalachia. Giardina, in her delineation of the social and physical structures of Appalachian coal mining camps and communities, illuminates how the combined forces of physical repression and ideological manipulation worked in tandem to create a system of lack, loss, and injustice for miners and their families.

When Raymond Williams states that the industrial novel is concerned with the actual work relations and familial patterns in working communities, he points to two key areas Giardina explores in *Storming Heaven.* For her, work relations and familial patterns are inseparable. The narrative in *Storming Heaven,* for example, operates in such a way that work and family are inextricably linked. The relationship between siblings Carrie and Miles Bishop, for example, is fraught with complexity. Miles, a firm believer in the idea of "progress" for the Appalachian mountains, returns from Berea College and becomes a mine boss while Carrie, a more introspective observer of the transformation of their community, works as a nurse in the coal camp repairing miners' injured bodies. The Bishops are a family divided. Following Williams's formulations on patterns in the industrial novel, this comes as no surprise. "The family," he writes, "is an epitome of political struggle, and the conflicting versions and affiliations of that struggle are represented not only generally—in the events of the lockout and the struggles in the Miners Federation and between parties—but inside the family" (Williams, 225).

A good deal of scholarship on the industrialization of central Appalachia indicates that local mountaineers were pressured by outsiders (middle-class benevolence workers, missionaries, and capitalists from the northeastern United States) to shed their local habits and customs and to accept the idea of "progress" for the mountains. The rift between Miles and Carrie offers readers an example of how families experienced the pressures associated with class and culture during the industrialization of central Appalachia. Delineated in a dual relationship between work and family, many of the characters in *Storming Heaven* arrive at decisions under the pressure of economic necessity and familial constraint. Giardina makes clear the forces that divide families when Carrie aligns herself politically with Rondal Lloyd, a union organizer fervently opposed to the practices associated with Miles's coal company. Through this depiction and others, Giardina poignantly demonstrates some of the ways that families face certain pressures during industrialization, something Williams describes as "the spread of alternatives, the pressures to go different ways, including going away altogether, solving their problems differently" (224).

Studies of middle-class intervention in central Appalachia illuminate how schools function as locations where particular kinds of values are created. One of the key issues that divide Carrie and Miles, for example, is Miles's education at Berea and his subsequent belief in the idea of "progress" for the central Appalachian mountains. C. J. Marcum, on the other hand, had hoped that Rondal would go away for a college education and then come back to help the local population and serve their needs instead of the needs of coal companies. But as the narrators in *Storming Heaven* demonstrate, if Rondal receives an education anything at all like Miles's education, then Rondal, like Miles, would do little to help local inhabitants in West Virginia. In a particularly revealing statement, Miles tells Carrie that his becoming a mine superintendent at Pond Creek (a mine owned by a Bostoner) is what education is all about: "To prepare mountain youth to take their place in the modern world" (Giardina, 60). What that means for Miles, as demonstrated in the way he answers to the needs of the coal company rather than to the needs of the local inhabitants, is that local folks must continue to accept the grinding realities associated with industrial capitalism.

Storming Heaven functions effectively when Giardina contrasts the different kinds of living conditions in coal camps. On her way to Miles's house, for example, Carrie walks through a coal camp where clouds of coal dust whip through the streets and, she reports, when the wind is right, sulphurous fumes from a burning slag heap choke the air in the camp. Carrie's thoughts about the living conditions she sees on the way to Miles's house ("Negroes in board and batten shacks down in Colored Bottom, mountain people in squat four-room houses on Tipple Hill, Hungarians in tall thin double houses up Hunkie Holler. None of the houses sat on foundations, but instead balanced on small piles of bricks set at each corner") situate her brother's company-provided residence in sharp contrast to miners' company-provided homes. Miles's house differs significantly in size, condition, and cleanliness when compared to the company housing for miners. Carrie reports: "I moved into the big house on the hill where Miles lived, above the noise and dirt, three stories and fifteen rooms, green shingles outside with white gingerbread trim and scalloped eaves. From the bottom it appeared to be a castle, floating behind its brown stone wall on a moat of green grass" (90).

Carrie expresses her discomfort about living there, for she has never seen chandeliers and she has never used crystal drinking glasses. After Carrie guiltily accepts an offer to live in the "clubhouse" where miners are not allowed to board because it is "reserved for the 'better sort' of employee," she forces readers to think of this coal camp in terms of colonialism: "Although I knew I should disapprove, I accepted this distinction. It added a touch of the exotic, as though I had set down in imperial India amid the sahibs and the natives, and all this in Paine County, just across the mountain from where I had been born" (90).

Once Carrie is settled in Miles's home, the distinction between Miles and Carrie is even more sharply drawn. Miles, who had come back with his corn-colored hair parted in the middle and cut short "like they wear in Boston," tells Carrie about his visit to his employer's summer cottage in Maine where he ate lobster and had Baked Alaska for dessert. Carrie responds angrily: "Well, while you was having Baked Alaska, we was having typhoid . . . five cases. . . . Two died and one is like to go anytime." Carrie explains to Miles that his coal company had made the mistake of building privies over the creek where miners and their families retrieved their drinking water.[2] Carrie pushes a reluctant Miles to write a letter to the coal company asking for money to build privies in a proper location. The company responds within a week, stating that there is no money in the budget for such "frills" and that disease in the camp is caused by "the filthy habits of the miners and their families" (93). The company's retort that miners are "filthy" demonstrates at least one of the ways that class figures in constructions of the Appalachian "other." This incident and others like it demonstrate how the class divide between Miles and Carrie increases as Miles moves further away from ministering to the needs of miners and their families.

The events in *Storming Heaven* span three major periods of central Appalachia's transformation to industrial capitalism: (1) from 1865 to 1890 land speculators and railroad owners "purchased" land deeds from local inhabitants of the mountains; (2) from 1890 to 1910 financial capitalists and outside investors took control of the land, imported labor from the Deep South states and Europe, built company towns, and began speeding up the process of industrialization; and (3) from 1910 to 1925 absentee corporate ownership and even more strict disciplinary measures in the mines and company towns prevailed.[3] All of these periods are known as times of strife; the latter two periods especially are characterized by bloody civil unrest, with labor strikes a basic fact of life in company towns and outlying areas.[4]

Priscilla Long reports that, throughout the periods described above, miners' concerns about quality of life clashed with operators' concerns about profits (63). Ralph Henry Gabriel echoes Long's sentiments when he contends that transformations to industrial capitalism create situations in which the "mores of a simpler agricultural and commercial era [do] not fit the conditions of an age characterized by the swift accumulation of industrial power" (146). Richard Simon writes that "whether during periods of strikes or long periods of undisturbed production, [West Virginia coalfields] were characterized by force, repression, and the resistance of the mine workers in the 'labor wars.' The long periods of calm reflected *not* the willing cooperation of the miners but the dominant power of the operators to prevent strikes before they started" (174). During the late nineteenth century and continuing into the early decades of the twentieth century, central Appalachians lived through the transformation from an economy based largely on low-level agricultural production and characterized by self-sufficiency to one based on coal mining and characterized by dependency. As such, they experienced a transition to industrial capitalism, a process that cuts across social relations of power, meanings, attitudes, and values.[5]

According to E. P. Thompson, "there is no such thing as economic growth which is not, at the same time, growth or change of a culture" (403). There is no doubt that central Appalachia's shifting economy altered local cultures. How one thinks about changes in economic structures and "growth" depends, of course, on the angle from which one views such changes. Absentee and local coal camp owners experienced economic growth in that they skimmed a considerable profit from the various industries related to central Appalachian coal mining. It has been documented that even when coal capitalists made little or no profit from the sale of coal, profits from home rentals and sales at company stores—practices that Richard Simon calls "audacious robbery"—more than made up for the lost revenue in the mines (170). Miners, on the other hand, inherited a legacy of chaotic work cycles, landlessness, poverty, broken bodies, black lung disease and, of course, death. The landscape of central Appalachia fares hardly any better than miners: scarred hillsides, diminished forests and animal life, and polluted streams provide visual reminders of central Appalachia's "economic growth" in the twentieth century.

The turn to industrial capitalism has forever altered the culture and landscape of central Appalachia. Economies based largely on subsistence farming and low-level capitalism gave way to single-industry coal camps where a lack of industry diversification caused a "development of underdevelopment." By 1930, underemployment rather than employment, surplus labor, and the suppression of union representation best defined many coal camps (Simon, 175). Alan Banks has pointed out that the structural changes that must occur for industrial capitalism to succeed include the separation of labor from control over the instruments of labor, the freeing of capital to be invested for its own self-expansion, and the foundation of an infrastructure for the maintenance and reproduction of new class relations—the construction of laws, schools, housing, and roads (321–22). All of these developments occurred in central Appalachia. The reshaping of class relations, the increasing size of the working class, the rise of company towns, and the creation of infrastructural foundations for the maintenance and reproduction of new class relations in the mountains occurred as miners sometimes rebelled against and sometimes acquiesced to these changes.

A particularly troubling aspect of the turn to industrial coal mining in Appalachia is that between 1880 and 1915, the period when industrial capitalism made its biggest impact in the region, Appalachia was also "discovered" as a "strange land inhabited by a peculiar people, a discrete region, in but not of America" (Shapiro, xiv). In *All That Is Native and Fine,* David Whisnant demonstrates that at the end of the nineteenth century there were four important and interrelated processes taking place in the mountains: "economic colonization by northeastern capital; the rise of indigenous resistance among workers and farmers; the discovery of indigenous culture by writers, collectors, popularizers, and elite-art composers and concertizers; and the proliferation of (mostly Protestant) missionary endeavors" (6). During this period of profound change for farmers, miners, and their families, the discovery of particular kinds of culture directed "attention away from dominant structural realities, such as those associated with colonial subjugation or resource exploitation or class-based inequalities" while offering a "warm glow upon the cold realities of social dislocation" (Whisnant, 260). Giardina's assertion that myths and stereotypes mask an economic structure that functions to increase the development of the central Appalachian region at the expense of a majority of its inhabitants echoes Whisnant's account of the development of the region and resonates vividly in *Storming Heaven.*

A particular power of *Storming Heaven* lies in its ability to subvert Appalachian stereotypes. Through the delineation of struggles for justice in the central Appalachian region, Giardina moves beyond dated assumptions and worn-out cultural beliefs about central Appalachia and its people. *Storming Heaven* enables readers to better understand how miners and their families negotiated the rise of industrial coal mining in central Appalachia.

If fiction is a means to a better understanding of a region and its people, then Tal Stanley's succinct assessment of Giardina's fictional account of the central Appalachian region is suggestive: "From Giardina's narrative emerges a place constructed out of and signifying the real connections and losses, the pressures and limits exerted by capitalism through a history of colonization, industrialization, and deindustrialization among the people located on a particular geography." Out of all of this, Stanley contends, "Giardina recovers in her writing a past usable for place-based struggles for social democracy" (360). In the latter half of the twentieth century, economic crises in many regions of the United States, particularly in the Rust Belt and the Sagebrush states, demonstrated that the instability of capitalism produces

what Giardina and others aptly call the "Appalachianization of America."
"When the American people seek images of poverty and powerlessness on
the nightly news," Giardina writes, "they now see their own faces looking
back" (21). Viewing Giardina's delineation of labor, familial relationships,
and the rise of industrial capitalism in *Storming Heaven* through a class-
based lens reveals that, indeed, the myths and stereotypes of the Appalachian "other" have, for far too long, incorrectly and unjustly characterized
the central Appalachian mining family.

Notes

Acknowledgment: I would like to thank Allen Tullos and Catherine Nickerson for their in-
cisive and helpful comments on a longer version of this essay.

1. Giardina puts Appalachia's economic structure into perspective when she states in the
New York Times: "Appalachia is a land owned by large corporations. More than 80 percent of
my native county in West Virginia is absentee-owned. We have a wealth of experience with
economic forces well beyond our own control" (21).

2. For a provocative discussion of coal camp waste facilities and typhoid, see pages 36–41
in Winthrop D. Lane's *Civil War in West Virginia.* Lane writes: "In Mingo County the death
rate from typhoid fever in 1919 was thirty; it is normally about ten in counties with safe clos-
ets [indoor flush toilets]. In Logan County the death rate from typhoid in 1918–1919 was
twenty-two" (40).

3. Numerous sources indicate this general pattern of development. See, for example,
Corbin, Eller, and Seltzer.

4. For detailed accounts of the mine wars in West Virginia from 1890 to 1921, see
Corbin, Lane, Lee, Lunt, and Savage.

5. Here I broadly generalize the preindustrial period of central Appalachia. A recent trend
in Appalachian studies reveals that the economic and cultural milieu of the preindustrial period was not homogenous or wholly without inegalitarian forms of cultural and economic
power. For discussions on this and related topics, see Dunaway.

Works Cited

Banks, Alan. "Class Formation in the Southeastern Kentucky Coalfields, 1890–
1920." In *Appalachia in the Making: The Mountain South in the Nineteenth Century,* ed. M. Pudup, D. Billings, and A. Waller, 321–46. Chapel Hill: University of North Carolina Press, 1995.

Corbin, David Alan. *Life, Work, and Rebellion in the Coal Fields: The Southern West Virginia Miners, 1880–1922.* Urbana: University of Illinois Press, 1981.

Dunaway, Wilma. "Speculators and Settler Capitalists: Unthinking the Mythology
about Appalachian Landholding, 1790–1860." In *Appalachia in the Making:
The Mountain South in the Nineteenth Century,* ed. M. Pudup, D. Billings, and
A. Waller, 50–75. Chapel Hill: University of North Carolina Press, 1995.

Eller, Ronald D. *Miners, Millhands, and Mountaineers: Industrialization of the Appalachian South, 1880–1930.* Knoxville: University of Tennessee Press, 1982.

Gabriel, Ralph Henry. *The Course of American Democratic Thought: An Intellectual History since 1815.* New York: Ronald Press Company, 1940.

Gaventa, John. *Power and Powerlessness: Quiescence and Rebellion in an Appalachian Valley.* Urbana: University of Illinois Press, 1980.

Giardina, Denise. *Storming Heaven.* New York: Ivy Books, 1987.

———."Appalachian Mirror." *New York Times,* 31 October, late edition, 1992.

Gramsci, Antonio. *Selections from the Prison Notebooks.* Ed. and trans. Q. Hoare and G. N. Smith. New York: International Publishers, 1971.

Lane, Winthrop D. *Civil War in West Virginia.* New York: Arno Press, 1969 [1921].

Lee, Howard B. *Bloodletting in Appalachia: The Story of West Virginia's Four Major Mine Wars and Other Thrilling Incidents of Its Coal Fields.* Parsons, W.Va.: McClain Printing Co., 1969.

Long, Priscilla. *Where the Sun Never Shines: A History of America's Bloody Coal Industry.* New York: Paragon House, 1989.

Lunt, Richard D. *Law and Order vs the Miners: West Virginia, 1907–1933.* Hamden, Conn.: Archon Books, 1979.

Pudup, Mary Beth, Dwight B. Billings, and Altina L. Waller, eds. *Appalachia in the Making: The Mountain South in the Nineteenth Century.* Chapel Hill: University of North Carolina Press, 1995.

Savage, Lon. *Thunder in the Mountains: The West Virginia Mine War, 1920–1921.* Pittsburgh: University of Pittsburgh Press, 1990 [1986].

Seltzer, Curtis. *Fire in the Hole: Miners and Managers in the American Coal Industry.* Lexington: University Press of Kentucky, 1985.

Shapiro, Henry D. *Appalachia on Our Mind: The Southern Mountains and Mountaineers in the American Consciousness, 1870–1920.* Chapel Hill: University of North Carolina Press, 1978.

Simon, Richard M. "Uneven Development and the Case of West Virginia: Going Beyond the Colonialism Model." *Appalachian Journal* 8 (Spring 1981): 165–86.

Stanley, Talmage A. "The Poco Field: Politics, Culture and Place in Contemporary Appalachia." PhD diss., Emory University, 1996.

Thompson, E. P. *Customs in Common: Studies in Traditional Popular Culture.* New York: New Press, 1993.

Whisnant, David E. *All That Is Native and Fine: The Politics of Culture in an American Region.* Chapel Hill: University of North Carolina Press, 1983.

Williams, Raymond. *Problems in Materialism and Culture: Selected Essays.* London: Verso Editions, 1980.

CORMAC MCCARTHY

Restless Seekers

JOHN G. CAWELTI

Southerners have a favorite set of self-images involving associations with stability, tradition, and dedication to local communities, all the symbology of "down-home." But in fact the South was founded by a horde of restless seekers who left their homeplaces behind them in pursuit of a plethora of dreams: wealth and grandeur, religious salvation, utopia, or all three in various combinations. Faulkner understood this well, and two of his most significant characters, Thomas Sutpen and Flem Snopes, represent different generations of poor whites seeking to rise in the world. Even Faulkner's great aristocratic families, the Sartorises, the Compsons, and the McCaslins, were founded by such pilgrims.

These men and women were driven by a restlessness and desperation of spirit that urged them on to glorious accomplishment or catastrophic destruction. Such extremities have also been a fundamental part of Southern culture and history. From the beginning, a key dynamic of southern evangelical Protestantism featured saintly figures like Billy Graham vying for control of the southern conscience with men with a thirst for wealth, lust, and power like Jim Bakker, Jimmy Swaggart, and Pat Robertson. The drive toward extremes may also account for the way in which southern

Originally published in a slightly different form in *Southern Writers at Century's End,* ed. Jeffrey J. Folks and James A. Perkins, 164–70, 174–75 (Lexington: University Press of Kentucky, 1997). Reprinted by permission of the author and the publisher.

literature has been pervaded by a fascination with the gothic and the grotesque, plumbing the lower depths of society as well as fantasizing about chivalry and nobility. Flannery O'Connor, generally recognized as the most important southern writer of the generation between the age of Faulkner and the present, was deeply imbued with this fascination, as her parables of redemption and damnation in a modernizing South reveal. The most important contemporary inheritor of this stream of Southern literature and culture is a man many consider the most important living Southern writer, Cormac McCarthy.

McCarthy has developed in a very complex fashion, embarking in the last two decades on an almost completely new set of literary ventures, marked by his own restless quest from Knoxville, Tennessee, to El Paso, Texas, from the heart of the South to the edges of the West. In this way, McCarthy not only exemplifies some important aspects of the Southern identity as it is reshaping itself in the era of the Sunbelt, but in a deeper sense can be seen as a postmodern avatar of that restless drive toward the West that has been a key motive in Southern culture since the first hunters crossed the Appalachians in search of more game and the plantations began their long push from the Tidewater through the deep South to the plains of Texas.

McCarthy's literary journey embodies this great migration in mythical terms. In his first three novels, *The Orchard Keeper* (1965), *Outer Dark* (1968), and *Child of God* (1973), the protagonists are mountaineers driven or drawn out of their isolated homeplaces into the modern world. *Suttree,* published in 1979, was McCarthy's most ambitious novel up to that time and it was also, as it turned out, his valediction to the middle South; for with his next novel, *Blood Meridian, or The Evening Redness in the West* (1985), McCarthy set forth on the fictional western quest that would soon lead to the first two novels of his announced "Border Trilogy," *All the Pretty Horses* (1992) and *The Crossing* (1994). The last two novels not only rise out of the Southern tradition, but are major reinventions of the western, reminding us how the great tradition of the modern western began when a Philadelphian went to Wyoming to recover his health and came back with a novel called *The Virginian* (1902), an epic account of a former Southerner's heroic encounter with badmen (and a New England schoolmarm) in the Wild West.

As McCarthy develops his mythos of the pilgrimage through the fictional world of his imagination, we realize that such quests are never simple. It is often difficult to tell whether McCarthy's seekers are mainly driven by something they flee or drawn by something they seek. Is their quest best defined in terms of a journey through space or into the soul? Is this journey best understood as moving into the future or into the past? Is it toward salvation or damnation? Are these mysterious quests ultimately as incomprehensible as life itself, or is there, in the end, some point to it all? One of the fascinating things about McCarthy is that the quest continues but each new book slightly shifts the grounds traversed by its predecessors. He too still seems to be engaged by the very quest he writes about with such mystery and passion.

Suttree (1979) is McCarthy's longest and most ambitious novel to date.[1] It is also, along with *Blood Meridian,* a major work of culmination and transition in his career. It is in this novel that McCarthy says his symbolic farewell to the South and begins his move from the gothic world of the Southern literary tradition to the leaner, more action-filled style of the western. As a novel, *Suttree* is a culmination and transformation of literary modernism as well as of important aspects of its Southern inheritance. The McCarthy Home Page on the World Wide Web likens *Suttree* to Joyce's *Ulysses*—"the novel's evocation of Joyce's masterpiece, *Ulysses,* is often palpable"—with Suttree "like some latterday Bloom" and Knoxville as a Southern version of "dear, dirty Dublin." There's certainly some truth in this assertion,[2] but McCarthy's most direct predecessors are much closer. McCarthy himself offers homage to the greatest Southern modernist by making Suttree's very name allude to one of Faulkner's most important restless seekers, Thomas Sutpen. But Suttree is in some ways more like Henry than Thomas Sutpen, a latter-day revenant to the family home and the scene of the crime, though it's not at all clear what the crime is. However, the most direct prototype of *Suttree* is Flannery O'Connor's *Wise Blood.* Like an inverted Hazel Motes, Suttree is unwillingly driven toward a goal he does not want to seek. In addition, he is plagued by a sort of disciple whose penchant for the subhuman world takes Enoch Emery's gorilla suit several steps further and includes sexual intercourse with watermelons, a bizarre pursuit of pigs, and an explosion in the Knoxville sewers. Suttree even has relationships with women that are eerily reminiscent of Hazel's involvements with Leora Watts and Sabbath Lily Hawks. *Suttree*'s Knoxville is as much a variation of O'Connor's Taulkinham as it is of Joyce's Dublin.

Like O'Connor's major characters, Suttree is trapped in a world that has lost the sense of the presence of God. However, O'Connor's devout if offbeat Catholicism leads her to frame her stories of modern alienation by constantly hinting that, if we can look beyond the deceptive lights of the modern city, we can always see that "the black sky was underpinned with long silverstreaks that looked like scaffolding and depth on depth behind it were thousands and thousands of stars that all seemed to be moving very slowly as if they were about some vast construction work that involved the whole order of the universe and would take all time to complete" (*Wise Blood*, 24).

In O'Connor's world it is always possible for the seeker to encounter transcendence. Sometimes even a person who is not actually seeking, like Ruby Turpin in the story "Revelation," is gifted with a moment of grace. McCarthy was raised a Catholic, but in his cosmos the audience sits in an empty and decaying theater and the minstrel show is long over. There's nothing left but death and silence. Whatever ultimate meaning there may be can be summed up only in such enigmatic axioms as "ruder forms survive."

> The rest indeed is silence. It has begun to rain. . . . Faint summer light-
> ning far downriver. A curtain is rising on the western world. A fine rain
> of soot, dead beetles, anonymous small bones. The audience sits webbed
> in dust. Within the gutted sockets of the interlocutor's skull a spider
> sleeps and the jointed ruins of the hanged fool dangle from the flies,
> bone pendulum in motley. Fourfooted shapes go to and fro over the
> boards. Ruder forms survive. (*Suttree*, 5)

Suttree takes place in Knoxville in the early 1950s, a city on the verge of dramatic changes.[3] The novel ends in 1955 with the tearing down of the old slums in McAnally Flats in order to construct a new expressway, symbolizing Knoxville's hopeful participation in the Sunbelt South with its increasing commercial and industrial linkages to the rest of the country. However, the novel is not primarily concerned with the impinging of modernization on a traditional culture as it might have been had it been written by Bobbie Ann Mason, Lee Smith, Wendell Berry, or any number of other contemporary Southern writers. McCarthy chooses instead to deal with a protagonist and a group of characters whose impoverished marginality makes the new developments wholly irrelevant to them until they are suddenly dispossessed of the decaying area of the city where they live. The inhabitants of McAnally Flats form a grotesque community of exiles and escapees from the modern social order. Suttree is temporarily at home with the anarchic drunkards and grotesque thieves and madmen who live on the flats and on the wastelands along the floodplain of the Tennessee River. Deeply wounded in spirit and a restless seeker himself, Suttree is a kind of fisher king of this community of wasteland outcasts. Though scion of a respectable old family, he has left the upper-middle-class world behind and become a derelict fisherman, selling carp and catfish he takes from the river to local butchers.

Yet Suttree is only hanging on in Knoxville, living marginally on its decaying fringes, held by a few residual family ties and by his loyalty to the fellow outcasts and rebels he has met along the river. Everything seems to conspire against his establishing any lasting relationships: his friends are killed by the police, hauled off to prison, or victims of exposure and alcoholism; a perversely idyllic love affair with a beautiful girl he meets while catching mussels upriver ends tragically when his lover is killed in a rockslide; he almost settles down with a prostitute from Chicago, but just as things are going very well for them she goes violently insane and Suttree has to run for his life; finally, Suttree himself contracts typhoid fever and nearly dies. When he recovers, it is as if he has been inversely born again and everything in his former life has become dead for him. As the novel ends, Suttree passes the site of his former riverside shanty, now the construction site of a new expressway; a car stops for him, though he has not lifted a hand to signal it, and he is gone.

Whether Suttree's incessant seeking is primarily a quest for something beyond or a flight from the demons that haunt him is never fully clear. In fact, at the level of McCarthy's narrative quest and flight, seeking and running away seem to be interchangeable aspects of the same desperation of spirit. The source of this despair is McCarthy's overpowering sense of the brevity, fragility, and impermanence of human order in face of the vast but profoundly beautiful abyss of the cosmos. Above all, McCarthy's narrative gives us a sense of the macroscopic and microscopic, of the reality beyond human culture, the truth of "things known raw, unshaped by the construction of a mind obsessed with form" (427). In sudden flashes his characters reveal a primordial savagery that lurks beneath the surface of civilized society, as if "they could have been some band of stone age folk washed up out of an atavistic dream" (358). Suttree, more than most of the other characters, seems possessed with this sense of ultimate insecurity that pierces him at any moment when he lets his guard down: "he lay on his back in the gravel, the earth's core sucking his bones, a moment's giddy vertigo with this illusion of falling outward through blue and windy space, over the offside of the planet, hurtling through the high thin cirrus" (286).

Through McCarthy's vision we see that it is not the thriving New South city but the outcasts' "encampment of the damned" that is closer to reality, because it reveals the truth of man's folly and mortality: "this city constructed on no known paradigm, a mongrel architecture reading back through the works of man in a brief delineation of the aberrant disordered and mad" (3). In this world the most permanent and lyrical thing is decay, and any belief in permanence is delusion and madness. McCarthy is a veritable Tolstoy of Trash, and his pervasive and redolent poetry of rubble, garbage, and detritus are an ode to the haunting but futile beauty of the brevity and emptiness of human accomplishment against the vast geological panorama of rocks and stars.

However much he may reflect certain aspects of the Eliotic wasteland version of the grail legend, Cormac McCarthy's *Suttree* is no longer a Christian, nor is the possibility of Christian revelation held out to him, as is the case with Flannery O'Connor's characters. In one especially poignant scene, Suttree wanders into the unused Catholic school where he once studied, and there at this "derelict school for lechers" he finds his old desk and sits at it for a while before he notices a pathetic figure standing in the door of "this old bedroom in this old house where he'd been taught a sort of christian witchcraft." The figure is an old priest who still apparently lives in the deserted school. But there is no contact and no word. "When he came past the stairway the priest was mounted on the first landing like a piece of statuary. A catatonic shaman who spoke no word at all. Suttree went out the way that he'd come in, crossing the grass toward the lights of the street. When he looked back he could see the shape of the priest in the baywindow watching like a paper priest in a pulpit or a prophet sealed in glass" (304–5).

In *Suttree,* McCarthy's world is that of a scientific rather than a religious millennialist, though the biblical overtones of his novel are at times almost overwhelming. McCarthy views human life from the perspective of eternity, yet his version of eternity is the cosmic, geological, and biological immensity that derives from a purely naturalistic vision of the universe. In a way his characters, like O'Connor's, are "god-haunted," and his novels are secular allegories of driven souls fleeing the devil and seeking salvation in a realm across the borders of human good and evil where it is increasingly difficult to distinguish between the holy and the diabolical. This apocalyptic sense, with its implications of violence and destruction, is one aspect of the tradition of extreme individualism in religion and personal violence which John Shelton Reed identifies as a central component of the "enduring South," and which, he suggests, may be becoming an even more important characteristic of Southern culture in the postmodern era.[4]

Though he is haunted by the absence of God from the moment he first appears as a fisherman on the horribly polluted Tennessee River until he shakes the dust of Knoxville from his feet, Suttree has one significant moment of revelation during a trek up into the mountains in his second year on the river. This restless trip becomes a vision quest as Suttree gets increasingly lost and fatigue and hunger undercut his sense not only of where he is but of how long he has been there. Finally a storm that seems to have been following him for days breaks over him, and as he "crouched like an ape in the dark under the eaves of a slate bluff and watched the lightning" he has a vision of the world as a bizarre witches' sabbath with all the eras of evolutionary history mixed together:

> The storm moved off to the north. Suttree heard laughter and sounds of carnival. He saw with a madman's clarity the perishability of his flesh. Illbedowered harlots were calling from small porches in the night, in their gaudy rags like dolls panoplied out of a dirty stream. And along the little ways in the rain and lightning came a troupe of squalid merrymakers bearing a caged wivern on shoulderpoles and other alchemical game, chimeras and cacodemons skewered up on boarspears and a pharmacopeia of hellish condiments adorning a trestle and toted by trolls with an eldern gnome for guidon who shouted foul oaths from his mouthhole and a piper who piped a pipe of ploverbone and wore on his hip a glass flasket of some smoking fuel that yawed within viscid as quicksilver. A mesosaur followed above on a string like a fourlegged garfish helium filled. A tattered gonfalon embroidered with stars now extinct. Nemoral halfworld inhabitants, figures in buffoon's motley, a gross and blueback foetus clopping along in brogues and toga. Attendants attend. Suttree watched these puckish revelers pass with a half grin of wry doubt. Dark closed about him. (287–88)

After such knowledge, what forgiveness? This vision might serve as a symbolic prophecy of the things experienced by the protagonists of McCarthy's next three novels. For Suttree, his final year on the river brings "a season of death and epidemic violence" (416). Increasingly he feels the coming of the hunter who in some mysterious way has been dogging his steps from the beginning. Finally the destruction of McAnally Flats, the one place in Knoxville he has been able to live in, drives him off the river and onto the road, where "out across the land the lightwires and road rails were going and the telephone lines with voices shuttling on like souls" (471).

Like his own protagonist, McCarthy pulled up stakes in Knoxville, leaving there in 1976, around the same time he was completing *Suttree*. At this point he made a major geographical and creative move to the Southwest, settling in El Paso, Texas, where he continued to write, but more in the traditions of western literature. Thus, McCarthy linked those traditions with those of the South, continuing to express in western terms his central themes of the failure of white American civilization and its inescapable burden of guilt. The guilt comes from its destruction of nature and its tragic heritage of human waste represented by the extermination of great traditional cultures and by the pervasive racism of modern America. Other contemporary literary explorations of the history and culture of the South and the West, regions which were once so important as sources of romantic myths of otherness in American culture, have also produced compelling reevaluations of the basic myths of American exceptionalism and superiority and powerful critiques of the multiple failures of the American dream. It is striking, though perhaps not surprising, that these deeply critical literary movements have emerged almost simultaneously with a new surge of political conservatism and fundamentalism in America, also centered in the South and the West and seeking to manipulate the same symbolic and ideological traditions for their own very different purposes. As many commentators have noted, Ronald Reagan tried to reenact the western myth of the shootout between the heroic marshall and the outlaw on the national and international scenes. The new breed of Southern Republicans who have recently become so important in American politics has found that a traditional Southern rhetoric of states rights, less government, family values, localism, and even a coded white supremacy skillfully disguised as opposition to affirmative action has proved highly effective on the national scene. These reactions are almost antithetical to those of serious contemporary Southern and Western writers, but they are probably different responses to the same uncertainties that have beset America in the last quarter of the twentieth century: a profound loss of confidence in America's uniqueness, moral superiority, and global omnipotence. In the context of this ongoing spiritual crisis, the South and the West, which once helped define America mythically and symbolically through their otherness, are now being pursued by both intellectual critics and conservative fundamentalists as symbols of the real truth of America.

Notes

1. Cormac McCarthy, *Suttree* (New York: Vintage Books, 1992).

2. Passages like the following clearly reflect the influence of Joyce's method of amassing incredibly detailed catalogues of the people and things that haunt the Dublin streets:

> Every other face goitered, twisted, tubered with some excrescence. Teeth black with rot, eyes rheumed and vacuous. Dour and diminutive people framed by paper cones of blossoms, hawkers of esoteric wares, curious electuaries ordered up in jars and elixirs decocted in the moon's dark. He went by stacks of crated pullets, plump hares with ruby eyes. Butter tubbed in ice and brown or alabaster eggs in ordered rows. Along by the meatcounters shuffling up flies out of the bloodstained sawdust. Where a calf's head rested pink and scalded on a tray and butchers honed their knives. (*Suttree*, 67)

In spite of the Joycean model, McCarthy imparts his own distinctive aura to the scene.

3. Perhaps there is some hint of James Agee's nostalgically beautiful "Knoxville: Summer, 1915," that haunting evocation of a bygone way of life from *A Death in the Family,* in McCarthy's Knoxville of the 1950s.

4. Cf. John Shelton Reed, *The Enduring South: Subcultural Persistence in Mass Society* (Lexington, Mass.: Lexington Books, 1972). Also Clyde N. Wilson, ed., *Why the South Will Survive by Fifteen Southerners* (Athens: University of Georgia Press, 1981).

CLAIMING A LITERARY SPACE

The Affrilachian Poets

THERESA L. BURRISS

In 1991 Frank X Walker created a new word. It was a word that came to him as he forged a space for himself in his native Appalachia. As an African American, Walker had tired of African Americans' exclusion from Appalachian literature and sought to eliminate their marginal status within the scholarship. According to Kentucky scholar and writer Gurney Norman, Walker turned to poetry to relieve his frustration; consequently, "a synapse fired in Frank's brain" (Norman) to create this new word. And the word was *Affrilachia.*

Many outside the region view Appalachia as distinctly white, homogenous. Even many white Appalachians have fallen prey to such a myopic vision and remain unconscious of the diversity within the mountains. Scholars of Appalachian history typically focus on the Scots-Irish descendants who inhabit the region. Only recently, within the surge of postcolonial studies, have the Cherokee offered their voices, a counter-discourse, to remedy these exclusionary practices of many scholars. Edward Cabbell and William Turner's work, *Blacks in Appalachia,* published in 1985, serves as the primary scholarly work devoted exclusively to African Americans in Appalachia. As we enter the twenty-first century, though, when multiculturalism stands at the forefront of much social and political consciousness, a new generation of scholars and writers is beginning to realize the true diversity of Appalachia. Frank X Walker has contributed to this awakening.

Soon after Walker's creation of *Affrilachia,* a group of African American writers in Lexington, Kentucky, began meeting to share their work, to critique and encourage each other. Consequently, in 1991 the Affrilachian Poets were born. And their birth spawned a new focus in Appalachian literature. Until this time, Nikki Giovanni served as the only recognized black poet from Appalachia. Yet, she did not emphasize her tie to the region and rarely focused on her life in Knoxville, Tennessee, or southern Ohio. Giovanni's poems dealt and continue to deal with a national black struggle, often with strong feminist overtones. Indeed, black Appalachian writers are conspicuously absent from such well-respected anthologies as *Voices from the Hills.* Edward Cabbell does note in the *Voices from the Hills* sequel, *Appalachia Inside Out,* "Unlike white Appalachian literature, which has been discovered and rediscovered many times, black Appalachian literature has yet to be revealed and appreciated. . . . Thus, literature, the chief interpretative agent for understanding the history and culture of any region or locale, has failed adequately to explore the black Appalachian experience" (Cabbell, 241).

As a direct result of the formal organization of the Affrilachian Poets, African American writers in Appalachia are finally finding recognition both within and outside the region. Black Appalachian experience finds expression through literature. Critical responses to Crystal Wilkinson's two books of short stories, *Blackberries, Blackberries* and *Water Street,* and to Nikky Finney's book of poems, *Rice,* illustrate this long-awaited acknowledgment.

And despite certain distinctions among the Affrilachians, the poets exhibit commonalities in their writing. A focus on ancestors, common people, and their role in shaping identity pervades their writing. Members express deep ties to the land based on the certainty of their heritage. They substantiate their identity and subjectivity through the land on which they live. And lastly, their writing is infused with the postcolonial notion of cultural hybridity, where two, and often more, cultures merge within one individual. Each of these characteristics can be traced to long-standing Appalachian cultural traditions and sociological characteristics. In the introduction to *Old Wounds, New Words: Poems from the Appalachian Poetry Project,* George Ella Lyon describes the themes of 1930s and '40s Appalachian poetry as "reveal[ing] its origin in closeness to the earth and love of song" (1), while contemporary Appalachian poetry embodies diversity and "often contradictory visions" (9). Nevertheless, Lyon explains, "[t]wo things can be safely said" about this new poetry:

First, it most often concerns itself with revaluation or reclamation of the past, which includes strengthening or at least an exploration of the bonds between generations. Second, its strong tie to the land has continued, whether in the pastoral work of poets like Jeff Daniel Marion, Robert Morgan, Fred Chappell, and Maggie Anderson, or the more consciously political poems of Jonathan Williams, P. J. Laska, Mary Joan Coleman, and Bob Snyder. (9)

Though Lyon provides a viable framework in which to unite Appalachian writers, interestingly, black Appalachians are absent from the list.

The idea of Affrilachia opens Appalachia to more fluid ways of thinking about the area and its residents. Frank X Walker acknowledges that Affrilachia "does such a good job describing who we are, our space inside the space, and it does it in a dignified way. We don't give up our African heritage and we don't give up Kentucky" (Walker/Ledford).

Affrilachia embodies an idea of spirit, a realm where common experiences mingle and find expression. Though blacks in Appalachia share a heritage with white Appalachians, their experiences are inevitably different. Social and political cognizance of race by both blacks and whites throughout the world, along with the United States' history of slavery, dictates these differences. All Appalachians could be said to embody a hybridity because of their "othering" by mainstream America. Affrilachians, however, symbolize a great merging of more cultures. In *The Location of Culture*, Homi Bhabha explains, "It is in the emergence of the interstices— the overlap and displacement of domains of difference—that the intersubjective and collective experiences of nationness, community interest, or cultural value are negotiated" (2). When Frank X Walker created the word Affrilachia, he reclaimed subjectivity for blacks in Appalachia while acknowledging the intersecting cultures that make them American, black, and Appalachian, a merging of cultures that makes them unique.

Nikky Finney, Frank X Walker, and Crystal Wilkinson are three members within the larger group who have carved out a space in Appalachian literature. Not only do these poets offer new perspectives on Appalachian experiences; they challenge the very parameters of what it means to be Appalachian.

Nikky Finney became a member of the Affrilachian Poets when she moved to Lexington, Kentucky, to teach at the University of Kentucky. Although she grew up in Conway, South Carolina, the Low Country of coastal Carolina, Finney identified with Appalachians' tie to the land. She accepted as common her family's dependence on nature for their livelihood. Once she moved to Kentucky, she observed this same dependence. She recalls, "I witnessed how valuable the land was to our everyday eating as well as to my grandmother's livelihood. I remember not being amazed that the only thing they would buy in town was coffee and sugar, that everything else needed was either made or grown or bartered for" ("Salt-Water," 123).

Finney finds an ironic spiritual sustenance in the Atlantic Ocean, the waterway that ushered so many Africans onto American soil and into slavery. She explains, "My eyes are always stitched open when I move in this particular water because I know I am searching for the faces of my family. I am afraid to blink because I don't want to miss even one of the sixty million and more who jumped off the slave ships rather than be a member of the landing party" ("Salt-Water," 121). The coastal Carolina African diaspora culture that resulted from those who did not jump ship, however, also provides Finney with a sense of self. "This original culture fed me in a thousand invisible ways. . . . I was never ashamed to talk to the sea as if she could hear me" (122).

Importantly, too, Finney spent much of her girlhood on her grandfather's farm in the foothills of Appalachia, where she "could see the tips of the Great Smoky Mountains way off in the distance" ("Salt-Water," 122–24). Her summers in the Appalachian foothills serve as the link to her current Kentucky experiences. Finney notes, "I stared deep at these great slopes whenever they appeared into the frame of my life, creating stories about how they got there and who it was that lived deep inside their folds. Little did I know that years later I would relocate to the Kentucky River basin to live, listen, teach, and write side by side children of mountain people and recognize the curves and mounds in my own saltwater soul" (124). Through the adoption of Appalachian and Affrilachian culture, coupled with her inherited Low Country culture, Finney articulates in her memoirs the notion of migratory subjectivity. She has shaped her identity in the spaces between all these cultures, the "interstices," and where they confront traditional white culture.

Poet Kwame Dawes, in his *African American Review* article "Reading *Rice:* A Local Habitation and a Name," explains, "What a poet like you does is reinstate the concept of the poet as *griot*—as priest, not void of subjectivity and a private self, but able to contain the voices of the community, and able to be virtually empowered with the gift to become the soul of the people" (271). In her poetry, Finney draws from personal experience, from the stories of her life, yet explodes these words to speak for and to her community. Just as traditional griots of western Africa perpetuate oral traditions of family and village through storytelling, Finney passes down the history of her own people. So, too, she strengthens her ties to Appalachia's oral storytelling tradition and further represents a postcolonial hybridity of African and Appalachian culture.

Both Frank X Walker and Crystal Wilkinson grew up in the foothills of the eastern Kentucky mountains, Walker in an urban area and Wilkinson in a rural one. Born in Danville, Kentucky, a town near the Dix River, which is in the Kentucky River basin, Walker eventually made his way to the city of Lexington to attend the University of Kentucky. He considers his upbringing "very urban because I grew up in the housing projects most of my life versus the farm. That's the one image you don't get when you think of Appalachia. You think mostly rural" (Walker/Ledford).

And Walker's urban Appalachian experiences, coupled with a focus on family, take center stage in his poetry. He acknowledges, "The poem 'Affrilachia' talks about the worshipping of families and porches. Basically, it's some traditional values that have been swept away or lost in this other stuff that's happening in America" (Walker/Ledford). When describing the catalyst for his writing, he claims, "Family is still the foundation of my work. Anything else that evokes some kind of emotional response, be it political or social, those things happen, but they're usually isolated. I think every relative that I have, at some level there's a piece of writing about them at this point somewhere in my work" (ibid.). Clearly, Walker embodies the old Appalachian value of "familism" that Loyal Jones describes in his *Voices from the Hills* essay, "Appalachian Values": "Appalachian people are family centered. . . . Loyalty runs deep between family members" (511).

Walker's reliance on family for his creative muse also echoes renowned Appalachian poets like Jim Wayne Miller, Jesse Stuart, and Louise McNeill. In Miller's beautifully crafted collection *The Mountains Have Come Closer*, he pays homage to those who came before him. The poem "Bird in the House," especially, illustrates the traditional Appalachian familial theme. As the speaker of the poem reflects on the "[s]ubtraction of lives from the land," the loss of his ancestors, he finds solace in "their stories on the porch at night" (32) that persist long after their deaths.

In Jesse Stuart's poem "Builders of Destiny," the speaker acknowledges a type of universal ancestors and their intense labor in the making of America. Because they dared to dream and build, often at the cost of their own well-being, we enjoy "[a] land of dream and wealth and energy, / A land where freedom is the greatest greed" (316). Stuart's ironic positioning of freedom with greed speaks directly to Appalachians' historic deprivation of economic and social freedom by Northern industrial interests. Stuart queries, "What does it matter if their bones turn stone, / Their flesh be richer dust our plowshares turn" (316). We owe our very sustenance to the sacrificial nature of our ancestors.

Louise McNeill also recognizes ancestors' hard work in sustaining life. In "Katchie Verner's Harvest," the speaker catalogues the various fruits, vegetables, and meats lining the shelves or hanging from the rafters of Katchie Verner's store. Indeed, Katchie Verner offers a true smorgasbord of edibles, which is especially vital to fight "[a]gainst the mountain winter / When sleet-hard drifts will freeze / The deep loam of her garden / And gird her orchard trees" (320). In addition to placing value on Katchie Verner herself, McNeill connects Katchie Verner to the land and her dependence on it.

Though exhibiting the same loyalty to family as Frank X Walker, Affrilachian Crystal Wilkinson was born and raised on a sixty-acre farm on Indian Creek in rural Casey County, Kentucky. As she lived with her grandparents, Wilkinson recalls the encouragement provided by her grandmother. Though her grandmother wanted to become a schoolteacher, her parents would not allow her to live in the city on her own. Wilkinson notes, "My grandmother never had the opportunity to become what she really wanted to be. She became a wife at fourteen years old" (Wilkinson/ Ledford). Nevertheless, her grandmother's artistic drive manifested itself in other ways. "She used to write songs, make up church songs, on the back of envelopes. I had seen her write those songs, which were really poems, on the backs of envelopes that no one ever saw. That did kind of encourage me" (ibid.).

Her grandmother's furtive ways of releasing her creativity echo Alice Walker's essay "In Search of Our Mothers' Gardens: The Creativity of Black Women in the South." Many Southern black women had no outlet for their creativity, could not utilize their talents. And Walker explains this tragedy as she asks, "Did you have a genius of a great-great-grandmother who died under some ignorant and depraved white overseer's lash? Or was she required to bake biscuits for a lazy backwater tramp, when she cried out in her soul to paint watercolors of sunsets, or the rain falling on the green and peaceful pasturelands?" Although not born into slavery, Wilkinson's grandmother served as a maid for several white families for many years. Then, after cleaning other people's homes all day, she would return to her own home to continue working.

Wilkinson's grandfather had only a third-grade education and could not read or write, "though he was a mathematician out of this world" (Wilkinson/Ledford). As a result, her grandmother made sure that Wilkinson learned to read even before she entered school. According to Wilkinson, her early reading ability "encouraged the writing part," so she began crafting stories at an early age (ibid.).

Wilkinson continued to write creatively and nurture her creativity on her own, though she had received ill advice from a career counselor to major in journalism in college. She remembers, "I had all these poems in a box and every once in a while I would bring some out and let a friend read it, but no further than that" (Wilkinson/Ledford). Not until she read a short story at an open mic event at a Lexington restaurant, long after graduating from college, did Wilkinson emerge onto the literary scene. Recalling that night and her terror of reading before the audience, Wilkinson explains, "I read a short story and people clapped. So then I started getting into the literary community here in Lexington and I started doing more and getting my work out there, even though I was still doing that in my own little shell" (ibid.).

In a *Lexington Herald-Leader* article by Nicole Moran, Crystal Wilkinson describes her involvement with the Affrilachian Poets. "'It was just like going to church. You're never alone,' she said. In the early years, no matter how many people came to hear one of the poets read, there would be five or six members of the group there to support them, too, Wilkinson said" (13). As a result, the Affrilachian Poets forged their own community. Gurney Norman explains his philosophy about such community crafting: "If the dominant culture doesn't recognize you, refuses you space within its coterie, then create your own niche" (Norman). The Affrilachian Poets did just this.

Rice, Finney's collection of poetry published in 1995 by Sister Vision Press, contains powerful images of injustices suffered by blacks in the United States. In "The Afterbirth, 1931," Finney describes the birth of her father, a birth gone awry because of a drunk white doctor with "shiny" degrees. Forsaking their founded belief in midwives, listening instead to the learned doctor's appeal to advanced medicine, Finney's family allows the doctor into the pregnant woman's room despite great unease and instinctual distrust among all present. They are people of the country, criticized for their backward ways. Hence, Finney reveals her union with so many rural Appalachians as she documents in her poems the marginalization suffered by country folk. These wise, rural people with knowledge of the land and vital skills of survival so often are discounted as ignorant by industrial society.

So, the family attempts to trust this so-called progress, to discard old ways, and to wait for the doctor who "came when he wanted / the next day / after his breakfast / but what more / could we colored country folks ever want" (68). Tragically, however, advanced medicine turns into botched malpractice as the drunken, racist doctor "forgets" to remove the afterbirth from Finney's grandmother's womb, "somewhere he probably didn't want to touch" (68). Advanced medicine turns into murder as her grandmother dies from infection:

> Then he packed his bag and   left
> with all of his official training
> and gathered up gold stars   left
> the Virginia land of Cumberland county
> he left and forgot
> he left and didn't remember
> the afterbirth inside
> Carlene Godwin Finney
>
> to clabber
> gangreen
> close down
> her place
> her precious private pleasing place
> to fill the house to the rafters
> up past the dimpled tin roof
> with a rotting smell
> that stayed for nine days
> that mortgaged a room
> in our memories
> and did not die along with her
> (69–70)

Finney's grandmother falls victim to both racial injustice and medical abuse, just as rural Appalachians have suffered various doctors' ineptitude or lack of concern for decades. Appalachians in coal mining towns, under the "care" of company-owned doctors, come to mind most immediately.

Finney's daddy does not escape the doctor's incompetence either. The doctor's drunkenness infects everyone he touches:

> Then he pulled my daddy through
> somebody he probably didn't care to reach for
> and from the first he pulled him wrong
> and wrong
> shattered his collarbone
> and snapped his soft baby foot in half
> and smashed the cartilage in his infant hand
> (68)

Finney presents the particular tragedy of her father's birth and her grandmother's death, invoking her griot status as she reveals a life-death cycle of so many black Americans' experience.

In "'God Ain't Makin' No More Land' for South Carolina," Finney recounts through her poetry another tragedy as told by an elderly black woman she interviewed. The bond between the land and its people echoes this long-standing Appalachian cultural characteristic. Through the use of coastal Carolina vernacular, Finney gives voice to the woman sitting on her front porch. She details the appropriation of Low Country blacks' land for resort development, land held in their families since the Civil War. The woman cites the importance of the land to its people and grieves over the ills that befall a people when that land is gone.

> No Sa
> what we's speakin' of
> ain't like what glue is to paper or cement to brick
> cain't even leave it for the common prayer no more
> more like the death comin' on like a sneaky wave
> cause when the land go everythin' go
> (59)

The developers' greed envelops the land and catches the people like death—unawares. Even the common prayer to God Almighty does no good when the almighty dollar dictates economic outcome and rules in a capitalist society. The parallels with Appalachia are astounding. The exportation of raw materials like coal and timber from the mountains also brought about the exportation of wealth from the area and created dependent economies, depressed peoples.

Finney continues by describing the animals that suffer death and displacement, but then returns to the people who suffer similar fates. They are denied their dignity, are stripped of their ancestral ties:

> but the graveyard of the Gullah promise
> only the bulldozer with he own security guard
> just' so to keep us and lil' Buddy
> from visiting with Nana on Sunday
> then it all jus' 'bout gone
> City Man come tell me say
> lessen we know somebody behind the gate
> who can write us a go-through pass
> . . . .
> (us know somebody alright)
> behind and under and all around and about
> but we ground-up folks
> don't write nothing down not no more
> what for   long time for now give up on word
> (59–60)

With tragic irony, history repeats itself though the characters may be different. Just as plantations dotted the islands of the Low Country in the time of slavery, plantations are again resurrected through developers' dreams—only this time slavery remains a subtle reality and the word is never spoken. The Gullahs' burial grounds are sacrificed for the playgrounds of the rich. Blacks of the Low Country are denied access to their own lands.

Providing almost a mirror image, Appalachian writer Denise Giardina describes Appalachians' severance from their land in her novel *Storming Heaven.* Union organizer Rondal Lloyd reflects on the coal company's introduction to the mountains. One day, as he and his family were traipsing the hills of what used to be their land, gathering greens and intending to hike up to the family cemetery, he explains, "we . . . were stopped by a gate and barbed wire fence strung across the road, and a sign which read, NO

TRESPASSING. PROPERTY OF AMERICAN COAL. We never went to the cemetery again" (14). Like the Gullahs in Finney's poem, the Lloyds cannot even "visitate" with their dead.

Since Finney's move to Kentucky, and her consequent tie to the Affrilachian Poets, she finds creative fodder in the history of Kentucky. Her poem "Mary Mary Quite Contrary" describes the fortitude of a former slave who lived during the late 1700s. A *Lexington Herald Leader* article educates the reader on the plight of Slave Mary and sets the tone for Finney's poem. Mary sued her owner for her freedom. She won because the judge's "order contained verbatim a letter from Mary's owner relinquishing ownership of the slave, saying she wasn't worth the cost of contesting the suit" (73). From the start of the poem, Finney marvels at Mary's gumption and the unlikelihood of her success:

Wonder who she thought she was   Wonder
how it wasn't raped away
a long winding memory
spoken just as fresh
as a constitutional amendment
(73)

While she recounts the spirit of one Kentucky slave woman, Finney also catalogues one of the most horrendous injustices suffered by female slaves, rape by their owners. Moreover, Finney highlights the blatant hypocrisy of the time when the Constitution claimed all were equal, but in reality this "all" included only white men.

Finney plucks this woman from history to serve as inspiration to others, as Mary defied the suppression and oppression imposed on all peoples of color during the eighteenth and nineteenth centuries. Through her poem Finney offers Mary to readers and illustrates how one woman, despite her status, conquered evil and found both beauty and strength inherent in her being. Again, Finney relies on the gifts of the ancestors, a very distinct African *and* Appalachian trait, to make her way in the world through her art:

Wonder
what she knew she was guaranteed
Wonder
how she figured up

the total sum of her parts
and didn't bother
with the division
Wonder   Wonder   Wonderful
(73–74)

Just as Mary discovered her total self-worth, Finney motivates her readers
to act and find their own, not to merely wonder over the possibilities.

Although Frank X Walker does not experience Kentucky mountain life
in all the same ways white Appalachians do, in the title poem of his collection *Affrilachia*, he squarely situates himself as an African American Appalachian and binds himself to the culture:

anywhere in Appalachia
is about as far as you could get
from our house
in the projects
yet
a mutual appreciation
for fresh greens
and cornbread
an almost heroic notion
of family
and porches
makes us kinfolk
somehow
(92)

Walker will not be denied his Affrilachian heritage, but his claim to this
heritage is not without struggle. As many white Appalachians tend to
deny black Appalachians' existence, the media attempt to reductively car-
icature *all* Appalachians. Both groups omit entire peoples from the mountainous region:

that being 'colored' and all
is generally lost
somewhere between
the dukes of hazard

and the beverly hillbillies
(93)

He continues to play on outsiders' stereotypes of Appalachians, but then
manipulates the stereotypes to make a striking comparison:

but
if you think
makin' 'shine from corn
is as hard as kentucky coal
imagine being
an Affrilachian
poet
(93)

Amidst the humiliating labels crafted by outsiders and the denial of his
presence by insiders, Frank X Walker announces his existence. The poetry
of his Affrilachian voice claims a space in these mountains that demands
attention. And in his poetry, Walker exhibits W.E.B. DuBois's concept of
"double consciousness," though in actuality Walker's is a triple consciousness. Both African and Appalachian cultures are rooted within him as he
negotiates a white American world. DuBois explains in his seminal work,
The Souls of Black Folk, "It is a peculiar sensation, this double-consciousness,
this sense of always looking at one's self through the eyes of others, of
measuring one's soul by the tape of a world that looks on in amused contempt and pity" (DuBois, 3).

In "Statues of Liberty," Walker recognizes the black Appalachian women
in his life. Here, he demonstrates the timeless Appalachian trait of reliance
on ancestors. Throughout the poem he summarily recounts the details of
their lives, lives bound in service to others:

mamma scrubbed
rich white porcelain
and hard wood floors
on her hands and knees
hid her pretty face and body
in sack dresses
and aunt jemima scarves

from predators
who assumed
for a few extra dollars
before christmas
in dark kitchen pantries
they could unwrap her
present
(10)

Walker gives multiple meanings to the word service. Not only does his mother clean for these white families, she must dodge the advances of her male employers, a service in which she is not willing to engage. Interestingly, Walker's mother appropriates the Aunt Jemima character created by whites and utilizes it not only to protect herself but to subvert the power of her male employers. In donning this Aunt Jemima mask, his mother undermines the Aunt Jemima stereotype.

Walker continues his poem by remembering his aunts and their lifework of either washing clothes or taking care of others' children. Before they have an opportunity to relish the rewards of this life, however, they are transported to the next. Aunt Helen

waited patiently
for her good white woman
to die
and make good on her promise
to leave her
a little something
only to leave her first
(11)

And Aunt Bertha
spent every other moment
preaching about
the richness of the afterlife
before the undertaker
took her
to see for herself
(11)

Though Walker could end his poem by cataloguing the injustices suffered in this earthly life by his ancestors, he illustrates how their endurance
paved an easier path for the next generation. He venerates these women
who never made it into the history books or feminist manuscripts:

> this curse-swallowing sorority
> dodged dicks
> and bosses
> before postwar women
> punched clocks
> they birthed civil and human rights
> gave the women's movement
> legs
> sacrificed their then
> to pave the way for a NOW
> their hard-earned pennies
> sent us off to college
> and into the world
> our success is their reward
> we
> are their monuments
> but they
> are our statues of liberty
> (12)

Despite what others would deem the seeming insignificance of these
women's lives, Walker writes to testify to the contrary. He records their accomplishments and equates them with one of America's most enduring
symbols of freedom, Lady Liberty. The beacon of light they shine, the wisdom these ancestors impart, guides future generations and enables them to
achieve better lives. Walker continues the Appalachian tradition of honoring family.

Walker's voice does not end at the borders of Appalachia, however. Tes-
tifying to the richness and diversity of the Affrilachian Poets' work,
Walker infuses much of his poetry with the riffs of pop culture. Placing a
twenty-first-century spin on a poem in homage to Martin Luther King Jr.,
Walker muses over the possibilities of Dr. King as rap artist in "Lil'
Kings":

what if
the good revren doctah
mlk jr
was just marty
or lil' king
not a pastor
but a little faster
from the streets
quoting gangsta rap
not gandhi
(32)

Walker poses these possibilities and enriches the scenes with the vernacular of the streets. He suggests an unlikely union between the historical
pacifist figure of Dr. King and the gun-wielding gangsta rappers of modern society.

Walker continues to paint the twenty-first-century Dr. King, or "king
doctah," by asking:

what if somebody
screaming 'nigger'
hit 'im in the head
with a brick
and he pulled out a nine
and squeezed off
one or two rounds
not tears
praying
only that he
not miss
(32–33)

How would society react to this new Dr. King? In this new picture,
Walker poses questions to his readers that are not easily answered. Would
this be the same man? Can a man act in self-defense, utilize the protection
of a 9 mm gun, and still be honored as a great civil rights leader?

Interestingly, we do discover parallels. Walker asks what if this new Dr.
King "got arrested for / conspiring to incite riots / disturbing the peace /

and resisting arrest" (33). The real Dr. King did provoke these events through peaceful means, while Walker's imagined twenty-first-century King achieves the same end through other means. And this is perhaps where the similarities fall apart—in the means to the end. Walker chooses a play on words to pose his final question. What if Dr. King had his

> eyes on a prized new voice
> not no bel
> no peace
> of nothin'
> that just rings
> when it's hit
> a voice that hits back
>
> could he still
> be king?

The Nobel Peace Prize would elude this new Dr. King because his means to remedy injustices move beyond peaceful protest and civil disobedience. Hence, we are left to wonder whether this type of man, one who does strive for racial equality, could still be held in high esteem, could serve as an honorable role model.

Though these Kentucky writers are known as the Affrilachian Poets, and poetry unites them as a group, several members, including Crystal Wilkinson, explore meaning through other genres as well. The characters in Crystal Wilkinson's short story collection, *Blackberries, Blackberries,* are rural black Kentuckians. And these characters are definitely "country," in their mannerisms, speech patterns, and knowledge. Within the introduction, Wilkinson claims her Appalachian rural heritage as a very part of her physical stature. "Being country is as much a part of me as my full lips, wide hips, dreadlocks and high cheek bones" (1).

In an article in *Kentucky Living,* critic Liz Mandrell describes Wilkinson's writing as praising "the unsung humanity of country life through stories and characters that show its depth and diversity." Wilkinson does not shy away from the complexity of the human character and illustrates through her stories both the good and the evil possible in human beings. Consequently, her characters are real. Like Nikky Finney, Wilkinson creates stories based on the particulars of rural country living that reach to a universal audience and transcend their particularity. Wilkinson herself explains in her introduction to *Blackberries, Blackberries,* "These stories come from the ordinary and the extraordinary. From black, country women with curious lives. From struggle, from fear, from love, from life, from the gut, from the heart. Black and juicy, just like a blackberry" (2).

In "The Wonderer," Wilkinson challenges the traditional culture's notion of beauty as readers follow a little black country girl's thoughts before bedtime. While watching the glow of lightning bugs caught in a mason jar, Javeda "would wonder why white folks seemed to have life so easy and why black folks seemed to have so many stumbling blocks" (115). Reminiscent of Toni Morrison's tragic character Pecola Breedlove in her novel *The Bluest Eye,* Wilkinson's character Javeda mulls over the benefits of waking up the next morning white. She initially envies the little white girl who lives down the road, envies her straight hair and "china doll" existence.

But then, unlike Morrison's character, Javeda stops this wondering and begins to catalogue the various gifts associated with being black. She thinks about "the flip side of the coin," a side where the little white girl "would never know the love that comes outta them hour-long combing spells, be it Gran Nan or Granny Tine who was doing the combing. That's how Javeda got to the heart of her women folk" (116). Her grandmothers' struggles to tame her nappy hair invite wonderful opportunities for Javeda. "That's where souls got transferred. That's where knowledge was passed on. She liked that time between sturdy black legs, feeling the love being greased into her scalp. And what kinda patience could a fifteen-minute hair combing learn you anyhow" (116).

Though in one sense Javeda's grandmothers seem to succumb to white notions of beauty by attempting to "tame" her hair, because nappy hair is unacceptable, they do so only strategically. Javeda's tamed hair allows her to maneuver more easily in a white world and the grease on her hair ensures a healthy mane, not one burned up and made brittle by a hot iron. As a result of the love that emanates from her hair-combing sessions, Javeda comes to celebrate her own beauty, a distinct and natural beauty characterized by her blackness.

In a change of perspective, through the voice of a young boy named Brother (Butch to his friends), Wilkinson notes the wisdom of women in "Girl Talk." She begins the short story, "Now I'm not one to get too involved in much girl talk but being the only boy in the house, sometimes it

just can't be helped" (31). At first, Brother seems to dismiss the idle chatter of Ma Mae, Mama, and Hattie Lee. He remarks, "Usually, unless it's
supper time, lunch time or time to go to bed or church, I steer clear of the
whole bunch and hang out down on the lot with my boys. But every so
often I get an earful, when I'm in Mama's kitchen helping peel potatoes or
carrying in groceries" (31–32). Brother seems to believe that the "girl
talk" is just nonsense and compromises his male posturing and toughness.

As he walks his little sister, Hattie Lee, to school, his friends make fun
of him. "'Look at Butch holding his little sister's hand. Ain't that cute'"
(32). Such displays of affection are not a part of these boys' rough-and-
tumble world. Wilkinson provides poignant commentary on the social
rules and societal expectations for boys. The rules are rigid, and anyone
daring to defy them, whether on his own accord or through his mother's
mandates, finds himself the object of other boys' ridicule.

John F., another boy in the story, but not one of Brother's pals, discovers
the rigors of social standards as well. As the only child of Miss Beulah, an
older woman who had him late in life, John F. suffers a life of exclusion and
pampering. He was born prematurely and consequently is "sort of cripple.
Walks funny with a limp" (35). Brother recalls the words of his mother
when explaining the life of this child. "Mama says he could do better 'if his
silly old mama would let him out the house to run and play like normal'"
(35). But in the very next breath, Brother again excludes himself from involvement in such conjecturing. "Like I said before, I don't participate in
girl talk but in my house you ain't got much choice" (35). Though Brother
views girl talk as useless, he possesses an understanding of the ways of the
world because he listens to this girl talk. His boys don't understand John
F.'s nature or predicament, don't have insight into how such things work.
The women in Brother's life help him realize, "[Miss Beulah's] gonna treat
that baby like it was gold and keep it by her side always. And that John F.
sure was Miss Beulah's gold piece" (36).

When John F. ventures off the confines of his porch to seek out the other
boys, Brother feels uneasy about playing with him. His mother's and
grandmother's words of warning seem to haunt him. Nevertheless, he
chooses John F. to play on his team in a game of kickball. All seems to be
going well at the start of the game. Brother notes that John F. even kicks
the ball fairly well. But just when John F. has another turn to kick, events
turn bad. Instead of kicking the ball out into the field, "John F. kicks the
ball straight up and it comes back to him like a boomerang and hits him

right in the nose" (37). The blood starts gushing from his nose as the boys all stand around him, staring.

Just then, Miss Beulah finds the boys standing over her baby and starts screaming, "'Oh, my Lord. Oh, my Lord. Lord have mercy they done killed my baby!'" (37). Despite Miss Beulah's hysterical screaming, Brother notes that John F. "raises up a little and is still grinning all silly like he's proud of a bloody nose" (37). Brother now realizes that John F. just wants to be a part of the boys, to play and get dirty and risk bloody noses.

Brother doesn't have long to mull over these thoughts as Hattie Lee pulls on his arm to take her home to the bathroom. And then it hits him. "I'm walking her home, waving bye to my boys, thinking they ought to visit their mama's kitchens more often. Then they'd know about these things" (37). Even though in the beginning he views the girl talk in his own kitchen with cynicism, he comes to appreciate the wisdom and insight he gains by listening to this girl talk. In his rough, boyish way, he praises these women, their talk, and the knowledge he acquires as a result.

In the documentary film *Coal Black Voices,* Gurney Norman verifies the universality of the Affrilachian Poets and compares their work with that of the Harlem Renaissance writers. He cites a sense of urgency in the writing, where the poets bring community into their art and then take the art back to the community. Norman explains that this sense of community, coupled with an "enduring interest in the land," is distinctly part of the literary consciousness of Appalachia. Just as writers of the Harlem Renaissance spoke to their community with their jazz-infused poetry and their reclamation of black culture through art, the Affrilachian Poets follow similar routes. In his poetry, Frank X Walker focuses on current issues facing young urban blacks, issues such as peer pressure and gang violence. Yet, within the tradition of Appalachian literature, he also relies on his ancestors and their life stories to enrich his own life story and, more particularly, his life's work. Nikky Finney, Frank X Walker, and Crystal Wilkinson all honor the past and their ancestors' place in it. Community, whether present or past, is central in each of the poets' work.

C. Daniel Dawson, curator and African culture historian in Lexington, Kentucky, provides insight into the Affrilachian Poets' African inspiration, whether conscious or not. In *Coal Black Voices,* he explains the poets' use of the land in their writing, how the landscape is populated with the spirits of their ancestors, known as Simbi, twice-born ancestors. The Affrilachian Poets, through their ties to their ancestors in their work, have made a contract with the landscape. This contract also relates to Appalachians' deep sense of place, their instinctual tie to the land. Dawson calls the Affrilachians "avant garde," not because they are exclusive or promoting high theory, but because "they've gone back to find who they are" (Donahue).

As a result, the Affrilachian Poets give voice to a people historically unrecognized in the Appalachian region. They draw inspiration from the specific geography and culture of Appalachia, move into realms of Africa, acknowledge a dependence on their ancestors, and find their words contributing to a global literature. The Affrilachian Poets bring unique perspective to Appalachia, and consequently, energize the literature of the region with vitality inspired by their multiple consciousness.

Works Cited

Baber, Bob Henry, George Ella Lyon, and Gurney Norman, eds. *Old Wounds, New Words: Poems from the Appalachian Poetry Project.* Ashland, Ky.: Jesse Stuart Foundation, 1994.

Bhabha, Homi K. *The Location of Culture.* London: Routledge, 1994.

Cabbell, Edward J. "Black Diamonds: The Search for Blacks in Appalachian Literature and Writing." In *Appalachia Inside Out,* ed. Ambrose N. Manning, Robert J. Higgs, and Jim Wayne Miller. Vol. 1, *Conflict and Change,* 241–45. Knoxville: University of Tennessee Press, 1995.

"Coal Black Voices." Media Working Group home page, http://www.mwg.org (accessed 27 Dec. 2002).

Dawes, Kwame. "Reading *Rice:* A Local Habitation and a Name." *African American Review* 31 (Summer 1997): 269 (11). *Infotrac Database* (accessed Dec. 27, 2002).

Donahue, Jean, and Fred Johnson. *Coal Black Voices: A Documentary.* Videocassette. Media Working Group, Covington, Ky., 2001.

DuBois, W.E.B. *The Souls of Black Folk.* New York: Bantam, 1989.

Finney, Nikky. *Rice.* Toronto: Sister Vision Press, 1995. (Excerpts used by permission of the author.)

———. "Salt-Water Geechee Mounds." In *Bloodroot: Reflections on Place by Appalachian Women Writers,* ed. Joyce Dyer, 120–27. Lexington: University Press of Kentucky, 1998.

Giardina, Denise. *Storming Heaven.* New York: Ivy Books, 1987.

Higgs, Robert J., and Ambrose N. Manning, eds. *Voices from the Hills: Selected Readings of Southern Appalachia.* 2nd ed. Dubuque, Iowa: Kendall/Hunt, 1996.

Jones, Loyal. "Appalachian Values." In *Voices from the Hills: Selected Readings of Southern Appalachia,* ed. Robert J. Higgs and Ambrose N. Manning, 507–17. 2nd ed. Dubuque, Iowa: Kendall/Hunt, 1996.

Mandrell, Liz. "Clearly Crystal." *Kentucky Living,* Feb. 2001.

McNeill, Louise. "Katchie Verner's Harvest." In *Voices from the Hills: Selected Readings of Southern Appalachia,* ed. Robert J. Higgs and Ambrose N. Manning, 319. 2nd ed. Dubuque, Iowa: Kendall/Hunt, 1996.

Miller, Jim Wayne. *The Mountains Have Come Closer.* Boone: Appalachian Consortium Press, 1980.

Morgan, Nicole. "A Way with Words: Affrilachian Poets Band Together for Inspiration, Mutual Support." *Lexington Herald-Leader,* 22 Aug. 2001, http://www.ket.org/content/bookclub/books/2001_sep/extras.htm.

Morrison, Toni. *The Bluest Eye.* New York: Dutton/Plume, 1994 [1974].

Norman, Gurney. Telephone interview, 20 Feb. 2002.

Stuart, Jesse. "Builders of Destiny." In *Voices from the Hills: Selected Readings of Southern Appalachia,* ed. Robert J. Higgs and Ambrose N. Manning, 316. 2nd ed. Dubuque, Iowa: Kendall/Hunt, 1996.

Turner, William, and Edward Cabbell, eds. *Blacks in Appalachia.* Lexington: University Press of Kentucky, 1985.

Walker, Alice. "In Search of Our Mothers' Gardens: The Creativity of Black Women in the South." *Ms. Magazine,* Spring 2002 (1974), www.msmagazine.com/spring2002/walker.asp.

Walker, Frank X. *Affrilachia.* Lexington, Ky.: Old Cove, 2000. (Excerpts used by permission of the author and publisher.)

———. Unpublished interview with Katherine Ledford. University of Kentucky, Lexington, Ky., May 1996.

Wilkinson, Crystal. *Blackberries, Blackberries.* London: Toby Press, 2000.

———. "Humming Back Yesterday." In *Home and Beyond: An Anthology of Kentucky Short Stories,* ed. Morris Allen Grubbs. Lexington: University Press of Kentucky, 2001.

———. Unpublished interview with Katherine Ledford. Carnegie Center, Lexington, Ky., 9 May 1996.

NATURE-LOVING SOULS AND APPALACHIAN MOUNTAINS

The Promise of Feminist Ecocriticism

ELIZABETH ENGELHARDT

In 1955, Wilma Dykeman tried something different. Rinehart Books was in the midst of producing a series of coffee-table books called "Rivers of America." *The French Broad* is Dykeman's volume, and it focuses on the river of that name running through North Carolina and Tennessee, and drawing its watershed from parts of Virginia, South Carolina, Georgia, and Kentucky. Dykeman frequently wrote about the Appalachia she knew intimately. Having lived for most of her adult life in eastern Tennessee and western North Carolina, Dykeman expresses her dedication to the place by setting her novels there, mentoring young people in the region, and supporting education within and about Appalachia. Although best known for her novels, over the course of her career Dykeman has written everything from historical works and essays to letters in local newspapers—all important, all demonstrating her commitment to the people and places of Appalachia. Dykeman could simply have combined tourist-board descriptions with technical, geological, or geographical detail to complete Rinehart's volume. Instead, using dialogue, sketches of intriguing people, dramatizations of crucial historical moments, and personal reflection, Dykeman breathed life into the form Rinehart had established. In the process, Dykeman rewrote the history of the counties through which the French Broad flows to focus on the river and its human and nonhuman inhabitants.[1]

As different as it was to bring a literary eye to bear on the story of a geographical feature, perhaps the book's most radical move happens in its first chapter. After listing the various names given the river by its Cherokee communities, Dykeman writes:

> I should like to think that by some unmerited but longed-for magic I have spoken for a few of the anonymous dead along its banks and up its mountains. For the Negro baby drowned in the river when its mother tried to swim from slavery and bring it into freedom. For the sheriff who was shot in the back from a laurel-thicket ambush as he picked his way along a fog-blanketed early-morning trail. For the minister in a windowless log church who made foot washing a symbolic ceremony of humbleness and brotherhood. For the old taletellers around country stores and the urbane newcomers who seek but have not found as yet. For these and for the river itself, mountains, lowlands, woods, gullies, springs and ponds and brooks I should like to speak, to quicken understanding.[2]

Invoking the diversity of humans living near the river, and adding their voices to the stories of the earth itself, Dykeman radically broadens the definition of community. Today ecologists describe as "bioregional" such a view of community—one that organizes community more in terms of watershed than according to arbitrary political boundaries drawn by humans. In other words, Dykeman claims that humans are united less by state boundaries than by the shared experiences of living with specific trees, animals, mountains, and, above all, water. In addition, people who seem to have little or no connection with each other—white sheriffs, slave babies, or urbane visitors, for instance—are connected by virtue of their proximity to the river. As early as 1955, in poetic language evoking as well as describing the place, Dykeman celebrated life in a bioregion. Her celebrations, though, raise questions too, such as: what does it mean to speak for a river, mountain, woods, or pond? and, if those rivers and mountains have stories to tell, do they also have a say in the stories of the humans in the area? With her invocation, Dykeman suggests that these are the issues with which her text will struggle.

Further, writing before the full blossoming of the civil rights era, and well before today's focus on multiculturalism and diversity, Dykeman strikingly expands the definitions of human community on the river as well. In *The French Broad,* she emphasizes Appalachia's diversity—the book is peopled with Native Americans, black and white women and men, some educated in colleges and others in the woods, some traditional insiders and others perhaps surprising in their inclusion (tourists, would-be developers, and industrialists, for instance). By putting diverse characters on the stage, as it were, Dykeman opens investigation of how power in society is negotiated between them, for instance, between the "Negro baby," its mother, the sheriff, the minister, and the anonymous dead in the passage quoted above. She invites her readers to examine who along the river basin has more power and privilege, who has less, and why. Dykeman refuses to argue that any one group is inherently superior to the others (although that is precisely the argument many white southerners were making at the time), but she instead implies that such beliefs damage communities. Explicitly multicultural about the river's history, Dykeman's story begins before the Cherokees arrive, discusses African American history in the region, includes the nonhuman spirits of the place, and is particular about the economic and social differences between classes along its banks—even if social, political, or literary cultures would prefer to erase many of those differences.

The recent recovery of the works of Effie Waller Smith, African American poet and short story writer, suggests just what would be lost if stereotypes about Appalachia as exclusively white go unchallenged. Smith is the kind of mountain woman who for too long has been erased from the list of Appalachian writers. A schoolteacher from Pikeville, Kentucky, Smith was born in 1879 to a family of professional teachers; she followed a brother and a sister to college for her own teacher training. Before her death in 1960, Smith experienced marriage, divorce, adoption of a child, life in several states, the murder of a loved one, publishing success, and subsequent obscurity. She published short stories and poems in the leading journals of her day, such as *Putnam's,* the *Independent,* and *Harper's.* She also published volumes of her own poetry with national presses.[3] Yet, by 1991, only a handful of her volumes of poems could be located, and few people knew her name. As a part of the Schomburg series reprinting African American women's literature, and thanks to the work of David Deskins, Smith was brought back into print.

Smith was forthcoming about her race and how it affected the way people read her poems, and she discussed both her racial and her artistic identity. In "Answer to Verses Addressed to Me by Peter Clay,"[4] Smith describes her "dusky hue" and her "genius of the soul," not to be obscured by her skin color. Her poems move between the local (her grandmother's garden or her favorite foods) and the grand (celebrating majestic mountains). She writes national, historical poems (commemorating "colored soldiers" or the death of Frances Willard, the famous temperance activist) as well as personal ones (about the loss of a lover or the death of her brother). From living most of her life in eastern Kentucky and Tennessee, Smith often began her poems with the strength, joy, and comfort to be found from the mountains and rivers of Appalachia. Her poetry portrays physically active women, the dangers to women of bad marriages and alcohol addiction, strong and independent single girls, and a society in which race or gender does not preclude love of mountains and Appalachian cultures.

In 1909, Smith voiced sentiments about her native eastern Kentucky similar to the ones Dykeman would discuss forty-five years later in *The French Broad*. Smith rejoices in her poem "My Native Mountains":[5]

> I love my native mountains,
>> The dear old Cumberland,
> Rockribbed and everlasting,
>> How great they are, and grand!
> (16)

Striking a note of awe for the mountains surrounding her, Smith also signals the familiarity she has with the mountain range. The mountains are "dear" as well as "grand." Examining the importance of the physical mountains to life in Appalachia is a theme to which Smith returns frequently. In some poems, Appalachia's flora and fauna are comforting; for instance, they help mourners heal after the death of a loved one in "A Mountain Graveyard."[6] Smith points to the "dark boughs," which "with human hearts did share / Grief's long protest and despair" with mourners at graveside. Describing and defending her community's burial rituals, "A Mountain Graveyard" suggests that not all the mourners are humans.

If she had stopped with her feelings of awe and consolation, Smith could be mistaken for simply romanticizing nature. Instead, she presents a range of humans' interactions with the world around them. Even as the mountains provide comfort in times of mourning, they can also be physically challenging, even for local residents. Because "we had climbed a good long mile / of stony path," the narrator and her companions in the poem "Sunrise on the Cumberlands" find that "Tired were our feet and sore."[7] Although Smith uses the moment to make a religious metaphor, the poem also counters turn-of-the-century stereotypes that only tourists took time to or were mentally equipped to enjoy Appalachian scenery. In fact, Smith says, the mountains make life in eastern Kentucky substantially better than life in the cities, a fact she claims Appalachia's citizens know well. In poem after poem, she says as she does in "The Hills," "Far from the city's strife and care / . . . I breathe the sweet health-giving ai[r] / And drink the water pure."[8] Overall, for Smith, mountains inspire joy, unmitigated and unapologetic.

If Smith prefigures Dykeman in describing the nonhuman, geographical features of Appalachia, she also leads the way in redefining human community in Appalachia. Besides celebrating the "Rockribbed and everlasting" peaks, in "My Native Mountains" Smith continues:

But more than these old mountains
    Which with wonder I revere
I love with true devotion
    The people who live here.
(16–17)

For Smith, Appalachia's people combine with the nonhuman characteristics of the place to form a supportive community. Because she spent most of her life in Appalachia's African American communities, Smith's definition of "The people who live here" is more complex than in most of the literature about Appalachia written by her contemporaries. Throughout her body of work, Smith makes space for Appalachians of diverse races; she also insists that humans are interdependent with the places in which they live. With her poems, Smith questions how categories of identity—such as race, class, and gender—are entwined with places; in other words, how individuals or societies are inseparable from where they live.

Today's theoretical stance of feminist ecocriticism combines a focus on place—for Dykeman and Smith's texts, Appalachia—with an attention to the workings of social and cultural power in the place. Its methodology can be applied to any text; yet it is particularly interesting in terms of Dykeman's book and Smith's poetry. Using more traditional tools, it can be hard to know what to do with *The French Broad*. It cannot be called a historical text (because of its many fictionalized sections); it cannot be called a novel (because it sustains neither plot nor the goal of following characters over time); and it cannot even be called traditional nature writing (because it has many long sections that focus on humans). Similarly, Smith's poems are hard to analyze by using standard methods. What does one do with "Apple Sauce and Chicken Fried," light verse celebrating two common southern foods prepared "as mother used to"? Smith wrote short poems, rigorously rhymed, with strict rhythm about (superficially, I argue) straightforward subjects. However, bringing a feminist ecocritical lens to the texts pulls out the richness embedded in them. Dykeman's and Smith's contemporary critics recognized the texts' strengths by reviewing *The French Broad* widely and well and by comparing Smith to Paul Lawrence Dunbar, the most famous African American poet of her day. Revisiting their complexity and power can bring both the texts and the authors to more central positions in Appalachian literature.[9]

The project to unite literature and the environment gained focus in 1996 when Cheryll Glotfelty published the *Ecocriticism Reader,* the first text to systematically collect the field's founding essays. Glotfelty defines ecocriticism as theory with "one foot in literature and the other on land." In her introduction, she argues that the movement to preserve the earth's natural resources is the last major social change movement from the 1960s and 1970s to make its way into the theoretical toolbox of literary studies.[10] Ecocriticism now joins feminism from the women's liberation movement, African American studies from the black power and black arts movements, and queer studies from lesbian and gay liberation as theoretical perspectives through which to read texts. Much like those other movements, ecocriticism both analyzes known texts (such as Dykeman's) and looks to recover forgotten ones (such as Smith's).

However, much ecocriticism is weakened by its refusal to analyze and problematize differences in power and privilege between humans. That refusal builds into some ecocritics' work theoretical blind spots that can make it difficult to explain why unsustainable, damaging ways of thinking about the environment continue to take precedence. To address its blind spots, ecocriticism needs to be combined with feminist literary studies, and specifically it needs a complicated feminism, one that does more than look at women. The kind of feminism useful to ecocriticism avoids big statements about "all women" or "all men" and instead begins with the assumption that gender, race, class, and other categories of power and privilege are inseparable and must be analyzed together. Such a feminism foregrounds how race, class, and gender *intersect* in individuals and social systems.[11] Feminist ecocriticism's questions can be organized into two categories: how does an author talk about—in theoretical terms, "construct"—nature in his or her text? and, how does the author's discussion of race, class, and gender intersect with that construction of nature in the text? An exploration of how the construction of nature and the intersections of race, class, gender, and place bring out the complexities and strengths of Dykeman's and Smith's projects suggests the directions feminist ecocriticism can push the study of Appalachian literature.

CONSTRUCTING NATURE ON THE FRENCH BROAD RIVER

Dykeman departs from typical constructions of nature. Her contemporaries, and indeed many people today, imagine nature as something fundamentally "out there," as the environment separate from the viewer, something that exists to be viewed. This construction of the physical world is nature with a capital *N*. Much literature assumes that Nature is a vast, unpeopled land out there, waiting to be conquered, heretofore unseen by white (male) eyes. Not only can humans separate themselves from Nature, but it exists for the pleasure of certain groups of humans more than for others. Nature, in its traditional construction, is a dark, mysterious, unknown force that is so alien to humans (white, male, rich humans) as to be mortally dangerous. She—and it is remarkable how often Nature becomes gendered as female—is unexploitable because her resources seem never-ending. The effect of this traditional construction is to set up a binary relationship between man and Nature, in which the two are totally separate and opposed to each other.[12]

Of course, capital-*N* American Nature—vast, unpeopled, mysterious, dangerous—is just one of many possible constructions. It had such staying power because it supported the expansionist, colonialist agenda of a growing United States. Yet, even after the country's borders were set, the construction persisted in American literature. In part it was kept because it seemed to work so well—to explain Nature in some fundamental way—especially for the American West, out there, on which it was modeled. If a local environmental problem developed (the well dried up, the land stopped producing, the timber had all been taken), one did not have to change one's ideas about Nature. Rather, one could move on farther west and find new resources: the supply appeared inexhaustible. The original

Native American (and later Spanish) inhabitants were not all farmers or were few and far between, so one could imagine the land to be basically empty, ready to be filled by non-Hispanic European Americans, or, later, cordoned off as the "pristine" wilderness of national parks. The continent was large, it was difficult to map, and many visitors died because of the physical challenges it posed—the mystery and danger could seem ever-present and the construction of Nature seemed right.

Yet, Appalachian nature in particular has been difficult to fit into the typical construction of Nature. For more than a hundred years, Appalachian nature has been less than a day's rail ride from industrial centers of the eastern United States. Bounded by—and containing—cities, rivers, and development, it has always been peopled, not only with Native Americans, but for many years, European and African Americans as well. Further, most of Appalachia's residents lived in permanent homes, villages, or cities. As Dykeman says, "the French Broad is above all a live country" (25); it is fundamentally inhabited, not empty or unpeopled.

Departing from the binary that opposed man and Nature, Dykeman suggests that the very language available to construct Appalachian nature has been shaped by the people who lived here. She concludes her wish to speak for and with Appalachia's residents with the thought: "The Cherokees said, 'we have set our names upon your waters and you cannot wash them out'" (25). In other words, for Dykeman, Appalachian nature can only be talked of by using diverse language, recognizing diverse influences; it turns "Nature" into "nature"—something more complicated, existing not just for certain white people, but always already constituted by a range of human lives and languages. She continues, "They were right—the Nolichucky and the Swannanoa and the Estatoe—but they might also have said, for all of us, 'We have lived our lives along your rivers and you cannot wash the memory of us out'" (25). Individuals can find Appalachian nature mysterious and dark, but also comforting and familiar. It has been right-here, not out-there, in mainstream United States society. Appalachian nature can be dangerous yet safe, isolated and peopled. Dykeman makes space in her construction for all of these Appalachian natures; she explores various images in order to speak for and with nature's complexity.

Human interaction with Appalachian nature has not been free of costs. Appalachia has been mined, timbered, dammed, and polluted. In Appalachian nature, the massive chestnut trees all died, mines shut down when veins were exhausted, entire industries such as timbering closed up shop because the virgin stands were logged; resources can clearly be overtaxed, used up, and exploited. Dykeman explains how humans could be so callow by saying, "when we turned away from the spring at the edge of the kitchen yard and turned on the faucet in our porcelain sink, we turned off our interest in what came out of the spigot. One by one we allowed ourselves and others to begin the rape which finally (in places) ended in the murder of the French Broad" (25–26). *Rape* and *murder* are strong words, but since Dykeman has elevated the nonhuman world to equal footing with humans, she holds humans responsible for victimizing the place just as she would if they harmed other humans. Thus, she uses the same linguistic terms—rape and murder—to condemn destructive environmental actions.

Dykeman's own interest in questions about nature culminates in her chapter "Who Killed the French Broad?" Because she includes diverse humans, nonhumans, and long-term perspectives, Dykeman prefigures today's environmental justice movement, by indicting industry (in this case a paper plant) along the river for polluting the bioregion. Differing from mainstream environmentalism by its emphasis on race and class, environmental justice is generally characterized by diverse community participation, grassroots activism, and working-class voices. Although Dykeman does not explicitly discuss whether the poisoning of the river has been targeted to affect poor or nonwhite communities particularly, with her indictment she outlines the pollution's effect on the whole community. "Who Killed the French Broad?" turns Dykeman's text, despite its beginnings as a celebratory coffee-table book, into an explicitly political text, for which she encountered and resisted pressure to moderate its agenda.[13] She moves beyond pallid environmentalism that seeks only to preserve pretty vistas. Instead, Dykeman moves toward claiming that all community members should have the right to a safe environment regardless of race, class, or gender; with everyone included in the ecology, then, cleaning up the environment becomes a larger social justice issue.

Yet, since Dykeman has redefined community to include so many voices, some of the participants who weigh in on the environment in *The French Broad* are surprising. Dykeman herself might find it odd to be described as prefiguring the modern environmental justice movement, since she makes room for voices of industry and pro-business municipalities in her text. Nevertheless, as Dykeman argues, "industries and municipalities [must] accept their responsibilities to other industries and municipalities and to the region as a whole and embark on a program of each cleaning up its own waste" (288). Dykeman does not just argue that the environment should be cleaned for a single interest—whether that be tourists, industry, rich people, or old timers. She argues that it should be cleaned because it affects everyone and everything—and all residents have to live in the ecology. Therefore, her more complicated construction of nature supports and allows what is ultimately a more radical environmental solution.

RACE, CLASS, GENDER, AND NATURE IN THE APPALACHIAN CUMBERLANDS

Effie Waller Smith's poetry is as radical as *The French Broad,* but in a different direction. In her exploration of the intersections of race, class, gender, and nature, Smith provides not just a "black perspective" on Appalachia, nor simply an "Appalachian perspective"; rather, her poetry represents a black, female Appalachian viewpoint from the turn of the century. "Appalachian woman" brings to many people's minds a bundle of stereotypes—some positive (hard-working, strong, loyal), some negative (ignorant, always pregnant, old before her time), but almost always white, rural, and poor. Similarly, "Appalachia" brings visions of isolated mountain cabins. Yet both images deny the lived experiences of urban, sophisticated, educated, rich, Jewish, Native American, or black Appalachian women. Beyond asking different questions of texts by recognized Appalachian writers, feminist ecocriticism puts pressure on scholars to recover texts from largely forgotten writers who expand our senses of who Appalachians were and what their concerns were.

If "woman" or "Appalachian" does not mean the same to everyone, then the issues diverse women authors write about will not automatically overlap either. Smith's poem "On Receiving a Souvenir Post-Card"[14] from 1909, which begins, "On the little desk before me / A pictured post-card lies, /. . . It was sent from Kentucky, where / My childhood's home used to be" (45), could be mistaken for simple romanticizing of Appalachian nature. However, the poem's "rustic scene in black and white" is complicated by Smith's discussions of being African American at the turn of the century. In the first decade of 1900, lynch mob violence was rampant, as Smith's colleague Ida B. Wells was actively documenting (after Wells was forced to leave her home state of Tennessee by race rioting and threats). Smith had first-hand knowledge of the dangers faced by African American men and women, not only through her role as a schoolteacher, but also through the unsolved murder of her husband, a deputy sheriff.[15] The post-Reconstruction South was a difficult place for any African American. Nevertheless, Smith called for the freedom for African American women to feel about the mountains, "How sweet among their vales to roam, / And view their summits high; / Here may I ever have a home, / Here may I live and die!" ("The Hills," 49). "On Receiving a Souvenir Post-Card" illustrates how if race, class, gender, and nature truly intersect, then a poem seemingly discussing one (for example, nature) may simultaneously and profoundly be discussing others (in this case, race and gender).

Smith's poem "A Mountain Graveyard," about the mourning rituals of people and nature, also demonstrates the importance of analyzing the intersections in Smith's texts, as paying attention to intersections pulls out otherwise obscured layers of meaning. The poem describes a community's burial practices as not "tall marbles, gleaming white," but instead:

Rude, uncarven stones are seen,
Brought there from the mountain side
By the mourners' love and pride.
There, too, scattered o'er the grass
Of the graves, are bits of glass
That with white shells mingled lie.
(89)

The graveyard's location at the top of the mountain and the burial stones culled from the mountain signal that the community is an Appalachian one, imbedded in its place and drawing from it for resources. Other details mark the community as specifically African American Appalachian. Smith signals the intersection of race and place with a typical burial practice of turn-of-the-century black mourners, the scattering of glass and shells on a grave, in a location unmistakably, even stereotypically, Appalachian. The isolated, wind-swept graveyard, surrounded by mourning trees as well as people, argues that African American Appalachians must be included in any portrait of Appalachian societies—even the most common portrayals. In a final gesture, Smith implies that the rough stones and scattered glass are just as valid and important ways to mourn loved ones as tall and gleaming marbles are. In so doing, she moves beyond suggesting that African American Appalachian communities exist; she argues they are as cultured, valuable, and precious as any other community in the place. Although today her claim may not seem radical, at the turn of the century, against the backdrop of Jim Crow segregation, lynching, and scientific racism (the belief that science proved nonwhite people were closer to animals and less civilized than white people), Smith slipped a bold statement into her poem about graves on a mountainside.

Smith also regularly makes bold claims in her poetry about women, claims that are revealed when the intersections of race, class, gender, and nature are foregrounded. Smith pays particular attention to the experiences of women living in the mountains at the turn of the century; almost all of her poems have a female narrator, and many focus on topics specific to women's lives. "Apple Sauce and Chicken Fried" falls into the latter category of her poems, as it circles around a task many women face: providing good food for their families. The poem talks about class-based changes coming to the mountains, "cooking-schools and cook-books" for "farmers' girls," which make them look down on traditional, everyday foods. The narrator discusses her own occasional enjoyment of the new "dainty dishes" such as "Chicken a la Française, / And also fricassee" (129). However, unlike the farmers' girls, the narrator ultimately prefers the dishes her mother made so well, the applesauce and fried chicken. Unfortunately, she finds she cannot make them as well as her now absent mother did. The poem's note of sadness concerns this loss of knowledge between mothers and daughters; it has the effect of celebrating women's local knowledge and work in the mountains. By creating a narrative "I" who lives in Appalachia, cooks in the most modern style, and yet is sophisticated enough to develop her own aesthetic taste (to claim what she really likes even though it goes against the prevailing fashion), Smith expands the roles available to black women in Appalachia. In this one poem, women can be young, old, educated, fashionable, iconoclastic, or traditional, and all of it happens within Appalachia's black communities.

In other poems, Smith includes challenges women face. "Only a Drunkard,"[16] ostensibly about a man who is addicted to alcohol, becomes a poem about the effect of his choice on "a mother, a sister or wife." Smith does not turn away from the domestic violence that can accompany alcoholism, saying:

There once were days when those hands, those arms,
    (But those days are gone, are dead)

Caressed the delicate form of her,—
   Now they give her blows instead.
(103)

Because of the structure of marriage at the time, which gave women few options once the contract was signed, the "Only" in Smith's title becomes deeply ironic, as the poem discusses how many women's lives are affected by the actions of one man.

But Smith does not stop with realistic portrayals of the challenges that women faced at the turn of the century. In other poems, she counters restrictions on women's mobility and emphasizes their intellectual capacities. In "The Hills," celebrating "rugged, rocky peaks" (48), it is the female narrator who climbs them. Similarly, in "Sunrise on the Cumberlands," women are among the expeditionary party that has walked for many a "good long mile" to reach the peaks of Chimney Rocks. Once there, women lead the group's intellectual and spiritual conversation about the effect of Appalachian mountains on the human mind and soul (18–20). Smith's contemplative yet physically active women challenge prevailing ideas about all women's capabilities at the turn of the century. She goes even further to challenge racist notions about African American women in particular.

The combination of the challenges facing women and their innate capabilities is a considered argument about the need for and potential of what Smith names "Woman's Rights" in her poem "The 'Bachelor Girl.'" Within the poem's stanzas, Smith celebrates the independence and physical mobility women can claim for themselves. Because elsewhere in her poetry her narrator and characters are Appalachian and African American, Smith's feminism should be read through those categories as well; it is at the intersections that Smith's black Appalachian feminism resides. "The 'Bachelor Girl,'" a funny, pointed, and astute poem, reads in part, "She's no 'old maid,' she's not afraid / To let you know she's her own 'boss'" and "She talks and writes of 'Woman's Rights' / In language forceful and clean"; it ends, "And come what may, she's here to stay, / The self-supporting 'bachelor girl.'"[17] Once again, the questions emerge from the intersections, as feminist thinkers at the turn of the past century did not exist in vacuums—the cross-pollination of ideas from people of different races, places, classes, sexual orientations, ages, and abilities means that a poem like Smith's should be read for its intersections of feminism, nature, messages about class and race, poetics, and the position it occupies in the early twentieth century's social hierarchies.

Paying close attention to constructions of nature and to the intersections of categories of power in Dykeman and Smith can expand and may demand new definitions of literature. Unlike Dykeman's *The Tall Woman* or *The Far Family,* which in form at least are traditional novels, *The French Broad* is a cross-genre, multivocal, experimental way of writing. As if speaking to the book's role in a naturalist series on American rivers, Dykeman says, "You cannot know this river by simply sitting on the level banks of its lower body or by striking out on any straight road up its course; you must judge the 'lay of the land' and follow a wandering path that will take 'rounders' on its sources high in the mountains." She continues, "Likewise to know its people you cannot adopt quick attitudes or secondhand generalities, a frontal approach forespells failure in any friendship; you must take 'rounders' here, too, and find your way by easy conversation into their sources of character and life" (330). Dykeman's own "rounders" into alternate constructions of nature result in a particular Appalachian writing style that both challenges and validates Appalachian community members.

Smith titled her second collection of poems *Rhymes from the Cumberlands.* Certainly, her narrator in the poems follows through with the promise of speaking from mountain communities. Yet, in her dedication, Smith suggests that the poems circle around in ways similar to Dykeman's "rounders": Smith's poems become rhymes *for* the Cumberlands as well. Cumberland readers are among her target audience, despite the national publication of the book. Smith says the book is for "You" who "live among the mountains— / The dear old Cumberlands."[18] The poems stand, then, at a further intersection of race, class, gender, and nature because they assert a poetry-loving audience among people who love the mountains as well.

Dykeman ended her book by paraphrasing Robert Frost: "I'm going out to clean the spring and wait for it to flow clear again. . . . Won't you come too?" She continues, "I'm going out to hear the slow talk of some stranger becoming friend as I listen to his life; to see the wide sweep of the river's silent power around a certain bend beneath the sycamores. I'm going out to smell fresh rain on summer dust and the prehistoric water odors of the old French Broad in flood. Won't you come too?" (346). The way ecological challenges affect race, class, and gender dynamics, which Dykeman and Smith carefully outlined, becomes an additional intersection over which a theory combining constructions of nature with gender and other systems of power and oppression must struggle. In one of her final poems, "Autumn Winds," Smith wrote of her own desire to be like Appalachia's "giant trees" and "stand forth free to struggle and endure!"[19] She surely would have been saddened to see those trees logged, the lands they stood on strip-mined, or the very mountains removed to get at the last of the coal underneath. The complexities about which Dykeman and Smith wrote, the complexities that writers about Appalachia have been addressing for more than a hundred years, expose the tensions and fault lines we as readers face today in Appalachia and in the nation—as the intersections of race, class, gender, and place continue to challenge and locate us as societies and individuals.

Feminist ecocriticism's theoretical tools can be applied to any text and indeed should be. At its heart, though, Appalachian literature is defined by the mountains, rivers, and trees rising up through it and by the diversity of people who have fallen in love with those mountains. I want to see us build a theory of literary criticism that acknowledges and values those people and places, that "quicken[s] understanding" and finds that "unmerited but longed-for magic" of which Dykeman spoke so eloquently (*French Broad*, 25), so that each of us can find what Smith called our "nature-loving soul."[20]

Notes

1. Wilma Dykeman, *The French Broad*, Rivers of America series (New York: Rinehart, 1955); for biographical information on Dykeman see Patricia M. Gantt, "'A Mutual Journey': Wilma Dykeman and Appalachian Regionalism," in *Breaking Boundaries: New Perspectives on Women's Regional Writing*, ed. Sherrie A. Inness and Diana Royer (Iowa City: University of Iowa Press, 1997), 197–215; also see Oliver King Jones III, "Social Criticism in the Works of Wilma Dykeman," in this volume. On Dykeman's support for and identification with the region, see Danny L. Miller, *Wingless Flights: Appalachian Women in Fiction* (Bowling Green, Ohio: Bowling Green State University Press, 1996).

2. Dykeman, *French Broad*, 25; for a discussion of bioregions, see Gary Snyder, "Bioregional Perspectives," in *The Practice of the Wild* (New York: North Point Press, 1990), 37–44.

3. For biographical information on Smith, see David Deskins, introduction to *The Collected Works of Effie Waller Smith* [hereafter, *CW*], Schomburg Library of Nineteenth-Century Black Women Writers (New York: Oxford, 1991), 3–26.

4. Smith, "Answer to Verses Addressed to Me by Peter Clay," *Songs of the Months* (1904; reprinted in *CW*), 167–68.

5. Smith, "My Native Mountains," *Rhymes from the Cumberland* (1909; reprinted in *CW*), 16–17.

6. Smith, "A Mountain Graveyard," *Rosemary and Pansies* (1909; reprinted in *CW*), 88–89.

7. Smith, "Sunrise on the Cumberlands," *Rhymes from the Cumberland* (1909; reprinted in *CW*), 18–19.

8. Smith, "The Hills," *Songs of the Months* (1904; reprinted in *CW*), 48–49.

9. Smith, "Apple Sauce and Chicken Fried," *Songs of the Months* (1904; reprinted in *CW*), 129–30. On critics' reviews of the works, see Gantt, "Mutual," 213, and Mary Elliott Flanery, introduction to *Songs of the Months* (1904; reprinted in *CW*), xvi.

10. Cheryll Glotfelty, "Introduction: Literary Studies in an Age of Environmental Crisis," in *Ecocriticism Reader: Landmarks in Literary Ecology,* ed. Cheryll Glotfelty and Harold Fromm (Athens: University of Georgia Press, 1996), xv–xxxvii.

11. Other scholars working to bring feminism and ecocriticism together include Greta Gaard, Patrick D. Murphy, and Glynis Carr; see Gaard and Murphy's collection *Ecofeminist Literary Criticism: Theory, Interpretation, Pedagogy* (Urbana: University of Illinois Press, 1998) and Carr's special issue of the *Bucknell Review: New Essays in Ecofeminist Literary Criticism* (Lewisburg: Bucknell University Press, 2000).

12. For discussions on gendering, colonizing, and inserting race into constructions of nature, see Mary Louise Pratt, *Imperial Eyes: Travel Writing and Transculturation* (London: Routledge, 1992); Annette Kolodny, *The Lay of the Land: Metaphor as Experience and History in American Life and Letters* (Chapel Hill: University of North Carolina Press, 1975); and Carolyn Merchant, *The Death of Nature: Women, Ecology and the Scientific Revolution* (San Francisco: Harper and Row, 1980).

13. Gantt, "Mutual," 211.

14. Effie Waller Smith, "On Receiving a Souvenir Post-Card," *Rhymes from the Cumberland* (1909; reprinted in *CW*), 45.

15. On Smith's husband's death, see Deskins, introduction to *CW,* 8. For information on Wells, see Linda O. McMurry, *To Keep the Waters Troubled: The Life of Ida B. Wells* (New York: Oxford University Press, 1998). For Wells's own writing, see Ida B. Wells-Barnett, "Lynch Law in America," in *Words of Fire: An Anthology of African-American Feminist Thought,* ed. Beverly Guy-Sheftall (New York: New Press, 1995), 74.

16. Smith, "Only a Drunkard," *Songs of the Months* (1904; reprinted in *CW*), 101–3.

17. Smith, "The 'Bachelor Girl,'" *Rhymes from the Cumberland* (1909; reprinted in *CW*), 49–51.

18. Smith, "Dedication," *Rhymes from the Cumberland* (1909; reprinted in *CW*), n.p.

19. Smith, "Autumn Winds" (1917; reprinted in *CW*), 104.

20. Smith, "A Meadow Brook," *Rhymes from the Cumberland* (1909; reprinted in *CW*), 32.

The Wolves of Ægypt

John Crowley's Appalachians

RODGER CUNNINGHAM

One of the most significant writers of fiction about Appalachia today is seldom if ever mentioned by Appalachian literary critics, while his Appalachian connection is almost never mentioned by his own commentators. John Crowley's meditative postmodern novels are hard to classify as to genre. His first two, *The Deep* (1975) and *Beasts* (1976), are pretty strictly in the science-fiction and fantasy vein, but later the relation between reality and fantasy in his novels becomes more complex and rewarding. His next, *Engine Summer* (1979), is set in the future after the collapse of civilization as we think we know it. His fourth, *Little, Big* (1981), often called his masterpiece, is set in New York City and upstate in the nineteenth and twentieth centuries. In it a realistic story is set within a framework of the fairy mythology. It is, in James Hynes's words, "a long, gorgeously written, picaresque family saga, in the last fifty pages of which all the major characters, with one heartbreaking exception, turn into fairies" (Hynes, para. 1). With *Little, Big,* Crowley establishes himself as a master of a distinctly North American kind of postmodern magical realism (cf. Attebery, 44–48).[1]

Crowley continues his work in this vein in his next three novels, which form the first three volumes of a projected quartet: *Ægypt* (1987), *Love & Sleep* (1994), and *Dæmonomania* (2000).[2] In this *Ægypt* quartet, as it is generally called, a modern realistic story is intertwined, via a dead novelist's manuscript, with a magical plot based on the adventures of the Elizabethan magus John Dee and his still stranger and more brilliant contemporary,

Giordano Bruno. Each volume is divided into three sections named after one of the astrological houses (not signs) in order from first to, so far, ninth. The *Ægypt* quartet is a vast, multi-plotted story which will not lend itself to a complete synopsis or character rundown in an essay of this scope. What I intend to explore, at any rate, is only a single thread in the quartet—that neglected but important thread of Crowley's thematic treatment of Southern Appalachia. This is full of troubling aspects, but it still offers a fascinating and neglected metaphoric take on the region's place in the American *imaginaire* and the human imagination. Crowley's picture of the Appalachian region contains many disturbing stereotypical elements, but it is Crowley's approach to symbolic and imaginative realities that lifts this depiction out of stereotype and that points to important and seldom-stated truths about Appalachia, America, and the contemporary world.

The *Ægypt* quartet's protagonist is Pierce Moffett, once a New York history professor, now (in the late seventies) dropped out of the hopeless job race and settled in Blackbury Jambs, a little town in the Faraway Hills somewhere northwest of the city. There, through studying the papers of the late novelist Fellowes Kraft, Pierce comes to believe that the cycles of history are punctuated by moments at which the laws of cause and effect really change, and the past along with them. In the Middle Ages, magic really worked; now it doesn't, and not only that, *now it never did.* In medieval times, Pierce thinks, the Hermetic philosophy—the belief that imaginative correspondences among things are real and cause physical effects, making magic and alchemy possible—was actually true. This Hermetic philosophy originated two thousand years ago in Egypt, and Pierce comes to use the obsolete spelling "Ægypt" to denote in his mind the whole magical universe that he thinks once existed. Once, he decides, the Hermetic philosophy, derived from Ægypt, was true; now it never was, and "Ægypt" is only a shimmering mirage of the "real" Egypt, a tattered tissue of obsolete European misconceptions about that country. Only the odd manuscript or artifact survives the change to clue us to the fact that at one time things were different. Once alchemists could turn lead to gold; once Ægypt had been real.[3]

The last great change took place in the Renaissance, at just the time that John Dee and Giordano Bruno were cutting their strange swaths through Europe. Dee, an English mathematician and astrologer, grew obsessed with the ambition to understand the key to all knowledge, and he came to believe that only angels, contacted through mediums, could impart it to him. In the 1580s, searching for channelers of angel messages, Dee fell under the sway of a sociopathic graduate student, Edward Kelley, who led Dee and his crystal ball on a bizarre adventure with a series of royal patrons in Cracow, Prague, and elsewhere. During the same decade, the Italian monk Giordano Bruno was wandering Europe too, proclaiming his daring theories about the infinity of the starry universe, the consequent infinity of the human soul that could comprehend such a universe, and the superiority of "Ægyptian" wisdom to Christianity. Eventually Bruno was burned at the stake for heresy, and nine years later, Dee died in poverty and obscurity. But their ideas are still fascinating. Both the men and the ideas are complex mixtures of the old and the new, medieval and modern: excellent vehicles, therefore, for Crowley's themes.[4] Pierce holds that the last change in the world took place in Dee's and Bruno's time, and another such change, he begins to think, is on the point of occurring now. Once more the past will change; this time it is our own modern world that will never have been, and that will survive only as Ægypt survives next to Egypt, "like [it] but different from it, underlying it or sort of superimposed on it" (Æ, 183).

This notion is a powerful symbol of the shifts in our ways of thinking and feeling that follow upon shifts in society and economics; the changes in our experience-world and therefore in our memory-worlds. As for magic itself, Crowley has used it in many of his books to image forth humanity's natural but mysterious powers. "Magical beliefs," as the anthropologist Michael Taussig says, "are revelatory and fascinating not because they are ill-conceived instruments of utility but because they are poetic echoes of the cadences that guide the innermost course of the world. Magic takes language, symbols, and intelligibility to their outermost limits, to explore life and thereby to change its destination" (Devil, 15). The use of magic as a device in so much contemporary literature is part of its exploration of how language constitutes the human world, while itself being constituted by the cadences of our own innermost, and hence most objective, realities.

In an interview about Love & Sleep, Crowley says:

The basic idea of the book, besides the idea of time passing through a gateway, is the Gnostic mythology that we are really the gods, that human beings are final, and that the gods who come between us and the unknown, fore-existing God are really lesser than us and not our

masters, although we have let them become our masters. The gods
create the world by language, by imposing rules on us; we discreate the
world by language in the same way and create our own in its stead.
(Qtd. in Gehr, para. 10)

It all sounds very esoteric, but these Gnostic views are back with us today,
having resurfaced in the secularized form of existentialism (cf. Jonas,
320–40), with its emphasis on human responsibility in an indifferent universe. Crowley has simply re-clothed these ideas in some of their cast-off
mythology—a mythology now to be "believed" on the artistic level—and
combined that mythology with the postmodern emphasis on language to
create a powerful literary mixture.

As part of Crowley's project to re-cast old insights in new forms, there is
a great deal of Rosicrucian imagery in the *Ægypt* quartet. The Rosicrucian
manifestos, which show the influence of John Dee's thought, were published in the early 1600s just after the English philologist Isaac Casaubon
proved the supposedly primordial Hermetic treatises to be Christian-era
confections. Casaubon's discovery was a key event in the transition to modern thought. Reacting to this, the Rosicrucians' project was to keep
"Ægypt" alive on a new basis—to cut off its dependence on a literal historical transmission of hidden knowledge, now disproved, by basing that
magical and mystical teaching in a new kind of revelation and initiation.
Crowley, then, joins those who continue "Ægypt" into the modern era by
re-backing it again on the canvas of poetic metaphor, befitting a modern
age in which *literal* magic can only be a kind of bad poetry. And he brings
this idea further forward into the postmodern era—the new world-shift
he's writing about—by foregrounding metaphor itself, the metaphor-
making process, and the historical changes in that process.

What of Appalachia, then? When Crowley's protagonist, Pierce Moffett, was a young boy in New York City, his mother abruptly left his father
without telling Pierce why (years later he'd learn that his father had been
having an affair with another man) and moved in with her brother, a doctor at a Catholic mission hospital in Eastern Kentucky. Of course Pierce is
traumatized by being inexplicably snatched away and set down in this
utterly strange environment, and being a bookish, indoors boy and a
Catholic doesn't help his social integration any. But one of Pierce's most
important memories of this period is of the time when he and his cousins
took in a runaway local girl, Bobby Shaftoe, and hid her from the adults for

a period until she had to be given back to her grandfather, Floyd.[5] These matters are alluded to only occasionally in *Ægypt;* they first receive full treatment in *Love & Sleep,* as Crowley begins to work them into the magical contexts in which they appear in *Dæmonomania.*

As I have said, these parts of the quartet are both interesting and disturbing. While reading *Love & Sleep,* I kept thinking, "This reads exactly as if Crowley really did have some sort of close encounter he didn't understand with East Kentuckians and then went to Harry Caudill, God help us, for an explanation." The mark of Caudill was unmistakable. There was the same gritty, sour-smelling sharpness of detail illuminated by the same perpetually gray, bleak light; the same closeness of observation filtered through the same template of class division. And yet, coming to the note at the end of the volume, I was still surprised to find that I'd been exactly right. Crowley really did spend part of his youth in Eastern Kentucky (cf. Gehr, para. 9), and he thanks Caudill "for reminding me of much I had forgotten and explaining much that I had not understood" (*L&S,* 503).

If author Crowley's experiences were anything like his character Pierce's, it's no wonder that Caudill's picture of the region would resonate with his. But this also means, of course, that Caudill has only reinforced some of Crowley's most naïve youthful impressions. With Bobby Shaftoe we are immediately in the well-known stereotypical realm of opposite-sex Others like John Fox Jr.'s June Tolliver and her many later clones. And the stereotyping goes on from there, all the way into Crowley's further elaboration of his Appalachian theme, in the final chapters of *Love & Sleep* and on into *Dæmonomania.* Here he melds together his sixteenth-century magical plot and his twentieth-century realistic plot with the revelation that Floyd Shaftoe is one of a secret race of werewolves originating in the Eastern Europe of Dee and Bruno's adventures. Crowley's risky game with the all-too-familiar sign-system of wild-versus-tame, savage-versus-civilized, Appalachia-versus-America hardly needs pointing out.

And yet this is not all there is to be said about the matter; far from it. Crowley's game is a risky one, but not, I think, one doomed to failure. His use of the wolf motif will remind one apprehensively of another writer from elsewhere, shocked by Eastern Kentucky and turning to Harry Caudill for explanations: Robert Schenkkan. Just to mention the comparison, though, is to call up the contrasts. The *Ægypt* quartet is not *The Kentucky Cycle Meets the X-Files.* Crowley is a vastly better writer than Schenkkan, both stylistically and (more importantly) in his understanding of metaphor and symbol. His writing rises far above the dead level of signs that stand for thoughts, into the world of symbols that give rise to thought (cf. Ricoeur); beyond two-dimensional stereotypes into those three-dimensional structures of the human mind that, for lack of a better word, we can still call archetypes. In *Love & Sleep,* Pierce thinks:

> From age to age we pass on stories, which do not seem to be inside us; we seem instead to be inside them, taking place. What if (Pierce began to wonder) they turned out to be not primitive guesses about how things came to be, or ramparts shored up against darkness and fear, or lessons in life; what if they were true allegories (though you may not ever crack the code) about what the world is made of, why things are as they are and not some different way instead, which arise just because we are made by the same laws that made the universe? (151)

The same laws that made the universe, the cadences that guide the innermost course of the world. Magic is the power of language to constitute our world. And Crowley's technique bears many resemblances to Latin American magical realism, where, as Luis Leal says, "the main point is not the creation of imagined beings or worlds, but rather the uncovering of the mysterious relationship between man and his situation" (qtd. in Díaz 103n3; my trans.). By rising to the level of archetype, Crowley raises his treatment of Appalachia—at least in part—to something that has the same relationship to stereotype that a physical *fact* has to stereotype. That is, he invites us not to stop with his own treatment of the archetype—as if it were a flat picture whose eyes always face the viewer—but to deal with it as his own partial take on that mental fact, his own angle on a three-dimensional reality, and to go beyond that snapshot to walk around and explore the archetype from our own angles, in our own terms. So then, let us do so.

Crowley's version of the werewolf myth is based closely on the researches of the Italian historian Carlo Ginzburg. In *The Night Battles,* Ginzburg analyzed the records of the Inquisition to uncover the existence of a sixteenth-century agrarian cult, the *benandanti* or "good walkers." Four times a year, on the Rogation or Ember Days, the *benandanti,* men born with a caul, left their bodies in a trance state, often in the spiritual form of animals, and went to the world of the dead to battle the evil witches and sorcerers, in order to recover the fruits of the harvest that the latter had stolen or were about to. Under the pressure of the Inquisition and its forced confessions, these beast-shaped fighters for God were gradually assimilated to the devilish witches themselves, even in their own minds, before disappearing from records in the following century. This all took place in the Friuli, the northeast corner of Italy, on the borders of the Germanic and Slavic worlds, and Ginzburg connected the *benandanti* with similar phenomena in several parts of Central and Eastern Europe. In his later book, *Ecstasies,* he explored the roots of such phenomena further into Celtic and Central Asian religious currents, especially shamanism.

Crowley, then, works all this into his fiction by having John Dee, during his Prague years, meet Jan, a young werewolf, his ankle broken in a trap. Dee saves Jan from being killed by the Holy Roman Emperor and advises him to go to "Atlantis," as Dee believed America to be. Jan never does so, but his descendants do, taking the arts of mining with them. They settle up and down the Appalachian Mountains, where those born with the caul continue to go out in their wolf-shape to battle the Devil's hosts for the fruits of human labor.[6]

This is certainly a bold mythicization of history, and the very project may well put off many readers. On the other hand, perhaps it is precisely Crowley's use of myth *as historically recorded* that gives this aspect of the *Ægypt* quartet an opening to history. As the Mexican novelist and essayist Octavio Paz noted of the cult of the Virgin in Mexico, spiritual archetypes respond to concrete historical situations as much as material facts do (qtd. in Díaz, 96). What Crowley is working with is a mythic version of peasant resistance—a version not transformed into myth by literary elites, but rather developed by the peasants themselves, and always viewed with hostility by their "betters." It is a myth of shamans acting collectively for the material benefit of their people, and this motive has always been the key feature distinguishing true shamans from would-be ones, whether the latter are tribal eccentrics, modern surrealists, or postmodern deconstructionists.

What, then, of the myth Crowley uses? In the *Ægypt* quartet, the werewolves fight the Devil's agents in the land of the dead. Taking in turn each of these elements—lycanthropy, sorcery, and underworld—we shall see what Crowley makes of it, what Crowley makes of Appalachia with it, and what Appalachians can make of it and of Crowley.

Crowley's use of wolf imagery in connection with Appalachian people has its roots in Pierce's childhood memories. Again, these are expressed in a language close to stereotype, if not indeed residing firmly in it. When memories of Bobby Shaftoe start coming back to Pierce as an adult, he thinks that "he and his cousins had taken in a she-wolf cub, and kept it hidden in their rooms, and tried to tame it" (L&S, 5). Later, when he remembers Bobby more clearly, he recalls how the children

> look at her small feral teeth and the broken nails of her hands, the dull glow of her eyeballs moving in her head from one to another of them, the pulsebeat in her hollow temple. Her body isn't as theirs are. They smell her, not only her musty coat but some other odor that's hers alone, that makes their nostrils open and their heads bend toward her to learn more. (D, 357)

In all Pierce's memories of this episode, Bobby is frequently described in the imagery of a wild animal, a dog or wolf. She, with her whole culture, appears to the boy Pierce to be outside civilization and therefore almost outside humanity.

This is where it begins with Pierce, and where it probably began with his creator Crowley. What is important is that it doesn't stay where it began; it goes in a very interesting direction. And it is precisely by being consciously mythical that Crowley rises out of stereotype. Already in the quoted passage, the animal-human opposition is subverted: the "civilized" children are responding to Bobby like animals, like a litter of yard pups in the presence of a wolf cub. Bobby is an animal only as all children, indeed all humans, are animals. And this is a late passage; by the time we have read it, we have already gotten to know not only the adult Bobby, a nurse's aide living close to Pierce in the Northeast (unbeknownst to both of them), but also Floyd himself. And when Crowley gets inside the heads of adult mountain people, the animal characteristics disappear—even from Floyd, the werewolf.

For indeed, the legendary complex of the werewolf has nothing to do with that of the wild man. As Ginzburg points out, medieval references to werewolves depict them as innocent victims or beneficent figures; only at the dawn of the modern era do they come to be negatively stereotyped as ferocious monsters (Ecstasies, 154). Crowley follows the older tradition (cf. D, 180). In his account, the werewolves are descended from a wolf that felt remorse at killing a lamb, and was rewarded by being turned into a man by the Christ Child: "summoned . . . to do battle in the name of the Lamb, . . .

to suffer the hatred of all men, and be known as just only to Him" (*L&S*, 471). Jan's wounded foot will recall to us the enmity of Adam to the serpent (Gen. 3:15): thus the werewolf is marked as the paradoxical representative of general humanity, called by the Son of Man, Blake's "Universal Humanity," to combat the enemies of the human. Werewolves are (to recall another strange Appalachian book) the dogs of God (Eliade, 77). Their initiation is at once martial, shamanic, and divine (cf. Eliade, 71–72). They wear their fur on the inside, and their animal form is non-material: their real nature is their animal nature, but it is identical with their spiritual nature—always, as Jim Wayne Miller said, out of sight.[7]

The werewolves fight for God against the witches. They do so to recover the fruits of the earth which the witches have stolen to sell to their master the Devil. The metaphorical resonances of this are plain enough, and Crowley makes them explicit.

Crowley's witches take "the health and wealth of the earth" (*L&S*, 103) to the devil to receive their pay for it. Jan wonders: How are they paid? "Don't they too have to live on the earth with us, don't they too suffer when the earth is robbed?" An old werewolf explains it to him:

God forgive them . . . : they are that hungry, that everlastingly hungry, and nothing they can see or touch or taste can satisfy them; they must be always imagining some better food, some greater pleasure, sharper sauce, sweeter fruit than any know, and that's just what they're promised, though they never get it, never, for the Devil doesn't have it to give: he has only his promises. (*L&S*, 470)

Jan's descendant Floyd Shaftoe, Bobby's grandfather, asks the same question: "Why they should want to harm the world he didn't know . . . ; why they did harm that could bring no good to them, why they took the corn laid by in the earth to grow, took the starting farrow from the sow's belly, carried them off under the earth, though it meant no one could have them" (*L&S*, 111–12). But he immediately draws the analogy: "Like the great devil Hoover, who had brought ruin on the country, only to be turned out in disgrace himself: you wondered why" (112). The demonic force here is that of industrial capitalism, which fosters bottomless, insatiable desire as the engine of consumption; the force of what Crowley's late friend (murdered by Stalinists), the scholar of magic Ioan Couliano, called the "sorcerer-state" (*Eros,* 105), with its "impersonal systems of mass media, indirect censorship, global manipulation, and the brain trusts that exercise their occult control over the Western masses" (90). Michael Taussig, anthropologist and student of Latin American devil-beliefs, speaks too of "the sorcery-bundle of mythical representations on which Western culture is based" (*Shamanism*, 201), a culture in which "Adam Smith's invisible hand [is] the modern version of animism" (129). And he finds this metaphor to be more alive and conscious among the people in resource-extraction regions that are "not market organized but market dominated" (*Devil*, 10)—regions, that is, "where the rapid making of a wage-working class exposes and draws out the magic implicit in the commodity fetishism of capitalist culture and its organization of persons as things through the market mechanism" (*Shamanism*, 283); regions, of course, like Central Appalachia for the past century or so. Thus Appalachia is a natural place for the worst side of industrialism, and the resistance to it, to be shown forth imaginatively in witchcraft and the resistance to it. And this is what Crowley has done.

Floyd Shaftoe receives his first call to be a werewolf on the same day he goes to work for the coal company (*L&S*, 104). "Black gold" coal is called, and Crowley explains this phrase as meaning "earth transformed to worth by time" (*D*, 310), a phrase recalling the beliefs and goals of alchemy. Just before this passage in *Dæmonomania*, Crowley says that the gold that John Dee manufactures alchemically with Edward Kelley turns after a while to stinking slime (*D*, 308–9); like the black gold that is worth no more than slime for the places that produce it, the transformed earth whose production leaves seas of stinking slime behind. The modern industrial system, capitalist and socialist alike, claims to raise everything to perfected matter and only reduces it to undifferentiated matter; as it claims to raise human beings to a higher level of consciousness and only lowers them to material calculation, reduces them to things to be sold.[8] "What's yours is mine," says a witch to Floyd (*L&S*, 111); and one thinks of the coal companies' habit of referring to their extractive activities as "recovery," as if they, or we, had lost the mineral and were only getting it back. According to widespread folk theory, magic that is used to recover lost or stolen goods is innocent, but a treasure trove can be found only with demonic help.[9] The real recovery work, though, is that of God's dogs, who have to leave their bodies in order to recover their true form.[10]

The werewolves, the witches; and thirdly and finally, then, we have the Underworld. The werewolves fight the witches in the land of the dead, near the mouth of Hell. Once more Crowley's description of Appalachia in these terms—"ragged hills and coalsmoke and spoliation" (*D*, 351)—is derived from a combination of unhappy memory and the depressive vision of Harry Caudill. But once more, something else goes on behind that, and goes beyond that. As Ægypt to Egypt, so is Crowley's Appalachia to the real one, "like [it] but different from it, underlying it or sort of superimposed on it." To be exact, there is a *stereotype* superimposed and an *archetype* that lies behind and goes beyond. The world which Crowley's werewolves traverse under the moon, the land inhabited by all the dead that have died unjustly (*L&S*, 109, 112–13), is the under-weave of Caudill's dark vision. The land where only the *unjustly* dead are visible is a land where injustice appears on the surface, manifests its trace of the life that should have been. And this land is indeed, in some sense, closer to the surface in Appalachia. Eastern Kentucky is one of those places where the negative effects of the industrial system are more apparent than elsewhere—on the surface of the soil, and on the surface of the soul. It is therefore one of what Crowley calls "those lands that are not under the earth's skin but are nevertheless deep down" (*D*, 311)—the underside or Otherside of earth in general, of our human experience of being-in-the-world, and of our experience of modern life in particular. Some may object that Crowley's image of the malign force acting on Appalachia is abstracted from the economic relations it represents; but after it is made abstract in this way, it is *made concrete again* in a poetic metaphor that illuminates the nature of those relations.

And Appalachia includes not only Eastern Kentucky but Pierce's Faraway Hills near New York. They are part of the same range, a fact made explicit in descriptions of Pierce's and Bobby's travels between the two places. When Pierce nearly, but not quite, recovers his memory that he had lost his virginity with Bobby, during the week she had hidden with him (*L&S*, 304), this failed recovery images forth the secret repressed connection between Appalachia and America, and, more generally, all denials of connection with the Other. "Most secret of all," Pierce thinks, "is what's forgotten" (*D*, 30). If Appalachia—a regional culture founded deliberately in order to act out the repressed desires of American elites (cf. Cunningham, "View," 310–11n34)—if Appalachia, then, is America's Shadow in Crowley as it is in the American psyche in general, then at least in Crowley it is not a totally denied and rejected Shadow, but one whose acknowledgment—not as Other but as self—can help return to America, and to humanity, what has been stolen from it.

And something like this may be what Crowley has in the offing. Some readers have wondered where his plot could go now that he has killed Dee and Bruno off, but the fact seems to be that he is merging his sixteenth-century magical themes into his twentieth-century story precisely via his Appalachian subplot, which has been growing and growing. In *Dæmono-mania* a totally new element is introduced. First by allusion and then in scenes, it is revealed that in the highest and remotest recesses of the Eastern Kentucky mountains there exists a Gnostic sect resembling the medieval Cathars and Albigensians. Bobby has heard of them (*D,* 212), and then it emerges that Pierce's friend, the New Age thinker Beau Brachman ("Beautiful Brahmin"?), spent a year among them during his continent-wide pilgrimage of the sixties and even witnessed the ritual self-starvation of one of their spiritual leaders, Plato Goodenough (*D,* 372–73). For *Dæ-monomania* Crowley acknowledges the influence of another Appalachian book besides *Night Comes to the Chromosomes,* and of all things it's Deborah McCauley's *Appalachian Mountain Religion* (*D,* 453). He seems to have been impressed with McCauley's impassioned and erudite defense of the most traditional mountain churches against the strictures of "mainstream" Christianity (cf. especially Bobby's recollections of the former, *D,* 269), and McCauley's book seems to have inspired him to project a critique of mainstream Christianity in his own, quite different direction.

"Project" is of course the operative word here. Once more there is the element of stereotype, but this time it's positive stereotype. Appalachia has been seen again and again as some pure heart of America, some hidden innermost place in which the uncorrupted truth has been preserved—for America's sake, not for Appalachia's. On this level, the best that can be said for Crowley's contribution to this annoying tradition is that, as undisguised fabulation, it's not apt to be as damaging as many supposedly realistic fantasies have been. After all, no one is likely (one hopes) to go up into the hollers looking for real American Cathars.[11]

But again, on another level, Crowley's undisguised projection of an ideal may encourage us to consider it *as* an ideal in itself. On the one hand, Gnosticism shares with its secularized revival, existentialism, the quality of being a somewhat self-defeating response to alienation. As a general matter, the absolute opposition that both Gnostics and existentialists typically draw between humanity and the rest of the universe—the image of humanity being "thrown into" nature occurs in both—only reproduces the fundamental flaw at the bottom of modern attitudes. More specifically, real mountain religious attitudes toward Creation, which form an important site of resistance to commodification and destruction of the land, hardly seem compatible with the Gnostic hatred of the cosmos that Crowley foists on his most "perfect" of mountain Christians. In fact, the concept of "nature" as distinct from "Creation" has no place in traditional mountain language (cf. Cunningham, *Apples,* 92, 96–97).

On the other hand, the Gnostic/existentialist sense of being "thrown into" nature isn't the whole story. As the religious scholar and ecophilosopher Hans Jonas points out, the man/nature dichotomy, which this metaphor rests on, dissolves on examination. Conscious and moral life has not been thrown into nature but "has been 'tossed up' *by* nature" (339). The psychologist Joel Kovel finds the same false dichotomy in Karl Marx. Where Marx said that nature was "man's inorganic body," Kovel corrects him by declaring that humanity is "'nature's wandering spirit,' self-generating until it becomes capable of forgetting its attachment to the original ground of being and fancies itself the lord of creation" (226). This is precisely the Gnostic myth of the deluded creator-god, Jaldabaoth, turned upside down—or right side up. Insofar as we create our own world out of the illusion of our separateness from it, *that* is the world of dead "matter," "Egyptland where we are imprisoned," as Crowley's mountain Gnostic radio station, WIAO, calls it (*D,* 370):

> *The beautiful young foolish Wisdoma God! She had a partner now, and the partner was her own Anguish. And with that partner she brought forth a son! The lion-shaped lion-headed one, Jove Jehovah Jaldaboth, the maker and ruler of the heavens that we see and that we labor under.* (374)

Our alienation is the child of Wisdom and Wisdom's Anxiety, of consciousness and its own inevitable tension with the rest of the cosmos, sharpened in our case by the modern opposition between individual and society and the opposition between human labor and a world reduced to mere commodities for buying and selling. The visible heaven, Blake's "starry floor," is an optical illusion, an enclosure that (as Giordano Bruno was one of the first to know) does not exist. Hence it's a fit image of all the self-imposed, mind-forged limitations of consciousness in our civilization. Almost four centuries ago, not long after Dee's and Bruno's deaths, René

Descartes created our present mind-body, man-nature opposition out of his
acquaintance with "Ægyptian" Hermetic doctrines (cf. Keefer, 59). Thus
he took from ancient capitalism an alienated philosophy suited to expressing the self-alienation fostered by modern capitalism. The first step to freedom is to overcome this opposition.

And though Crowley spells none of this out, the attitude behind it
seems to me to be imaged forth in his werewolf myth. Again, the werewolves' true form is both spiritual and animal—as is the true form of each
of us. Modern spiritual alienation is rooted in alienation from body and
Creation—and hence from spirit and eternity as well—under the sign of
abstraction.[12] That alienation must be overcome, *first in imagination,* in
order to defeat the bewitchment that flows from that sign.

At the climax of the last section of *Dæmonomania,* Beau Brachman is
driving back to Kentucky to return to his Gnostic friends. He gets close
enough to start pulling in WIAO, but at the last minute he realizes that
instead of retreating to this refuge, he must use what he has learned from
these people back in his own home, and he turns around to return to the
Faraway Hills (375). This is the pivot of the plot of *Dæmonomania,* where it
turns toward the forthcoming volume. In other ways, too, people and
things are clearly being moved into position.

And for what? We are moving toward midwinter, the time of transformation, when the underworld is nearest to ours. What is to come in Crowley's fourth volume can hardly be any great apocalyptic change; the novel's
time frame is approaching 1980, and the twelfth and last astrological
house, fittingly, is *Carcer,* Prison. No doubt we will end up back in the
world again; but not quite the same world. Nothing, at any rate, is quite
the same after reading Crowley.

But is Appalachia any different after Crowley? Octavio Paz says that magic
is about the thirst to become Other (qtd. in Díaz, 10–11). How well does
Crowley's magic enable him to get inside the Appalachian Other? Certainly Appalachian culture is much more alive, and the Appalachian
people much more able to help themselves by natural means, than Crowley
will ever learn from reading Harry Caudill, or than most people are apt to
learn from reading Crowley. Some readers of this essay, indeed, may well
suspect that all along I have just been wishfully trying to redeem an unfor-
tunate part of a work that is so good in so many other ways. I freely ac-

knowledge that motive, but I do not think the result is wishful; I believe, or hope, that this motivation has a true impulse behind it, and that its pressure has caused me to uncover truths about Crowley's work. I have looked at the *Ægypt* quartet on levels that have not been explored before, perhaps even by Crowley himself; and, as a result, I hope I have illuminated both Crowley's opus and Appalachia, and maybe some other things besides. I have tried to show why I feel that, at least part of the time, Crowley's treatment of Appalachian things rises above, or out of, or gets below, the projection of undesirable (or idealized) features of oneself onto the other—rises or descends into the acknowledgment of those features as part of the universal human experience, and therefore of mountain people themselves in a truer way. The interest, for me, lies not so much in how well Crowley has gotten *inside* Appalachia as in how well he has gotten *under* it: not so much in what Crowley does with Appalachia as in what Appalachia has done to Crowley—not only on the conscious level but underneath, in that other realm—and in what Appalachians can do with, or make of, the result.

How should people who hope for justice look toward the future? Optimism of the will, pessimism of the intellect, said Antonio Gramsci. What, then, of the imagination? Yes, Floyd Shaftoe is right when he thinks that there is a new world coming (*L&S*, 113). The end of the world is under way everywhere, always, undetectably (cf. *D*, 30). There is a plane of existence on which the battle of the end is always being fought, and there is always a need there for the spiritual and animal being, the undivided self, to wage war against the bewitchments that rob the world of its substance, and to win back that substance in the name of the Divine Ground and the Universal Humanity.

Notes

1. Recently Crowley has also published *The Translator* (2002), which is in the spy-novel genre.
2. Hereinafter these novels will be referred to in citation as *Æ*, *L&S*, and *D*.
3. Cf. Goux: "What I mean by Egypt is the land of hieroglyphics or, in more general terms, the continent of cryptophoric symbolism, as opposed to the operative sign" (122).
4. Crowley's view of Dee and Bruno, and of their world in general, is largely based on the work of the late Dame Frances Yates. This is appropriate in spite of the justified criticism her work has received over the past dozen years. Dame Frances had a true instinct for the inner meaning of the age that fascinated her, and her increasingly anchorless speculations were

simply the result of trying to force into the frame of her generation's notions of intellectual history a phenomenon which could only be grasped properly by deploying our own concepts of paradigm, discourse, mentality, and consciousness. Dee and Bruno's fascinating dances through the period are the complex, gliding, hopping footwork of men perpetually struggling (and finally failing) to stay on their feet in the profound shifts of the discursive ground, of discursive space itself, in that epoch. Crowley's vast continuing novel about them and about us is one of the best literary meditations on such epochal themes that we have in this epochal time.

5. Floyd has adopted his granddaughter, born illegitimately in the North and virtually abandoned. The whole scenario seems to be borrowed from Caudill, 289.

6. Dee, by the way, did not die "near the winter solstice" (*D,* 349), as most standard reference sources still say, but on March 26 of the following year, 1609, as recorded in Dee's diary in a cryptic and hard-to-notice glyphic jotting (Roberts and Watson, 60). The note is by John Pontois, Dee's executor, in whose house Dee died and who inherited a great deal of Dee's magical apparatus. Pontois later sailed to "Atlantis" to become governor of Virginia; which would one day have a county called Kentucky . . .

7. As Laurette Séjourné notes of the eastward, Native American extension of this shamanic complex of ideas, "Quetzalcoatl does not succeed in his terrifying mission to the Land of the Dead until he has assumed the form of a dog. . . . This shows that, far from being a useless element that is only troublesome to the spirit, nature is necessary because it is only by the reciprocal action of one upon the other that liberation is achieved" (qtd. in Díaz, 94). The Mesoamerican *nagual* man-animal complex shares with its Old World analogues the fact that the *naguales* are beneficent beings, but are often looked on otherwise (Díaz, 42).

8. Crowley notes, too, how the eye of God ended up on the dollar bill (*L&S,* 172). And he also uses the idea that our dollar sign originated on the Spanish dollar as the Hapsburg Emperor's personal emblem, a picture of the Pillars of Hercules wreathed with the motto *Plus ultra,* "Further" (*L&S,* 419–20). Thus this image of Renaissance daring gradually wears down into the best known worldwide symbol of American power—worn down as an image on, and then of, gold.

Francis Bacon, by the way, used these same pillars on the frontispiece of his *Great Instauration,* a work which links the goals of medieval magic to the methods of modern science (cf. *L&S,* 159) by extending the idea of empire to Man's rule over Nature. Bacon, a younger acquaintance of Dee, took up not only Dee's goals of power and knowledge but his identification of America with Atlantis, and in the *New Atlantis* Bacon depicts a state ruled by techno-science, a Mr. Wizard's World like the one Couliano invokes.

9. A Holiness church member in Appalachia told sociologist Nathan L. Gerrard, "When I think of the devil, I think of Mr. Mullins, the coal company's lawyer" (Gerrard, 106). This sounds like something out of Taussig—or Crowley. But Gerrard simply remarks that "the devil . . . is hallucinated [*sic!*] in various forms."

10. One day Floyd's cabin is destroyed by a boulder rolling down from a strip mine, and Bobby shows Pierce and his cousins the print of the Devil's invisible hand on the rock (121): "Devil thowed it at my grandpap account of what he knows" (122).

11. Hmm, perhaps around Carcassonne, in the high borders of Letcher County? Don't even breathe it.

12. The adult Bobby remembers Pierce and his cousins as "those spectral children" (*D,* 206). If she seems like an animal to them, the "civilized," "American" children seem like ghosts to her. Each sees only a part of humanity, an inhuman-seeming part, across the cultural and class divide, which also encodes the mind-body opposition in the division between intellectual and manual labor.

Works Cited

Attebery, Brian. *Strategies of Fantasy.* Bloomington: Indiana University Press, 1992.

Caudill, Harry M. *Night Comes to the Cumberlands: A Biography of a Depressed Area.* 1962. Boston: Little, Brown, [1963].

Couliano, Ioan Petru. *Eros and Magic in the Renaissance.* 1984. Trans. Margaret Cook. Chicago: University of Chicago Press, 1987.

Crowley, John. *Ægypt.* New York: Bantam, 1987.

———. *Dæmonomania.* New York: Bantam, 2000.

———. *Love & Sleep.* New York: Bantam, 1994.

Cunningham, Rodger. *Apples on the Flood: The Southern Mountain Experience.* Knoxville: University of Tennessee Press, 1987.

———. "The View from the Castle: Reflections on the *Kentucky Cycle* Phenomenon." In *Confronting Appalachian Stereotypes: Back Talk from an American Region,* ed. Dwight Billings, Gurney Norman, and Katherine Ledford, 300–312. Lexington: University Press of Kentucky, 1999.

Díaz, Nancy Gray. *The Radical Self: Metamorphosis to Animal Form in Modern Latin American Literature.* Columbia: University of Missouri Press, 1988.

Eliade, Mircea. *Rites and Symbols of Initiation: The Mysteries of Birth and Rebirth.* Trans. Willard R. Trask. 1958. New York: Harper, 1965.

Gehr, Richard. "John Crowley." 11 July 1994. *Richard Gehr's Rubrics and Tendrils.* http://www.levity.com/rubric/crowley.html.

Gerrard, Nathan L. "Churches of the Stationary Poor in Southern Appalachia." In *Change in Rural Appalachia: Implications for Action Programs,* ed. John D. Photiadis and Harry K. Schwarzweller, 99–114. Philadelphia: University of Pennsylvania Press, 1970.

Ginzburg, Carlo. *Ecstasies: Deciphering the Witches' Sabbath.* 1989. Trans. Raymond Rosenthal. 1991. New York: Penguin, 1992.

———. *The Night Battles: Witchcraft and Agrarian Cults in the Sixteenth and Seventeenth Centuries.* 1966. Trans. John and Anne Tedeschi. London: Routledge, 1983.

Goux, Jean-Joseph. *Symbolic Economies: After Marx and Freud.* 1973, 1978. Trans. Jennifer Curtiss Gage. Ithaca: Cornell University Press, 1990.

Hynes, James. "Genre Trouble." *Boston Review* 25 (Dec. 2000/Jan. 2001). http://bostonreview.mit.edu/BR25.6/hynes.html.

Jonas, Hans. *The Gnostic Religion: The Message of the Alien God and the Beginnings of Christianity.* 1958. 2nd ed. Boston: Beacon, 1963.

Keefer, Michael H. "The Dreamer's Path: Descartes and the Sixteenth Century." *Renaissance Quarterly* 49 (1996): 30–76.

Kovel, Joel. *History and Spirit: An Inquiry into the Philosophy of Liberation.* Boston: Beacon, 1991.

McCauley, Deborah Vansau. *Appalachian Mountain Religion: A History.* Urbana: University of Illinois Press, 1995.

Ricoeur, Paul. *The Symbolism of Evil.* 1967. Trans. Emerson Buchanan. Boston: Beacon, 1969.

Roberts, Julian, and Andrew Watson. *John Dee's Library Catalogue.* London: Oxford University Press, 1990.

Taussig, Michael T. *The Devil and Commodity Fetishism in South America.* Chapel Hill: University of North Carolina Press, 1980.

———. *Shamanism, Colonialism, and the Wild Man: A Study in Terror and Healing.* Chicago: University of Chicago Press, 1987.

Harriette Simpson Arnow was born in Wayne County, Kentucky, in 1908. She attended Berea College from 1924 to 1926 and received her bachelor's degree from the University of Louisville in 1930. Her experiences as a mountain schoolteacher in 1926 served as the basis for her first novel, *Mountain Path* (1936). Her critically acclaimed second novel, *Hunter's Horn,* became a best-seller in 1949. *The Dollmaker* (1954) was cowinner of the *Saturday Review* national critics' poll for best novel and was runner-up for the National Book Award, which went to William Faulkner's *A Fable.* Though best known for her novels, she also wrote essays, short stories, and nonfiction books. Among her many honors are the Friends of American Writers Award, Berea College Centennial Award, Woman's Home Companion Silver Distaff Award, Mark Twain Award for Distinguished Midwestern Literature (Michigan State University), and three honorary degrees. She died in Washtenaw County, Michigan, in 1986.

Jo Carson was born in 1946 in Johnson City, Tennessee, and still makes her home there. She received bachelor's degrees from East Tennessee State University in both theater and speech in 1973. The author of short stories, poetry, children's books, and plays, Carson has worked as a television producer, visiting lecturer, performer on National Public Radio, and actor/playwright with the Road Company. Carson collected her "people pieces"—real-life dialogues or monologues from people in the Appalachian region—in the critically acclaimed book *Stories I Ain't Told Nobody Yet* (1991). Beginning in 1989 with the semiautobiographical *Daytrips,* she has written a series of award-winning plays, including *Preacher with a Horse To Ride* (1993), *The Bear Facts* (1993), and *Whispering to Horses* (1996). In 2000 she received a Theater Communications Group/NEA residency award to collaborate with 7 Stages in Atlanta, which bore fruit in a new play called *If God Came Down.* Carson's other honors include an AT&T Onstage Award, the Roger L. Stevens Award from the Fund for New American Plays, the Kesselring Award for best new American play, and an NEA fellowship.

Fred Chappell was born in Canton, North Carolina, in 1936 and earned bachelor's and master's degrees from Duke University. He has taught writing at the University of North Carolina at Greensboro since 1964. With the publication of his first novel, *It Is Time, Lord,* in 1963, Chappell gained critical attention as a fiction writer working in the Southern Gothic tradition. His latest novel, *Look Back All the Green Valley* (1999) completes a prose tetralogy centered around the Jess Kirkman family: *I Am One of You Forever* (1985); *Brighten the Corner Where You Are* (1989); and *Farewell, I'm Bound to Leave You* (1996). Chappell is most widely recognized as a poet, having produced a dozen volumes of verse between 1971 and 2000. His most acclaimed poetic work is *Midquest* (1981), a collection of four linked volumes reflecting on his thirty-fifth birthday. Among his many honors are a Rockefeller Foundation grant, a Bollingen Prize in Poetry, the T. S. Eliot Prize and the Sir Walter Raleigh Award. Chappell served as poet laureate of his home state from 1997 to 2002. His most recent poetry collection, *Family Gathering,* appeared in 2000.

John Crowley has been described as "one of the best, if not *the* best, contemporary authors of fantasy." Born in 1942 in Presque Isle, Maine, he received his BA from Indiana University in 1964 and published his first novel, *The Deep,* in 1975. With the release of the novel *Aegypt,* in 1987, Crowley embarked on a projected tetralogy that he regards as the principal undertaking in his creative work. Two more volumes in the series, *Love and Sleep* and *Daemonomania,* followed in 1994 and 2000. In addition to his fiction, Crowley is a freelance writer for films and television; he also serves as a visiting professor of creative writing at Yale University. He has received numerous honors for his work, including two World Fantasy Awards and the American Academy of Arts and Letters Award for literature. His most recent non-Ægypt novel, *The Translator,* was published in 2002.

Wilma Dykeman was born in Asheville, North Carolina, and educated at Northwestern University. Beginning in 1955 with the publication of her nonfiction book, *The French Broad,* Dykeman has long been a voice of conscience speaking out on environmental and social issues in Appalachia and the South. With her husband, the late James R. Stokely Jr., she coauthored *Neither Black nor White* (1957) and *Seeds of Southern Change* (1962). The first of her three novels, *The Tall Woman,* also appeared in 1962 and has been in print ever since. Dykeman has published nonfiction books about Tennessee history and has contributed articles and book reviews to the *New York Times Magazine, Harper's, New Republic,* and other periodicals. She has been awarded a Guggenheim fellowship, the Thomas Wolfe Memorial Trophy, the Hillman Award, the Waukegan Club Award (Chicago Friends of American Writers), and a National Endowment for the Humanities senior fellowship. She lives in Newport, Tennessee.

John Marsden Ehle Jr. was born in Asheville, North Carolina, in 1925. He holds an AB in radio, television, and motion pictures and an MA in dramatic arts from the University of North Carolina at Chapel Hill, where he later taught in the Communication Center. His writing traces the historical and cultural evolution of his native mountain region through nearly a dozen novels, beginning in 1957 with the publication of *Move Over, Mountain,* and reaching full development with works such as *The Journey of August King* (1971) and *The Winter People* (1982). Ehle has also voiced his social concerns through nonfiction books such as *The Free Men* (1965), an exploration of the struggle for racial equality in Chapel Hill, for which he received the Mayflower Award. He is the recipient of the Sir Walter Raleigh Award in fiction and two Freedom Foundation Awards. Ehle now lives in Winston-Salem.

Denise Giardina was born in Bluefield, West Virginia, in 1951. She received a bachelor of arts degree from West Virginia Wesleyan College in 1973 and a master of divinity degree from Virginia Theological Seminary in 1979. She is best known for her coal-mining novels, *Storming Heaven* (1987) and *The Unquiet Earth* (1992), the latter of which won the American Book Award from the Before Columbus Foundation. *Saints and Villains* (1998), her creative treatment of the life of theologian Dietrich Bonhoeffer, received the Boston Book Review Fisk Fiction Prize. A licensed lay Episcopal minister and social activist, Giardina ran for governor of West Virginia in 2000. She lives in Charleston and teaches at West Virginia State College. Her latest novel, *Fallam's Secret,* was published in 2003.

Cormac McCarthy was born Charles McCarthy Jr. in Providence, Rhode Island, in 1933. When he was four, his family moved to East Tennessee, a region that eventually would become the setting for much of his early fiction. McCarthy studied engineering at the University of Tennessee, served in the Air Force in Alaska, and later resumed his studies at UT, where he turned to writing. His highly acclaimed first novel, *The Orchard Keeper* (1965), won the Faulkner Foundation award and was followed by three other novels set in Appalachia—*Outer Dark* (1970), *Child of God* (1974), and *Suttree* (1979). In 1974 McCarthy moved to Texas and eventually gained further renown for his fiction set in the Southwest, winning the National Book Award and the National Book Critics Circle Award for *All the Pretty Horses* (1992). Often compared to Faulkner and O'Connor, McCarthy was the recipient of a MacArthur Foundation "genius award" in 1981.

Jim Wayne Miller was born in 1936 in Leicester, North Carolina. He earned a bachelor's degree from Berea College in 1958 and a doctorate from Vanderbilt University in 1965. Miller was a professor of German at Western Kentucky University and the author of several volumes of poetry, including *Dialogue with a Dead Ma*n (1974), *The Mountains Have Come Closer* (1980), and *Brier, His Book* (1988). He wrote two novels, *Newfound* (1989) and *His First, Best Country* (1993). At various times he was chairman of the Kentucky Humanities Council, board member of the Appalachian Community Service Network, a writer-in-residence at several colleges, and a consultant to poetry workshops and Appalachian Studies programs. A talented editor and translator, he worked in association with the Jesse Stuart Foundation to edit several books of Stuart's writing and translated the poetry of Emil Lerperger. Miller was Kentucky poet laureate in 1986 and won many other honors for his poetry, plays, and short stories, including the Thomas Wolfe Literary Award, Zoe Kinkaid Broackman Memorial Award for Poetry, Best Book of the Year citation (*Learning Magazine*), Editor's Choice citation, and Best Book of the Year citation (*Booklist*). He died August 15, 1996, in Louisville, Kentucky.

Robert Morgan was born in 1944 in Hendersonville, North Carolina. He received his bachelor's degree from the University of North Carolina at Chapel Hill and an MFA from the University of North Carolina at Greensboro. Since 1971 he has taught at Cornell University in Ithaca, New York. Beginning with his first book, *Zirconia Poems* (1969), Morgan focused his early writing career primarily on poetry. His first short story collection, *The Blue Valleys,* was published in 1989, and his first novel, *The Hinterlands: A Mountain Tale in Three Parts,* followed in 1994. Morgan received critical acclaim for his novels *The Truest Pleasure* (1995), and *Gap Creek* (1999), which were cited as notable books by the *New York Times. Gap*

Creek also won the Southern Book Critics Circle Award and was selected for the Oprah Winfrey Book Club. Among other honors, Morgan has received four grants from the National Endowment for the Arts, a Guggenheim fellowship, a Bellagio Conference Center fellowship, and the North Carolina Award in Literature. His most recent works are *Topsoil Road: Poems* (2000) and the novel *Brave Enemies* (2003).

Gurney Norman was born in 1937 in Grundy, Virginia, and grew up near Hazard, Kentucky. He was educated at the University of Kentucky and did graduate work as a Stegner Fellow at Stanford University, where he was immersed in the 1960s counterculture that would later figure in his novel, *Divine Right's Trip* (1972). Three stories from Norman's highly regarded short story collection *Kinfolks* (1977) have been adapted into short films for public television. Norman also has been a newspaper and book editor, a cultural activist, and a documentary filmmaker exploring the natural history of eastern Kentucky and southwest Virginia. A resident of Lexington, he currently directs the creative writing program at the University of Kentucky.

Mary Lee Settle was born in Charleston, West Virginia, in 1918 and attended Sweet Briar College from 1936 to 1938. In addition to serving in the Women's Auxiliary Air Force (1942–43), she has worked as a model, actress, assistant editor of *Harper's Bazaar,* freelance writer, professor, and lecturer. Although most widely recognized for her novels, including the five-volume Beulah Quintet, Settle has written plays, short stories, and autobiographical nonfiction. She is the recipient of two Guggenheim fellowships, an award from the Merrill Foundation, and the Janet Heidinger Kafka Prize for fiction by an American woman. Her novel *Blood Tie* won the National Book Award in 1978. She now lives in Charlottesville, Virginia.

Lee Smith was born in Grundy, Virginia, in 1944 and was educated at Hollins College and the Sorbonne, University of Paris. She is a former professor of English at North Carolina State University in Raleigh and also has worked as a newspaper feature writer, film critic, and editor. Her first novel, *The Last Day the Dogbushes Bloomed,* garnered a Book of the Month Club fellowship in 1968. Over the past three decades she has written several critically acclaimed novels that give a strong voice to women, including *Oral History* (1983), *Family Linen* (1985), and *Fair and Tender Ladies*

(1988). *Oral History* won both the Sir Walter Raleigh Award for Fiction and the North Carolina Award for Fiction. Smith also has received two O. Henry awards and a PEN/Faulkner Award for her short stories. Her most recent novel is *The Last Girls* (2003).

James Still was born in 1906, in LaFayette, Alabama, but lived most of his life in Hindman, Kentucky, where he died on April 28, 2001. He received his AB from Lincoln Memorial University in 1929; his MA from Vanderbilt University in 1930; and a BS from the University of Illinois in 1931. Still was closely associated with the Hindman Settlement School, where he worked as a librarian in the 1930s and again in the 1950s. He later taught English at Morehead State University and was an occasional commentator for National Public Radio.

Often considered the dean of Appalachian letters, Still made an auspicious entry into the literary world in the late 1930s with his first book of poems, the well-received *Hounds on the Mountain* (1937), and with the 1939 short story "Bat Flight," which won the O. Henry Memorial Prize. In 1940 he followed with the novel *River of Earth,* which has become a classic in Appalachian literature and is sometimes compared with Steinbeck's *The Grapes of Wrath.* Still's other works include the short story collections *On Troublesome Creek* (1941), *Pattern of a Man* (1976), and *The Run for the Elbertas* (1983), as well as *The Wolfpen Poems* (1986). He also wrote children's books and contributed to numerous periodicals such as *Atlantic, Esquire, Nation, Saturday Evening Post* and *New Republic.* His final book, *From the Mountain, From the Valley: New and Collected Poems,* was published in 2001.

Still received many awards during his long career, including the Mac-Dowell Colony fellowship, the Southern Authors Award (Southern Women's National Democratic Organization), two Guggenheim fellowships, the American Academy of Arts and Letters Fiction Award, the Weatherford Award, the Marjorie Peabody Waite Award (American Academy and Institute of Arts and Letters), the Milne Award (Kentucky Arts Council), and three honorary degrees. He is buried on the grounds of the Hindman Settlement School in a spot overlooking Troublesome Creek.

Jesse Stuart was born in W-Hollow, Greenup County, Kentucky, in 1906, and lived in the county most of his life. He received his AB degree from Lincoln Memorial University in 1929 and later attended Vanderbilt University and Peabody College. Beginning in 1934 with the publication of his sonnet collection, *Man with a Bull-Tongue Plow,* Stuart embarked on a prolific career. Over the next half century, he wrote nearly sixty books. Although he produced a second volume of poetry, *Album of Destiny,* in 1944, and continued to write verse throughout his career, Stuart became known primarily as a fiction writer. The author of 12 novels and more than 400 short stories, he won a Thomas Jefferson Southern Memorial Award for his best-known novel, *Taps for Private Tussie* (1943). In addition, Stuart drew from his experiences as a public school teacher and administrator to write autobiographical works such as *The Thread That Runs So True* (1949). He also was a farmer and visiting professor who traveled extensively to foreign countries as a goodwill ambassador for the U.S. government.

Stuart was poet laureate of Kentucky in 1954. He received the Academy of American Poets Award in 1961, and a collection of his poems, *The World of Jesse Stuart,* was nominated for a Pulitzer Prize in 1975. Among his other honors are the Jeannette Sewal Davis prize (*Poetry* magazine), a Guggenheim fellowship, an Academy of Arts and Sciences Award, and numerous honorary degrees. Stuart died in Ironton, Ohio, in 1984 after a long illness. Many of his books are still widely available today, both in the United States and abroad.

CONTRIBUTORS

Leslie Banner is a writer, editor, and higher education research specialist who retired from Duke University in 2004. She is the author or coauthor of four books. Her interest in Appalachian literature reflects family roots in Western North Carolina and influenced her choice of PhD dissertation topic at the University of North Carolina at Chapel Hill, "The North Carolina Mountaineer in Native Fiction."

Theresa Burriss lives in Wytheville, Virginia, with her two sons, Paul and Campbell. She is the director of the Learning Assistance and Resource Center at Radford University in Radford, Virginia, as well as an English special purpose faculty member. A doctoral candidate at the Union Institute and University, she is focusing on Appalachian Studies and Women's Studies. Much of her time is spent running and hiking the trails of the Appalachian Mountains.

Hilbert Campbell received his PhD from the University of Kentucky and for thirty years taught English at Virginia Tech, where he served as director of graduate studies and as department chair. His scholarly interests include eighteenth-century British literature, Sherwood Anderson, and Southern/Appalachian literature, especially the writers Fred Chappell, Clyde Edgerton, and Lee Smith. He now conducts a small mail-order bookselling business (summerleebooks.com).

John G. Cawelti retired from the University of Kentucky in 2000 after teaching at various universities since 1957. He has written several books and a sizable number of articles about various aspects of American literature and culture, particularly popular culture.

Cecelia Conway, professor of English at Appalachian State University, teaches contemporary American literature, including cultural perspectives, folklore, and film. Author of *African Banjo Echoes in Appalachia* and co-maker of award-winning films (*Sprout Wings and Fly; Julie*), she is currently working on the video *Robert Morgan's Lucid Poetry* (Cane Creek and ASU).

Ricky Cox teaches composition, American literature, and Appalachian folklore at Radford University in Radford, Virginia.

Rodger Cunningham teaches English at Alice Lloyd College in southeastern Kentucky. He is the author of *Apples on the Flood: Minority Discourse and Appalachia* and of many essays and reviews in Appalachian studies.

Corinne H. Dale is professor of literature at Belmont University in Nashville, Tennessee, and associate editor of *Journal of the Short Story in English.* She has published articles on women writers and ethnicity in literature and has edited *Women on the Edge: Gender and Ethnicity in Short Stories by American Women* and *Chinese Aesthetics and Literature: A Reader.*

Charles H. Daughaday has retired as professor of English at Murray State University. His major areas of interest are modern English and American literature, literary criticism, classical literature, and creative writing.

Tim Dunn is an associate professor of English at Hazard Community College in southeastern Kentucky. He teaches composition, American literature, and Appalachian literature.

Terry Easton is a doctoral candidate in the American Studies program of the Graduate Institute of the Liberal Arts at Emory University in Atlanta. His articles on work and class have appeared in *Teaching Working Class* (University of Massachusetts Press, 1999) and *Women's Studies Quarterly.*

Elizabeth S. D. Engelhardt is assistant professor of American studies at the University of Texas at Austin. Born and raised in western North Carolina, she received her doctorate in women's studies from Emory University. The author of *The Tangled Roots of Feminism, Environmentalism, and Appalachian Literature* (Ohio University Press, 2003), she studies women's literature, feminism, and ecological activism in Appalachia and the United States.

Patricia M. Gantt is the associate head of the English Department at Utah State University, where she also directs the Women and Gender Studies

Program. Her publications include work on August Wilson, William Faulkner, Thomas Wolfe, *Contempo* magazine, and women's oral histories from the Federal Writers' Project. With Lynn Langer Meeks, Gantt has co-edited two volumes of classroom ideas from award-winning English teachers, *Teaching Ideas for 7–12 English Language Arts: What Really Works* and *Teaching College English: Strategies for Literature and Composition,* both from Christopher-Gordon Publishers, 2004.

Robert J. Higgs is professor emeritus at East Tennessee State University where for twenty-five years he taught classes in Appalachian, Southern, and American literature. He is coeditor with Ambrose Manning of *Voices from the Hills: Selected Readings of Southern Appalachia* (Kendall Hunt, 2001, Twenty-fifth Anniversary Edition) and with Manning and Jim Wayne Miller of the two-volume *Appalachia Inside Out: A Sequel to Voices from the Hills* (University of Tennessee Press, 1995).

Dorothy Combs Hill received her PhD from the University of North Carolina at Chapel Hill and taught at Chowan College, the University of Missouri, and Georgetown University. Her interest in contemporary Southern women writers led to the publication of her book *Lee Smith,* a volume in the Twayne United States Authors Series, as well as numerous critical essays and interviews. Under her editorship, the *Carolina Quarterly* won the Best American Short Story Award (1980) and two O. Henry Awards (1979, 1980). Hill now lives with her husband Francis Anderson in the mountains of New Mexico, where she works as a freelance editor and writer. Her current book project is entitled *High White Sundays.*

Don Johnson is an English professor at East Tennessee State University, a poet, and longtime editor of *Aethlon: The Journal of Sport Literature.*

Oliver King (Chip) Jones III is documentation manager for Ceridian, a multinational human resources services company. He received a BA in English from Vanderbilt University and an MA in English from the University of North Carolina at Chapel Hill. Since 1987 he has worked in the technical communication field, specializing in online information design and delivery systems. Jones lives in Roswell, Georgia, with his wife and three children.

Nancy Carol Joyner is professor emerita of English at Western Carolina University. She has published extensively on Appalachian women writers, including several articles on Mary Lee Settle.

Dayton M. Kohler (1907–1972) was a professor of English at Virginia Polytechnic Institute and State University in Blacksburg. Considered an authority on modern American literature, he wrote and edited synopses of novels, short fiction, and plays for *Masterplots* and also edited the *Cyclopedia of World Authors*.

John Lang teaches American literature at Emory & Henry College, where he also edits *The Iron Mountain Review* and coordinates the college's annual literary festival. He is the author of *Understanding Fred Chappell* (University of South Carolina Press, 2000).

Jeff Daniel Marion lives in Knoxville, Tennessee, with his wife Linda. He is author of seven books of poems, the most recent being *Letters Home* (Sow's Ear Press, 2001) and *Ebbing & Flowing Springs: New and Selected Poems and Prose, 1976–2001* (Celtic Cat Publishing, 2002).

Danny Miller is chair of the Department of Literature and Language at Northern Kentucky University. A graduate of Berea College and the University of Cincinnati, he has published widely on Appalachian literature, including the monograph *Wingless Flights: Appalachian Women in Fiction* (Bowling Green State University Popular Press, 1996). He is a past president of the Appalachian Community Development Association and a member of the Jesse Stuart Foundation Board of Directors.

Jim Wayne Miller (1936–1996) was a professor of German at Western Kentucky University and the author of two novels and several volumes of poetry. A native of North Carolina, Miller was Kentucky poet laureate in 1986 and won many other honors for his poems, plays, and short stories.

Joyce Carol Oates was born in upstate New York and educated at Syracuse University (BA, 1960) and the University of Wisconsin (MA, 1961). Twice nominated for the Nobel Prize in literature, she is the author of many novels and short story collections, as well as books of poetry, plays, and literary criticism. Her writing has garnered many notable awards, including the PEN/Malamud Award for Excellence in short fiction, the Rosenthal Award from the American Academy-Institute of Arts and Letters, a Guggenheim fellowship, the O. Henry Prize for Continued Achievement in the Short Story, the National Book Award, and membership in the American Academy-Institute. She is the Roger S. Berlind Distinguished Professor of Humanities at Princeton University.

Barbara Hill Rigney is a professor of English at The Ohio State University. She has written five books, including *The Voices of Toni Morrison* (1994), and coedited *Exile: A Memoir of 1939* (1998), both published by Ohio State University Press.

Anita J. Turpin, a professor of English at Roanoke College in Salem, Virginia, grew up on a burley tobacco farm in eastern Kentucky and will always consider Kentucky home.

Jane Gentry Vance is a native of Athens, Kentucky, and now lives in Versailles, Kentucky. She teaches in the English Department and Honors Program at the University of Kentucky. Her criticism has appeared in *Mississippi Quarterly, Kentucky Review, Southern Literary Journal, The Iron Mountain Review,* and several collections and reference volumes. Her collection of poems, *A Garden in Kentucky,* was published by Louisiana State University Press in 1995.

Cratis Williams (1911–1985) is often referred to as "the father of Appalachian Studies." A native of Caines Creek, Lawrence County, Kentucky, Williams was educated at the University of Kentucky (BA, 1933; MA, 1937), and at New York University (PhD, 1961). He joined the faculty of Appalachian State University in Boone, North Carolina, in 1942, serving as instructor, dean of the graduate school, and acting chancellor during a 30-year tenure. Williams's comprehensive doctoral dissertation, *The Southern Mountaineer in Fact and Fiction,* and his master's thesis on folk music in eastern Kentucky are considered landmark contributions to Appalachian scholarship.

INDEX